WITCHCRAFT AND HYSTERIA IN ELIZABETHAN LONDON

Tavistock Classics
in the History of Psychiatry

GENERAL EDITORS:

W. F. Bynum and Roy Porter

Current interest in the history of psychiatry is growing rapidly both among the psychiatric profession and social historians. This series is designed to bring back into print many classic documents from earlier centuries. Each reprint has been chosen for the series because of its social and intellectual significance, and includes a substantial introduction written by an eminent scholar in the history of psychiatry.

Illustrations of Madness (1810)
by John Haslam (ed. Roy Porter)

An Essay . . . on Drunkenness (1804)
by Thomas Trotter (ed. Roy Porter)

Observations on Maniacal Disorders (1792)
by William Pargeter (ed. Stanley W. Jackson)

Lifes Preservative against Self-Killing
by John Sym (ed. Michael MacDonald)

Clinical Lectures on Diseases of the Nervous System
by J-M. Charcot (ed. Ruth Harris)

George Cheyne: The English Malady (1733)
edited by Roy Porter

*The Asylum as Utopia: W.A.F. Browne and the
Mid-Nineteenth Century Consolidation of Psychiatry*
edited by Andrew Scull

WITCHCRAFT AND HYSTERIA IN ELIZABETHAN LONDON

Edward Jorden and the Mary Glover Case

Edited with an Introduction by
Michael MacDonald

TAVISTOCK/ROUTLEDGE
London and New York

First published in 1991
by Routledge
11 New Fetter Lane, London EC4P 4EE

Simultaneously published in the USA and Canada
by Routledge
a division of Routledge, Chapman and Hall Inc.
29 West 35th Street, New York, NY 10001

© 1991 Introduction by Michael MacDonald

Printed in Great Britain by Antony Rowe Ltd

British Library Cataloguing in Publication Data

Witchcraft and hysteria in Elizabethan London: Edward Jorden
and the Mary Glover case. – (Tavistock classics in the
history of psychiatry)
1. Witchcraft – Sociological perspectives
I. MacDonald, Michael, *1945* – II. Bradwell, Stephen
III. Series
306

Library of Congress Cataloging in Publication Data

Witchcraft and hysteria in Elizabethan London : Edward Jorden and the
Mary Glover case / edited by Michael MacDonald.
p. cm. — (Tavistock classics in the history of psychiatry)
Reprint (1st work). Originally published: A briefe discourse of a
disease called the suffocation of the mother. London, 1603.
Reprint (2nd work). Originally published: A true and breife report
of Mary Glovers vexation and of her deliverance by fastings and
prayer. London? 1603.
(3rd work). Previously unpublished: Mary Glovers late
woeful case / Stephen Bradwell: 1603.
Includes bibliographical references
1. Hysteria—Case studies. 2. Witchcraft—England—History—17th
century—Case studies. 3. Psychiatry—England—History—17th
century—Case studies. I. MacDonald, Michael, 1945–
II. Jorden, Edward, 1569–1632. Briefe discourse of a disease called
the suffocation of the mother. 1991. III. Swan, John, d. 1671.
True and breife report of Mary Glovers vexation and of her
deliverance by fastings and prayer. 1991. IV. Bradwell, Stephen.
Mary Glovers late woeful case. 1991. V. Series.
RC532.W58 1991   90–8435
616.85'2409—dc20   CIP

ISBN 0–415–01788–2

CONTENTS

ACKNOWLEDGEMENTS

For permission to publish Sloane MS 831, 'Mary Glovers Late Woeful Case' by Stephen Bradwell, I am grateful to the British Library Board. I am obliged to Anne Summers, Curator of the Manuscript Collections, for her prompt assistance in obtaining the Board's permission. The University of Michigan supplied a small grant on short notice to pay for some of the costs of preparing the transcription. *A True and Breife Report* by John Swan is reproduced by kind permission of The British Library. I am grateful as well to the general editors for their patience and help.

Professor Paul S. Seaver read the introduction in spite of many more pressing obligations and lent me his unrivalled knowledge of the religious scene in Elizabethan London. He saved me from several foolish errors; no doubt I slipped others past him. Without the help of Carol W. Dickerman, who retyped a huge portion of my transcription of Bradwell's treatise that was lost in a computer disaster and read the entire manuscript aloud with me to check for errors of transcription, I do not know how or when I might have finished.

INTRODUCTION

Michael MacDonald

Edward Jorden is one of the most celebrated obscure physicians in medical history. The author of just two brief books, he has been widely hailed by modern scholars as a key figure in medical opposition to superstition and in the development of the concept of hysteria. Richard Hunter and Ida Macalpine, for instance, assert that Jorden's *Briefe Discourse of a Disease Called the Suffocation of the Mother* (1603) 'was the first book by an English physician which reclaimed the demoniacally possessed for medicine'.[1] They also single Jorden out as the physician who, 'for better or worse', introduced the concept of hysteria into English medicine.[2] In her authoritative history of hysteria, Ilza Veith echoes both of these kudos and adds another first to the impressive list of innovations attributed to Jorden's book. She points out that he went beyond classical discussions of the pathology of hysteria and rejected the notion that the malady was primarily a disturbance of the uterus. 'Jorden's transfer of the seat of all hysterical manifestations from the uterus to the brain', she lauds, 'constituted a major turning point in the history of hysteria.'[3] In histories of witchcraft, Jorden is enshrined among the pantheon of rationalists who opposed the witch hunt long before it petered out; in histories of mental illness he is presented as the leading early modern precursor of Thomas Willis and Thomas Sydenham in the development of medical understanding of hysteria. Few authors can have won such an enduring reputation for precocious sagacity on the basis of a short and technical pamphlet that was never reprinted and cannot have been very widely read, even in its own time, much less in subsequent decades.

Introduction by Michael MacDonald

Jorden was born in 1569 at High Halden in Kent and received his education at Cambridge. After taking his BA there in 1583, he studied at Padua, where he received his MD in 1591. He became a Licentiate of the College of Physicians in 1595 and a Fellow two years later. His brilliant performance on his examinations was praised in the Annals of the College. He practised in London for some years before removing to Bath, where he spent the bulk of his long career. While he was in London he won the confidence and favour of King James, and although he was never officially a Royal Physician, he treated the Queen on her visits to Bath. He died there in 1632. In addition to the *Briefe Discourse*, Jorden published in 1631 *A Discourse of Natural Bathes and Mineral Waters*, a book that was far more influential than the former tract. It went through five editions in the seventeenth century and was an important contribution to the development of chemistry in its day. Its fourth edition includes a brief biographical notice of Jorden, written by the editor, Thomas Guidott. Jorden had a great deal of experience at 'mineral works', and tried unsuccessfully to obtain a monopoly on the profits of alum from King James. Despite his complaints about the huge expenses he had incurred in studying alum and pursuing its patent, Jorden was a successful and prosperous physician. He married a gentlewoman with a substantial fortune and wed his daughter to a mayor of Bath. It was a distinguished career, particularly for a provincial physician, and it won hyperbolic praise from Guidott: 'He had the Applause of the Learned, the Respect of the Rich, the Prayers of the Poor, and the Love of all.'[4]

The aim of this book is to challenge the prevailing view of Jorden's achievements. It seeks to explain why and how he came to advance the opinions that have won him such acclaim in our own century. For it is my conviction that modern assessments of Jorden have misunderstood his motives for writing his *Briefe Discourse* and the considerations that prompted him to reassess the cause and symptoms of hysteria. I shall argue here that Jorden's book is in the first instance a work of religious propaganda. It grew out of an episode in a bitter and protracted struggle between the church hierarchy and its Catholic and Puritan opponents, and it was almost certainly commissioned by the Bishop of London, Richard Bancroft. Jorden provided scientific arguments for disputing the validity of cases of possession, witchcraft and dispossession that both Catholics and Puritans were exploiting to win public approval and make converts. This interpretation of Jorden's motives is advanced with allusive brevity by the preacher John Swan and with infuriated prolixity by the physician Stephen Bradwell. Both of their works are reprinted here, so that the *Briefe Discourse* may be seen in its original context and its arguments and significance clarified.

To argue that the *Briefe Discourse* is on one fundamental level a work of religious propaganda is not to denigrate either Jorden's scepticism or his insights into hysteria. There is no doubt that he genuinely believed that in the principal case he had in mind the apparently possessed victim of witchcraft actually suffered from a natural disease and that the woman convicted of bewitching her had been wrongly accused. Nor is there any doubt that his discussion of the causes and effects of hysteria was scientifically sound by the standards of his time and innovative in several respects. But when the *Briefe Discourse* is seen for what it was – one blast in a bitter pamphlet battle – one can appreciate why Jorden was prompted to advance opinions about witchcraft and hysteria that were so innovative and unusual. D. P. Walker has suggested that the controversy over possession and witchcraft in which Jorden took part helped to create, for religious reasons, a climate of opinion that was 'unfavourable to witch-hunting and demoniacs' and 'favourable to the development of modern science'.[5] This introduction and the tracts that are gathered together in this volume substantiate his claim. They provide a case study in the development of psychiatric thought and its relationship to religious and magical beliefs that reveals the importance of power politics in shaping beliefs and opinions. They deepen our understanding of Jorden's motives while they confirm his reputation as a humane sceptic and innovative medical theorist. Seen in this light, Jorden is a man of his times who was prompted by compelling circumstances to champion ideas that have in retrospect rightly made him a man for all times.

The bewitching of Mary Glover

The *Briefe Discourse* was written, Jorden declares on its title page, because of a recent incident in which the effects of hysteria were confused with 'possession of an evill spirit, or some such like supernaturall power'. Its aim, the long title continues, is to show 'that divers strange actions and passions of the body of man, which in *the common opinion, are imputed to the Divell, have their true naturall causes, and do accompany this disease*', which he calls the suffocation of the mother. Although he never again alludes to the case to which he refers, everyone knew that he meant the alleged possession and bewitchment of Mary Glover, the teenage daughter of a London shopkeeper, whose affliction and cure had caused a sensation in the metropolis at the end of 1602. Glover's spectacular fits, her accusations of witchcraft against an old woman called Elizabeth Jackson, the dramatic trial and conviction of the 'witch' and Glover's eventual dispossession by a group of Puritan preachers had captured the attention of London's leading citizens, enraged the church hierarchy and alarmed the government. Jorden himself had testified at Jackson's trial, swearing that the girl was not possessed or bewitched, and he had been personally rebuffed by the judge, who ridiculed his argument that she had a natural disease. The *Briefe Discourse* was Jorden's response to the humiliating repudiation of his testimony, partly an effort to restore his credibility by expanding and documenting the scientific reasoning behind the arguments he had made in court. To understand the book, therefore, it is first necessary to describe the incident that occasioned it.

Mary Glover was fourteen years old at the end of April 1602, when she fell ill following a dispute with Elizabeth Jackson. According to Stephen Bradwell, who provides the fullest (if least objective) narrative of the episode, the girl had accused Elizabeth Jackson of fraud, tattling to one of her mistresses about 'a certaine fashion of her subtile and importunat begging' (fol. 3r).* Enraged, the old woman confronted her when she was sent to her house on an errand. Locking the door after Glover, Jackson railed at her for meddling with her daughter's apparel. She shouted terrifying and malevolent curses, wishing an evil death on the girl, sending her away finally with this threat: 'my daughter shall have clothes when thou art dead and rotten' (fol. 3v). Badly shaken, Glover made her way home, stopping to tell a servant from the house next door that she felt unwell. Apparently Elizabeth Jackson overheard this exchange, for she rushed into the neighbour's house and boasted that she had 'rattled up' one of the gossips who had somehow meddled with her daughter's clothes, declaring again that she hoped Mary Glover died an evil death (fol. 3v). Back home at her father's shop, Glover evidently suffered no further symptoms until three days later, when Elizabeth Jackson came in as she was drinking posset and asked to see her mother. The girl told Jackson that her mother was not at home, and the old woman glared at her and snapped that she must see her mother.

After she left, Glover tried to drink her posset again, but she found that her throat was constricted, and she could not swallow any more of it. She went to the house of a friendly neighbour for help, where her affliction worsened. She was struck dumb and blind, and the neighbours brought her back to her own home. Her neck and throat then appeared to swell, as they did every day after that for eighteen days, during which time she seemed to eat nothing at all. Mysteriously, she did not show any of the usual effects of fasting. Still, her fits were so terrifying that her parents believed she was about to die; they had the churchbell tolled, the customary announcement of death or of approaching death. Jackson, who lived nearby, heard the bell and the rumours that rang through the neighbourhood, telling the inhabitants of the parish who was ill and what was wrong. She crowed triumphantly, boasting to her next-door neighbour: 'I thanck my God he hath heard my prayer, and stopped the mouth and tyed the tongue of one of myne enemies' (fol. 4v). She allegedly repeated her boasts in other people's homes, including that of William Glover, a city alderman and a kinsman of the afflicted girl. At one of them she added the ominous curse, 'The vengeance of god on her, and on all the generation of them. I hope the Devill will stop her mouth' (fols. 4v–5r). Mary Glover's mother was, understandably, upset, and she hurried to confront Jackson, who denied that she had made the boasts and curses reported to Mrs Glover. But Elizabeth Jackson was, whatever else may have been wrongly claimed about her by her enemies, a woman with a towering temper. 'You have not crosses ynow', she fulminated, 'but I hope you shall have as many crosses, as ever fell upon woman and Children' (fol. 5r).

Most Elizabethans believed that curses could kill, and Elizabeth Jackson's raging threats would by themselves have raised fears of witchcraft. Suspicion was beginning to grow. It was intensified by Mary Glover's physicians, who struggled unsuccessfully to relieve

xi

her symptoms. The first doctor who treated her was Robert Shereman, a fellow of the College of Physicians, and as such a member of the country's medical elite.[6] Assisted by a surgeon, he treated the girl for quincy (supperative tonsillitis), but her difficulties in swallowing persisted, and soon new symptoms appeared, notably frequent abdominal distortions, movement in her chest, and loss of speech and sight. Shereman suspected that these symptoms might be supernaturally caused, but he knew also that they could be caused by hysteria, and so he tried hard 'to cleare the point touching *hystericall* passions'. When his attempts to cure the mother also failed, 'he pronounced and was plainely of that mind that som cause beyond naturall was in it' (fol. 5v). Interestingly, the family did not immediately agree with him, and so they brought in an even more distinguished doctor, Thomas Moundeford, seven times President of the College of Physicians and an expert on melancholy, which was another natural disease widely believed like hysteria to produce apparently supernatural symptoms.[7] He attempted for over two months to discover the precise nature and cause of Glover's malady and to cure it. He concluded that the disease was not hysteria, but that some other natural illness, which he could not identify, might be responsible for her symptoms (fol. 102r). After several months of treatment by two of the most eminent physicians, therefore, medical opinion about Glover's illness was divided, and the doctor who believed it was supernatural was more confident than the one who thought it could have some natural cause. The division of medical opinion was to persist throughout the episode.

Meanwhile, as the doctors were trying and failing to diagnose and cure Mary Glover, her fits became more regular, more spectacular and more frightening. Bradwell divides them into two main kinds, which he calls ordinary and extraordinary. The former were more vigorous and protracted on one day, less vigorous and shorter on the next. They involved apparent unconsciousness, swellings, contortions, writhings and an elaborately choreographed pattern of hand motions. Glover also fell into trance-like states and suffered contortions every time she ate. Her extraordinary fits occurred whenever she was in the company of Elizabeth Jackson. They involved seemingly unconscious spasms and convulsions, tossing Glover's body away from Jackson's touch, which continued until the old woman left the Glover house. Ominously, during these fits, Mary Glover began to speak the words 'hang her', almost inaudibly, in a voice that seemed to observers to be coming from her nostrils. This lethal litany also ceased when Jackson left the house.

As Glover's seizures became more intense and more plainly linked with Elizabeth Jackson's presence, observers who believed that her symptoms had a supernatural cause began to believe that the girl had been bewitched. They staged trials in which the unwilling old woman was dragged to the Glover house and forced to touch the girl. These 'trials' or 'experiments' were spectacular events, and Glover's fits became a kind of show. The house was jammed with people: pious Puritans awestruck by the evident power of Satan, more sceptical observers wanting to see for themselves whether Glover's illness was natural or supernatural and the merely curious. The spectators included some men and women of high rank, such as Lady Brucknard, and eminent divines and physicians. The diarist John Manningham recorded a joke he read in a lost narrative of the affair that shows that the Glover house had become a kind of theatre, where the spectators had to cope with all the usual hazards of the London crowd:

> A gentlewoman which had bin to see a child that was sayd to be possessed with the Divel, told howe she lost hir purse while they were at prayer. 'Oh', said a gent[leman], 'not unlikely, for you forgott halfe your lesson: Christ bad you watch and pray, and you prayed onely; but had you watched as you prayed, you might have kept your purse still'.[8]

City authorities soon became concerned about the Glover case. Both the girl and the old woman were first summoned to the house of William Glover, an alderman and former sheriff, who was Mary's uncle. Mary Glover herself seems to have precipitated the confrontation, accusing Jackson of having bewitched her, and when they were brought face to face, she fell into an extraordinary fit, repeating 'hang her, hang her', in her nasal voice. Soon afterwards, Sir John Harte, a former Lord Mayor long a leader in City government, staged another meeting between Glover and Jackson at Mary's house, with the same results.

The episode was becoming more serious, and the suspicions against Jackson were mounting. But not everyone was easily convinced. Richard Bancroft, the Bishop of London, believed that she was innocent. At his urging, the City's chief legal officer, the Recorder John Croke, staged a remarkable set of rituals to test the validity of Glover's claim to be possessed and bewitched. The trials proceeded by stages. He first tested the effect that Elizabeth Jackson had on the girl by disguising another woman as Jackson, bringing her into the room and having her approach and then touch Mary. The girl did not respond. Croke then brought in the real Elizabeth Jackson, dressed in the clothes of another woman. No sooner had she entered the room than Mary fell into her extraordinary, accusatory fit. Croke next tried to establish whether or not Glover's affliction were supernatural and genuine by seeing if she were impervious to pain. He applied a hot pin to her cheek and lit papers and burned her hand, scrutinizing her for any sign of a response. She remained impassive, even when the ordeal was repeated and her flesh was burned. Evidently convinced that Mary was not faking, Croke then turned the hearing into a test of Elizabeth Jackson. Her hand was burned, and he admonished her for being unable to endure the pain – disproof of her allegation that the girl had been faking. He then ordered the terrified old woman to repeat the Lord's Prayer, and when she skipped the phrase 'deliver us from evil', he had her say it, causing Glover's body to convulse, as it always did when that phrase was recited. The apparently senseless maid then spoke in her nostril voice, demanding that Jackson be hanged. Croke, who had obviously begun his tests with the suspicion that the girl was dissembling, ended them with the conviction that Jackson had bewitched her. The old woman was indicted and remanded for trial on 1 December 1602.

The trial was another dramatic confrontation between the girl and the old woman. But by now both parties had expert supporters as well as ordinary witnesses to corroborate their testimony. On Mary Glover's side were two physicians, Francis Herring and a Doctor Spencer, who had been officially summoned to state the nature and cause of Glover's illness.[9] Both testified that her disease 'proceeded of som cause supernaturall, having stranger effects than either the mother, or any other naturall disease'. On the other side appeared two members of the College of Physicians, Jorden and John Argent (already a Censor and eight times President of the College in the 1620s and 1630s),[10] and a noted divine, James Meadowes, DD.[11] The doctors had been ordered by the College to examine Glover, and although they were not officially summoned to testify at Jackson's trial, they were, in effect, government witnesses, procured by Bishop Bancroft. Both physicians denied that Glover was the victim of a supernatural disease. 'These Phisitions', grumbles Bradwell, 'sought earnestly, to make the case a meere naturall disease. ... But above all others, Doctor Jorden earnestly contended with reasons, which when they were delivered, argued not somuch a naturall disease, as som minde (rather) of dissimulation and conterfetting' (fols. 37r–37v). Their testimony was supported by Meadowes, who sought to prove that Jackson had not practised witchcraft.

The confrontation between the physicians at the trial perpetuated a division that had begun in a meeting of the College of Physicians two weeks earlier. On November 13 Elizabeth Jackson had petitioned the College, naming Moundeford, Herring and Bradwell as her accusers, and asking the physicians to consider her case. Moundeford was absent, but Herring and Bradwell were examined by about a dozen fellows. Herring explained that he had accompanied the girl during her first test by the Recorder, at her parents' request. He had been convinced then, and not before, that she was really bewitched and that Jackson was the culprit. Bradwell had also become involved at this relatively advanced stage in the affair, and he, too, was persuaded by what he saw. He explained Mary Glover's symptoms to the fellows and stressed that whenever Jackson came into her presence, she said 'hang her, hang her' through her nostrils. The petition and support for it had been carefully planned, almost certainly by Bishop Bancroft or his agents. Many of Jackson's neighbours and friends were in attendance; ten elders among them testified that they had known her for twenty years and had heard nothing against her. According to Sir George Clark, the majority of the fellows took Jackson's side, maintaining 'that Mary Glover was not bewitched but afflicted with some natural disease'. These included, again according to Clark, 'men of great learning', who were among the most eminent members of the College.[12]

Of the physicians actively involved in the case, the leading figures were more or less evenly matched in terms of their standing in the College, but Mary Glover also attracted one or two supporters who were not as respected by their colleagues as her adversaries. Argent and Moundeford had already served as Censor and were on their way to becoming President of the College. Jorden was remembered for his brilliant examinations; Herring had a highly successful career in the College and as a medical author. Bradwell had been admitted to the College without an MD in 1594, partly because of his courageous service during a serious epidemic of plague that struck London a year earlier. He had been practising for some time without a licence, and he had stepped in when many of the regular physicians had refused to serve. Despite his lack of academic credentials, he had considerable influence and intellectual ability. He was the son-in-law of the distinguished City physician John Banister, [13] and he had published religious and scientific works. The latter included a preface to Gerard's *Herbal*, advocating that the College found a lectureship in chemistry. His interest in a science associated with Paracelsianism may have been one of the reasons why he was often at odds with the Fellows. Numerous complaints about his insolence, alleged ignorance and unseemly advertising were laid against him between 1607 and 1610.[14] Finally, if the Dr Spencer at the trial was Ethelbert Spencer, as seems likely, then he was hardly an unalloyed asset to Mary Glover's team. He had failed his examinations as a candidate for a fellowship twice; the second time after he had received his MD.[15]

The principal judge at the trial was Sir Edmund Anderson, the Chief Justice of the Court of Common Pleas. He presided because the system for trying felonies in London relied on commissions of oyer and terminer that included one or more of the judges of King's Bench and Common Pleas and various officials of the City. Serving with Anderson were Croke the Recorder and a number of other eminent men, including Sir William Cornwallis and Sir Jerome Bowes, famous as Elizabeth's ambassador to Russia.[16] Anderson's role in the trial is important, because his power was vast and his opinions were strongly against Elizabeth Jackson. Anderson had been the presiding judge in many witchcraft trials, including two involving victims who had been exorcised by the famous Puritan thamauturgist, John Darrell. Anderson was something of an expert inquisitor.

The trial was unusual in many respects, not the least because it quickly turned into a ritualized confrontation between Mary Glover and Elizabeth Jackson. When the latter entered the courtroom for the arraignment, the girl cried out, asking where she was, and fell into a swoon, writhing and contorting, repeating 'hang her' through her nose increasingly loudly. After a break, the eminent justices subjected Mary Glover to a terrifying test, crying out that she was a counterfeit and burning her hand once more to prove that she was senseless. Impressed by the girl's response to these ordeals, Anderson then led the accused through a series of standard tests for witchcraft, similar to those Croke had administered, demanding that she repeat the Lord's Prayer and the Creed. Like countless other laymen, Jackson proved herself woefully ignorant of these crucial formulae. She forgot the verse asking forgiveness for our sins and mangled the phrases, 'the communion of saints, the forgiveness of sins' in the Creed. Her mistakes were deemed significant proof of a devotion to Satan rather than simple ignorance. Mary Glover dramatized their significance by writhing in torment when Jackson was led through certain passages in both the Lord's Prayer and the Creed. The ominous implications of these religious ordeals were further reinforced by the testimony of witnesses against Jackson, including the young Puritan divine, Lewis Hughes, who described how her malevolent gaze had rendered him speechless when he visited her home to remonstrate with her concerning her 'lewed tongue'.[17]

The most important evidence in Jackson's defence was the assertions of Jorden and Argent that Glover's ailment was not supernatural. The doctors were unable to make a convincing case for their diagnosis. Jorden in particular was fatally evasive and indecisive. Pressed by the judge, Jorden asserted that Glover's symptoms had a natural cause and identified her malady as 'passio hysterica'. But he would not confirm that the disease could be cured, and he declined to treat her himself. Anderson seems to have suspected that his reluctance might arise from a suspicion that the girl was faking, and he asked Jorden directly whether he thought she was counterfeiting. Although at other times, Jorden had said that he believed her symptoms were produced by a combination of hysteria and fakery, he now answered that she was not a fraud. Anderson pounced on the doctor: 'Then in my conscience, it is not naturall; for if you tell me neither a Naturall cause of it, nor a naturall remedy, I will tell you, that it is not naturall' (fol. 38r). The belief that the acid test whether or not a disease was natural was that it could or could not be cured using natural means was widely shared by laymen and physicians alike. The Judge was on firm ground.

Anderson then turned to address the jury, instructing them on the perils of witchcraft and its characteristics, and explaining why he rejected Jorden's diagnosis of the girl's disease. 'The Land is full of Witches', he began, 'they abound in all places.' He announced that he had hanged over two dozen of them himself, and boasted that he knew more about witches than any man present. He explained the theology of witchcraft and the significance of the witches' mark, examples of which had been found on Elizabeth Jackson's body. He reminded the jury that her personality fitted the stereotype of a witch: she was an ill-tempered, bad-tongued woman. There had also been testimony that her threats had made a neighbour who had taken Mary Glover's side in a quarrel violently ill and her curse had caused one of Lady Bond's men to break his leg. Finally, Anderson asked the jury if they had ever heard of a case of the mother in which hysterical fits occurred regularly, in different forms, on alternating days and intensified when one particular person was present. 'Divines [and] Phisitions', he concluded, 'I know they are learned and wise, but to say this is naturall, and tell me neither the cause, nor the Cure of it, I care not for your Judgement' (fols 38r– 39r). The Recorder finished the summation, describing once more the tests he had arranged to see if Mary Glover's symptoms might have been caused by fear or dissimulation. He asserted that every natural explanation for her malady had been eliminated; only supernatural causes, namely witchcraft, remained. 'The presumptions and probabilities (as we all see) are very great and pregnant' (fols 39r–39v). Understandably, after receiving this guidance, the jury quickly found Elizabeth Jackson guilty of bewitching Mary Glover, and she was sentenced to a year's confinement, during which she was several times to stand in the pillory and endure the abuse of the crowd. This was the maximum penalty she could have received for a first offence under the witchcraft statute of 1563. Witchcraft that did not result in the victim's death was not made a capital crime until 1604.

The conviction of Elizabeth Jackson was not, however, the end of the incident. She had acquired powerful supporters during her ordeal, and she was quickly released from prison. She probably received a royal pardon; she certainly escaped punishment. Meanwhile, Mary Glover continued to suffer her 'ordinary fits', as Bradwell calls them. Finally, on 14 December 1602, a group of Puritan divines and godly laymen cured the girl by holding a session of prayer and fasting, the only method of exorcism approved by any Protestant theologians. The dispossession itself was a dramatic ritual confrontation between the godly preachers and the devil in Mary Glover. All day the clerics preached and prayed; the girl's fits were worse than ever before, as the power of prayer battled against the power of evil. The struggle continued in stages, each one of which she marked with a prayer. Finally, after her last and most intense contortions, the devil seemed to leave her body and the girl revived, crying out in joy that God had come and the Lord had delivered her. At the moment of her deliverance, she used the same words that her grandfather, a victim of the Marian persecutions, had uttered as he died on the pyre. The equation of the famous martyr and the godly young demoniac was significant, and it was seized upon by all of the Puritan writers who described her dispossession. To Puritan eyes – including Mary Glover's – the girl had become the central figure in a struggle between religious truth and official persecution.

The politics of exorcism

The possession and dispossession of Mary Glover were acted out in a politically supercharged atmosphere. The Church of England was being challenged from within and without by thaumaturgists who claimed to have the power to cast out devils, and its leaders had embarked on a campaign to discredit and silence them. Exorcism had been controversial ever since the mid-sixteenth century, when it was struck out of the English rite by Protestant reformers. They objected to the Catholic ritual of exorcism mainly on the grounds that it was an idolatrous ceremony that had no biblical sanction. The Protestants' scruples, however, proved the papists' opportunity. The demand for spiritual remedies for supernatural afflictions did not diminish merely because reformers had foresworn exorcism. Throughout the late sixteenth and early seventeenth centuries, Catholic priests exploited that demand, performing well-publicized exorcisms. The Jesuit missionaries who began to infiltrate England after 1580 were especially active as exorcists, staging spectacular dispossessions that dramatically confirmed the authority of their church and attracted, it was claimed, large numbers of converts. The high point of Catholic thaumaturgy came in 1585 and 1586, when a dozen priests led by William Weston, SJ, exorcised six demoniacs in the homes of prominent recusants. Their feats were described in a manuscript prepared for publication but subsequently seized by the government. The propaganda element was very prominent in these rituals, which were presented as a highly theatrical contest between the champions of the rival confessions. 'A pox on you all for popish priests', cries a demon named Modu just before Weston casts him out, adding that 'my fellowes the protestants' welcome the devils that provoke deadly sins, whereas 'you scurvy priests can neither abide them your selves, nor suffer them to be quiet whensoever you are conversant'.[18]

To counteract the propaganda advantage that the Catholics had won for themselves, Protestant divines devised a new means of casting out devils that had scriptural authority and so was acceptable to scrupulous reformers. They seized on a passage in Mark (ix, 14–29), in which Jesus cures a youth afflicted with a 'dumb and deaf spirit', whom his disciples had been unable to relieve. When the apostles ask him why they failed, he explains 'This kind can come forth by nothing, but by prayer and fasting'.[19] Fortified by faith, polemical purpose and scriptural authority, Protestants began to exorcise possessed and bewitched people in marathon sessions of prayer and fasting. One of the earliest and most influential dispossessions was led by the martyrologist John Foxe in 1574. The patient was a law student called Briggs whose actions and words were controlled by the devil. Foxe and his assistants confronted Satan directly, in a dramatic dialogue that climaxed hours of fervent prayer. 'Thou most retched serpant', cried Foxe, 'O thou foul devil, I command thee to depart'. The devil would not budge, and counterattacked, accusing Foxe of witchcraft. Finally, when Briggs himself was made to order the Satan to depart in God's name, the devil fled. As Keith Thomas has pointed out, accounts of this miracle circulated in Protestant, particularly Puritan, circles and strongly influenced subsequent dispossessions. These took on an increasingly partisan character in the latter part of Elizabeth's reign, when they become a central issue in the intensifying struggle between the Puritan faction in the church and the conservative clergy.[20]

Introduction by Michael MacDonald

The struggle became an open battle in the 1590s, when the ecclesiastical authorities assailed the Puritan exorcist, John Darrell. Darrell had been dispossessing patients since 1586, but it was the appearance in 1597 of a pamphlet describing how he had cured Thomas Darling, a thirteen-year-old witchcraft victim, that finally provoked the fury of the bishops. Copies of the offending pamphlet were destroyed, and the printer was imprisoned. Darrell and his associates were arrested or threatened with arrest. Men who merely expressed belief in Darrell's powers were cast into gaol or driven into hiding.[21] These oppressive measures did not stop Darrell. The stakes were too high. However much the misguided authorities objected, Darrell was convinced that exorcism was the weapon that would vanquish the papists. 'If the Church of Englande have this power to cast out devils', wrote his closest ally, George More, 'then the Church of Rome is a false Church, for there can be but one true Church, the principall marke whereof (as they say) is to worke miracles, and of them this is the greatest, namely to cast out Devills.'[22] Darrell went on to exorcise no fewer than seven children in a Lancashire family and a troubled young Nottinghamshire apprentice musician named William Somers in 1597. These incidents prompted the authorities to renew their attacks.

Darrell, his patients and his associates were harried in the courts and excoriated in print.[23] The assault on him was carefully co-ordinated. Somers was arrested in January 1598 and accused of witchcraft by supporters of the woman he had accused of bewitching him. The mayor and three aldermen of Nottingham examined him in prison and induced him to confess that he had simulated his possession. In March, the Archbishop of York, Matthew Hutton, established a commission to investigate the matter. Hutton was accused by conforming hardliners of being soft on Puritans; that may explain why Somers withdrew his confession in the hearings he held.[24] Within a fortnight the mayor, two justices of the peace and an assize judge interrogated him and extracted fresh admissions of fraud and even got him to demonstrate his skill as a fake demoniac. As D. P. Walker points out, the harassment of Somers divided Nottingham into factions of believers and doubters; the Mary Glover case divided London in just the same way four years later.[25] Darrell and More were arrested and tried before the High Commission in 1599. The trial was presided over by his most

xxi

powerful enemies, the Archbishop of Canterbury, John Whitgift, and Bishop Bancroft, and included two other arch-anti-Puritans, Chief Justices Popham and Anderson. There is no doubt that Bancroft was Darrell's main adversary; rigidly, even fanatically, hostile to Puritans, he had taken charge of most of the significant work of the church, because of Whitgift's age. He was, Thomas Fuller remarks, 'the soul of the high commission'.[26] He was also, in all probability, a sceptic about witchcraft – or at least about its occurrence in the modern world. In May, the commission denounced Darrell as a counterfeit. He was suspended from the ministry, briefly imprisoned and driven underground. Meanwhile, the government launched a noisy barrage of propaganda against him. Bancroft's chaplain Samuel Harsnet was encouraged to write *A Discovery of the Fraudulent Practises of John Darrell* (1599), which demolished four earlier pamphlets by Darrell and his supporters that had publicized his cures and defended their genuineness. Darrell and More answered Harsnet's book after their trial, and two hired pens, John Deacon and John Walker, published attacks and refutations in 1601, supporting the bishops' position. Darrell wrote a final defence in 1602; he seems to have died soon afterwards.[27]

Memories of the Darrell case were still strong and still divisive when Mary Glover's possession occurred, and the two episodes became intermeddled in the minds of participants and observers. To Bancroft and his allies, the possession of a girl from a prominent Puritan family must have signalled a renewal of the Lancashire episodes and the Somers case. Mary Glover's fits turned into just the sort of dumbshow that Darrell had exploited so successfully. It is highly probable that the appearance of Jorden, Argent and Meadowes at Jackson's trial was Bancroft's attempt to keep the episode from going any further. If so, the attempt failed, as we have seen, and Mary Glover's successful dispossession soon afterwards must have realized his worst fears. When he heard about it, he was furious. Advised by Croke 'to goe to the Bishop before he was misinformed, and to shew him the passages of the day from the beginning to the ending', the naive young Lewis Hughes suffered the full blast of Bancroft's rage. 'I did so, but I could have no audience, and for my paines I was called Rascall and varlot, and sent to the Gatehouse, where he kept mee foure monthes.'[28] The Bishop also suspended him from his position as curate and lecturer at

St Helen's Bishopsgate; after ten years of oblivion, he surfaced again finally as an immigrant in Bermuda, a newly-discovered colony. He spent the rest of his life diligently advancing an uncompromisingly Puritan programme of liturgical reform there and at home and recruiting godly ministers to serve in the islands.[29] Another of the Puritan exorcists, a Mr Bridger, was also imprisoned. How many others may have suffered for their part in the affair is impossible to determine. Swan, however, makes it clear that Bancroft threw a deep scare into the Puritans (pp. 60–4).

Punishing those involved was less important and perhaps more difficult than winning the struggle for the support of the citizens of London and the King. The authorities therefore launched a new offensive from the pulpit, the pillory and the press to advance their interpretation of the miracles wrought by Catholic and Puritan exorcists. As early as November 1602 Dr Thomas Holland, Regius Professor of Divinity at Oxford, had preached a sermon at St Paul's Cross denouncing exorcism. 'Some have gon about to shewe the truth of relligion by casting out divels', Holland told his auditors. 'David must come out with his two stones, the old and the newe testament, before Goliah [sic] can be slayne.'[30] Henoch Clapham and Dr Giles Thompson, newly-appointed Dean of Windsor, both doubted that possession occurred 'nowe adayes' in sermons preached in February and March 1603.[31] In February as well, Thomas Darling, whom Darrell had dispossessed, was sentenced to lose his ears and suffer a public whipping in London for libelling almost all of the principal officials of the crown and the church in a private letter. He had charged that Whitgift and Bancroft, among others, 'made the way for Papistry'.[32] Jorden and Harsnet finished their attacks on possession and exorcism in the next month. Both books were almost certainly commissioned by Bancroft; they expounded his views and won his official approval. There are several bits of evidence that suggest the Bishop commissioned Jorden's pamphlet. Jorden himself announces on the first page of the *Briefe Discourse*, 'I have not undertaken this businesse of mine owne accord', and as Bradwell insists, Bancroft is the most likely person to have urged him on. Moreover, Bancroft passed the book himself, an act that was somewhat unusual; censorship was a task he frequently delegated to subordinates.[33] There is even less doubt about who was behind Harsnet's pamphlet. Harsnet was Bancroft's assistant, and he was producing what was, in effect, a sequal to his earlier blast against Darrell on the Bishop's behalf. *A Declaration of Egregious Popish Impostures* was published by order of the Privy Council in 1603 and reissued in 1604 and 1605. The book was aimed chiefly at the Catholics and was part of Bancroft's masterly attempt to exploit the division in their ranks known as the Archpriest Controversy. At some point in its composition, probably very soon before publication, Harsnet inserted a page extending his attack on Weston and his fellow papists to include the divines who exorcised Mary Glover. Linking their names with Darrell's supporters, he declares that '*Skelton, Evans, Swan, & Lewis*' are creduluous frauds, 'devil-finders, the devil-puffers, or devil-prayers'.[34]

According to Henry N. Paul, both books were presented to James during his progress from Scotland to Westminster.[35] The moment was a crucial one. For Whitgift, Bancroft and their allies, the change in regime was fraught with peril. Plotters and clerical politicians threatened the security of the state and the church and endangered the anti-Puritan policies that Whitgift and the old Queen had been pursuing for more than a decade. Their most immediate concern was to detect and expose the machinations of Catholic priests. By July Bancroft had become heavily involved in exposing the Bye Plot, a confusing conspiracy to seize and perhaps to kill or depose the King, led by the secular priest William Watson.[36] Bancroft himself had been dealing with Watson's allies in the Archpriest Controversy, and he was deeply alarmed that he would be implicated in this treasonous business, despite the fact that he was acting as the agent of Whitgift and Sir Robert Cecil in apprehending the plotters. On July 21 he wrote to Cecil, seeking the King's signature on a letter that would exculpate him, if his enemies tried to discredit him.[37] At the same time, the manoeuvring that culminated in the Hampton Court Conference had begun. In May the Puritans had presented to the King the famous Millenary Petition, calling for reforms in the liturgy and an end to the persecution of Puritans, and by July Whitgift and Bancroft had grown afraid that James might acquiesce to its demands. The aged and ill Archbishop roused himself to denounce the Puritans in correspondence with the King and leading figures of the government. He was assisted by Bancroft, who was to become the church's principal spokesman at the Hampton Court Conference in January

1604. A sense of high anxiety over the future of the church pervades the correspondence of both Whitgift and Bancroft throughout the tense months that followed the Queen's death.[38]

It is easy to see why Bancroft encouraged the publication of Jorden and Harsnet's tracts in the spring of 1603. The battle, however, did not end with their coordinated shots. Swan fired back with his pamphlet soon after theirs appeared. It was a secret publication, printed clandestinely to avoid Bancroft's censorship. About Swan, little is known with certainty. He seems to have hailed from Wye in Kent, notorious for its popery earlier in the century. He undertook to edit for the press the sermons of his friend and fellow Puritan, Thomas Jackson, who preached there. The book appeared some months after the Mary Glover case. He had also translated Lambert Danaeus' treatise on the Antichrist in 1589.[39] His account of Mary Glover's dispossession was not entered in the Stationers' Register and lacks the printer's name and address.[40] It was dedicated to the King, and Swan immediately drew James' attention to the essential issue at stake. 'The cause which is controverted concerneth even the glory of Christ Jesus, of late manifested', Swan declares, railing bitterly at Bancroft, Jorden and Harsnet. 'The cause hath bin blasphemed, our persons pursued, and our names traduced, and that openly in print by one S. H. a Chaplain (as I take it) of the Bishopp of London, whose evill dealinge I think not fit, to lay open to your Princely selfe' (p. 2). Harsnet, Swan complains, has depicted holy prayer for poor distressed creatures as mere devil-puffing; equally disturbing, 'he compts Witches to be but *Bul-beggers*, and the opinions of witcherie, to be *brainles imaginations*'. In these endeavours he has been assisted by Jorden, who has accused Mary Glover of counterfeiting and has maintained 'that her affliction proceeded onely from a naturall cause' (pp. 2, 3–4). Swan also grumbles that a preacher holding forth at St Paul's Cross in London has recently publicized the government's sceptical views, charging that Elizabeth Jackson was wrongly convicted (p. 5). This may refer to one of the sermons mentioned above, heard by John Manningham, or to yet another, more specific, government attack.

In his preface, Swan also refers to Bradwell's treatise, which was to complement his pamphlet, much as Jorden's complemented Harsnet's. The weaknesses of Jorden's arguments, he announces, are 'to be layed open, by the labours of two other learned and christian, professors likewise of physicke' (p. 4). Their pamphlet will refute Jorden's contention that Mary Glover suffered from a natural illness and will recount the full details of her possession, the trial of Elizabeth Jackson and her sentencing. Swan therefore will concentrate his attention on the exorcism itself. Who the other physician may have been, we do not know, but the description of the work in progress fits Bradwell's so exactly that it is surely the same. It is possible that Swan's second author was William Scott, who wrote a narrative of Mary Glover's possession that Bradwell used and Manningham quoted.[41] Scott was a barrister of the Inner Temple, and not a physician, though. His views probably coincided with Bradwell's, since the latter quotes the lost narrative as an authoritative account. The fact that neither Bradwell's tract nor Scott's narrative was printed testifies to Bancroft's renewed determination to suppress books critical of official ecclesiastical policy. The effectiveness of censorship waxed and waned during the Elizabethan and early Stuart period. In 1599 Whitgift and Bancroft had been forced to issue an order that certain sorts of books should not be printed without proper authorization, an indication that authors were finding ways to avoid the rules of publication.[42] This was what John Swan had done; Bancroft evidently made sure that Bradwell and Scott did not follow his lead.

Arguments for and against witchcraft

In attacking the belief that Mary Glover had been afflicted by a supernatural illness, Jorden was attempting to shift the field of combat to compensate for the inherent weaknesses in the official position. The decision to abandon exorcism of any type limited the possible responses that the church could make to Catholic and Puritan exorcists who claimed that they enjoyed the assistance of God, whose intervention proved the righteousness of their cause. The church's spokesmen therefore sought to cast doubt on the genuineness of the marvellous results its rivals claimed. They adopted two tactics, which they sometimes combined. The first was to charge that the bewitched and possessed persons whom the exorcists cured were fakers. This was the main thrust of the attacks on Darrell in the 1590s. It gained plausibility from the very thing that made the afflictions of Darrell's patients seem supernatural – their highly stylized, symbolically meaningful manifestations, and the incredibility of some of their symptoms. William Somers' confession was crucial confirmation of the conviction that such dramatic and amazing actions could only be produced by conscious effort. The second and more radical tactic was to question the existence of witchcraft and diabolical possession in the modern world. Deacon and Walker had already advanced along this path in their assaults on Darrell. It was a tortuous track, and it is not easy to simplify their arguments or the issues they raised. The key point is succinctly stated by D. P. Walker. Both Darrell and his adversaries agreed that miracles had ceased at the end of the apostolic age. Protestants of all hues maintained this argument tenaciously, since it was the basis of their claim that Catholic wonders were not miraculous. But Darrell defined the miraculous narrowly, to exclude dispossession by prayer and fasting, whereas Harsnet, Deacon and Walker defined it broadly, to include diabolical actions and divine counteractions.[43] From their point of view, therefore, the Protestant insistence that miracles had ceased required one to believe that Darrell's patients were not supernaturally afflicted.

None of Darrell's adversaries openly denied the existence of witchcraft, but Darrell and his supporters accused them of disbelief anyway. They were probably right about Deacon and Walker. They rely heavily on Reginald Scot's sweepingly sceptical *Discoverie of Witchcraft*, and they attribute the symptoms of bewitchment to natural diseases and malevolent guile. Following Levinus Lemnius and Johann Weyer, they invoke epilepsy, hysteria and melancholy as the causes of apparently diabolical signs. Like most other sceptical or selectively sceptical authors, they place greatest emphasis on melancholy, which had anciently been supposed to cause delusions and a kaleidoscope of other odd and changing symptoms.[44] Harsnet insists that contemporary cases of witchcraft and possession are sheer fakery. Exorcism is a Popish plot to establish false religion, 'a singular foundation to uphold the Pope his play-house, and to make religion a pageant of Puppittes'.[45] Darrell has adopted the same conning ploy for the same reason, and like the papists he has coached his live mannequins in the gestures of possession. Mostly the young people on their side are motivated by laziness or cravings for celebrity. Sometimes, however, diseases assist them to master the more spectactular signs of affliction. If an idle girl, he declares disgustedly, 'have a little helpe of the *Mother, Epilepsie,* or *Cramp*, to teach her to role her eyes, wrie her mouth, gnash her teeth, startle with her body, hold her armes and hands stiffe, make anticke faces, girne [sic], mow and mop like an Ape, tumble like a Hedgehogge, and can mutter out two or three words of gibridg, as *obus, bobus* ... the young girle is Owle-blasted, and possessed'.[46] Harsnet also denies that possession can be caused by witchcraft. In his 1599 attack on Darrell, he asserts that the best authorities insist on the independence of the two sorts of supernatural harm.[47] This was obviously relevant to the Mary Glover case. Other experts, however, disagreed with Harsnet, and there were spectacular instances of possession caused by witchcraft about which everyone knew, although the combination was rarer in England than it was in France.[48]

Jorden's aim both in court and in his *Briefe Discourse* was to mount a convincing scientific case to support Harsnet's arguments. He makes this as clear as anyone could wish. He has set down the medical facts about hysteria, he tells us, because the disease has been 'so great occasion of distraction among many good men'. The unlearned in particular have been deceived by it. They 'are apt to make every thing a supernaturall work which they do not under-stand', and hence they are vulnerable to those who abuse God's name and would 'make us to use holy prayer as ungroundedly as the Papists do in their prophane trickes; who are readie to draw forth their wooden dagger, if they do but see a maid or woman suffering one of these fits of the Mother, conjuring and exorcising them as if they were possessed with evil spirits' (sigs A2v–A3r). He announces in the Epistle Dedicatorie that he will show not merely that apparently supernatural afflictions are caused by the mother but that 'deliverance upon fasting and prayer' is a 'naturall remedie' (sig. A4r). He devotes the entire seventh chapter of his treatise to this point. When prayer and fasting, as well as the whole magazine of magical and religious cures, 'prevaile in the cure of diseases, it is not for any supernaturall vertue in them, either from God or from the divell ... but by reason of the confident perswasion which melancholicke and passionate people may have in them' (pp. 24–5). In other words, Jorden does not deny that prayer and fasting work, he argues instead that they work *naturally*. Indeed he recommends that persons afflicted with hysteria 'use much fasting and prayer' because they may calm the passions (p. 24). This argument was consistent with the views of many other physicians, who maintained that the imagination, which was particularly powerful in people of a melancholy temperament, could work physical effects on the body, causing illnesses and curing them in certain circumstances.[49]

Explaining the cure was one thing; explaining the illness was another, trickier problem. At Elizabeth Jackson's trial Jorden had been humiliated by Chief Justice Anderson because he could not account persuasively for Mary Glover's symptoms. It was a mistake he did not repeat. In his published treatise, he maintained steadfastly that the cause of symptoms like Mary Glover's was hysteria – the suffocation of the mother. He thus rejected Deacon and Walker's scattershot approach – naming all the possible culprits – and dropped his earlier suspicions that Glover might have been both ill and faking. The choice of hysteria rather than melancholy, the disease singled out as the cause of apparent witchcraft by Harsnet and most other sceptics, is more difficult to understand. It was a much less well-known malady, and Jorden was one of the first physicians to write about it in English. Other physicians had blamed apparent witchcraft cases on the mother, and more would do so in future, but it was a decidedly less common diagnosis than melancholy. The specific circumstances of the case probably influenced his choice. The crucial problem was Mary Glover's age. Although medical authorities had precious little to say about mental illnesses in children and nothing to say about them in girls, their discussions of melancholy implied strongly that it was not an illness of prepubescent females. Writing a scant generation later, Robert Burton summarized conventional wisdom: melancholy afflicted men more often than women, the old more often than the young.[50] He acknowledged a kind of melancholy that plagued young, unmarried women – 'Maid's, Nun's, and Widow's Melancholy' – but this could not have been Mary Glover's disease. For melancholy in these women was distinct from the other varieties of the disease precisely because it had 'one only cause proper to women alone': corrupted menses. 'Those vicious vapours which come from menstruous blood' caused symptoms similar to Mary Glover's: their victims become persuaded that they are vexed by an evil spirit, 'surely forspoken or bewitched'.[51] But Mary Glover was not old enough to have this disease, an illness of 'more ancient maids, widows, and barren women'.[52]

The fact that Mary Glover had not reached menarche when her attacks began thus made melancholy an unlikely explanation for her symptoms.[53] But it also tended to cast doubt on the diagnosis Jorden chose instead, the suffocation of the mother. The ancients had agreed that hysteria was a disease of the uterus (or mother), and that it therefore tended to afflict 'mature women who were deprived of sexual relations; prolonged continence was believed to result in demonstrable organic changes in the womb'.[54] Nevertheless, this choice gave Jorden some room to manoeuvre, for the ancients had not been unanimous about the exact aetiology of hysteria, although they agreed on the site of the disease.[55] Moreover, the literature about hysteria was much less familiar to laymen than the lore of melancholy, which had become an immensely fashionable illness in Elizabethan England. It seems likely that it was Mary Glover's youth that drove Jorden to take the innovative step of arguing that the brain played a prominent role in producing the characteristic symptoms of the mother. Indeed, he went on to argue that amenorrhoea and sexual abstinence were not the only causes of the disease. It might also arise from strictly psychological stresses: 'Lastly the perturbations of the minde are oftentimes to blame both for this and many other diseases', he concludes his discussion of the causes of the mother (p. 22). After citing classical authorities to prove this, Jorden adds: 'My selfe do know a Gentlewoman, who upon the sight of one particular man would alwaies feele an uterin affect: and another that upon feare of been chidden, or seeing another in the fit of the mother, would also fall into it herselfe' (p. 16 [23]). The close analogy with Mary Glover's situation could hardly be accidental.

Jorden's insistence that the brain played a leading role in producing the symptoms of the mother also enabled him to explain some of the peculiar features of Mary Glover's affliction, such as her reaction to the presence or touch of Elizabeth Jackson. He believed that her convulsions were expressions of a psychological aversion to Jackson that was expressed by an extreme physical reaction.[56] He therefore dwelt at some length on the ways in which the 'animal functions' that register perils and control the movements of the body 'may be abused both by our own will, and by the violence of some disease, and by both' (p. 12). His examples, several of which are drawn from Reginald Scot, all involve a kind of preternatural fakery, in which people were able to mimic the symptoms of diseases in ways that evidently went beyond the simple play-acting Harsnet emphasizes. Thus ordinary counterfeits who can act mad or drunk are paired with those who display much more remarkable symptoms, such as Hippocrates' ventriloquists, who talked from their stomachs and throats – as Mary Glover spoke through her nostrils – and, even more to the point, famous fake demoniacs, such as Agnes Briggs, Rachel Pinder and Martha Brossier (p. 12). One advantage of stressing the role of the imagination and the animal faculties in the false manifestation of illnesses (natural and supernatural) is that it enables Jorden to explain why such phenomena occur even when the counterfeit apparently has no motive for the deceit. They may be the secondary effect of another illness – a mental disturbance brought on by extreme fear, for instance – as well as simple fraud (p. 12).

Bradwell seizes on Jorden's innovations and charges that they extend the concept of hysteria arbitrarily in order to encompass Mary Glover's symptoms. He points with disdain to Jorden's sweeping assertion that 'whatsoever straunge accident may appeare in any of the principall functions of mans bodie, either animall, vitall, or naturall, the same is to be seene in this disease' (p. 1). He rightly complains that this opening assertion amounts to a declaration that all of Mary Glover's symptoms were necessarily manifestations of the mother. If, therefore, 'he shall not satisfie the expectation of his reader in everie particular ... yet this generall rule shall serve, in sted of all', Bradwell grumbles (fol. 66v). Bradwell also challenges Jorden forcefully at his most vulnerable point: the difficulty of Mary Glover's age. Although he acknowledges that the girl had her first period at some time during her illness, he is entirely correct to argue, as he does at length, that none of the authorities imagined that the mother could afflict a prepubescent female. Nor did any of them provide case histories that would support the diagnosis in a person so young (fols 119r–126v). As usual in this angry tract, he loses his way several times, but in the meanderings he manages to fortify his case with some notable generalizations about the coming of age of girls in Elizabethan England, the most interesting of which is the remark that they did not normally mature enough to suffer from sexual deprivation until they were about eighteen (fols 120v–121r).

Bradwell's fiercest attack on Jorden is reserved, however, for his views on the relationship between the natural and supernatural causes of disease. The issue was a complex one, on which there was an array of learned opinions. Although Jorden is careful to acknowledge that God may permit Satan to possess human beings, he believes that even very strange symptoms have natural causes, except in very rare cases. 'They which are ignorant of the strange affects which naturall causes may produce', he charges, 'have sought above the Moone for supernaturall causes, ascribing these accidents either to diabolicall possession, to witchcraft, or to the immediate finger of the Almightie' (p. 2). This incredulity enrages Bradwell. He argues that strange symptoms are indeed caused supernaturally and, besides, Satan can cause perfectly ordinary, natural diseases as well. His insistence that possession and witchcraft may be manifested by remarkable and distinctive signs was obviously important to his argument that Mary Glover was actually bewitched. But it also matched the opinion of legal and medical authorities. Thus although the Northamptonshire physician John Cotta admitted that natural afflictions could be very similar to diabolical ones, he maintained adamantly that 'it is impossible that the finger or power of the Devil should be in any malady, but such a cause must needs produce some effect like itself'.[57] Bradwell's other claims were more controversial. His fundamental point is that 'Naturall and supernaturall causes maie Concur, to the production or generation of sicknes ... and are not contraries that expell one another' (fol. 74v). Many lay authors would have endorsed this statement, but dual causation was gradually becoming less attractive to the medical profession. Still, Bradwell had ample authority for his somewhat less sweeping assertion that the devil could cause or amplify natural disorders: '*Sathan* the Ocean sea of subtleties, can ... hide his own ougly shape, under the leaves of ordinary symptomes' (fol. 74v). He points to Biblical passages proving that the evil spirits cast out by Christ himself had caused natural diseases such as epilepsy and blindness (fol. 70v). Moreover, he marshals modern medical experts, including Johann Weyer, a limited sceptic about witchcraft, to prove that even in these days 'the Divell maie be found to have his hand in sundry bodely afflictions which have no supernaturall symptomes to discover them' (fol. 74r). He could have gone still further. Some leading demonologists argued that Satan caused illness by manipulating the humours, and one modern scholar has asserted that 'the great principle laid down by theology ... was that whatever Satan did in the realm of physical nature he did by solely natural means'.[58]

Mary Glover's 'good possession'

On one point the supporters and adversaries of Mary Glover agreed: there was method to her madness. Her behaviour conformed to widely recognized signs of possession and bewitchment, and it implicated Elizabeth Jackson. To her supporters, the expressive aspects of her fits proved that they were supernatural and that Jackson had bewitched her; to her adversaries, they proved that she was faking, mentally ill or both. The unavoidable question is, was she mad? Did she suffer from hysteria as Jorden alleged? I am certainly less qualified to answer that question than many of the readers of this book, and the problem is compounded by the fact that the diagnosis is controversial and seldom used any more. The standard diagnostic manual for American psychiatrists goes so far as to claim that conversion disorder (or hysterical neurosis, conversion type) 'was apparently common several decades ago [but] is now rarely encountered'.[59] The changes in the extent to which hysteria is diagnosed and other, earlier variations in its symptomology suggest that it is a malady responsive to cultural conditioning.[60] Mary Glover's behaviour matched in striking ways modern accounts of hysterical neurosis of the conversion kind. The context in which the case began and developed also seems consistent with accepted aetiological models of hysteria. Psychiatrists argue, for instance, that conversion neurosis charactistically occurs among adolescents, particularly adolescent girls, and that it is a kind of defence that originates in repression. They distinguish between a 'primary gain' that the patient achieves by repressing disturbing sexual urges, and a 'secondary gain' that she enjoys by virtue of her illness and the response of others to it. Mary Glover was precisely the right age to be a victim of the malady, and she found herself in an extremely distressing situation. Whether there was a sexual conflict underlying her illness is impossible to determine. There were, however, plenty of more immediate tensions from which she escaped by falling ill. She avoided punishment by her parents and became the centre of attention. Like modern hysterics, her fits were timed to avoid distressing confrontations – or rather to control them so that she could not effectively be accused of the offence that began her conflict with Elizabeth Jackson. Her adversaries pointed to her tendency to evade trouble by having a seizure as evidence of her duplicity.[61]

On the other hand, there were aspects of her behaviour that do not seem to fit the stereotype of conversion neurosis. Her bodily movements, for example, were too deliberate and stylized to be entirely consistent with modern descriptions of the illness. Moreover, it is almost impossible to believe that the girl was not conscious of what she was saying and doing at some points in her fits. Her demand 'hang her' whenever Elizabeth Jackson was present is perhaps the most obvious example.[62] The safe conclusion – although it can never be satisfactorily substantiated – was the one that Jorden seems to have had in mind at the trial and that Chief Justice Anderson ridiculed. The girl did really suffer from hysteria, but she also wittingly employed her role as a demoniac in order to impress adults and attack her enemy Elizabeth Jackson. The problem, unresolvable in retrospect, is to determine how much of her illness was an act and how much of it was not. In terms of what can and cannot be said with certainty today, a more productive approach to Mary Glover's malady is to examine how it was influenced by cultural factors and the immediate circumstances and what her symptoms signified to others.

Diabolical possession is one of the most perplexing mental phenomena. Almost everywhere it has occurred – or still occurs – it is distinguished by extremely abnormal behaviour that signalizes violent emotions and bizarre, indeed alien, ideas. Spirit possession only happens in cultures that entertain the belief that supernatural entities might invade people and overwhelm their personal identities. This is an important point, no matter how simplistic it may sound. For it should warn us against proceeding too rapidly to translate what is essentially a religious experience into the terms of modern psychiatry, equating it with a disease entity in cultures that do not accept the possibility of possession. The signs and significance of possessed behaviour are strongly shaped by the stereotypes of the culture in which the possessed person and the people who observe him live.[63] There were quite striking variations in the manifestations of diabolical possession between early modern European nations and even within a single culture, depending on the setting in which the possession happened.[64] Possession in Elizabethan England, like spirit possession elsewhere in the world, was a 'culture-bound syndrome', an illness that was manifested in specific cultural settings and had very specific cultural meanings. A wider claim, which would be accepted by anthropologists and many psychiatrists, is that the symptoms of psychiatric illnesses are strongly influenced by social factors and cultural expectations.[65]

The signs of diabolical possession were very unusual and highly stereotyped. The classic symptoms were familiar enough to be listed in contemporary handbooks and depicted in popular literature and drama. They included extraordinary strength, convulsions and violent motions, knowledge of facts and languages the victim could not naturally have learned, speaking in strange voices, vomiting foreign objects such as nails or pins, insensitivity to pain and revulsion at sacred things.[66] Despite the reservations of demonologists, to which Harsnet pointed, few authors of handbooks about witchcraft aimed at laymen made any great distinction between the effects of bewitchment and possession. To some writers, the most important indications of supernatural affliction were speaking in strange voices or tongues that the possessed person cannot have learnt and extreme revulsion at holy words and things. These symptoms were crucial, both because they decisively distinguished supernatural from natural maladies and because they plainly proved that the devil was the source of the affliction. Moreover, as D. P. Walker points out, the religious signs also served as the basis for 'scientific' proofs that the person was possessed, experimental tests of the circumstances in which his or her symptoms manifested themselves.[67]

Authors of eyewitness descriptions of the behaviour of demoniacs and of some witchcraft victims claimed to have observed the stereotypical symptoms described in the handbooks. Undoubtedly, this is partially the result of selective observation and imitative reporting.[68] The impression one gets from many tales of possession and dispossession is that they were scripted, and that naturally arouses in modern readers – as it did in contemporary disbelievers – the conviction that they were deliberately staged. The problem of fakery – or at least of conscious manipulation of symptoms that originated in an underlying disease – is complicated for us as it was for contemporaries by the fact that some people undoubtedly did mimic the illness of possession in order to gain the attention and authority it conferred. The confessions of putative demoniacs that they had been coached and the exposure of the pathetic attempts at deception by others cannot be dismissed as propaganda. Nevertheless, it is likely that both Mary Glover and the would-be healers were entirely sincere. The Puritans, after all, were notorious for their abhorrence of dramatic fakery. The situation is hard to understand partly because our sympathy must be with the Elizabeth Jacksons of the period and partly because like their supporters we presume that learning a complex sickness role must take a conscious effort and that anyone capable of doing it must not therefore be sick. This is, however, an unrealistically simple conception of learning. Sickness roles are usually quite stylized and they are learned in complex cultural and social processes that are seldom consciously recognized by the participants.

Possession, I suggest, was learned as the illness developed. The basic features of the affliction were widely known, and the demoniac was helped to master them by the reactions of concerned and curious onlookers. Bradwell's narrative shows quite clearly how Mary Glover's fits strengthened and changed over time, so that they confirmed with increasing clarity that she was bewitched. The distress she experienced in the first eighteen days after her traumatic confrontation with Elizabeth Jackson was manifested in bodily signs of extreme anxiety and in transient periods of unconsciousness. These symptoms were sufficiently undistinctive to cause one of her physicians to think that they were natural, and to cause her parents to proceed cautiously, minimizing publicity and calling in medical men and a folk healer of some kind to cure her. The confrontation between the girl and Elizabeth Jackson at Sheriff Glover's house recreated the original trauma and caused her ordinary fit to be 'strengthened and lengthened, yea with som new addicons, more and more augmented by her [Jackson's] contagious coming to her' (fol. 12v). Her behaviour became more dramatic, but it is notable how variable it was at first. It seems that it was only after she began to be tested by adults that she manifested the unmistakable symptoms of possession, reacting violently to the petition in the Lord's Prayer, 'deliver us from evil', for instance (fol. 11r). Further confrontations with Jackson and experiments with the usual tests for possession and bewitchment led to more spectacular fits and elaborations on her regular seizures. Her apparently uncontrolled and amazingly energetic behaviour thus developed and changed in response to the actions and expectations of others, some of whom as magistrates, physicians and divines were experts in what to look for.

To be recognized as the victim of possession or witchcraft sick people had therefore to master a difficult set of extreme behaviours. They were challenged and helped by the reactions of others to their illness, and they either perfected their roles or abandoned them in one way or another, being demoted to mere mad folk or counterfeits. There were, accordingly, good possessions and bad. Mary Glover's was undoubtedly a good possession. It involved all of the classical physical and psychological symptoms of diabolical illness. Glover apparently lost control of her body and yet she moved in patterns, elaborately described by Bradwell, that followed rigid conventions, so that her gestures suggested that external forces were controlling her limbs. Although she did not speak in unknown tongues, she did utter strange words – 'Tesh', she moaned loudly during her fits – and she urged in a preternaturally soft voice, 'hang her, hang her'. She also lost sensation in her limbs, so much so that she could without flinching submit to having her flesh roasted. Finally, at the very climax of her illness, recorded in Swan's pamphlet, she managed the transition from torment to transported, pious joy with consummate skill, changing from a violently raging devil into the very image of the pious Puritan daughter, singer of psalms, reciter of prayers.

The religious context of Mary Glover's good possession was vital. Keith Thomas has observed that a great many of the most highly publicized possessions occurred in intensely pious environments.[69] Mary Glover's household was certainly exemplary in this respect. She was the grand-daughter of Robert Glover, the Somerset Herald and a famous Marian martyr, who was burned at Oxford in 1555. In his lengthy account of Glover's sufferings for the faith, John Foxe argues that Robert's two brothers, John and William, were also martyrs for the true faith. For although neither of them was executed, both were resolute Protestants who were hunted by the authorities and disinterred and disgraced after their deaths. To Glover's family, militant Protestantism was an inescapable heritage.[70] Her uncle William Glover is known to have been a Puritan, and Mary and her parents had worshipped with Lewis Hughes, the godly young lecturer at St Helen's Bishopsgate, a rich parish inclined to Puritanism.[71] Thomas suggests that such backgrounds led to possessions in which the victim, controlled by diabolical forces, could lash out against the oppressive piety and obsessive control that characterized them. Children who normally lacked the authority to defy the oppressive demands of their parents suddenly became the frightening instruments of supernatural force.

Mary Glover's possession was rebellious in the sense that she obviously exercised her power over her parents and attendants, keeping them in a state of terror and wonder during her fits. She also obviously retaliated against Jackson for rebuking her and rallied her parents and other adults to her side. But in her case, bewitchment was a means of proving her godliness. She accused Elizabeth Jackson – probably not a Puritan and certainly beyond the pale of Mary's social circle – of causing her illness. Her fits and her many public confrontations with Jackson became a contest in which she played the part of a pious innocent harmed by an evil and sinful old woman, famous for her temper and her 'lewed tongue'. For instance, as she perfected her 'ordinary fits', she punctuated the stages in them with expressions of thanks to God and pleas to Him to deliver her from her affliction (Bradwell, fols 17v–18r). The Puritan magistrates and preachers rallied round her; it was the prayers of the latter that led to her triumphant reintegration into her original social circle. The climax of her good possession was her deliverance at the exercise organized by the Puritan divines. Swan presents it as an almost Manichaean struggle between the devil in Mary Glover and the power of God, which is roused by the supplications and brave words of the ministers. Mary herself is at once the embodiment of Satan, the tormented site of the struggle, and a child of God. She emerges from the battle as an exemplar of holiness, singing His praises. Moreover, at the moment of her triumph, she cries out 'he is come, he is come ... the comforter is come, O Lord thou hast delivered me', and her father exclaims 'this was the crye of her grandfather goeing to be burned' (Swan, 47). Identified now with the martyr, she has been transformed into a Puritan saint. Her prayer of thanksgiving asks God for a new birth and sanctity, which in the eyes of the observers she had just dramatically obtained. In the poems of prayer Swan appends to her account, she is cast as the champion of the saints:

> Let all thy sainctes rejoyce to heare,
>   and see thy gratious hand,
> and let thy foes be smitt with feare,
>   that did thy worke withstand. (unpaginated)

Scepticism, credulity and power

In a brilliant and well-known essay, Stephen Greenblatt has stressed the way in which Harsnet seized upon the theatricality of exorcism. He argued that Darrell's patients and the demoniacs that the Jesuits had dispossessed were mere actors; the theatrical features of possession and exorcism were proof of its falsity. Greenblatt summarizes his view succinctly: 'performance kills belief; or rather acknowledging theatricality kills the credibility of the supernatural'. A central device of Harsnet's polemic was therefore to expose the artifice that the participants in the rituals of possession and dispossession refused to recognize.[72] Harsnet was, of course, absolutely right about exorcism: it was a kind of sacred theatre. His aim was to discredit it by equating it with the secular stage. To the performers themselves, however, it was a spectacle of supernatural power. Indeed, Darrell's language even betrayed recognition of the performative qualities of William Somers' possession: 'This evening, he acted many sins by signs and gestures, most lively representing and shadowing them out unto us.'[73] The question for the Puritan exorcists and for the non-sceptics who crowded in to see Mary Glover and other demoniacs was not whether or not possession and exorcism were theatrical but who wrote the script and directed the action. Genuine performances had been scripted by God: they recreated the miracle stories in the New Testament. They were staged by Satan, and the exorcists attempted to play the part of the

Apostles as best they could in a corrupt age. Bogus performances, on the other hand, had been devised by the participants for reasons that might be mistaken or deceitful. They could be recognized when the demoniac fell out of character.

Performance itself, in other words, could create belief as well as kill it. If the possessed person played his part recognizably and well, he convinced his audience that his disease was authentic and that his deliverance was genuinely marvellous. To those who were prepared to believe in the reality of possession and exorcism, the performative aspects of the phenomena and the unfolding of the drama in scenes and acts familiar from accounts of other cases were precisely what made them convincing as demonstrations of supernatural power at work. Exposing bogus cases involved detecting flaws in the demoniac's performance. Hence the repeated attempts to discover inconsistencies in Mary Glover's behaviour. What was happening in the Glover case, therefore, was a contest between two conflicting interpretations of a ritual performance, one of which was sanctioned by an appeal to biblical authority, the other by a rival set of theological arguments and by medical science. It is necessary to insist on this to understand the pattern of events in the case and to grasp why the testimony of an expert like Jorden failed to convince the judge and jury. A crucial problem, which Jorden tried and failed to solve, was that medical arguments against supernatural maladies were simply not conclusive. Nor could they have been. Mental illnesses could not be diagnosed scientifically, which is to say in a way that negated the interpretation that the sufferer placed on them and substituted instead a label that was recognized to have greater authority than lay explanations. This was brought home all too clearly by the division of opinion among the physicians at Mary Glover's trial. In such a situation, the interpretation triumphed that explained most persuasively to lay observers events that were played out on a public stage.

The theatre of possession and exorcism was theatre in the world, and it was consequently acted out by and before people whose social roles and prestige differed widely. The extent to which a possession was judged to be persuasive or unpersuasive was determined partly by a shifting matrix of power relations. From the very beginning, the possession of Mary Glover was a power struggle. The interpretation of her malady was contested by Mary

Glover and Elizabeth Jackson, by the physicians who treated her and testified at her trial, by the political authorities and the neighbours of the accuser and the accused, by the church hierarchy and the Puritans. The story reveals a good deal about how different ideas served different ends and how they were shaped by social and political factors. On the most fundamental level, Mary Glover's affliction was a contest between the girl and an old woman. It pitted the generations against one another quite explicitly. At first, the conflict was a complicated, but nevertheless normal, case of adult discipline. Although she was merely a charwoman, Elizabeth Jackson's age authorized her to scold Mary for mistreating her daughter. Jackson's visit to Mary's house after she had scolded her illustrates her confidence that she was in the right; she was seeking and evidently expected Mistress Glover's support. Confronted with the prospect that Jackson would be joined by her parents in admonishing or punishing her, the girl was terrified and her fits began. The belief that they had a supernatural cause enabled Mary Glover to reverse the normal relations of authority and to exert power over her adversary. Convincing her elders that her disease was supernatural, however, was difficult and protracted. Her parents seem initially to have been very reluctant to upset the usual relations of generational power. They called in experts to diagnose her ailment and persisted in seeking a natural remedy for it even after Dr Shereman had declared that it was supernatural.

As the case developed, increasing numbers of more and more powerful adults became involved in the struggle to identify her disease and its cause. One of the most striking features of Bradwell's partisan account is his inadvertent acknowledgement of how many people rallied to Elizabeth Jackson's side. As the incident developed, it pitted her neighbours against the Glovers and their allies. At her final public tests and the trial itself angry spectators denounced Mary Glover as a counterfeit. The ordeals and the trials were thus social confrontations. They were also highly politicized confrontations, since public authorities of great prestige and power rapidly became involved and took control of them. On her side Mary Glover began with significant advantages. She was the niece of William Glover, who was sheriff in 1601–2 and was still an alderman of the City in 1603,[74] and she convinced notable Puritan divines and a majority of the physicians who examined her. As she passed the tests that Recorder Croke and Chief Justice Anderson set for her, she won their backing, which was decisive in the trial. Croke's views must have impressed the jury especially strongly. Not only had he been an MP, he had also served as the Speaker of the House of Commons in the parliament of 1601.[75] On the other hand, these influential men, although they were able to help her win the contest in court, were unable to triumph in the long run against the still more powerful supporters whom Jackson acquired. Bancroft, Meadowes, Argent and Jorden made up for their smaller influence in the courtroom and over London opinion by their institutional authority. They possessed lofty credentials to validate their opinions, and they held positions superior to their adversaries in the church and in the College of Physicians. More to the point, Bancroft controlled the press and had the power to imprison offending divines, ruin the careers of men hopeful of favour at court and set aside judgements at law. By the time it was through, the disturbed antics of a fourteen-year-old girl had become a contest of power between the church and the criminal courts of the City of London.

The contest was only possible because incompatible explanations for apparent bewitchment already existed and were vigorously contested. There never had been a time when supernatural beliefs had been the only possibility: Jorden himself calls attention to the discussions of the alternatives of the natural and the divine in Hippocrates and Galen. Outright scepticism was admittedly rare in print. The most important English sceptic was Reginald Scot, whose *Discoverie of Witchcraft* (1584) is a brave and brilliant dismissal of popular beliefs about witches. Scot's central theme is that ignorance has prompted men illegitimately to expand the realm of the supernatural. He makes this perfectly plain in the opening sentences of his book:

> The fables of Witchcraft had taken so fast hold and deepe root in the heart of man, that fewe or none can (nowadaies) with patience indure the hand and correction of God. For if any adversitie, greefe, sicknesse, loss of children, corne, cattell, or libertie happen unto them; and by and by they exclaime uppon witches.[76]

Scot brusquely dismisses the diseases caused by witches as natural maladies: 'As apoplexies, epilepsies, convulsions, hot fevers, wormes, &c. Which by ignorant parents are supposed to be the vegeance of witches.' And he inveighs against the 'unskilful physicians' who lend their authority to such superstition.[77]

Scot's opinions eventually became so widely held that it is necessary to recall just how unpopular they were with British intellectuals when they first appeared. In the decades that followed the publication of the *Discoverie of Witchcraft*, prominent authors, including the King of Scotland, introduced a new doctrine of witchcraft to English-speaking readers. This explanation of the crime attributed the powers of witches to a diabolical compact, and it tended to present witchcraft as a religious offence, a kind of devil-worship. Although this notion and its elaborations never captured the English imagination as strongly as it fascinated Continental minds, the wave of publications propounding it in English and in Latin surely limited the influence of Scot's scepticism.[78] He was attacked explicitly by King James and many other authors, including Henry Holland and Robert Burton, who rightly remarked of Scot and the handful of other notable sceptics: 'They laugh at all such stories; but on the contrary are most lawyers, divines, physicians, philosophers.'[79] Scot was already notorious by the time that Jorden wrote his treatise, and he was one of only a handful of writers who dared appeal to him as an authority. Bradwell was amazed that Jorden had the temerity to cite Scot: 'Let him not be angrie with me, that I compare him to that notable witchwarder *Reinold Scott* [sic] (sith him selfe busheth not to use his authoritie sometime)' (fols 167v–168r). The ultimate objection to the arguments of Scot and Harsnet was that they promoted atheism. The author of *The Triall of Maister Dorrell* called attention to a worry shared by many pious men when he asked: 'If neither possession, nor witchcraft ... [are real] why should we thinke that there are Divells? If no Divells, no God.'[80]

And yet despite the weight of learned opinion in favour of witchcraft and possession, their identification and prevalence were matters of intense debate. Swan reports that a Cambridge scholar 'had even his hands full' disputing whether possession and dis-possession occurred ordinarily in modern times. The University officials had refused to allow him to debate the broader question of whether they had ever occurred or did now (pp. 57–8). According to Swan, the heads of the universities also refused a challenge by the Puritan John Ireton, a prebend of Lincoln, to dispute the existence of witchcraft and possession (p. 3). The sermons reported by Manningham, although stimulated by Bancroft in all probability, also show that there was considerable room for incredulity. Thus Henoch Clapham declaimed that 'there can not be assigned anie proper token or signe to knowe that anie is essentially possessed'.[81] Furthermore, there were less sweeping kinds of scepticism that were more readily acceptable than Scot's arguments. Demonologists themselves disagreed about Satan's powers and had developed a subtle set of distinctions between supernatural, preternatural and natural effects. On a more mundane and immediately germane plane, many Englishmen apparently agreed with Scot that the danger of witchcraft had been amplified unreasonably by popular credulity, even by those who rejected his scepticism.[82] Nor were these debates theological aridities. In practice English judges and juries showed themselves to be strikingly reluctant to conclude that charges of witchcraft had been proven. Even when trials were at their height on the Home Circuit, around 1600, almost sixty per cent of accused witches were acquitted.[83] Incredulity was thus directed less at the existence of witchcraft than at its particular manifestations.

These competing views of witchcraft had become deeply embroiled in the power politics of late Elizabethan England, as the debate over the Mary Glover case plainly shows. Under the spell of Michel Foucault, historians have in recent years come to insist more loudly, frequently and crudely that knowledge and power are identical. There are manifold difficulties in the way of a conventional historian who seeks enlightenment and inspiration from Foucault's treatments of this theme, not the least of which – as his more perceptive disciples often remind us – is that he regarded the attempt as contemptible. Nevertheless, in some obvious ways, the competition over the classification of Mary Glover's illness illustrates the usefulness of the Foucauldian dyad and some of his insights into it.[84] The arguments for and against possession were adopted explicitly to vindicate the claims to religious authority of both sides. Jorden and Harsnet provided the medical and theological basis for Bancroft's effort to discredit Mary Glover, secure the release of Elizabeth Jackson and depict the girl's exorcism as a

fraudulent act. Bradwell, Swan and Hughes insisted on the supernatural character of their adversary in Mary Glover and Elizabeth
Jackson and on the marvellous victory that they had achieved in the
end, a triumph over Satan that demonstrated the righteousness of
their cause. In seeking to win the victory for its own interpretation,
each side exploited the techniques of power that were available to it.
The supporters of Mary Glover relied extensively on ritual to
capture the minds of their audiences. They transformed her fits into
a bedroom spectacle, and then transferred the show out of the
Glover residence to locations that were the arenas of greater
authority and public visibility. The ordeals moved from Sheriff
Glover's home, to the Recorder's lodgings in the Inner Temple and
finally to the Sessions House, the Old Bailey. The audience at each
of these venues was different, giving way in the last stages from a
ritual test presided over by Croke in which women played a
prominent part to an arraignment and trial presided over by men of
great judicial, political and social prestige. At the trial the chorus of
women and men who had participated in the Recorder's test was
replaced by a jury of men, selected and sworn to their special
role, whose job it was, in effect, to validate the opinion of the
court. Finally, frustrated by the suspension of Elizabeth Jackson's
sentence, the Puritans resorted to sacred ritual, dispossession, that
they publicized as best they could, appealing to the King and
perhaps to the universities for recognition of its wondrous authority.
Bancroft and his men asserted their authority in other ways, as we
have seen, broadcasting their views from the pulpit and in print and
deploying their superior institutional power to quash the Puritans'
victory in court and drive them underground.

But it would be a mistake to try to reduce the conflict to a
confrontation between Puritan believers and Anglican sceptics
whose outcome was determined by their relative power. The
equivocal outcome of the struggle demonstrates above all that the
capacity to shape public perceptions of the meaning of an incident
was diffused among different kinds of people and social, judicial,
ecclesiastical and political institutions. The conviction that Mary
Glover had been the victim of witchcraft could not be demolished
by an exercise of political repression. It surfaced and resurfaced
for the rest of the century in publications by Puritans and Nonconformists, testimony no doubt to how tenaciously it survived in

the oral traditions of those groups.[85] Moreover, the positions that individuals adopted were complicated by other considerations that affected their relationship to the shifting political contest that underlay the case. The most revealing examples are Chief Justice Anderson and Recorder Croke. Anderson was a notorious anti-Puritan as well as an adamant foe of witchcraft. He had been equally prominent as a prosecutor of a woman accused of bewitching Thomas Darling and as a member of the team who condemned Darrell three years later at his trial before High Commission. In 1599, at the trial of a woman called Anne Kerke, he had fallen into a debate with Bancroft over the reality of witchcraft; the Bishop ridiculed the accusations against her, and Anderson stoutly defended them, winning her conviction.[86] On the other hand, he and Bancroft had been partners in crushing the separatists in the 1580s.[87] The thread that seems to connect his passionate denunciation of the Brownists and other Puritan nonconformists and his alarmist remarks about witches to Jorden at Mary Glover's trial was a strong conviction that the land was threatened with subversion. Croke presents even more complications. He was a man on his way up, who wanted and needed royal favour. As we have seen, after an initial phase of cautious scepticism, which may have been heightened by an intervention by Bancroft, he became convinced that Mary Glover was genuinely bewitched and played a leading part in securing Elizabeth Jackson's conviction. He may have been a Puritan, which would help to explain why he urged the Puritans to exorcise her when the girl's fits continued after the trial.[88] 'We should be ashamed to see a child of God in the clawes of Sathan, without any hope of deliverance, but such meanes as God had appointed, fasting and prayer', he told Lewis Hughes.[89] But as soon as the excited Hughes returned to him with the news that he and his colleagues had cast the evil spirit out of Mary Glover, Croke sent on to tell the Bishop the news, 'and not to go my self, but from him, and tell the Lordship that he did send me'.[90] Thus he seems to have been working at once to undercut Bancroft's attempt to discredit the verdict and also to bring down the hierarchy's wrath on its opponents, since he must surely have known that the Bishop would not be pleased by Hughes' news. Perhaps he misjudged Bancroft or perhaps he was protecting himself by sending the zealous young man to the Bishop as a way of disassociating himself from the

Puritans. He certainly did not lose favour as a result of his part in the affair. He was made a serjeant and knighted in 1603.[91]

The Mary Glover case, Edward Jorden and the decline of witchcraft

All of this suggests, I think, how right Foucault is to insist on the fluidity of the relationship between power and knowledge. He urges looking for 'local centres' of power and 'patterning of transformation' and observes that no real transformation of knowledge is possible unless the strategies at work in the interaction of local centres of power are reinforced by an overall strategy.[92] How this happens in Foucault's scheme is by no means clear, at least to me, but once more his insight does provide a hint about how we can understand the importance of the Mary Glover case and Jorden's role in it in the history of witchcraft and psychiatry. For if one looks at the problem in the usual way, the upshot is, frankly, to reduce Jorden to insignificance. Despite the celebrity it has gained in this century, Jorden's *Briefe Discourse* had little lasting influence on the diagnosis of either witchcraft or hysteria. Subsequent opponents of witchcraft concentrated their attention on its common features. Medical arguments did play a part in their attacks on witch beliefs, but they generally followed Scot's lead rather than Jorden's, attributing the unusual symptoms of witchcraft victims to melancholy rather than hysteria. It is easy to understand why. The putative victims of witchcraft and of demonic possession were mostly too young or too old to fit the profile of hysterics, and many of them were male. The diagnosis was used by sceptics now and then, but it was not a prominent part of the attack on witchcraft beliefs, nor was Jorden cited as an ally by later champions of scientific rationalism. Nor was his influence over the subsequent history of hysteria as great as Veith's superb survey implies. For although he added mental disturbances to the aetiological factors of the disease, he did not renounce traditional uterine explanations. And those who did, Thomas Willis and Thomas Sydenham, offered completely different explanations for the nervous and psychological basis of the illness. The most that can be said for Jorden is that he may have encouraged English physicians to pay greater attention to the classical literature about hysteria and to have sanctioned a certain flexibility in its study. But here, too, establishing his influence in any conventional way is frustrated by the fact that the leading figures did not cite him and may have been entirely ignorant of his work, which was, after all, never reprinted.[93]

Jorden nevertheless played a major part in events that began the decline of witchcraft. The Mary Glover case was not the end of his career as a semi-official government sceptic, and he was able to impress his opinion that much apparent witchcraft and possession was caused by hysteria on the new King. When in 1605 James learned of a young woman in Berkshire named Anne Gunter who was supposed to be bewitched, he enlisted Jorden's help to discover whether her illness was genuine.[94] Her symptoms closely resembled Mary Glover's except that she also vomited pins. According to his biographer, Jorden immediately suspected that Gunter was faking. He gave her neutral potions that he said were strong medicine, which she said greatly relieved her symptoms. His conviction fortified, he tried one of the tests to which Mary Glover had been subjected, reciting the Lord's Prayer and the Creed. When she reacted with the expected convulsions, he modified the test by repeating the texts in Latin. She did not understand and failed to respond. It was axiomatic that the devil was an expert Latinist, and so Jorden told the King that Gunter was a counterfeit. The whole crew that had opposed Mary Glover reassembled. Bancroft and Harsnet were called in and the girl was examined in Star Chamber. The King became highly interested in the case and questioned her himself. Subjected to so much pressure from the great men of the realm, she confessed. James later summarized what they had concluded in a letter to the Earl of Salisbury: 'Wee find by her confession that shee holdeth herselfe perfectly cured from her former weakness by a potion given unto her by a phisitian and a tablet hanged about her neck [and] that she was never possessed with anie divell, nor bewitched.'[95] James also concluded that her fakery had been compounded by 'the disease called the mother, wherewith she was oftentimes vehemently afflicted', the diagnosis suggested by Jorden.[96]

Anne Gunter was not the only pretender James exposed. Soon after he ascended the English throne, he abandoned or greatly moderated his earlier enthusiasm for witch-hunting and turned

Grand Inquisitor, delighting in uncovering false claims of bewitchment. His methods were, at times, characteristically prurient. He
exposed one woman who pretended to have spells not unlike Mary
Glover's trances by whipping away the bed-clothes and displaying
her naked to the crowd. He induced a courtier to seduce another
purported witchcraft victim. In both cases, the women dropped
their charades, the one in embarrassment, the other (allegedly) in
the confusion of passion. His most renowned success as a counterfeit-
finder fortunately did not need his notorious sexual imagination to
solve. In 1616, his royal bearing alone overawed John Smith, a
teenage boy whose accusations had sent nine innocent people to
their deaths and caused six others to be arrested. At Leicester on a
progress, he summoned the lad to witness his strange fits. 'Possibly
daunted by his presence or terrified by his words', Francis Osborne
reported, 'the boy began to falter, so as the King discovered a
fallacy.' There were other incidents in which James himself caused
witchcraft victims to fall out of character and confess that they were
frauds, and he ordered his servants to investigate other claims as
well.[97] At some point early in his reign he urged his son and heir,
Prince Henry, to follow his example. After reacting with pleasure to
the exposure of a 'litle counterfitte Wenche', the new King advised:

> I pray God ye maye be my aire in such discoveries. Ye have
> ofte hearde me saye that most miracles nou a dayes proves
> but illusions, and ye maye see by this hou waire judgis should
> be in trusting accusations withoute an exacte tryall; and
> lykewayes hou easilie people are inducid to trust wonders.[98]

It has always seemed remarkable to historians that James should
have switched so rapidly from an enthusiasm for demonology to
limited scepticism. But the timing of his change of heart, which
coincided with his arrival in England, is significant. He was surely
persuaded by Bancroft that fakery and credulity were rife and
dangerous to the church. As early as 1604, in his *Counterblast to
Tobacco*, he fulminated that the weed's foul smoke might 'serve for
a precious Relicke, both for the superstitious Priests, and the
insolent Puritanes, to cast out devils withal'.[99] This passage is
interesting because it suggests how Bancroft might have presented
his case to the new King. Christina Larner has shown that James'
passion for witch-hunting in Scotland was aroused in 1590–91,

when over three hundred people were charged with treason for having attempted to kill him by sorcery. 'James early fell into a state of mind in which any attempt on the part of the judiciary to acquit an accused witch was seen as a failure to take seriously the treasonable threat to the king's majesty.'[100] Bancroft believed just as strongly that Catholic and Puritan exorcists were seditious, and he may well have convinced the King that the danger in England came not from supposed witches but from those who exploited the lies and delusions of their alleged victims. Jorden may have had a hand in his conversion as well; that would explain why he was called in so promptly to investigate the Anne Gunter incident. Whatever Jorden's involvement may have been before then, the King had been convinced by early in 1605 that some examples of putative bewitchment could be explained medically. In February of that year some physicians of Cambridge reported to the King that they had examined an allegedly bewitched girl, as he had instructed them to do, and found that her disease was not supernatural.[101]

At the very least, Jorden helped foster the King's newly cautious attitude to witchcraft. He may therefore also be claimed to have had some responsibility for the waning of witchcraft prosecutions during James' reign.[102] The number of trials on the Home Circuit – the only region for which we have data – declined during James' reign and was very low in the 1620s and 1630s, when acquittals soared. There were no executions for witchcraft in Essex, the most witch-ridden county on the circuit, after 1626, except during the witch-hunts organized by Matthew Hopkins in the 1640s.[103] This pattern probably held nation-wide, and leaving aside the Hopkins hunts as anomalous, it is evident that James' reign witnessed the advent of a growing trend towards judicial scepticism. Moreover, although the law was made harsher in 1604, its full, lethal potential was rarely fulfilled. The dangerous Continental doctrine of witchcraft as a diabolical plot was never admitted into English trials. For these linked developments, King James earns much of the credit. After his exposure of Smith in 1616 James admonished the judges, Sir Humfrey Winch and Sir Randolph Crew, for allowing themselves to be deceived and innocent people to be hanged.[104] His displeasure was court gossip, and it must rapidly have reached the ears of other members of the bench.[105] The King's sceptical attitude was very widely known. Richard Bernard felt constrained to chart a

1

narrow passage between Scot and James in his 1627 guide to grand juries in witchcraft prosecutions. He was no disciple of Scot, he declared, but at the same time he complimented the late King for his skill at uncovering counterfeits and included a thorough discussion of the sorts of fraud and illness that might be mistaken for witchcraft.[106] James also limited the application of the 1604 statute. According to Osborne, he warned the Judges of Assize 'to be Circumspect in Condemning those, Committed by Ignorant Justices, for Diabolical Compacts'.[107] And indeed, such accusations were extremely rare: fewer than five per cent of the Home Circuit convictions involved dealings with the devil (again excepting the Hopkins' convictions).[108]

The conflict over Mary Glover's affliction may therefore be seen as a turning-point in the history of witchcraft. Even more than the famous conflict between the bishops and John Darrell, it resulted in a shift in the alignments of power that promoted scepticism and defended witch beliefs. In a remarkably short time, this shift had eroded the confidence of the bench in the evidence that was presented to convict witches. It also probably encouraged medical sceptics to advance their cause. Writers like John Cotta who strove to circumscribe the illnesses that could be attributed to witchcraft were well aware that King James felt that its incidence was exaggerated by ignorant people. The practice of exorcism by prayer and fasting was also officially forbidden as a result of the case. Bancroft inserted into his draft for new canons of the church, which were promulgated in 1604, a prohibition against 'any privatt fastinge and prayer under pretence of Castinge out Devilles under payne of suspension and deprivation from the ministre'.[109] This is not to say that the contest over the prevalence of witchcraft and possession had been decided in the reign of King James. Writers who commanded immense respect continued to maintain the reality of those spiritual perils throughout the century. But the examples of Mary Glover, Anne Gunter, John Smith and the others contributed to the emergence of an overall strategy of the kind Foucault might have had in mind. In simple terms, they helped to increase the burden of proof and in doing so to redefine the debate in terms that made it harder and harder to resolve individual cases decisively in favour of the supernatural.

Historians have pointed out that the decline in witchcraft

prosecutions was the consequence of the ruling elite's waning confidence in the evidence on which they were based, rather than a rejection of beliefs in the supernatural. Thus Keith Thomas argues that the mounting rate of acquittals was a consequence of a growing awareness of alternative explanations for illnesses allegedly caused by witchcraft and for the usual proofs of witchcraft, including confessions, which could be regarded as melancholy delusions. He suggests several factors that contributed to this trend. First, the 1604 witchcraft statute, with its emphasis on the diabolical compact, actually demanded a higher level of proof than the 'presumptions' that were the basis for convictions of *maleficium* under the 1563 law. Second, the credibility of witchcraft accusations was eroded by overuse and fraud. Transparently malicious charges were frequent enough to call into doubt a crime that was easy to suspect and very hard to prove. Finally, two new attitudes became increasingly widespread among the educated classes. Even before the new science had been popularized, they had begun to believe that the world was orderly, regular and 'unlikely to be upset by the capricious intervention of God or Devil'. Moreover, this reluctance to credit supernatural intervention was complemented by a growing confidence that natural explanations would one day be discovered for even the most mysterious events and illnesses.[110] Barbara Shapiro has amplified Thomas' arguments, tracing the emergence among judges and the ruling elite generally of a 'family of ideas' that emphasized empirical evidence and probability. This new epistemology, which was obviously the basis for the new science, provided the intellectual foundation for the growing scepticism Thomas discerns.[111]

These ideas are undoubtedly correct. At the trial of Mary Glover Chief Justice Anderson had reasoned that since Jorden could not prove conclusively that her malady was a natural disease, the circumstantial evidence that constituted the case against Elizabeth Jackson should be interpreted as evidence of supernatural malevolence. Increasingly in the seventeenth century, it was natural explanations – principally fraud and melancholy – that got the benefit of the doubt. What has, I think, been underemphasized is that the decline of witchcraft beliefs was in the broadest sense of the term a political event. Witchcraft accusations were based on a collective 'reading' of the behaviour, relationships, personality and appearance of the accused witch and her alleged victim. Typically, the evidence presented at trials, like that introduced against Elizabeth Jackson, included nasty gossip about quarrels with neighbours, angry confrontations and eccentricities. Because outbursts of temper and unusual behaviour were commonplace and mundane, a successful witchcraft charge depended on a fragile consensus among a large number of people about the malevolence and dangerousness of the accused. Moreover, in the vast majority of instances, the injuries that the witch was supposed to have inflicted were easily explained on perfectly ordinary grounds. They were mainly mental disorders, neurological afflictions and chronic diseases that caused people to waste away, although they also included a wide range of ordinary diseases and traumas, like the broken leg Jackson was supposed to have caused.[112] There was, therefore, plenty of room for alternative points of view, both about the accused witch herself and about the injuries that she was supposed to have caused.

Although the records do not permit one to reconstruct the social dynamics that preceded witchcraft trials except in a small number of cases, it seems plain enough that many, if not most, witchcraft accusations were contested at every level from the informal conflicts of the village community to the ritual confrontation of the Assize trial. Many more accusations were made than ever came to trial; except during a brief period during Elizabeth's reign, more women were acquitted at the Assizes than convicted. A witchcraft trial was a complex social struggle over the meaning of misfortune – of death and disease and loss. A conviction was unlikely to follow from an accusation unless the accusers (and in cases like Mary Glover's the putative victim) could gain the support of their neighbours and powerful men in the county: justices of the peace who forwarded the charges to the grand jury and the jurors themselves, as well as manorial lords, ministers, physicians and others who commanded respect among the elite.[113] The gradual process of building a coalition in support of a witchcraft charge and the manoeuvring by supporters of the 'witch' and the 'bewitched' that is so conspicuous in Mary Glover's case was very likely the norm rather than the exception. In such circumstances, the shift in the crown's position to outright scepticism about the generality of supernatural harm must have made it much more difficult to form and sustain a deadly coalition of neighbours and grandees. Furthermore, the reversal in the political force field in which witchcraft accusations developed meant that natural explanations for strange illnesses were invoked with increasing frequency. And every time that they were validated by the King, the magistrates and jurors, they gained in social authority what they so conspicuously lacked as yet in scientific precision. As late as 1669, the sceptic John Wagstaffe confessed: 'The truth is, want of knowledge in the Art of Physick makes me attribute unto Spirits meer natural distempers: ... we are still in the dark as to the abstruser distempers of humane bodies, especially as arise from melancholly.'[114] The decline of witchcraft was a complex cultural event that was caused more by religious politics than by progress in medical science. In fact D. P. Walker was surely correct to believe that the political controversy over exorcism created conditions favourable to medical speculation by creating a ready and powerful audience for alternatives to witchcraft and possession.

The current of scepticism gathered power in the roiling disputes that decided between guilt and innocence, the supernatural and the natural, the absolute and the doubtful. Edward Jorden helped it to gain momentum more by what he did than by what he wrote. The fact that the *Briefe Discourse* has been presented in our century as a shining example of rationalist prescience tells a great deal about the historiography of science and medicine and reveals very little about the book or its author. His arguments were not more persuasive intrinsically than those of his opponents; they could not be verified, and they rested on ideas that were rapidly discarded. Nor was he more intelligent than the defenders of witchcraft. He was not even a disinterested champion of reason and a foe of superstition. He hoped to advance a political religious cause and to win the favour of powerful men, both of which he accomplished. His intentions were therefore complicated and qualified by the situation in which he found himself. This is not to say that he did not really believe that Mary Glover was suffering from hysteria and that Elizabeth Jackson was innocent. But the political circumstances of the case were the force that translated his private convictions into action. If his book did not save demoniacs for medical science or advance the development of clinical psychiatry it nevertheless contributed to the alternative explanations for the signs of apparently supernatural illnesses.

More importantly, Jorden was able directly to influence the course of events. Ideas are inert. They lie on the printed page and can make nothing happen. They are the essential conceptual tools with which men and women change the world, but they can accomplish nothing unless their uses are recognized and exploited by people engaged in the complex struggles of social life. The Mary Glover case presented Jorden with an opportunity to shape the way in which such incidents were decided in future. He used his opportunity effectively, and as a single move may be seen in retrospect to have decided the outcome of a long chess match, his association with Bancroft and King James had repercussions far greater and for far longer than anyone could have predicted. It was one of those pivotal events whose repetition leads to the eventual dominance of one kind of discourse over another. In Foucault's terms, the Mary Glover case forwarded a pattern of transformation within a larger matrix, a 'strategic envelope', that was also changing because of the dynamics of religious politics. To see Jorden's accomplishments as part of this process, rather than as part of the emergence of scientific psychiatry, may seem to diminish his significance. In fact, I think, it magnifies it by demonstrating how and why they mattered at the time. By placing Jorden back into history, we can see more clearly how he made history.

Notes

* References in brackets refer to pages or folios of the tracts printed in this edition. Where confusion seemed likely to occur, the author's name has also been supplied. Following the usual conventions, references to the front (recto) and back (verso) of folios have been given. Thus fol. 5r refers to the front of folio 5. In some instances, where there are no page numbers but signatures have been numbered, references are to the signature and folio within it. Thus sig. A3v is the back of the third folio of the signature marked A.

1. Richard Hunter and Ida Macalpine (1963) *Three Hundred Years of Psychiatry, 1535–1860*, London, p. 68.
2. Ibid., p. 69.
3. Ilza Veith (1965) *Hysteria: The History of a Disease*, Chicago p. 123.
4. *Dictionary of National Biography* (hereafter *D.N.B.*) and John Venn

and J. A. Venn (1922) *Alumni Cantabrigienses*, 4 vols, Cambridge, art. Jorden, Edward (note that the latter corrects errors in the other sources and adds that he was the son of Edward Jorden of Cranbrook, Kent); William Munk (1861) *The Roll of the Royal College of Physicians of London. Vol. I. 1518 to 1700*, London, p. 109 (hereafter Munk, *Roll*); Edward Jorden (1669) *A Discourse of Natural Bathes, and Mineral Waters*, (ed.) Thomas Guidott, 4th edition, London, Preface; *idem* (1676) *A Discourse of Bathe*, London, pp. 166–7; Anthony Wood (1815) *Athenae Oxonienses*, new edition, 4 vols, vol. 2, Oxford, cols 548–50.

5. D. P. Walker (1981) *Unclean Spirits: Possession and Exorcism in France and England in the Late Sixteenth and Early Seventeenth Centuries*, Philadelphia, p. 73.

6. Shereman received his AB (1579), AM (1583) and MD (1599) from Trinity College, Cambridge; he became a Fellow of the College of Physicians in 1599: Venn and Venn, *Alumni Cantabrigienses*, art. Shereman, Robert; Munk's *Roll*, p. 112.

7. Moundeford received his AB (1572), AM (1576) and MD (1584) from King's College, Cambridge, which he also served as a Fellow and as bursar before marrying and moving to London. He became a Fellow of the College of Physicians in 1594. He published in 1622 *Vir Bonus*, a non-medical work dedicated to James I: Munk's *Roll*; Venn and Venn, *Alumni Cantabrigienses* and *D.N.B.*, art. Moundeford, Thomas.

8. John Manningham (1976) *The Diary of John Manningham of the Middle Temple, 1602–1603*, (ed.) R. P. Sorlien, Hanover, New Hampshire, p. 120.

9. Francis Herring (d. 1628) took his BA (1585), MA (1589) and MD (1597) at Christ's College, Cambridge, and he was admitted to the College of Physicians as a Fellow in 1599. He was the author of half a dozen books, on pious and medical subjects: Munk, *Roll*, 111–12; *D.N.B.*, art. Herring, Francis. Doctor Spencer is more difficult to identify. He was probably the astonishingly named Ethelbert Spenser (or Spencer), who took his BA (1586) and MA (1589) at Jesus College, Cambridge. Clark notes that according to the Annals of the College of Physicians, he received an MD from Cambridge in 1598 or 1599. He evidently never became a member of the College, but Whitgift had licensed him to practise in the province of Canterbury in 1591: George Clark (1964) *A History of the Royal College of Physicians of London*, vol. 1, Oxford, p. 143; John H. Raach (1962) *A Directory of English Country Physicians, 1603–1643*, London, p. 84. Another possibility is John Spencer, who had BA and MA degrees from

Oxford and an MD from Leiden. He evidently practised in Windsor from around 1600: Raach, *Directory of Country Physicians*, p. 84.

10. John Argent took his AB (1591) and MD from Cambridge, and was admitted as a Fellow of the College of Physicians in 1597: Munk, *Roll*, 108–9; Venn and Venn, *Alumnae Cantabrigienses*, art. Argent, John.

11. James Meadowes was a graduate of Oxford, who was incorporated as a DD at Basel. He was rector of St James, Eastcheap at the time of the Mary Glover affair, and he also became rector of St Gabriel, Fenchurch Street in 1603, possibly as a reward for his services at the trial: Joseph Foster (1891–2) *Alumni Oxonienses*, London, art. Meadowes, James.

12. Clark, *College of Physicians*, vol. 1, pp. 168–9.

13. *D.N.B.*, art. Banister, John.

14. Ibid., pp. 138–9, 142, 200–1; Stephen Bredwell (1586) *A Detection of Ed: Glovers Hereticall Confection*, London; *The Rasing of the Foundations of Brownisme*, London; John Gerard (1597) *The Herball or Generall History of Plants*, London, 'To the Well Affected Reader', unpaginated; Charles Webster (1979) 'Alchemical and Paracelsian Medicine' in his *Health, Medicine and Mortality in the Sixteenth Century*, Cambridge, p. 329. Probably fearing a backlash, Bradwell tries to disassociate himself from the Paracelsians in his preface. Bradwell's name is rendered variously as Bradwell, Bredwell and Bredwall. His son, Stephen Bradwell, was the author of a handbook on treating injuries and two plague tracts, the more famous of which contains references to his father: Stephen Bradwall (1636) *Physick for the Sicknesse, Commonly Called the Plague*, London, pp. 30, 48. Webster notes that he, too, was frequently prosecuted by the College.

15. Clark, *College of Physicians*, p. 143.

16. *D.N.B.*, art. Bowes, Sir Jerome. There were two notables named Sir William Cornwallis, the son of the more famous Sir Thomas, who had been knighted in 1599 for his services in Ireland under Essex, and the essayist and MP, who was a friend of Ben Jonson. It is impossible to tell which of them served at Jackson's trial: *D.N.B.*, art. Cornwallis, Sir Thomas; Cornwallis, Sir William.

17. Bradwell refers to Lewis Hughes as Mr Lewes. Hughes was Welsh, and throughout his career he was referred to as Lewis or Hughes or variations, English and Welsh, on either name: Henry N. Paul (1971) *The Royal Play of Macbeth*, New York, p. 104n; G. W. Cole (1927) 'Lewis Hughes, The Militant Minister of the Bermudas and his Printed Works', *Proceedings of the American Antiquarian Society*, New Ser., 37: 248–9.

18. Harsnet (1603) *A Declaration of Egregious Popish Impostures*, London,

p. 280, quoted in Walker, *Unclean Spirits*, p. 49. See also, ibid., pp. 47–8. Following the passage quoted, Modu goes on to mock Catholic idolatry and thus to question the authority of the priesthood. The religious politics of exorcism in England are discussed sensitively in ibid., pp. 43–73, 77–84 and K. Thomas (1971) *Religion and the Decline of Magic*, New York, pp. 477–92, and I have relied greatly on them for this account. Because of this, I have often quoted sources that are cited in their books; whenever possible, however, I have examined the originals in their entirety.

19. A different version of this miracle is in Matthew, xvii, 14–21. For a discussion of the significance of fasting in Protestant and especially Puritan religious practice, see Patrick Collinson (1982) *The Religion of Protestants*, Oxford, pp. 260–3.

20. Thomas, *Religion and Magic*, pp. 481–3.

21. Thomas, *Religion and Magic*, p. 414.

22. G. More (1600) *A True Discourse Concerning the Certaine Possession and Dispossession of 7 Persons in One Familie in Lancashire*, London, p. 5, quoted in Thomas, *Religion and Magic*, p. 484.

23. This account follows closely Walker, *Unclean Spirits*, pp. 62–6.

24. *D.N.B.*, art. Hutton, Matthew.

25. Walker, *Unclean Spirits*, p. 64.

26. Thomas Fuller (1952) *The Worthies of England*, (ed.) John Freeman, London, p. 301.

27. John Darrell (1601) *A Detection of that Sinnful, Shamful, Lying and Ridiculous Discours, of Samuel Harshnet*, London; John Deacon and John Walker (1601) *Dialogicall Discourses of Spirits and Divels, Declaring their Proper Essence*, London; John Darrell (1602) *The Replie of J. Darrell to the Answer of J. Deacon and J. Walker Concerning Demoniackes*, [London?]. This list by no means exhausts the magazine; there are as many as twenty publications in all, including some that have been lost. They are conveniently listed in the otherwise disappointing Corinne Holt Rickert (1962) *The Case of John Darrell*, University of Florida Monographs, Humanities, 9, Gainesville, Fla., pp. 64–7.

28. Quoted in Cole, 'Lewis Hughes', p. 253. Cole reprints a full transcript of Hughes' narrative on pp. 250–3; it originally appeared in Lewis Hughes (1641) *Certaine Grievances, or Errours of the Service-Booke*, 3rd edition, London, pp. 12–15.

29. Cole, 'Lewis Hughes'; Guildhall [London] MS, 6836, fols 64v–67v. Hughes was probably the clergyman's son from Cardigan of that name who matriculated at Jesus College, Oxford in 1582. He was then twenty-one years old; he apparently left without taking a degree:

Foster, *Alumnae Oxonienses*, art. Hughes, Lewis. For information concerning Hughes and the citation to the Guildhall MS above, I am grateful to Paul Seaver.

30. Manningham, *Diary*, p. 198. Divines who preached at Paul's Cross were carefully selected and monitored by Bancroft and Sir Robert Cecil; they were dismissed if their sermons failed to please: Historical Manuscripts Commission, Report 9, *Salisbury* 12: 312–13.

31. Manningham, *Diary*, pp. 185, 211.

32. Henry Foley (1877) *Records of the English Province of the Society of Jesus*, vol. 1, London, pp. 18–19; John Chamberlain (1939) *The Letters of John Chamberlain*, (ed.) Norman Egbert McClure, Philadelphia, pp. 186–7.

33. Paul, *Royal Play*, p. 109n; Edward Aber (1876) *A Transcript of the Register of the Stationers' Company of London, 1554–1640*, vol. 3, London, p. 93; F. S. Siebert, *Freedom of the Press in England, 1476–1776*, Urbana, Ill., pp. 62–3.

34. Harsnet, *Declaration*, p. 166. See also, Paul, *Royal Play*, p. 109.

35. Paul, *Royal Play*, p. 107. The evidence supporting this contention is lamentably circumstantial: see J. Nichols (1828) *The Progresses Processions, and Magnificent Festivities of King James the First*, vol. 1, p. 106.

36. R. G. Usher (1910) *The Reconstruction of the English Church*, vol. 1, New York, pp. 302–6.

37. Usher, *Reconstruction*, p. 305.

38. Historical Manuscripts Commission, Report 9, *Salisbury*, vols 12–14, *passim; Calendar of State Papers, Domestic, James I, 1603–10*, p. 63; Usher, *Reconstruction of the Church*, pt 1, ch. 8, pt 2, ch. 1.

39. Thomas Jackson (1603) *Davids Pastorall Poeme*, London; 'To the Christian Reader' (which Swan signs from London in September); Lambert Danaeus (1589) *A Treatise Touching Antichrist*, London, sig. A3v. The latter is signed from 'the Colledge of Wye'. It is possible that this John Swan is to be identified with the man of that name who took his BA (1573), MA (1576) and BD (1583) from Cambridge and who served as recorder of South Hanningfield in Essex: Venn and Venn, *Alumni Cantabrigienses*, art. Swan, John.

40. Paul, *Royal Play*, pp. 108–10.

41. For the identification of Scott, see Manningham, *Diary*, p. 354.

42. Siebert, *Freedom of the Press*, p. 63.

43. Walker, *Unclean Spirits*, pp. 66–73.

44. Walker, *Unclean Spirits*, p. 69; John Deacon and John Walker (1601) *Dialogicall Discourses of Spirits and Devils*, London, pp. 206–8, 325, 355.

Introduction by Michael MacDonald

45. Harsnet, *Discovery*, sig. A3r.
46. Harsnet, *Declaration*, pp. 136–7; Walker, *Unclean Spirits*, p. 71.
47. Harsnet, *Discovery*, p. 36; Walker, *Unclean Spirits*, p. 72.
48. Thomas, *Religion and Magic*, pp. 478, 489–90, 542.
49. Thus Robert Burton explains and dismisses the cures of mountebanks, wizards and empirics with exactly the same argument: Robert Burton (1978) *The Anatomy of Melancholy*, (ed.) Holbrook Jackson, 3 vols, vol. 1, London, pp. 256–7.
50. Burton, *Anatomy of Melancholy*, vol. 1, pp. 172, 210–11.
51. Ibid., pp. 414, 416.
52. Ibid., p. 414.
53. Bradwell says that Mary Glover experienced her first period several months after her illness began: Bradwell, fols 80v, 123r, 126r.
54. Veith, *Hysteria*, p. 10.
55. Ibid., ch. 2.
56. See Bradwell's account of Jorden's views, which although it is hostile to them nevertheless makes sense of his testimony at Jackson's trial and accords with the arguments in his pamphlet: Bradwell, fols 37r–38r, 65v, 85r–87r.
57. John Cotta (1616) *The Triall of Witch-craft, Shewing the True Method of Discovery*, London, p. 75.
58. Paul H. Kocher (1953) *Science and Religion in Elizabethan England*, San Marino, Calif., p. 120; Stuart Clark, 'The Scientific Status of Demonology', in Brian Vickers (1984) *Occult and Scientific Mentalities in the Renaissance*, Cambridge, ch. 12.
59. American Psychiatric Association (1987) *Diagnostic and Statistical Manual of Mental Disorders*, 3rd edition, revised, Washington, p. 258.
60. Cf. John G. Howells (1989) *Modern Perspectives in the Psychiatry of the Neuroses*, New York, p. 16.
61. For standard discussions of the aetiology and symptomology of hysteria, see Armand M. Nicholi, Jr (1978) *The Harvard Guide to Modern Psychiatry*, Cambridge, Mass., pp. 181–5; Michael Gelder, Dennis Gath, and Richard Mayou (1983) *Oxford Textbook of Psychiatry*, Oxford, pp. 169–80; Michael I. Weintraub (1983) *Hysterical Conversion Reactions*, New York; D. Wilfred Abse (1987) *Hysteria and Related Mental Disorders*, Bristol, ch. 2.
62. These objections also apply to the very recent assertion by Mary Kilbourne Matossian that Jorden was in fact describing not hysteria but ergotism, a polymorphous disorder caused by eating tainted rye. There are other objections to make to Matossian's assertion that in explaining Mary Glover's illness, Jorden wrote 'the earliest detailed account by an English physician of what may have been ergotism'.

Glover was the solitary victim of the malady; no one else in her family fell ill; she was the daughter of a substantial tradesman and unlikely to have been consuming rye bread; the development of her illness, as it is described by Bradwell, points to a very particular psychological stress as the immediate cause of her affliction. Her fits did not simply begin; they were plainly reactive. The principal difficulty with Matossian's arguments, here and elsewhere, is that ergotism is presented as a malady so elusive that almost any strange behaviour can be said to match its symptoms. At the same time, it is impossible to establish that any of its supposed victims were in fact eating spoiled grain. The very detailed description of the circumstances of Mary Glover's illness and its signs in Bradwell's treatise ought to make it as clear as it can ever be that the assertion that Jorden's discussion of her malady was an account of ergotism is extremely unlikely: Mary Kilbourne Matossian (1989) *Poisons of the Past: Molds, Epidemics, and History*, New Haven, Conn., pp. 65–6.

63. A classic study is I. M. Lewis (1971) *Ecstatic Religion: An Anthropological Study of Spirit Possession and Shamanism*, Harmondsworth, especially ch. 7.

64. The best discussion of this issue is Mary O'Neil (1989) 'The Devil in the Cloister: Possessed Nuns in Early Modern Italy', unpublished paper presented to the American Historical Association, Pacific Coast Branch, Portland, Ore.

65. Perhaps the most impressive recent arguments in favour of this notion have been advanced by Arthur Kleinman (1980) *Patients and Healers in the Context of Culture*, Berkeley; *idem* (1986) *Social Origins of Distress and Disease*, New Haven. For a compelling plea that we stop trying to diagnose demonic possession in early modern Europe using modern psychiatric terms and see it as a cultural phenomenon in its own right, see H. C. Erik Midelfort (1981) 'Madness and the Problems of Psychological History in the Sixteenth Century', *Sixteenth Century Journal* 12: 9–12.

66. Walker, *Unclean Spirits*, pp. 12–13; Richard Bernard (1627) *A Guide to Grand-Jury Men ... In Cases of Witchcraft*, London, pp. 49–52; William Drage (1665) *Diamonomagiea. A Small Treatise of Sickeness and Diseases from Witchcraft and Supernatural Causes*, London, pp. 3–10.

67. Walker, *Unclean Spirits*, p. 13.

68. Thomas, *Religion and Magic*, p. 481, remarks on the influence early cases had on later accounts.

69. Thomas, *Religion and Magic*, p. 480.

70. John Foxe (1877) *Acts and Monuments*, vol. 7, London, pp. 385–402. There seems to be some confusion about the identities of the

descendants of Robert Glover, but the contemporary sources are unanimous in agreeing that Mary was his grand-daughter.

71. Frank Freeman Foster (1977) *The Politics of Stability: A Portrait of the Rulers in Elizabethan London*, London, p. 129n; Cole, 'Lewis Hughes', especially p. 251, Guildhall [London] MS, 6836, fols 64v–67v. For the Puritan heritage of the parish, and the militancy of its lecturer at the time, see P. S. Seaver (1970) *The Puritan Lectureships*, Stanford, California, pp. 209, 210.

72. Stephen Greenblatt (1988) *Shakespearean Negotiations*, Berkeley, pp. 96–114.

73. Darrell, *Discovery*, p. 118.

74. Alfred B. Beaven (1913) *The Aldermen of the City of London*, vol. 2, London, p. 48. Glover died in December 1603.

75. *D.N.B.*, art. Croke, Sir John.

76. Reginald Scot (1964) *The Discoverie of Witchcraft*, (ed.) Hugh Ross Williamson, Carbondale, Ill., p. 25.

77. Ibid., p. 30.

78. Thomas, *Religion and Magic*, pp. 439–49.

79. James VI and I (1597) *Daemonologie*, Edinburgh; Henry Holland (1590) *A Treatise Against Witchcraft*, London, sigs A3r–B1v, B4v–F4r; Burton, *Anatomy of Melancholy*, vol. 1, pp. 202–3. For other critics, see Robert H. West (1984) *Reginald Scot and Renaissance Writings on Witchcraft*, Boston, pp. 110–11.

80. *The Triall of Maist[er] Dorrell* (1599), London, p. 8, quoted in Walker, *Unclean Spirits*, pp. 71–2. For the same sentiment, in almost identical language, see John Gaule (1646) *Select Cases of Conscience Touching Witches and Witchcrafts*, London, pp. 1–2. See also, Thomas, *Religion and Magic*, p. 573.

81. Manningham, *Diary*, p. 185.

82. See, for example, Holland, *Treatise Against Witchcraft*, sig. E2r; John Cotta (1612) *A Short Discoverie of the Unobserved Dangers of Severall Sorts of Ignorant and Unconsiderate Practisers of Physicke in England*, London, p. 58.

83. Thomas, *Religion and Magic*, pp. 451, 573–4.

84. The texts I appropriate are Michel Foucault (1977) *Discipline and Punish: The Birth of the Prison*, translated by Alan Sheridan, New York, especially pp. 26–8; *idem* (1978) *The History of Sexuality, Volume I: An Introduction*, translated Robert Hurley, New York, especially pt 4, ch. 2. For an excellent explanation of why this appropriation is emphatically *not* Foucauldian, see Allan Megill (1985) *Prophets of Extremity*, Berkeley, pp. 247–52.

85. See, for example, George Sinclair (1685) *Satans Invisible World*

Discovered, Edinburgh, pp. 94–100, which relies heavily upon Hughes, *Certain Grievances*, whose publication history, popularity, and subsequent influence are discussed quite fully in Cole, 'Lewis Hughes', pp. 249–57, 298–304.

86. Walker, *Unclean Spirits*, p. 72.
87. Stuart Barton Babbage (1962) *Puritanism and Richard Bancroft*, London, p. 21; *D.N.B.*, art. Anderson, Sir Edmund.
88. A contemporary biographer praises the godliness of 'Judge Croke', but there is some doubt as to whether he was referring to John or his brother George: Wilfrid R. Prest (1986) *The Rise of the Barristers*, Oxford, p. 229.
89. Cole, 'Lewis Hughes', pp. 251–2.
90. Ibid., p. 253.
91. *D.N.B.*, art. Croke, Sir John.
92. Foucault, *History of Sexuality*, pp. 98–100.
93. Jeffrey M. N. Boss (1979) 'The Seventeenth-Century Transformation of the Hysteric Affection, and Sydenham's Baconian Medicine', *Psychological Medicine* 9: 223–5. Boss also argues that Jorden's work is a particular response to the Mary Glover case and notes no links with later writers. For Willis and Sydenham, see Veith, *Hysteria*, ch. 7; Thomas Willis (1689) *The London Practice of Physick*, London, pp. 297–307; Thomas Sydenham (1696) *The Whole Works of Thomas Sydenham*, London, pp. 440–78.
94. Among the most informative treatments of this episode are C. L'Estrange Ewen (1938) *Witchcraft in Star Chamber*, London; Paul, *Royal Play*, pp. 118–27.
95. A facsimile and transcription of the letter are printed in Richard Hunter and Ida Macalpine (1963) *Three Hundred Years of Psychiatry*, London, pp. 76–7.
96. Ibid. Gunter was imprisoned briefly after James's investigation and examined, at the request of the new Bishop of London (Bancroft having been elevated to Canterbury), by the College of Physicians, who judged her a fraud. Because of this William Harvey was familiar with the case and mentioned it in his *Praelectiones*: Clark, *College of Physicians*, p. 198.
97. G. L. Kittredge (1956) *Witchcraft in Old and New England*, New York, pp. 320–1; David Harris Willson (1963) *King James VI and I*, London, pp. 309–12; Paul, *Royal Play*, pp. 113–30; T. Fuller (1845) *The Church History of Britain*, (ed.) J. S. Brewer, vol. 3, Oxford, pp. 448–52; F. Osborne (1659) *A Miscellany of Sundry Essayes, Paradoxes, and Problematicall Discourses*, London, pp. 4–9. The most recent authoritative discussions of evolution of the King's views on

witchcraft are Christina Larner, 'James VI and I and Witchcraft' in Alan G. R. Smith (1973) *The Reign of James VI and I*, London, ch. 4; S. Clark (1977) 'King James's *Daemonologie*: Witchcraft and Kingship', in S. Anglo (ed.) *The Damned Art*, London, pp. 156–81.

98. Quoted in Kittredge, *Witchcraft in England*, p. 319; J. O. Halliwell [Phillips] (1818) *Letters of the Kings of England*, vol. 2, London, p. 102.

99. Quoted in ibid., p. 319.

100. Larner, 'James VI and I and Witchcraft', pp. 82–3.

101. Ewen, *Witchcraft and Demonianism*, p. 451.

102. For the most detailed account of James's interest in witchcraft and his influence on its decline, to which I am much indebted, see Kittredge, *Witchcraft in England*, ch. 17.

103. Thomas, *Religion and Magic*, pp. 451–2; Alan Macfarlane (1970) *Witchcraft in Tudor and Stuart England*, New York, ch. 3.

104. Kittredge, *Witchcraft in England*, pp. 322–3; Ewen, *Witchcraft and Demonianism*, pp. 228–9.

105. Kittredge, *Witchcraft in England*, p. 323; see also Osborne, *Miscellany*, p. 4.

106. Kittredge, *Witchcraft in England*, p. 325; Bernard, *Guide to Grand-Jury Men*, sig. A4r, pp. 12–18, 29–48. See also G. Goodman (1839) *The Court of James the First*, (ed.) J. S. Brewer, vol. 1, London, p. 3; Halliwell [Phillips] *Letters of the Kings of England*, vol. 2, pp. 124–5; Fuller, *Church History*, vol. 3, pp. 451–2; Osborne, *Miscellany*, pp. 4–5.

107. Kittredge, *Witchcraft in England*, p. 315.

108. Thomas, *Religion and Magic*, pp. 447, 456, 460.

109. Babbage, *Puritanism and Bancroft*, p. 381. Slightly moderated, this draft became canon 72: Thomas, *Religion and Magic*, pp. 485–6.

110. Thomas, *Religion and Magic*, pp. 576–8.

111. Barbara J. Shapiro (1983) *Probability and Certainty in Seventeenth-Century England*, Princeton, ch. 6.

112. Ronald C. Sawyer (1989) '"Strangely Handled in All Her Lyms": Witchcraft and Healing in Jacobean England', *Journal of Social History* 22: 467–9.

113. Some insight into the importance of gaining the support of such figures is presented by Joyce Gibson (1988) *Hanged for Witchcraft: Elizabeth Lowys and her Successors*, London, pp. 217–18, which is otherwise tendentious and unreliable.

114. John Wagstaffe (1669) *The Question of Witchcraft*, pp. 66–7.

A BRIEFE DISCOURSE OF A DISEASE CALLED THE SUFFOCATION OF THE MOTHER

Edward Jorden

A BRIEFE DIS-COVRSE OF A DIS-EASE CALLED THE Suffocation of the *Mother*.

Written vppon occasion which hath beene of late taken thereby, to suspect possession of an euill spirit, or some such like supernaturall power.

Wherin is declared that diuers strange actions and passions of the body of man, which in the common opinion, are imputed to the Diuell, haue their true naturall causes, and doe accompanie this disease.

By EDVVARD IORDEN Doctor in Physicke.

LONDON.
Printed by *Iohn Windet*, dwelling at the Signe of the *Crosse Keyes at Powles Wharfe*. 1 6 0 3.

TO THE RIGHT WOR-
shipfull the President and Fellowes of the
Colledge of Phisitions in
London.

S I am desirous to satisfie all indiffe-
rent men concerning the occasion and
intent of this my discourse : so I
thought good to direct the same especially vnto this societie, whereof I am
a member; to testifie both how iustly or
rather necessarily I haue beene drawn
to the vndertaking and publishing hereof : as also how
willing I am to submit my selfe to your learned censure;
the argument of my writing being such as none can better
iudge of then your selues.

    And first I protest vpon that credit which I desire to
haue among you, that I haue not vndertaken this businesse
of mine owne accord, as if I esteemed of mine owne knowledge and obseruation in this case aboue other mens. For
(if it had beene thought good to haue imposed it vppon o-
thers) I do acknowledge that there are many among vs
better able then my selfe to haue written in this kind, vnto
whome I would willingly haue put ouer my taske. Neither did I euer find my selfe prouoked hereunto vpon any
A 2

peeuish

peeuish humor to contradict or to disgrace any who doe
iudge otherwise of some pointes contained herein, then my
selfe doe : many of them being such as I do loue and affect
well. Neither vpon any fawning humor to please or flatter any person whatsoeuer; which I doe esteeme more base
then begging. But disclayming both hony and gall, I haue
plainely set downe the true doctrine of Phisicke concerning
that disease which giues so great occasion of distraction a-
mong many good men: especially such as haue not learning
sufficient to resolue them of this point, or not that moderation and humilitie of spirit to acknowledge their insuffici-
encie, and to hearken vnto others whom in all reason they
might thinke able to direct them better in such a case.

For if it be true that one man cannot be perfect in e-
uery arte and profession, and therefore in cases out of our
owne callings, we do depend vpon those which haue beene
trayned vp in other particular subiects, beleeuing men in
their owne profesions: Why should we not prefer the iudgements of Phisitions in a question concerning the actions
and passions of mans bodie (the proper subiect of that profession) before our owne conceites; as we do the opinions of
Diuines, Lawyers, Artificers, &c. in their proper Elements.
Neither haue I done this as taking vpon me to reforme the
mindes of men which are not vnder my charge (for I could
willingly haue permitted euery man to enioy his owne opinion:) But being a Phisition, and iudging in my conscience
that these matters haue beene mistaken by the common people; I thought good to make knowne the doctrine of this
disease, so farre forth as may be in a vulgar tongue conue-
niently disclosed, to the end that the vnlearned and rash
conceits of diuers, might be thereby brought to better vn-
derstanding

derstanding and moderation ; who are apt to make euery
thing a supernaturall work which they do not vnderstand,
proportioning the bounds of nature vnto their own capacities: which might proue an occasion of abusing the name
of God, and make vs to vse holy prayer as vngroundedly
as the Papists do their prophane trickes; who are readie to
drawe forth their wooden dagger, if they do but see a maid
or woman suffering one of these fits of the Mother, coniu-
ring and exorcising them as if they were possessed with euil
spirits. And for want of worke, will oftentimes suborne o-
thers that are in health, to counterfait strange motions
and behauiours: as I once saw in the Santo in Padua fiue
or sixe at one sermon interrupting and reuiling the Preacher, vntill he had put them to silence by the signe of the
Crosse, and certaine powerlesse spelles.

　Wherefore it behoueth vs as to be zealous in the truth,
so to be wise in discerning truth from counterfaiting and
naturall causes from supernaturall power. I doe not deny
but that God doth in these dayes worke extraordinarily,
for the deliuerance of his children, and for other endes best
knowne vnto himselfe; and that among other, there may
be both possessions by the Diuell and obsessions and witchcraft, &c. and dispossession also through the Prayers and
supplications of his seruents, which is the onely meanes left
vnto vs for our reliefe in that case. But such examples being verie rare now adayes, I would in the feare of God ad-
uise men to be very circumspect in pronouncing of a possession: both because the impostures be many, and the effects of naturall diseases be strange to such as haue not looked throughly into them.

　But let vs consider a little the signes which some doe
shew

ſhew of a ſupernaturall power in theſe examples. For if they ſay there neede no ſuch ſignes appeare, becauſe the Diuill by witchcraft may inflict a naturall diſeaſe : then I ask them what they haue to doe with the Diuell, or with diſpoſſeſſing of him, when he is not their preſent, but hath beene onely an externall cauſe of a diſeaſe, by kindling or corrupting the humours of our bodies; which diſeaſe as well as other will ſubmit it ſelfe to phyſicall indications : as is ſhewed, cap. 1. Wherefore they muſt needes make him to be an internall cauſe, and to poſſeſſe the members and faculties of the bodie, and holde them to his vſe : or elſe they vnderſtand not what they ſay, when they doe peremptorily diſclaime naturall meanes, and auouch that they ſpeake certaine wordes, and performe certaine voluntarie motions vpon his incitation, and are hindred by him from ſpeaking other wordes which they would ſaine vtter. And therefore to this end diuerſe ſignes and Symptoms are alledged by them, as arguments of a ſupernaturall and extraordinarie power inhærent in the body.

One of their ſignes is Inſenſibilitie, when they doe not feele, being pricked with a pin, or burnt with fire, &c. Is this ſo ſtrange a ſpectacle, when in the Palſie, the falling ſickeneſſe, Apoplexis, and diuerſe other diſeaſes, it is dayly obſerued? And in theſe fits of the Mother it is ſo ordinarie as I neuer read any Authour writing of this diſeaſe who doth not make mention thereof. This poynt you ſhall finde proued both by authorities and examples in the, 4. Chapter.

There alſo you ſhall find conuulſions, contractions, diſtortions, and ſuch like to be ordinarie Symptoms in this diſeaſe.

Another

The Epiftle Dedicatorie.

Another figne of a fupernaturall power they make to be the due & orderly returning of the fits, when they keepe their iuft day and houre, which we call periods or cicuits. This accident as it is common to diuerfe other chronicall difeafes, as head. aches, gowtes, Epilepfies, Tertians, Quartans, &c. fo it is often obferued in this difeafe of the mother as is fufficiently proued in the 2. Chapter.

Another argumnt of theirs is the offence in eating, or drinking, as if the Diuell ment to choake them therewith. But this Symptom is alfo ordinarie in vterin affects, as I fhew in the fixt Chapter: and I haue at this time a patient troubled in like maner.

Another reafon of theirs is, the comming of the fits vpon the prefence of fome certaine perfon. The like I dee fhew in the fame Chapter, and the reafons of it, from the ftirring of the affections of the mind.

Another maine argument of theirs, is the deliuerance vpon fafting and prayer: which we will imagin to be fo in deed, without any counterfeiting in that point. You fhall fee in the 7. Chapter, how this may be a naturall remedie two maner of wayes: the one by pulling downe the pride of the bodie, and the height of the naturall humors therof; a verie conuenient meanes, and often prefcribed by our Authcurs in yong and luftie bodies: the other by the confidēt perfwafion of the patient to find releafe by that means: which I fhew in that Chapter by rules and authorities in our profession and alfo by examples, to be a verie effectuall remedie in curing diuerfe difeafes of this nature.

Many other fuch like inftances they may produce, according vnto euerie ones feuerall conceit: which were in vaine for me to repeate perticularly: vnleffe I knew where-

The Epistle Dedicatorie.

in they would principally insist. But in the discourse following I haue as neare as I could described al the Symptoms
of this disease; whereby euerie man may readily find an-
swers to his seuerall obiections.

Now to testifie my loue and affection to this societie
of ours, and that I esteeme more of the censure of a fewe
learned and graue men, then of the opinions of a multitude
of other people: I thought good to choose no other persons
to patronize this slender discourse then your selues, who are
best able of any in this land, or any such like societie elsewhere (that euer I could find) to iudge whether I write true
doctrine or no.

Wherefore desiring you to accept it in good part, and
as occasion may serue to giue testimonie vnto it according as your iudgements and consciences
shall lead you, I take my leaue this
2. Martii, 1602.

Your louing friend and Colleague.

Ed. Iordes.

Of the suffocation of
the Mother.

Cap. 1.

That this disease doth oftentimes giue occasion vnto sim-
ple and vnlearned people, to suspect possession, witch-
craft, or some such like supernaturall cause.

THE passiue condition of wo-
mankind is subiect vnto more
diseases and of other [a] sortes
and natures then men are: and
especially in regarde of that
part [b] from whence this disease which we speake of doth
arise. For as it hath more va-
rietie of [c] offices belonging vnto it then other
partes of the bodie haue, and accordingly is supplied from other partes with whatsoeuer it hath
need of for those vses: so it must needes thereby
be subiect vnto mo infirmities then other parts are:
both by reason of such as are bred in the part it selfe,
and also by reason of such as are communicated vnto it from other parts, with which it hath corre-

B　　　　spondence.

a *Hyppocrat. 6*
Vulgar.part.7.
b *Galen 6. lo-*
corum affect.
cap.5. radix
suffocationum
vterus.
c *Mercatus de*
muliebr.lib. 2,
cap. 1.
1. *Ad sui ipsius*
alimoniam.
2. *Ad speciei*
propagationem
3. *Ad benefi-*
cium indiuidui
per euacuatione
superfluitatum.

spondence. And as thole offices in their proper
kindes are more excellent then other; so the difeafes whereby they are hurt or depraued, are more
grieuous. But amongeft all the difeafes wherevnto
that fex is obnoxious, there is none comparable
vnto this which is called *The Suffocation of the mother*, either for varietie, or for ftrangeneffe of accidents. For whatfoeuer ftraunge accident may appeare in any of the principall functions of mans bodie, either animall, vitall, or naturall, the fame is
to bee feene in this difeafe, by reafon of the communitie and confent which this part hath with the
Altomarus de braine, heart, and liuer, the principall feates of
medend. hum. thefe three functions; and the eafie paffage which
corp .malis it hath vnto them by the Vaines, Arteries, and
cap. 110. Nerues. And whatfoeuer humor in other partes
Barth. Mon- may caufe extraordinarie affects, by reafon of the
tagnana Con-
filio.226. abundance or corruption of it, this part will affoord
the like in as plentifull a manner, and in as high a
degree of corruption: and with this aduauntage
that whereas in the other, fome one or two of the
faculties onely one are hurt (as in *Apoplexies, Epilep-
fyes, Syncopyes,* fubuerfions of the ftomacke, &c.) and
not all (vnleffe as in *Syncopyes* by confent, where the
vitall function ceafing, all the reft muft needes
ceafe) in this cafe all the faculties of the bodie doe
fuffer; not as one may do from another, but all directly from this one fountaine, in fuch fort as you
fhall often tymes perceyue in one and the fame
Mercatus lib. perfon diuerfe accidents of contrarie natures to
2.cap.2.& 3. concurre at once.

And

And hereupon the *Symptoms* of this disease are
sayd to be monstrous and terrible to beholde, and
of such a varietie as they can hardly be comprehended within any method or boundes. Insomuch
as they which are ignorant of the strange affects
which naturall causes may produce, and of the manifold examples which our profession of Phisicke
doth minister in this kind, haue sought aboue the
Moone for supernaturall causes : ascribing these
accidents either to diabolicall possession, to witchcraft, or to the immediate finger of the Almightie.

Valetius scof-
fing at their
ignorance cal-
leth this dis-
ease a kind of
diuell. *in Hol-
ler.cap.59.*

But it is no maruell though the common people
and men also in other faculties verie excellent may
bee deceyued by the rarenesse and straungenesse
of these matters, which are hidden out of their Ho-
rizon amongest the deepest mysteries of our profession : when as Phisitions themselues, as *Cornelius
Gemma* testifieth. If they bee not verie wel exercised
in the practise of their profession, are oftentimes
deceyued, imagining such manifolde straunge accidents as their hee mencioneth to accompanie this
disease, (as *suffocation* in the throate, croaking of
Frogges, hissing of Snakes, crowing of Cockes, bar-
king of Dogges, garring of Crowes, frenzies, convulsions, hickcockes, laughing, singing, weeping,
crying, &c.) to proceede from some metaphysicall
power, when in deede (as hee there sayeth) they are
meerely naturall.

Cosmocrit. li.1
cap.7.pag.153
Inexperto me-
dico sæpe suspi-
tionem numi-
nis prabuerunt

Auicen also in his Chapter of this disease, speaking of the causes of it, sayth, that there were some
wise Phisitions in his time which said, that the cause

Fen.21,3 cap:
26:tract:4:

of this difeafe was vnknowne : Becaufe as *Iacobus de Partibus* expoundeth it, they did thinke it to be inflicted from aboue, yet notwithftanding he fetteth downe naturall caufes of it, and a naturall cure.

Hippocrates alfo long before finding this error to bee helde by fome in his time maketh mention of diuerfe of thefe *Symptoms*, and fayeth, that hee doth not fee anie thing in them more fupernaturall, or more to bee admired, then there is in Tertians, and Quartans, and other kindes of difeafes : imputing it either vnto ignorance, and want of experience that Phifitians of his time did iudge otherwife; or vnto a worfer humor, when as beeing loath to bewray their owne defects through pride and arrogancie: and not knowing what to prefcribe would flie vnto diuine caufes, and neglecting naturall meanes for their reliefe, would wholy relie vpon expiations, incantations, facrifices, &c. cloaking their ignoraunce vnder thefe fhadows, and pretending both more knowledge, and more pietie then other men : by which courfe they gained this aduauntage, that if the patient chanced to recouer, they fhould bee highly renowmed for their skill; if not, their excufe was readie that Gods hande was againft them.

This hee fpeaketh of the Phifitions of his time, whome he confuteth principally by two reafons, which may ferue for excellent rules for all men to difcerne fuch cafes by. The firft is, that there is no fupernaturall Character in thefe *Symptoms*, as hee proueth by an induction of diuerfe of them,

Lib. de morbo facro in principio.

Infcitiæ palliū maleficium & incantatio.
R. Scili, 1. cap. 3

them, which in the cómon opinion were thought to be aboue nature: yet hee proueth to haue their naturall causes in the bodie of man aswell as others haue.

The ſtrength of this argument will better appeare hereaſter in the particular *Symptoms*, which we are to entreate of: where it ſhallbe made manifeſt that the moſt of them doe both depende vpon ſuch naturall cauſes as other diſeaſes haue in our bodies, and alſo are oftentimes mixed with other diſeaſes which are accompted naturall.

It may likewiſe appeare by this, that whereas all other diſeaſes are knowne by their notes and ſignes which reſemble their cauſe (as *Choller, Flegme, Melancholy, &c.* haue their proper markes, corruption and putrefaction, their proper notes and malignity his Character) ſo there muſt be ſome Character or note of a ſupernaturall power in theſe caſes (as [a]extraordinary ſtrength or knowledge or ſuffering) or elſe we haue no cauſe but to thinke them naturall. If the diuell as an externall cauſe, may inflict a diſeaſe by ſtirring vp or kindling the humors of our bodies, and then depart without ſupplying continuall ſupernaturall power vnto it; [b] then the diſeaſe is but naturall, and will ſubmit it ſelfe vnto Phyſicall cure. For externall cauſes when they are already remoted, giue no indication of any remedy.

The ſecond argument of this is, that theſe *Symptoms* do yeeld vnto natural cauſes, and are both pro-

a Luk.8.27. 28. &c.
Ternel.de abditis rerum cauſis lib.2 cap 16
Platerus de mentis alienat.pag. 102.
Beniuenius de abditis morborum cauſis cap. s. Alſharauius, C. de Epilepſia.
b *Auicen.C.de melancholiſi contingat a Demonio ſufficit*

nobis quod conuertat complexionem ad choleram nigram,&c. Vide Iacobum de partibus inhunc locum, Valeſius meth; medendi lib,2. cap.2.

cured

cured and also eased by such ordinary meanes, as other diseases are: and ^c therefore they must needs be naturall.

c *Fernel loco ci tato matheus de Grad.ex A- zar…io.C.de E pilepsi…. d Hippo.de n… tura huma… circa medium. De statibus pau lo post principi um. e Gal.de Vena sectione aduersus Era- sistric…:8,in arte medicin… li cap:8 9.in constitutione artis cap:13. methodi med: lib.9.10.11. &c. f Valesius meth.med:lib: 1.cap:4:g Mercatus meth med:pag:42: 43:Gal,Simp- licium lib.3: cap:11:Vales us controwers: lib.1.cap.4 Luk,11.vers. 21.22.*

The strength of this argument is grounded vpon the very foundation of our profession which hath beene layd by ^d *Hyppocrates* and ^e *Gallen* long agoe and euer since confirmed by the practise and obseruations of all learned men; that diseases are cured by their contraries. I say contrary ^f both vnto the disease, vnto the cause, and vnto the *Symptom*. And the more exact the contrarietie is; the more proper is the remedy: as when they are equall in ^g degree or in power. But what equality of contrariety either in degree or in power, can there be betweene a supernaturall suffocating power, and the compression of the belly or throate. They are disperats in Logicke, but not contraries. For contrarietie is betweene such as are comprehended vnder one generall. And where one is opposed vnto one alone, and not indifferently vnto many. Neither doe I thinke, that any man wel aduised, will say that by compression of those parts, he is able to suppresse the power of the diuell. The like may be saide of the application of cupping glasses, of sweete plaisters, of ligatures,&c. beneath, and of euell smelles aboue; by all which we do obserue those kindes of fits to be mitigated: and yet there can bee no such contrary respect in thē against a supernatural cause, as is betweene a remedy and a disease. They are also procured vpon sweete smelles, vpon pleasant meats and drinkes, vpon feare, anger, iealousie,&c. as in the

parti-

particular caufes fhall bee farther declared: and yet
no fuch confent can bee fhewed in them with any
fupernaturall affect, as that they may any way caufe
or encreafe it. Wherefore the rule of *Hyppocrates*
muft needesbe true; that if thefe *Symptoms* do yeeld
vnto naturall remedies, they muft alfo bee naturall
themfelues. And thus much in explanation of
thefe two arguments of *Hyppocrates* againft the errour of his time: which notwithftanding hath been
continued in the mindes of men vntill this day, and
no maruell: vnleffe the fame corruption which
bred it at the firft, had beene remoued out of the
world. And therefore diuers of our Authors doe
make efpeciall mention of this cafe wherein they
report the common people to haue beene deceiued
by imagining witchcraft or poffeffion, where indeed there was none.

    Amatus Lufitanus reporteth of one *Dina Clara*, a
maide of 18. yeares of age, which had euery day
two or three fuch ftrange fits, as thofe that were a-
bout her, gaue out that that fhe was haunted with
an euill fpirit.

    In thofe fits euery part of her body was diftorted,
fhe felt nothing, nor perceiued any thing: but
had all her fences benummed, her hart beating, her
teeth clofe fhut together: yet for an houres fpace or
two fhe would haue fuch ftrong motions, that fhee
would weary the ftrongeft men that came at her.
When fhe had beene three weekes in this cafe, her
left arme began to be refolued with a palfie, &c. He
being called vnto her prefcribed fuch remedies as

Georg. Godel-
man. de magis
&c. lib 1. cap
8.
Bruno Seideli-
us de morbis
incurab. pag. 29
Centuria 5, cu-
rat: 75.

are.

are vſuall in this caſe, and within few dayes recoue-red her, to the great admiration of the beholders.

Obſeruationū medicin:lib: 10 *obſeru:* 30.

Petrus Forreſtus maketh mention of another maid of 22. yeares old, which dwelt with a Burgermaſter of *Delſt* in *Holland,* who falling in loue with a yong man, fell alſo into theſe fits of the Mother : which held her many houres together with ſuch violent horrible accidents, as hee neuer ſawe the like : her whole body being pulled to and fro with convulſiue motions, her belly ſometimes lifted vp, and ſometimes depreſſed, a roaring noiſe heard within her, with crying and howling, a diſtortion of her armes and handes : inſomuch as thoſe about her thought her to be poſſeſſed with a diuell, and out of all hope of recouery. He being called vnto her in Ianuarie 1565. applied conuenient remedies as there he ſetteth downe, and in a ſhort time reſtored her to her health againe.

Thaddæus Du-nus miſcull:cap 9.

Many more ſuch like examples might bee pro-duced both out of authenticall writers in our pro-feſsion and out of our own experiences, which yet do liue (were it not that late examples would bee offenſiue to rehearſe:) but theſe may ſuffice to ſhow how eaſily men vnexperienced in thoſe extraordi-narie kindes of diſeaſes, may miſtake the cauſes of them: when through admiration of the vnwonted and grieuous accidents they behold, they are caried vnto Magicall and Metaphyſicall ſpeculations. But the learned Phiſition who hath firſt beene trained vp in the ſtudy of Philoſophy, and afterwards con-firmed by the practiſe and experience of all manner of

of naturall diseases, is best able to discerne what is
naturall, what not naturall, what preternaturall, and
what supernaturall, the three first being properly
subiect to his profession : and therefore they doe
wrong vnto the faculty of Phisicke, and vnto them
selues, and oftentimes vnto others, who neglecting
that light which wee might yeeld them, doe runne
headlong and blindefold into many errors and absurdities. For preuention whereof I haue breefly set
downe what the doctrine of Phisitions is concerning this disease of the Mother, which of all other
is most subiect vnto misconstruction. For that as
Forrestus saieth it is a harde matter to discerne in
what maner the Mother may occasion such strange
and manifold accidents.

Lib.28.obseru. 26.

Cap. 2.

What this disease is, and by what meanes it causeth such varietie of Symptoms.

His disease is called by diuerse
names amongst our Authors. *Passio Hysterica, Suffocatio, Præfocatio,*
and *Strangulatus vteri*, *Caducus
matricis, &c.* In English the Mother, or the Suffocation of the
Mother, because most common-
ly it takes them with choaking in the throat : and
it is *an affect of the Mother or wombe wherein the principal parts of the bodie by consent do suffer diuersly according*

*Cardanus
de causis sig: et
locis morborum
cap.114.
Altomarus cap.
110. Guayneri-
us cap. de suffe:
matricis.*

*Ætius tetr.4
Serm.4.cap.68
P. Ægineta
lib.3.cap.71
Victor Trinca-
uel.lib:5.sect.5
cap.9.*

C

ding to *the diuersitie of the causes and diseases wherewith the matrix is offended.*

I call it an *affect* in a large signification to comprehend both *morbum* and *Symptoma*. For sometimes it is either of them, and somtimes both. For in regard the actions of expulsion or retention in the *Mother* are hurt. It may be called a *Symptoma in actione læsa*: in regard of the humor to be expelled which corrupteth and putrifieth to a venemous malignitie. It is likewise a *Symptom in excremento vteri mutato*. And in regard of the perfrigeration of the Mother, and so of the whole bodie. It is also a *Symptom* [a] *in qualitate tangibili mutata*, not *morbus ex intemperie*:[b] because it is suddenly inflicted &suddenly remoued. But in regard of the rising of the Mother wherby it is somtimes drawn vpwards or sidewards aboue his natural seate, compressing the neighbour parts, & so consequently one another. It may be said to be *morbus in situ*, in respect of the compression it selfe, causing suffocatió and difficultie of breathing. It may be [c] *causa morbi in forma* by causing *coarctation* of the instruments of breathing. And sometimes these are complicated and [d] together with a venemous vapour, arising from this corrupt humor vnto diuers parts of the bodie, there will be an euill position of the matrix also: either because the ligaments, vaines and arteries beeing obstructed: [e] by those vapours are shortened of their wontedlength, and so draw vp the part higher then it should be; or [f] for that the matrix being grieuously anoyed with the malignity of those vapours doth contract it selfe

and

a *Albert. Bottonus cap. 39.*
b *Gal. locorum affectorum 3. cap. 7.*
Petrus Salius pag. 467.
Altomarus cap 110.
Horatius Augenius Epist. 6
c *Gal. de causis morb. cap. 7*
d *Altomarus c cit. ato. Rondeletius methodo curand. morb. cap. 69. matheus de grad. in 9 Rhasis.. cap. 28*
e *Mercatus lib 2. cap 3.*
f *Matheus de grad. in 9. Rhasis cap. 28. Hor. Augenius sibi offensum fugiens ũt et iucundum inse quens.*

and rise vp by a locall motion towards the midrif.

I say of the *Mother* or wombe because although the wombe many times in this disease doe suffer but secondarily, yet the other parts are not affected in this disease but from the Mother: (*Radix suffocationum vterus*) which finding it selfe anoyed by some vnkind humor, either within it selfe, or in the vessels adioyning or belonging vnto it, doth by a naturall instinct which is ingrafted in euery part of the body for his owne preseruation, endeuour to expell that which is offensiue: in which conflict if either the passage be obstructed, or the humor inobedient or malignant, or the functions of the wombe any way depraued, the offence is communicated from thence vnto the rest of the body. The principall part of the body are the seates of the three faculties, which do gouerne the whole body. The braine of the animall, the hart of the vitall, the liuer of the naturall; although some other parts are plentifully endewed with some of these faculties, as the stomacke, entrailes, vaines, spleene, &c. with naturall faculties, the instruments of respiration with animall and naturall. These parts are affected in this disease, and do suffer in their functions as they are diminished, depraued, or abolished, [h] according to the nature & plenty of the humor, and the temperament and scituation of the Mother: and that *diuersly* : For somtimes the instruments of respiration alone doe suffer, sometimes the heart alone, sometimes two or three faculties together, sometimes successiuely one after another, sometimes one part suffereth both

Galen.6.loc.af fert.cap.5.
Auicen.Fen.21 3.cap.16.tract 4.initium est ex matrice et peruenit ad communitaté sortem cordis et cerebri &c.
Horatius Ange nius Epistol.16

g Gal.de dissi cultate respirá dis lib.1.cap.7. Trincauel.li.4 cap.12.Felix platerus ca.de respira.defectu Gal.de sympt. differentiis Cap 2.3. h Gal.5.loc.af sect.6 Mercatus pag. 173.

C 2   a

Petrus ſolius diuerſus pag. 400
Merc. it. pa. 170
Merca. pa. 174

a reſolution and a conuulſion in the ſame fit , or when as it ſuffereth in one part and not in another , as we ſee oftentimes ſence and motion to bee taken away and yet hearing and memorie to remaine ; the ſpeech faiiing and reſpiration good. Sometimes reſpiration, ſence, and motion do altogether faile, and yet the pulſe remaine good : So that the varietie of thoſe fits is exceeding great , wherein the principall parts of the body doe diuerſly ſuffer.

Ætius lib. 26.
ap. 70
P. Agineta. lib.
3. cap. 71.
Rhaſis cont. l. b.
22. meſue ſum.
4. part. 3. ſect. 1
cap. 8.
Auicen Fen. 21
3. cap. 16. tract
4. quandoque
ſunt period. eius
tardis, quando-
que accidit om
ni die.

Another diuerſitie there is , in the order of theſe fits : for ſomtimes they keep due periods or circuits yearly or monthly, according to the falling ſicknes, and ſometime euery weeke, ſometimes euery day, &c. I know a gentlewomã in this towne, who for 2. yeares together neuer miſſed a fit of the Mother in the afternoone. The like is hereafter mentioned in the Eſſex gentlewo. who for 16. years together had euery day a fit of the Mother at a certaine houre. *D. Argent* and I had another patient, in whome for 10. weeks together we obſerued a fit of the mother euery ſaturday. I adde *by conſent of the Mother* to diſtinguiſh thoſe *Symptoms* or diſeaſes from ſuch as are cauſed originally by the part affected. For being procured but by conſent, they endure no longer thẽ the fits of the mother do continue. The conſent or communitie which the matrix hath with thoſe principal parts of the body is eaſily perceiued, if wee conſider the anatomy of that part, & the diuers waies wherby it may and doth communicate with them. The ſuctions of this part, beſides that which is commõ to all other for their nutriment deriued from the naturall

faculdie

facultie, are 2. the one respecting the preseruatiō of the whole body, as it is an *Emunctory* of diuers super-fluities which do abound in that sex. The other for the propagation of mankind, where it is to be con-ceiued and nourished vntill it be able to appeare in the world. In regard of these offices this part hath neede of great varietie of prouision, according as the vses are manifold. The substance is neruous, for the great necessitie it hath of sence and motion.

Gabr. Fallopius de med. purg. Cap. 17. et 23. via euacuatio-nis.

It is also *Porous* for the better entertaining of the vitall spirits, and the necessitie it hath of distenti-on and contraction.

Constant. Vare-lius lib. 4. cap. 3

It is tied vnto diuers partes of the body that it might the better beare the weight of an infant: backwards by little strings vnto the lower gut, vnto the loines and *os sacrum:* forwardes vnto the necke of the bladder and *os pubis* by certaine membranes deriued from the *peritoneum:* on each side it is tyed vnto *ossa illii* by a ligament growing from the mus-cles of the loynes. It recciueth also for the former v-ses, vaines from the liuer, arteries from the hart, and nerues from the braine and backe, which are all in-serted into the substance of the part, to deriue vnto it the benefit of those 3. faculties, both for the pro-per vse of the part, and for the vse of propagation and to discharge the whole bodie of diuers superflu-ities, which otherwise would be an occasion of ma-ny infirmities in them.

Gasparus Bau-hinus historia anatom. p. 71.

Now according to this description let vs consi-der how by consent, the principall partes of the bodie may bee affected from the matrix.

The

b *Trincauel.l.3*
Sect.2.cap.2.
c *Auicen.Fe.1.*
3.tract.2.ca.6
Mont.ign.an.
consil.226

The partes of our bodie doe suffer by consent [b] two manner of wayes. The one is when they doe receyue some offensiue thing from another parte which is [c] called *Communitas non absoluta.* And this is either a qualitie as in venemous and infectious diseases, where the malignitie creeping from one part to another doth alter the qualitie of the parts as it goeth, and at the last is comminicated to the principall parts, as the head, heart, liuer, longs, &c. or a substance which either by manifest conducts, as vaines, nerues, arteries, &c. or by insen-

Fernel.p.atho-
logia li.6.ca.6

sible pores (as *Hyppocrates* saith, our bodies are transpirable, and transmeable) is conuaied from one part to another: whether it be a vapour or a humor, as wee doe commonly obserue in the fits of feuers, where a vapour arising from the part affected, disperseth it selfe through the whole body, and affecteth the sensiue parts with colde or heate, the motiue parts with trembling, the vitall parts with fainting, sounding, inequalitie of pulse, &c. the naturall parts with deiection of appetite, subuersion of the stomacke, &c. vntill nature haue ouercome and discussed it. In these Feuers also many times hu-

Forestus lib.10
obseru:115: in
scholiis.

mors are so plentifully sent vp vnto the braine, as by custome or long continuance they breede some proper affect there.

 The other kinde of communitie is that which they call *Communitas absoluta*, wherein the part consenting receiueth nothing from the other, but yet is partaker of his griefe: either for *similitude* of substance or function, which causeth mutuall compassion;

fion : as all neruous partes haue with the braine:
whereby if any Nerue or neruous part bee hurt or
pricked, the braine fuffreth a convulfion, or *for
neighbourhood* and vicinitie, whereby one part may
offend another, by comprefsion or incumbencie :
as in the prolapfe of the Mother, the bladder or fun-
dament is oftentimes offended in their naturall excretion. And in this difeafe which we haue in hand
by the locall motion of it vpwardes, the midriffe
is ftraightned of his fcope, whereby the lunges doe
faile in their dutie, or by *reafon of connexion or conti-
nuitie* which it hath with other parts, by Vaines,
Nerues, Arteries, Membranes, Ligaments, &c.
whereby the offence is eafily imparted vnto other
partes. Or laftly by priuation of fome *facultie or* Gal: loebrum
matter, whereof the part hath neede. As in the ob- affect: 1: cap: 6
ftruction of the *Spina Dorfi* there followeth a refolution or palfie of the legges or armes, by reafon
that the animall facultie that fhould giue fence or
motion to the part is intercepted and hindered in
his paffage. Likewife in a refolution of the Mufcles
of the breft, as in a wound of that part, or in fwoun-
ding the voice is taken away, becaufe the matter of Rondeletius
it which is breath, is either not fufficiently made, or cap 6 9. Trinc
is carried another way, or not competently impel- cauell loco
led to the organs of voyce.

All thefe manner of wayes hath the Matrix by
confent to impart her offence vnto other parts. For
there wanteth no corruption of humor, vapour, nor
euill qualitie, where this part is ill affected, to infect other partes withall, there wantes no oportunitie

nitie of conueyance or paſſage vnto any part, by reaſon of the large Vaynes, Arteries, and Nerues, which are deriued vnto it, with which it hath great affinitie and ſimilitude of ſubſtance, beſides the connexion it hath with the heart, liuer, braine, and backe. It is linked alſo in neighborhoode with diuerſe partes of great vſe, as the bladder, gutres, midriffe, &c. which are likely to bee warmed when this part doth burne. *According to the varietie of cauſes and diſcaſes wherewith the wombe is offended*, theſe *Symptoms* doe differ in nature, or in degree. [a] A plentifull matter produceth a vehement *Symptom* : a corrupt matter according to the degree of corruption, and the qualitie of the humor corrupted, cauſeth like accidents. The diſeaſes alſo of the Mother being cõplicated with the former corrupt humors do yeeld varietie of *Symptoms* : as the riſing of the Mother, which alwayes cauſeth ſhortnes of breath: [b] Empoſtumes of the Mother according to the place where they are bred, and the quality of them, doe alſo bring a difference in *Symptoms*. And thus much for explanation of the definition.

a Mercatus pag. 165:

Mathæus de gradi. & Auicenna locis citatis,

Cap. 3.

Cap. 3.

Of the kinds of this diseafe, and firft of that wherein the vitall facultie is offended.

Ow I come to the kinds and forts of this diseafe, which may bee reduced vnto three principall heades, according as euerie part of the bodie belongeth vnto fome of the three principall functions which do gouerne the bodie of man. Not that euerie *Symptom* in this diseafe doth hurt fome of the three functions, for fome are onely moleftations or deformities, as fudden *Affectus corporis vel excretionum vitia.* Collickes, windie humors, noyfes, alteration of colour, &c. But becaufe euerie part may well bee muftred vnder fome of thefe generals: and we doe feldome fee any hyftericall affect wherein fome one or mo of the functions are not affected. Thefe functions as they are diftinct in office, fo they poffeffe in our bodies feuerall feats and haue feuerall inftruments belonging vnto them.

1 The vitall function which by preferuing naturall heat in a due temperature, maintaineth the coniunction of foule and bodie togither, hath his principall manfion in the heart, and from thence by his Arteries conueyeth vitall fpirites vnto euery member. So as without this wee could not liue: and therefore it is accounted the principalleft func-

D tion

tion, becaufe the reft receyue their being from this, and this fayling they muft needes all ceafe. This function is performed by the motion of the heart, and Arteries, which in this affect of the Mother is drawne into confent as it is either diminifhed, abolifhed, or depraued. The deprauation of this motion is either when it is too faft and quick, or when it beates diforderly. The pulfe in this difeafe is oftentimes too quicke, although it bee weake withall : but feeing it brings no great offence with it, the patient doth feldome complaine therof. The greater offence is when it beates diforderly, and keepes no equall nor orderly ftroke, but either trembleth and daunceth in the motion, or elfe is violently impelled : infomuch as it doth not onely remoue ones hande being applied to fome part where the Arteries are great, and neare to the skinne) as lately appeared in a noble Gentleman of this lande now dead) but as *Fernelius* teftifieth, hath fometimes difplaced the ribbes, and fometimes broken them through the violent motion of the heart.

Trincauel.li.4 cap.24.

De partium morbis et fymp. lib.5:cap.12.

This *Symptom* is called the palpitation or beating of the heart, or Arteries whereof *Maximillian* the Emperour died as *Crato* reporteth, and wherewith *Charles* the fift was oftentimes molefted, as *Vefalius* writeth. It is chiefly to bee perceyued where the Arteries are great & neare the skin: as vnder the left ribbes towards the backe, and in the necke : as you may obferue in Maides that haue the greene fickeneffe, by the fhaking and quiuering of their ruffes, if they fit clofe to their neckes : where fometimes

times through the dilatation of the Arterie there ariseth a [a]tumour as bigge as ones fist. This *Symptom* is euerie where mentioned by our [b]Authours in this disease and our dayly experience confirmeth it.

This motion of the heart 'and Arteries in this affect of the Mother is oftentimes diminished either in part or to sense totally. In part, where the pulse in this disease is weake, slow, obscure, intermittent, &c. and the whole bodie accordingly feeble and slow in euery action, for want of influence of vitall facultie from the heart. It is totally diminished in that *Symptom* which is called *Syncope* or swounding, the very image of death, where the pulse is [c]scarcely or not at all perceyued; the breath or respiration cleane gone: by reason that the heart wanting his motion, hath no neede of the helpe of the lungs to refresh it withall, all the facultics of the body sayling, it selflying like a dead corpse three or foure houres togither, and [d]sometimes two or three whole dayes without sense, motion, breath, heate, or any signe of life at all (like as wee see Snakes and other creatures to lie all the winter, as if they were dead, vnder the earth) insomuch as diuerse [e]errors haue beene committed in laying foorth such for dead, which haue afterwards beene found to haue life in them, and haue risen vp in their burials, whereupon there haue beene lawes enacted, as [f]*Mercurialis* reporteth, that no woman which was subiect to this disease should be buried vntill she had beene three dayes dead. Or as [g]*Alexander Benedictus*

ot

a *Aneurisma.*
Fernel. loco citato.
b *Petrus Salius pag. 429.*
Shinckius de cordis palpit. obs. 211. item 218. 222.
Forestus lib. 17 obs. 8.

c *Gal. loc. affect. 6. c 5. pulsum six perceptibilem habent &c* item de compos it. pharmac. f. l. lib. 9. in finit.
d *Antho. Guaynerius. cap. de suffoc. matricis.*
Albert. Bottonus loco infra citato.
Gal. loco citato.
Altomarus loco citato.
e *Ambrof. paraeus li. 24. c. 10*
f *De morbis muliebr: lib. 4. cap. 22.*
Iacobus Syluius de mensibus mulierum.
g *De morbis medicandis. lib. 10. cap. 10.*

of *Bolonia* fayth 72. houres, which commeth to the same reckoning. [a] *Petrus Bayrus* fetteth downe diuerfe reafons why they fhould not be buried before three dayes bee ended, befides the experience of fome (as hee faith) that haue beene found aliue in their graues after they had beene buried. I will refer the reader for the reafons to the author himfelf, and to [b] *Forreſtus* in his obferuations. [c] *Plinie* maketh mention out of *Heraclides*, of a woman who for feuen dayes together lay for dead in a fit of the mother, and was reftored againe to life : which (faieth [d] *Marcellus Donatus*) is not to be thought a fabulous tale, feeing it is not repugnant to the rules of Philofophie and Phificke. And [e] *Galen* making mention of the verie fame hyftorie vnder the name of *Apnæa*, difcourfeth of the reafons of it.

[f] *Rabbi Mofes* an ancient Author in Phyficke, reporteth alfo of a woman, that in the fitte of the mother, did lie fix dayes without fenfe and motion, her Arteries being waxt hard, and fhe readie to be buried, and yet recouered.

[g] *Bottouus* a late profeſſor of Phyficke in Padua, reporteth of a woman that beeing giuen ouer for dead in a fit of the Mother, was by fuch conclufions as he tried, difcouered to be yet aliue, and recouered her former health againe by fuch remedies as he prefcribed.

[h] *Foreſtus* of *Alkmar* in north *Holland*, but lately dead, fetteth downe the like example of another, that lay in that maner 24. houres, and was by him reftored to health againe.

The

(marginal notes, left column:)

Practica lib. 2. cap. 17.

b Lib. 10. obfer. 79. in fcholiis. c Hiſtor. nat. lib. 7. cap. 52. d De medica hyſtoria mir. 12 bili. lib. 4. ca. 11 e 6 Locorum affeɛt. cap. 5.

f Ioh. Schinckius refert ex picto-rio. obferuat. med. lib 4. cap. 288.

g De morbis muliebribus cap. 43.

h Obferu. li. 10. in fcholiis ad obferuat. 79. Iacobus Ruffius teſtatur fe plu-res huiuf. nod. vidiſſ. muliebr. lib. 6. cap. 8.

The like also he citeth out of *Leouellus*, in that place, of one that lay with her eyes shut, and dumb a whole day, and by conuenient remedies was deliuered from her fit, and could rehearse all that was done about her in the time of her fit. But the most pitifull example of all other in this kinde, is that which *Ambrose Paræe* reporteth of *Vesalius* a worthie Physition, & for anatomicall dissections much renowmed, who being called to the opening of a Gentlewoman in Spaine, which was thought to be dead through the violence of one of these fits, began to open her, and at the second cut of the knife she cried out, and stirred her limbes, shewing manifest signes of life to remaine. The beholders were exceedingly amazed at the sight, and blamed the Physition much for it: who though hee tooke her for dead, yet tooke he great apprehension of sorrow for that accident, that he estranged himselfe. After through griefe and remorse of conscience for his error, pretended (as others say) a pilgrimage for the absenting of himselfe, and therein died. Many more examples to this end could I produce out of *Authenticall* writers, and late experiences, if it were free for mee to mention them: but these may suffice to shew how wonderfully the vitall facultie is ouerthrowne in this disease, and withall respiration, sense, motion, and all the functions of the bodie by reason of this.

De hominis generat.cap.46.

Of that kind of this disease wherein the animall facultie is offended.

He second kind of this disease is, where the animall facultie doth principally suffer; and it is that faculty whereby we do vnderstand, iudge, and remember things that are profitable or hurtfull vnto vs, whereby also we haue sence and do feele the qualities of things, and moue to and fro, & performe diuers other voluntary actions for the comoditie of the bodie. For nature had made vs but base creatures, if she had giuen vs onely the vitall facultie barely to liue, and the naturall to grow, and to supply the expence that is daily made of naturall moisture: If she had not withall giuen vs knowledg and vnderstanding of such things as we are subiect vnto, and abilitie to moue our bodies at our pleasure, to apprehend that which is profitable & to shun that which is offensiue, &c. And therefore as a facultie making most for the dignitie and vse of man, it is placed principally in the braine; from whence it disperseth his beames of influence into euery part of the bodie, according to the seuerall vses and necesitie of each part.

This animall facultie hath this peculiar difference from the vitall and naturall faculties, that the functions
ons

ons of it are subiect vnto our wil, &may be intēded
remitted, or peruerted at our pleasure, otherwise thē
in the other faculties ⁘ For no man can make his
pulse to beate as he lift, or alter the naturall functions at his will and pleasure. But these animall functions may be abused both by our owne will, and by
the violence of some disease, and by both, as *Galen*
testifieth, *lib.2.de Symptomatum causis cap.12.* That it
may be abused by our owne will, he proueth also in *De motu muſ-*
another place, where he bringeth an instance of a *culorum lib.2.*
seruant (*serui barbari*) who killed himselfe to anger *cap.7.8.*
his maister by holding of his breath. S. *Augustine* *De ciuitate*
saith that he knew a man that could make himselfe *Dei lib.4:*
to sweate when he lift, by his imagnation only. *Cor-* *Cosmocrit.lib.*
nelius Gemma saith, that he knewe one that could *1.pag.156.*
weepe when he lift : others that could make their
bodies stiffe like an image, imitate the voyces of all
kinde of creatures, raise a hickocke, and breake wind
as often and in what maner they would. And S.
Augustine tels of one that would make a kinde of *Medici parisien-*
musicke that way. *Adrian Turnebus* saw a rogue *Martha.Bros-*
that gayned much money by shewing this feate, we *ser.*
do also daily see that some can counterfait madnes, *1.Sam.21.13.*
some drunkennesse, some the falling sicknesse, some *Gal.lib quomo*
palsies and trembling, some can play the fooles and *do deprehendū-*
supply the roomes of innocents , some can make *tur qui ægrota-*
noyses & speake in their bellies or throates, as those *re se fingunt.*
which *Hyppocrates* calleth *Engaſtrimuthoi ventri loqui,* *Epidemiorum.*
such as was the holy maid of Kent, and *Mildred* of *5.R.Scot.lib.7:*
westwall, &c. And it is strange to see how young *cap.1.*
bodies will be bowed and writhed diuersly, as wee
see

see in tumblers iuglers, and such like companions.
Hereupon diuers haue counterfaited diseases as I
once saw a poor fellow being arested for a small debt
counterfaited a fit of the falling sicknes, with strange
and violent motions : whereby the creditor in
compassion was moued to release him. Being released he was well againe, and vnto his friendes seemed to confesse the cousonage : others haue counterfaited possessions, either vpon meere deceit or
inticed therto through the conceite of some disease
wherewith they haue beene troubled. But for this
point I referre you to the histories of *Agnes Brigs* ,
Lib.16.cap.4. *Rachel Pinder*, *Martha Brossier*,&c. *Ren.Scot* tels of
one that being blind, deafe, and dumbe, could reade
any canonicall Scripture, but no Apocripha : But
was discouered by inserting a leafe of Apocrapha :
among the canonicall.   Another faining her selfe
to be possessed with a diuell, would answere to any
question made in English, but vnderstood no latine.
Diuers such like examples might bee procured to
shew how the animall functions may be abused by
our owne will.   But against our willes this faculty
doth suffer by consent in the suffocation of the Mother diuersly according to the varietie of offices or
functions which it performeth.

The functions of it are three, the first is called *Internall* and principall sence which doth gouerne
and direct all the rest by *Imagination*,*Reason* and *Memory*: which if it bee hurt either by imminution or
deprauation or total abolishment, then the inferior
functions doe necessarily participate with the offence.

fence. They are hurt by Imminution when a man doth not *Conceiue, Iudge,* or remember fo well as hee ought to doe, as in dulneffe or blockifhneffe, as wee call it in vndifcretion, foolifhnes or want of iudgement, in obliuion or forgetfulnes, &c. They are abolifhed either in thofe drowfie affects which wee call *Caros, Coma, veternus, Lethargus* &c. or in thofe aftonifhing *Symptoms* wherein all the animall faculties are at once taken away, fometimes with a generall refolution or palfie, as in *Apoplexies :* fometimes with a generall conuulfion, as in the falling ficknes: fometimes with a *Stifneffe or congelation* of the body, wherein they lie like an image in the fame forme they were taken.

These internall fences are ouerthrowne either in part or in whole in this fuffocatió of the mother : and thereupon it is likened vnto thefe former difeafes : and this kind is accounted by *Auicen* to be the moft grieuous of all other, where the imagination and reafon is hurt : and the other which holds them with conuulfions, contractions, &c. he accounts to bee the milder and the more vfuall. And therefore he faith that commonly they can remember what was done about them in their fit : vnleffe it be of this moft grieuous kinde.

The Internall fence is depraued when a man doth imagine, iudge, or remember thinges that are not as if they were, or things that are, otherwife then they are indeed. Whether they do it in cogitation alone, or do expreffe it by word or deede. As

Hebetudo mentis.
Imprudentia obliuio.

Sopor.

Apoplexia.
Epilepfia.

Catalepfis.

a *Hypp. de morbis muliebr. lib 1 et 2. Torpor occupat caput mes percellitur et improba fit non facile intelligit. De Virginum morbis cor fatuum fit, ex fatuitate torpor. Gal. loc. affect. 6.5. De compofit. pharm. f. L. lib. 9. in fine Rhafis continet 22. Egineta. li. 3. ca. 71. Ætius tetr. 4 Serm 4. cap. 68. pafchaliuslib. 11*

cap. 58. *Valefcus de Taran. Iacobus Syluius Altomam. Augeni. Aui. Fen. 21.3. cap. 16. tract. 4. Idem. Petr. Salius de catelepfi. pag. 384.*

E.

wc

Infania.
Delirium.
Melancholia.
Furor.

we see in those fooles which wee call naturals, in mad men, in melancholike men, in those that are furious, in such as do dote, in such as are distracted through loue, feare, griefe, ioye, anger, hatred, &c. In some of which they will laugh, crye, prattle, threaten, chide, or sing, &c. according to the dispofition of the party or the caufe of the affect.

Vigilia.
Insomnium.

These functions are also depraued in too much wakefulneffe through the commotion of the animall fpirits, also in dreames, where fomtimes besides the deprauation of the fantafie they wil walke, talke, laugh, crye, &c.   And laftly in that difeafe which is

b *Saltus Viti.*
F. *Platerus de ment is aliena-tioue, pag.* 103

called b *Saltus Sa*ti *viti*, or *Saltuofa difpofitio membrorum* wherein they will daunce, and leape, and cannot endure to be quiet.

This deprauation of the internall fences, is fo ordinary in the fits of the Mother, as *Horatius Augenius Epiftola. 6.* feemes to make it of the effence of this difeafe, that the imagination is euer depraued in it.

c *Hippocrat.de morbit Virg: pra acut a infla matione in fa nit pra putredi ne clamat, &c De morbis mu liebr.lib.1.men te alienatur in hoc morbo et de bria fiunt furi ofa dentibus friendet Vigila-*

But c *Hyppocrates, Galen, Auicen,* and moft of the beft Authors in our profeffion, do affirme that very often there happeneth an alienation of the minde in this difeafe, whereby fometimes they will waxe furious and raging depriued of their right iudgement and of reft.

The fecond function of the animall facultie is the externall fenfitiue function; which giueth to the eye the facultie of feeing, to the eare of hearing, to

bit anxia erit &c. *Auicen loco citato facit accidere alienationem per communicatem corebri, &c. Aetius garrula inquiete & iracunda fiunt.lib.16.7 4 Hier.mercurialis mor uerborum muliebr.lib.4.c.10. Iacobus Syluius dementibus. Mathaeus de grad. confilio 80. hiftoriam narrat furiofi.*

the

the tongue of tasting, to the nose of smelling and to diuers parts of the bodie the power of feeling.

This function in all these kindes is diminished, depraued, or cleane abolished, but especially in this disease of the mother, we do obserue the offence which is done to the feeling facultie, when the parts are benummed or do not feele at all, or when they feele ᵈ paine and offence, or when they feele things falsely and otherwise then they are.

Concerning heating, although ᶜ *Hyppoc. Rhasis* and diuers others doe obserue that sometimes it is hindred: yet it seemes to be in the former kinde where the internall facultie doe suffer. For *Merca-tus* puts it as a difference from the falling sicknes, that in this suffocation of the matrix they doe commonly heare. The priuation of the other sences of seeing, tasting, smelling and feeling, are verie ordinarie in this disease, as you may obserue in the Histories following, and in these quotations.

The third function is that which giues motion to the whole bodie. This motion serueth either for a voluntary vse onely, or for a naturall vse also. The motions for the voluntary vse are the free motions of the externall members of our bodies: as to bowe the whole bodie and the head by meanes of the backe, to apprehend with the hand, to stand and goe with the feete and legges, to chewe with the iawes, to open & shut the lips & eyelids, to moue the eies, &c. This functiō is *diminished* in that affect which we cal *lassitudo*, werines or vnweldines,

Horatius Angenius Epist. 6, Gal. de motu musc. lib. 2. cap. 6. et 8.

E 2 wherein.

Priuatio visus
Auditus.
Gustus.
Olfactus.
Tactus.
ᵈ *Iuxta receptam a medicis sententiam dolorem hic infero licet videatur potius ad simplices corporis affectus referendus.*
ᶜ *Hyp. morb. mu-liebr. lib. o. ca-ligo ante oculos obuersatur et Vertigo, oculi non acute videt nihil olfaciunt Vocat. s non audit Rhasis 22. cont. in hac pas-sione non audit quando datur in auribus eius Vox terribilis AEgineta loco citato. Instru-mentorum sen-sus apprehensio. &c. Auicen narrat plurimum eius quod fuit in ea nisi sit maxima et immoderata AEtius sensus et motus inter-cipiuntur. Gal. immobiles sine sensu iacēt.*

wherein we are not able to moue so strongly and nimbly as we should.

It is *abolished*, either by a *resolution* or *palsie* where the sound part drawes the sickly part, that is the part resolued, & depending draws the muscles & nerues &c. or by a *Spasmus* or *contractiō* of them g where the sick part drawes the soundpart, that is, the muscle which is affected, drawes the member which is wel.

A resolution or palsie is either generall of both sides of the bodie h exempting the head, or of one side called *Hæmiplegia*, or yet more particular of the hand, legge, finger, &c. called i *parapligia*.

A *Contraction* or *Spasmus* is also of like sortes, sometimes the bodie is held vpright and cannot be bowed any way in that affect which is called *Tetanos*, sometimes it is bowed forwardes *Emprostotonos* sometimes backward *Opistotonos*, somtimes the back is crookt in some part of it, as in *Gibbo*, sometimes the iawes, lips, face, eyelids, &c. are contracted, wherby they make many strange faces and mouthes sometimes as though they laughed or wept, sometimes holding their mouthes open or awry, their eyes staring, &c. Sometimes the handes, armes, legges, fingers, toes, &c. are contracted, sometimes particular muscles in the sides, backe, armes, legs, &c. one or more at once, as in crampes.

It is *depraued* where the motions are immoderate, peruerse, inordinate, or indecēt, as when they are *vnquiet*, & cannot abstaine frō motions and gestures, casting their armes and legges to and fro, vp and downe

Paralysis.

g *Contract io. platerus. Gal. de causis morborū lib. 2. cap. 7. et loc. affect. li. 34.*

h *Petrus Salius pag. 40 [...] tanquam leuis Apoplexia Fern. de part. morbis & sympt. li. 5. cap. 3.*

i *Gal. 1. prorket com. 2. 50. et com. 3. 26. de Victus rat. tom. 4. 27. de morb. Vulg. com. 2. 56 Gybbus. Trismos. Tortura oris. Strabismus. Spasmus Cynicus.*

downe, dauncing, capring, vawting, fencing, and in
diuerfe maners forming their motions. Alfo in *Con-* *Marcellus Do-
natus.li.2.ca.4*
vulfions of the members, where they are fhaken and
pulled by inordinate motions, as wee fee in the fal-
ling ficknefle. Alfo in *trembling*, *palpitation*, *rigor* *Felix Platerus
de motu depra-
uato.pag.401.*
where the teeth do chatter, horror where the haire
ftandes vpright, ftretching, yawning, gafping
twinckling of the eyes, &c. Thefe impediments
and deprauations of motion are dayly obferued in
vterne affects : as may appeare by thefe teftimonies.
*Hyppocrat.de morbi muliebr.lib.1.Albas oculorum par-
tes fubuertit,dentibus frendet,& fimilis fit his qui hercu-
leo morbo detinentur. Item fit conulfio fortis articulorum
corporis, claudam facit aut impotentem pra rigore, alias
atque alias feipfam iactabit.Horror.Erecta ceruicis fpira-
tio ipfam tenet, & quicquid ederit aut biberit ipfam mo-
leftat.Torpor occupat manus & inguina,& crura & pop-
lites. Magnis pedum digitis conuelluntur gybbofa fit, de
nat.muliebr. Gal.lib.de femine cap.3. Tenfiones lumbo-
rum & manuum,& pedum viduam apprehendebant loc.
affect. 6.5. Aliis crura & bracchia contrahuntur. Auicenna, minor fuffocationum eft qua facit accidere fpaf-
mum & tetanum, fine nocumento in ratione & fenfu.
Quandoque claudit oculos & non aperit eos.Stridor dentium,percufsio oculorum,& motus innoluntarius lacerto-
rum.Rhafis. Stridor dentium cum fpafmo & torquedine
extremitatum, dolores fortes adeo vt mulierem torquere
faciant vndique & caput genibus implicari.&c. Mefue
loco fuperius citato.Aetius. Oculi poft multam grauitatem
attolluntur, vterus paulatim laxatur & intellectum &
fenfum recipit.&c.*

E 3   The

Of the Suffocation

The animall motions which doe serue for naturall vse, haue their power from the animall facultie, but their vrging and prouoking and cause from the naturall, and are either *Respiration, Ingestion, or Excretion.* Respiration hath annexed vnto it voyce, and speach, this is diminished or abolished in *Suffocation* or choaking, from whence this disease which we intreat of taketh his name, as from the most cōmon *Symptom* which appeareth in it. In *difficulty* of breathing. In priuation of *voyce and speach.*

Suffocatio. Anthon, Guaynerius.cap.de suffocatione.

Priuatio Vocis·

It is depraued when it is done immoderately or inordinately, whether it be voluntarie, or inuoluntarie, as in *shortnesse of breath, sighing, yawning, the hickock, sneesing, coughing, belching, vomiting, making of noyses, blowing, and reaching, &c.*

Cita respiratio, suspirium. Oscitatio. Singultus. Sternutatio, Ructus, Tussis. Deglutitio. Excret. o.

Ingestion, or swallowing, is also hurt in this affect, when either they cannot swallow meate, or drinke at all, or with great difficultie.

Excretion is also hurt in this case, by vomit, seege or vrine, &c. when either they cannot performe it being prouoked, or do it out of season, or more then is conuenient. &c.

These *Symptoms* also appeare in the Suffocation of the Mother. *Hyppocrat. de nat. muliebri. Muta de-repentè sit, de morbis muliebr. lingua ipsius refrenatur & hanc non claram habet. Aliquibus etiam vocis priuatio. Spiritus sublimis it, et suffocatio et anhelatio densa ipsam corripit. De nat. muliebr. Tussis detinet & contabiscit & videtur peripnumonia esse, &c. Gal. 9. de compis. Ph. s.l. aliquibus vox intercipitur. loc. affect. 6.5. aliæ interceptas habent spirationes aliæ suffocationes, &c. Hyppoc.*
                                                                        de

de nat. muliebr. quicquid ederit aut biberit ipsam molestat.
Auicen. Abscinditur loquela &c. Rhasis, Strictura arhe-
litus, squinantia, peripneumonia, apostema in gutture ex
comunicatione Diaphragmatis cum matrice. Gal. Loco ci-
tato humiditas quædam è locis muliebribus excurrit. &c.
Rondalat. cap. 6 9. Hollerius. cap. 59. Syluius suspirium.
Montagnana consilio. 22 5.

These motions as they belong to the animall facultie are principally hurt by *Resolution, contraction,*
or *conuulsion*, according as the simple motions are,
and therefore we shall not need to stand any longer
vppon them in this place : as they belong vnto the
naturall facultie, and do receyue offence in that respect shall be declared hereafter in the third general
faculty. In the mean time let vs producesome examples of this 2. kind of *Suffocation*, where the animall
faculty doth principally suffer : for examples many
times do perswade more then doctrine. *Hollerius* reporteth that the gouernour of *Roan* in France had
two daughters which were helde with these fits,
in such sort as they would laugh an houre or two togither, and confessed that they could not refraine
from laughing, although diuerse means to that end
were vsed, both by entreaty, and by threates. He tels
also of a gentlewoman *de Rochpot*, who being in
these fits would raue, laugh, & weep, her eies being
shut. *Forestus* maketh mention of one *Alcida Theodo-*
rici at Alkmare a yong lusty maid who was held 2 4.
houres in a most grieuous fit of the mother, wherin
she lay as if she had beene halfe dead, hearing what
was said about her, but could not speake, nor enioy
　　　　　　　　　　　　　　　　　　　her

De morbis in-
ternis lib. 1. ca.
59. in scholiis.

Lib. 2 8. obseru
26.

her other senses. Sometimes she would bee pulled
as if she had the falling sickenesse, sometimes would
lie still as if she were in an *Apoplexie,*sometimes she
would onely stirre her legges, the rest of her bodie
being dull: and although she could not speake, yet
she would crie and laugh by turnes,and then be sul-
len and dumpish,as if she were dead againe.

Aliam egregiã
mutuum covul-
siuorũ ab Vtero
hystor.Vide
apud eandem.
li.10.obser.116
Lib.26.cap. 16.

    Alexander Benedictus veronensis testifieth,that
he saw a woman in a fit of the Mother, that was besides her selfe, and would sometimes laugh & sometimes crie. Those that attended her, applied Par-
trige feathers vpon coales vnto her nostrilles,and by
chance through want of care there fell a great coale
out of the Chafingdish into her bosome, where it
burnt her,and made a great blister, but she perceyued it not vntill the next day,and then complained
of her breasts. My selfe had a patient in this Citie
yet liuing and in good health(whome I will name
vnto any whome it may concerne)that endured a
violent fitte of the Mother a whole day together:
wherein shee had many strong conuulsions, and
sometimes did lie as if she had beene dead. Infomuch as the midwiues would haue giuen her ouer,
and imputed ignorance vnto mee that I woulde
attempt any thing for her recouerie. But her huf-
band being perswaded by me to make triall of some
meanes which I had prescribed for her , shee was
within three or foure houres deliuered of a childe;
yet knew not of it, vntill shee was throughly recouered of her fit, which was fourteene or fifteene
houres after,and then she asked her husband what
                                was

was become of her great bellie. I could rehearse two other such like examples within this citie, which happened not many moneths since.

But we had of late a most rare example of this disease in an Essex Gentlewoman of good note, who being once frighted by squibs, fell into these fits of the Mother, which held her euery day, and whensoeuer else she did eate any comfortable meat, for the space of fifteene or sexteene yeares togither, with such violent conuulsions, as fiue or six strong men could scarce hold her downe. Sometimes her limbes would be contracted, sometimes perticular Muscles, which would cause swellings in diuerse parts of her bodie, sometimes she would be without all maner of sense. And being made beleeue by a stranger Physition that she was bewitched, her fits increased vpon her, and grew to bee stronger then before.

Bartholomeus Montagnana reciteh vp 31. seuerall *Symptoms* of this disease which hee obserued in a Gentlewoman which was his patient. Conuulsions, swoundings, choaking in the throate, sadnesse and lamentation, coldnes ouer her whole bodie, dumb-nesse, and yet could heare, drowsinesse, beating of the heart, trembling of the handes, contraction of the fingers, &c.

It were in vaine to heape vp many examples to this purpose, seeing our daily experience doth yeeld vs sufficient store of proofe of the varietie of these *Symptoms* in the animall facultie.

F   Cap. 5.

Cap. 5.

of that kind wherein the naturall facultie is offended.

He third kinde of this difeafe is, where the naturall facultie doth principally fuffer. This facultie is of great neceffitie for the maintenaunce of mankinde and according to the diuerfe vfes thereof is diftinguifhed . For feeing that nature bringes vs not forth into the world perfect men, in that ripeneffe and integritie, of all humaine actions which afterwards we attaine vnto, when wee come to full growth, it was meete to be prouided of fuch a facultie in our bodies as might encreafe our ftature, & ftrengthen the inftruments of the whole body, for the better perfection of the actions thereof. And this is called *facultas auctrix.* Seeing alfo that wee are made of a fluxible moulde which wafteth and fpendeth it felfe many wayes, whereby it ftandeth in neede of continuall refection and replie : Therefore it was meete to be furnifhed with fuch a facultie as might repaire the decay and expence of our fubftance, by yeelding continually apt matter for the nourifhment of the bodie. And that is called *facultas altrix.* And thirdly feeing, notwithftanding our bodies are continually nourifhed with the beft food, yet they muft once die as well as other inferiour

creatures

creatures doe : therefore God hath indued vs as
well as other creatures with the facultie of generation : whereby wee may bee able to make our
kind to continue as long as the world ſhall endure.

Theſe three naturall faculties haue diuerſe o-
thers attending vpon them, as the faculties of *Attraction, Retention, Concoction, Expulſion, Alteration,
Formation, &c.* Which I will for breuitie ſake ouerpaſſe with their bare mention, becauſe the *Symptoms* of theſe faculties are not ſo euident to the beholders eye, nor ſo ſtraunge as thoſe of the vitall
and animall faculties are, yet that theſe are alſo hurt
in the ſuffocation of the Mother, appeareth both
by dayly obſeruation, and by the authorities of all
both auncient and late phyſitions who haue written of this diſeaſe.

Gal. de tremor Palp.tit.&c. cap.2.ſenſibus non expoſita.

And to this place may we referre thoſe accidents
often mentioned in this diſeaſe. [a] *Gnawing in the
ſtomacke,* and paines in diuerſe partes of the bodie,
breaking of wind, vomiting, purging by ſiege, vrin,
or other excretion, loathing of meate, thirſt, extraordinarie hunger, ſwelling in the throat, ſwelling in
the body, in the feet, obſtructions in the vaines, cō-
ſumptions, tumors, feuers, priuation of voice, pale-
neſſe of colour, rumbling and noiſe in the belly or
[b] throat, like vnto frogs, ſnakes, or other creatures,
or as if they woulde ſpeake as *Hyppocrates* reporteth
of *Polymarchus* wife.

Some of theſe are Symptoma-ta in qualitate mutata, ot in extremento vitiato: but be-cauſe they are in the naturall parts, and ari-ſing from er-rors of that fa-cultie, I haue inſerted them here. a Hypp.de mor-bis mulieb.lib.1 Rhaſis con. li.22.Fernel.de partium morb.

And theſe are three principall kindes of this

lib.6.cap.16.Mercatus lib.2.cap.2.& 3. Bottonus,& Mercurialis lociscitatis. Sylutus de menſibus. b Schenkiusobſer. deptiſiobſer.137 1 Cornel. Gema. Coſmoer. Hyppocrat. Epidem.5.expectoreobſtrepebat.&c.

diſeaſe

diſeaſe wherevnto moſt of the *Symptoms* which euer
do appeare therein may be referred.

Cap. 6.

Of the cauſes of this diſeaſe.

He cauſes of this diſeaſe and
of the *Symptoms* belonging
therunto, haue euer bin found
hard to be deſcribed particularly: and eſpecially in a vulgar
tongue, I hold it not meete to
diſcourſe to freely of ſuch matters, and therefore I doe craue
pardon if I do but ſlenderly ouerpaſſe ſome poynts
which might be otherwiſe more largely ſtood vpon

The cauſes of this diſeaſe are either internall,
or externall. The internall cauſes may be any thing
contained within the bodie, as ſpirit, blood, humors
excrements, &c. whereby this part is apt to be offended, but principally they are referred vnto theſe
two, a blood, and nature.

Blood is that humor wherwith we are nouriſhed:
without which the infant in the mothers wombe
could neither grow & increaſe in bigneſſe, nor yet
liue: and therefore it was neceſſarie that thoſe that
were fit for generation, ſhould be ſupplied with
ſufficient ſtore of this humor, for the vſe of this part
wherin the infāt is to be nouriſhed, for which cauſe
there are large vaines & arteries deriued vnto it for

the

a Gal. loc. affec.
6. cap. 5. Holle-
rius, de morbis
internis. lib. 1.
cap. 59.
Paſchalius li. 1
cap. 57.
Altomarus. ca.
x 10. Item de
vtero gerenti-
bus. cap. 2.
Iacobus Sylutus
de menſibus.
Hor. Augenius
epiſt. 6.
Cardanus de
cauſis, &c.
morberum.
cap. 134.

the conueyance of bloud thereunto , and there is
greater prouision thereof made in womens bodies
then in mens : leaft this part fhould bee forced to
withdraw nourifhment from other parts of the bodie, and fo leaue them weake and confuming.

But this prouifion of nature is oftentimes de- *Defectus.*
fectiue : as when it is cut off by violent caufes , and
the part left deftitute of this familiar humor, which
fhould ferue both for the comfort of the infant, and
of the part it felfe : which finding offence thereby
doth communicate it vnto the other partes with
which it hath affinitie according to *Hyppocrates* doc-
trine.1.*Morborum muliebrium,*and *Ariftotle,de gene-*
rat. animal.cap. 11.*vteri euacuati furfum afcendunt &* *Holleriuser*
præfocationes faciunt. *Cordæus* giues vs an example *Rondelet.loci*
of one who by chaunce cutting a vaine in her leg, *citatis.*
Comment.2 in
whereupon fhe did bleede plentifully , fell into a fit *lib.1.Hypp.de*
of the Mother, and by moift and nourifhing diet *morb. muliebr.*
was recouered.. The reafon whereof *Hyppocrates*
referreth to the ouerdrying of thofe parts through
large euacuatiou of bloud,wherby the matrix doth
labour by fuch motion as it hath to fupply it felfe
with moyfture from other parts of the body : or as
Mercurialis doth enterpret it,doth impart by com- *Lib.4.cap.22.*
munitie (as is aforefaid) the offenfiue qualitie vnto
the braine, and by that meanes procures convulfi-
ons,&c. *Gallen* referreth it vnto the ouercooling
of thofe parts which neceffarily muft follow a large *2.loc.affect.*
euacuation of bloud,which coldeneffe being very
offenfiue vnto the nerues and neruous partes by
confent and compaffion offendeth the braine alfo ,

and

and by that meanes may procure the former *Symptoms.*

Excessus.

And as the want and scarsitie of bloud may procure this griefe, so the abundance & excesse thereof doth more commonly cause it, where the patients do want those monethly euacuatiōs which should discharge their bodies of this superfluitie: as we see in strong and lustie maidens, who hauing ease and good fare inough, haue their vaines filled with plen-

Gal.loc.affect.6
Pereda in paf-
chalinm lib.I.
cap.58.
Altomarus.
Syluius.

ty of bloud, which wanting sufficient vent distēdeth them in bulck and thicknes, and so contracteth them in their length, whereby the matrix is drawne vpwards or sidewards, according as the repletion is, whereupon followeth a compresion of the neighbour parts, as of the midrif which causeth shortnes of breath, by straightning the instruments of respiration of their due scope.

But if this bloud wanting his proper vse doe degenerate into the nature of an excrement, then it offendeth in qualitie as well as in excesse, and being detayned in the bodie, causeth diuers kinds of *Symptoms*, according to the qualitie and degree of the distemperature thereof.

Alteratio.

Hypp.de morbis
virginum.
Altomarus
Corruptio.

Mercatus loco
citato.

This distemperature is either in manifest qualities, of heate, colde, moisture, drines, according vnto which it is said to be, *Melancholicke, Flegmaticke, Choloricke, &c.* producing *Symptoms* of the like nature, or in corruption and putrefactiō of this bloud which breedeth diuers strange kinds of distēperatures, according to the diuersity of the humor putrefied, the degree of putrefaction or the condition

of

of the caufe or author thereof.

The other fubftance which moft commonly is found culpable of this difeafe, is nature or *fperma:* which befides the fufpition of fuperfluitie in fome perfons, may alfo receiue diuers fortes of alteration, and likewife of corruption, able to worke moft ftrange and grieuous accidents in our bodies. For as it is a fubftance of greateft perfection & puritie fo long as it retayneth his natiue integritie: So being depraued or corrupted, it paffeth all the humors of our bodie, in venom and malignitie. For it muft needs be a vehement and an impure caufe that fhal corrupt fo pure a fubftance, which would eafily refift any weake affault: and a fubftance fo pure and full of fpirits as this is, muft needes proue moft malitious vnto the bodie when it is corrupted. And therefore it is compared to the venom of a ferpent, a Scorpion, a Torpido, a madde dogge, &c. which in a fmall quantitie is able to deftroy or depraue all the faculties of our bodies at once.

Galen comparing the corruption of thefe two together, affirmeth that although from the putrefaction of bloud, diuers moft terrible accidents doe arife, yet they are not fo deadly as thofe which proceede from the corruption of nature; and proueth it by this obferuation that diuers women enioying the benefit of mariage, yet through the fuppreffion of their ordinary euacuation falling into this difeafe, had their refpiration and vitall faculties vntouched, although otherwife they were moft grieuoufly affected.

Others

Rondeletius c. 69. Platerus. Pereda in pafch alia. Valefius de Tarantia. lib 6. Velafcus teftatur fe deprehendiffe circa Stedii hyftericarii croceum humorem fœtidiffimii & c. lib. 5. c. 15. Mathœus de grad. in. 9. Rhafis. ca. 28. Item confilio 8.4. Mercatus. Gal. Auicen. Mercurialis. Bottonus locis citatis. Hercules Saxonia de plica. ca. 14. et. 34.

Syluius, &c.

others alſo hauing thoſe ordinarie matters in good
ſorte, yet being widdowes and taken with this grief
haue felt decay in thoſe faculties as well as in the
reſt.

How theſe two ſubſtances by conſent may affect the whole bodie according to their ſeuerall natures, hath beene ſhewed before : But one ſcruple
remaineth here to be diſcuſſed, namely how this venemous matter may lurke ſo long in our bodies in
ſilence not ſhewing it ſelf but at certaine times only.

Galen in the former place declareth this by the
example of a mad dogge, whoſe venom being recei-
ued of us, although but by the foame of his mouth,
will remaine ſometimes ſixe moneths within our
bodies vndiſcouered, and then hauing gotten more
ſtrength and ripenes vnto it ſelfe, and opportunitie
of conuaying his euil quallity vnto the parts, breaketh forth to open view by diminiſhing or peruer-
ring the faculties of thoſe parts. I had once a patient in Kent who feeding vpon a mad hogge which
hee had killed for couetouſneſſe ſake, found himſelfe diſtempered therewith at the firſt, but within
fiue or ſixe moneths after grew ſuddenly to be ſtarke
madde, and before his death, being by Phiſicke reſtored to ſome reaſonable vnderſtanding, he confeſſed the eating of that hogge to haue beene the true
cauſe of his diſeaſe. Diuers reaſons may bee yeelded of this as well as of the fits of intermittent agues
of *Epilepſies*, of ſweating, &c. which oftentimes haue
their due recourſe by the yeare, moneth, weeke, day
or houre, according to the nature of the humor :
which

Loc. affect. 6. 5.
Petrus ſalius de
affect. particu.
laribus pa. 326

Diſcordius.

which being crude expecteth his concoction in our
bodies and giues no signe of his presence vntill such
a proportion of it be digested and resolued into vapours, as for the office therof the part affectedis not
able to brooke and for the weakenesse of the expul-
siue facultie not able to auoide out of the bodie: but
filling the vaines, arteries, and the habit of the body,
is communicated to the principall parts; diminishing or depraving their functions so long, vntill that
portion of vapours be discussed through naturall
heate: and ceasing againe so long vntill by firmen-
tation and concoction, another portion of the corrupt humor shall be digested.

The vniformitie of this humor and of the
heate of concoction causeth the vniformitie of fits.
And this is the cause of the due periods or circuites
which oftentimes are obserued in this disease,
whereof wee haue spoken before : according also
to the condition of the part affected, which seruing
as an euacuatorie to the whole bodie, is accustomed
to such kind of humors and therefore can endure
them better then other parts can. And this is another cause why this humor giues no signe of his presence vntill it may communicate with the principall
partes : which are soone offended either with the
plenty of those vapours, or with the malignity, or
with the vnwonted and vnaccustomed approach of
them.

The externall causes of this disease are either such
things as are ordinary and necessary for our life and
which we cannot shun, as our meate and drink, mo-

tion

Gal.loc.affe.l.2.6
Felix Platerus
de causi febri
um.pag.6 3. 65
66.&c.
Mercatus.
Fernel.pat.ho-
leg.li.6,cap.18

Quia multum.
Quia prauum.
Quia insuetū.

tion and reft, fleepe and watching, euacuation and
perturbations of the minde : or fuch things as happen vnto vs accidentally, and may bee fhunned by
vs, as bathes, ointments, plaifters, cloathes, fmelles or
vapours, medicines, venus, noyfes, riding, fwim-
ming, fayling, wounds, contufions, falles, biting of
venomous beafts, &c, which may be alfo referred to
the former kindes. Thefe and fuch like as they are
the externall caufes of all difeafes, our bodies being
fubiect to be hurt and offended by euery one of
them : fo they are oftentimes acceffary to this particular difeafe.

The aire which compaffeth our bodies and
which we breath into our bodies is the occafion of
Vernelli 1 de many infirmities in vs, if either it be diftempered in
morbit caufis qualitie or corrupted in fubftance, or fuddenly altered. And this may be the caufe why women are
more fubiect vnto this difeafe at one time of the
yeare then at another, according to the conftituti-
on of the ayre : as in the winter time , by reafon of
colde and moyft weather the humors of our bodies
are increafed and made more crude and grofe, and
our pores ftopped , whereby expiration is hindered, &c.

Mathaus de But efpecially wee doe obferue that breathing
gradi. Mercat. in of fweete fauours doth commonly procure thefe
confiel.cap.69 fittes , either for that the matrix by a naturall propertie is delighted with fweete fauoures , as the li-
fitor. Mercuria uer and fpleene with fweete meates , or becaufe the
animall fpirites of the braine beeing thereby
ftirred

ftirred vp to motion, doe by confent affect the matrix with the like.

And therefore wee doe efpecially forbid
that they may not fmell vnto any fweet thing that
are fubiect vnto this griefe: but rather vnto euill
fauoures: which as *Platerus* thinkes by ftirring vp
the expulfiue facultie of the matrix, are a meanes
of the fhortening of the fit.

Meate and drinke is the Mother of moft difeafes, whatfoeuer the Father bee, for the conftitu-
tion of the humors of our bodies is according
to that which feedes vs. And therefore it is
reckoned as a principall externall caufe of difeafes.

And *Hippocrates* in this difeafe forbids fweete
and futte meats (*a dulcibus et pinguibus abftineat, donec
fana fit*) *Forreftus* telles vs of a Bruers wife of *Delft*,
who could neuer eate or drinke any thing that
was fweete or pleafant but her fit would take her
a frefh, and thereuppon was faine to mixe
wormewood with euery thing that fhe did eate or
drinke.

The *Effex* Gentlewoman of whome I fpake
before, could neuer take any comfortable fufte-
nance, but fhe was fure to haue a fit of the mother.
The reafon of this may be the fame which we haue
alleaged of fweet vapours.

The errours about euacuation are alfo an externall caufe of difeafes, and doe breed an internall
caufe afterwardes.

*Plater.p.a. 145
Iacobus Rueffi-
us de muliebri-
bus lib.6.cap.3
Sylvius
Guaynerius.*

*De ut.mulien
bri.
lib.2.obferu.
28.
Hipp.libro cita-
to quicquid eda
rit aut liberit
ipfam maleftat*

}

*Heurnius de
morbis capitis
pag.310.*

G 2 A3

As in this diſeaſe the want of due and monethly euacuation, or the want of the benefit of marriage in ſuch as haue beene accuſtomed or are apt thereunto, breeds a congeſtiō of humors about that part, which increaſing or corrupting in the place, cauſeth this diſeaſe. And therefore we do obſerue that maidens and widdowes are moſt ſubiect thereunto, motion and reſt being well ordered do preſerue health, but being diſordered do breed diſeaſes, eſpecially to much reſt and ſlothfulneſſe is a meanes of this griefe, by ingendering crudities and obſtructions in womens bodies, by dulling the ſpirits and cooling naturall heate, &c. So likewiſe ſleepe and watching, the one by benumming, the other by diſſipation of the ſpirits and natural heate, may occaſion this griefe.

Laſtly the perturbations of the minde are oftentimes to blame both for this and many other diſeaſes. For ſeeing we are not maiſters of our owne affections, wee are like battered Citties without walles, or ſhippes toſſed in the Sea, expoſed to all maner of aſſaults and daungers, euen to the ouerthrow of our owne bodies.

We haue infinite examples among our [a] Hiſtoriographers, and Phiſitions of ſuch as haue dyed vpon ioy, griefe, loue, feare, ſhame, and ſuch like perturbations of the mind : and of others that vpon the ſame cauſes haue fallen into grieuous diſeaſes : as [c] women deliuered of their children before their time, vpon feare, anger, griefe, &c. others taken with the

1 Falling ſickeneſſe , 2 Apoplexies , 3 Madneſſe, 4 Swounding, 5 Paities, and diuerſe ſuch like infirmities vpon the like cauſes.

And concerning this diſeaſe whereof we doe intreate, 6 *Iohannes Montanus* tels vs of a patient of his, who fell into the fits of the Mother vppon iealouſie. 7 *Forreſtus* of another, who had her fits whenſoeuer ſhee was angred : and of another that vpon loue fell into this diſeaſe. My ſelfe do know a Gentlewoman, who vpon the ſight of one particular man would alwaies feele an vterin affect:
and another that vpon feare of being
chidden, or ſeeing another in the
fit of the mother, would
alſo fall into it
her ſelfe.

1 Gal. loc. affec. 5. de Grammas tico Ioh. Montanus cōſileo. 50 Matheus de grad. de proprio filio. cap. de Epilepſis.
Amatus luſit. cent. 1. cap. 90.
2 Procopius de bello Gothorum lib. 1. Amatus luſit. cent. 3.
3 Chriſtoph. à Vega. li. 4 ca. 14 Corn. Celſus.
4 Gal. loco cit 4.
5 Areteus lib. 1 cap. 7.
6 Conſilio 3 11 i
7 Lib. 28. obſer. 28. lib. 10.
obſerv. 30.

G 3   Chap. 7.

Cap. 7.

Of the cure of this disease, so much as belongeth to the friends and attendants to performe.

He signes of this disease, seeing they are drawne principally from the causes and *Symptoms* before declared shall not neede any particular discourse, especially considering the vse of them belongeth properly to the Physition, to direct him in his cure. And therefore I thinke good to ease my selfe of this labour, which would bee altogither vnprofitable to the reader.

Concerning the cure also I thinke it not meete to say more then may concerne the friends and assistants vnto the patient to looke vnto: referring Physitions workes vnto Physitions. There are some things by the friendes to bee performed vnto the patient in regard of the [a] presēt fit, & some things in regard of the cause. In the fit let the bodies bee kept [b] vpright, straight laced, and the belly & throat held downe with ones hand. Let heed be taken that they hurt not themselues by biting their fingers, striking their armes & legs against hard things, &c. apply euill smels to their nostrils, and sweet smels beneath [c] tie their legs hard with a garter for reuulsion sake, &c.

Out of the fit, in regard of *Externall* causes, remoue from them all occasions of breeding or increasing

a Valesius in Hollerium.c.59 Valescus de Tarenta.lib.6. b Paschal.li. 1 ca.57 Altomar.

c onde le Hollerius.

c Rhasis ad Almansor.cap.28.

creasing the disease: as sweet sauors, pleasant meats and drinks, much rest and slouthfulnesse, &c. Also if [a]discontinuance of any thing accustomed bee the cause of this disease, bring it into custome againe: if want of any thing necessary for their health, let it be supplied, [b]let their diet be sparing and vpon cooling things, let them vse much fasting and prayer, and all other meanes to pull downe their bodies: and contrariwise abstaine from egges, wine, flesh, &c. If the perturbations of the mind be any occasion hereof, let them haue their proper remedies, as anger and iealousie are to be appeased by good counsell and perswasions: hatred and malice by religious instructions, feare by incouragements, loue [c]by inducing hatred, or [d]by permitting them to enioy their desires, &c. *Galen* boasteth that he did euery yeare cure many diseases by this stratagem of moderating the perturbations of the mind by the example of *Æsculapius* who deuised many songs and ridiculous pastimes for that purpose. To which end also other phisitions haue vsed diuers sorts of fallacies to encounter the melancholike conceits of their patients. *Cardan* tels of a Gentlewoman, who finding her selfe vexed with many grieuous *Symptoms*, imagined that the Diuell was the author thereof, and by *Iosephus Niger* was cured by procuring her son to make her beleeue that he saw three diuels in her looking glasse, & one great one to driue them out. Another like policie *Marcellus Donatus* tels vs of, which a Physition vsed towardes the Countesse of *Mantua*, who being in that disease which we call *melancholia Hyppechon-*

[a]*Hollerius nullum remedium melius mutatio. Valesens de exarnia Sylua.*

si nubilis est nec monialis nubat simon licet aut non licet nubere statur frigidis &c.

[a]*Mer. Rochius de morb. mul. cap. 5.*

Guaynerius suppositis in hoc casu principali obtinet, &c.

[b]*Valesens in Hall. Cap. (9. istud genus dicuntur maxime icterum nisi multo teineus.*

Paschali. Sim. pfinter &c. probat &c ita sunt curandi, &c.

Guaynerius.

Corpus macescribus &c. cur.

Auicen. ben (3.c.14.tract.4.

[c]*de 3 lisco.*

[d]*Aretæus. lib.1.cap.5.*

De sani tuenda lib.1.cap.11.

De subtilit.l.19

De medica historia mira. bili.lib.2.cap.1.

Hyppocrondriaca did verily beleeue that she was bewitched, and was cured by conueying of nayles,
needls, feathers, and such like things into her close
stoole when shee tooke physicke, making her beleeue that they came out of her bodie. The like
there he mentioneth also out of *Trallian*, of a woman who did thinke that she had a serpent within
her, and was cured by the like meanes.

So that if we cannot moderate these perturbations of the minde, by reason and perswasions, or
by alluring their mindes another way, we may poli-
tikely confirme them in their fantasies, that wee
may the better fasten some cure vpon them as *Con-*
stantinus Affricanus (if it be his booke which is inserted among *Galens* workes, *De incantatione, aduratione*
&c.) affirmeth, and practized with good successe,
vpon one who was *impotens ad Venerem*, & thought
himselfe bewitched therewith, by reading vnto
him a foolish medicine out of *Cleopatra*, made with
a crowes gall, and oyle : whereof the patient tooke
so great conceit, that vpon the vse of it he presently
recouered his strength and abilitie againe.

The like opinion is to bee helde of all those superstitious remedies which haue crept into our
profession, of Charmes, Exorcismes, Constellations,
Characters, Periapts, Amulets, Incense, Holie water, clouts crossed and folded superstitiously, repeating of a certaine number and forme of prayers or
Aue Maries, offering to certaine Saintes, pissing
through the wedding Ring, and a hundred such
like toyes and gambols : which when they preuaile
in

in the cure of diseases, it is not for any supernaturall
vertue in them, either from God or from the diuell
(although perhaps the Diuell may haue a collate-
rall intent or worke therein, namely to drawe vs
vnto superstition) but by reason of the confident
perswation which melancholike and passionate
people may haue in them: according to the saying
of *Auicen*, that the confidence of the patient in the
meanes vsed is oftentimes more auailable to cure
diseases then all other remedies whatsoeuer.

4. *Natural.* 6.

Another course hath beene taken sometimes in
these cases, by remouing the cause of these affections, or by inducing of other perturbations of a diuerse nature. Whereby as (experience teacheth vs)
most grieuous diseases haue beene oftentimes cured
beyond expectation.

A yong man falling out of fauour with his father, fell thereupon into the fits of the falling sicknesse, and continued long and often molested there
with; vntill a reconciliation was wrought with his
father: who sending him a kind letter to that effect,
the yong man was presently deliuered from that
fearefull disease.

A yong Maiden also vpon some passion of the
minde, as it was credibly reported, fell into these
fits of the Mother, and being in one of them, a Physition then present modestly put his hand vnder her
cloathes to feele a windie tumor which shee then
had in her backe. But a Surgeon there also present
not contented with that maner of examination, offered to take vp her cloathes, and to see it bare:

H   where-

whereupon the Maid being greatly offended, tooke such indignation at it, as it did put her presently out of her fit.

And it is no maruel that the affections of the mind doe beare such rule in this disease, seeing we doe obserue that most commonly besides the indisposition of the bodie: here is also some Melancholike or capricious conceit ioyned withall of loue, feare, hatred, iealousie, discontentment, witchcraft, poysoning, &c. which being by policie or good instructions and perswasions remoued, the disease is easily ouercome.

Other matters of gouernment of them either in the fit or out of the fit, together with the cure in regard of the internall causes, because they are properly belonging to the Physition, I do purposely omit.

FINIS

Faults escaped.

Fol. 11 b. lin. 22. dele *one*.
Fol. 3 a. lin. 27. *remoued for remoued*.

A TRUE AND BREIFE REPORT OF MARY GLOVERS VEXATION

John Swan

A

TRVE AND
BREIFE RE-
PORT, OF *MARY GLO-
VERS* VEXATION, AND
of her deliuerance by the meanes
of fastinge and prayer.
Performed by those whose names are
sett downe, in the next page.

By *Iohn Swan* student in
Divinitie.

Psal.34.6
*This poore man cried, and the Lord hearde
him, and saued him out of all his
troubles.*

IMPRINTED: 1603.

These six were imployed about preachinge and prayer.

M {
Barber.
Evans.
Lewes.
}

M {
Skelton.
Bridger.
Swan.
}

These other were inhabitants (men and women) in and about London.

Rob. Oliver.
Ioh. Badger.
Ioh. Bradshaw.
Rob. Midnall.
Ioh. Leigh.
Ioh. Gawthren.

Hen. Hale.
Ioh. Palmer.
Pet. Lamslet.
Tim. Glouer
the maides
father.

Mistris |
Barber.
Ratclife.
Moore.
Hill.

Mistris |
Bradshaw.
Birde.
Gawthren.
Glouer, with

her afflicted daughter, Mary Glouer.

Neither can they proue the thinges whereof they now accuse me. Actes. 24.13.

I will heare thee (saide he) when thine accusers come. actes, 23.35.

TO THE *KINGES* MOST EXCELLENT MAIESTIE, *MY GRACIOVS SOVE-RAIGNE LORD.*

*I*t was farre from my meaning (most deere and dread Soveraigne) to haue penned any thing of this argument, that euer might be presented to your Maiesties sight: But be-inge heerin ruled (or rather over-ruled) by others: I am forced to offer it to your High-nes, as it was purposed and addressed for the common view of all. For neither would time permitt me to cast it (as it were) into a new mould, neither if it did, could I frame it in such a forme, as might abide your high-nes censure.

Notwithstanding (most gratious King) how soever the manner of my inditinge may be defectiue, yet the matter is such, as is not vn-worthy a Princes knowledge and protecti-on. For the cause which is controverted con-cerneth even the glory of Christ Iesus, of late manifested, and who can be a fitter Iudge in such a cause, then a Prince, whose booke (of the like case) proclaymes his knowledg, and whose Princlye disposition and resolu-tion, is to find out and mantayne all truth.

Proſtrating my ſelfe therfore on my ben-
ded knees (moſt wiſe and righteous Sove-
raigne) I doe, in the name of many others al-
ſo, moſt humblie beſeech your Highnes, to
take knowledge hereof, and accordingly, to
take into your Maieſties protection both it
and vs, who hauinge been imployed therin,
haue been and are like to be expoſed to ma-
nifold moleſtations. For, the cauſe hath bin
blaſphemed, our perſons purſued, and our
names traduced, and that openly in print
by one S. H. a Chaplain (as I take it) to the
Biſhopp of London, whoſe evill dealinge I
thinke not fit, to lay open to your Princely
ſelfe, but haue ben bolde (in hope of your
Maieſties leaue and fauour) to deale with
him and his booke in another treatiſe: for
I could not in ſilence let paſſe his ſpeach,
wherein he termeth the holy practiſe of
prayer (vſed on the behalfe of poore diſtreſ-
ſed creatures) Deuill-puffinge, and De-
vill-praying: as alſo that, wherin he compts
Witches to be but Bul-beggers, and the
opinions of witcherie, to be brainles imagi-
nations.
And heerin, I am as it were enforced to flie
to your Highnes, and appeale for protecti-
on, becauſe (as I vnderſtand) they haue not
for

forborne to offer that immodest booke to your Maisties owne handes, notwithstanding the same (in the 2 1 *cap pag.* 1 37. *lin.* 8.) *giueth a most dishonorable counterbuffe, to your Highnes* Treatise, *which handleth that argument. But if they had ben willing to haue the truth of their controuersie to appeare (*viz. *whether there be any witches: or whether there may be any possessions & dispossessions in these dayes,) they had done better in my poore opinion, and more like christian schollers, to haue accepted an offer which was tendred vnto them, by a worthy* *preacher; *namely, to haue the question handled by a sett, and solemne conference or disputation in either of the vniuersities: rather, then with an heauie hand, a partiall pen, and arguments of violence; to striue to over-beare, both the men and the cause: insomuch, as it hath ben much maruiled at, what the matter might be, that hath stirred them to this vehement and æger opposition, in this and such other cases: wher by they haue as it were, euen shaken the land. Yet (as I heare) they haue now giuen over their first charge of this* Mary Glouer *touching any counterfeiting: and now they maintaine (and that specially by the*

M. Iohn Ireton.

meanes

meanes of a phisitian) that her affliction pro-
ceeded onely from a naturall cause: who also
hath written and published to that effect,
notwithstandinge he could not be ignorant,
that two phisitians of his acquantance and
Colledge, as great Clarkes as himselfe, did
trye their vtmost skill vppon her with their
phisicall receiptes, (yea, with some practises
beyond good arti) for the space of 9. or 10.
weekes in the time of her deepest distresse, &
in the end pronounced, that her affliction
did exceed both arte and nature.

But the weaknes of this mans opinion is rea-
dy to be layd open, by the labours of two o-
ther learned and christian, professours like-
wise of phisicke, who also haue taken twen-
tie times more paynes, care, and diligence,
about the afflicted party in time of her vex-
ation to find out the truth, then this man
hath done. Which booke of theirs, handlinge
the meanes of her first being taken, the man-
ner of her strange and fearfull fittes, by the
space of almost 8. monthes: the proceeding in
Iudgment against the VVitch, the evidence
brought in against her, the greivous afflicti-
on of the maide even in presence of Courte,
the verdict of the Iurie, the speech of the
Iudge, and sentence of the Recorder (not yet
ful-

fullye executed, (I know not vppon what cause:) will I hope, fullie giue information and content, to any indifferent reader: notwithstanding I am not ignorant, that one, very lately at Pauls crosse, spake much to the taxing of the Iudge, Iurie, and witnesses, and clearinge or acquittinge the Witch.

Thus, while these, and other more weightie controuersies continewe vndecided amongst vs, God hath ben provoaked at last to begin a controuersie with vs, by sending a contagious sicknes, that hath turned our triumphs into dayes of heavines: the which, when and wher it will cease, he onely knoweth. The Lord make vs all wise harted (by redressinge what is a misse, in publicke and private) to meet him betimes, especially such, as whose armes he hath strenghtened to that end, and that in the meane time, leaue and libertie may be had, for the inferiours to meet together without feare of men, in choice companyes, either publicklye, or (if that be not thought meet in this so infectious a time) in private families according to their desires, to humble themselues by prayer and fasting, that so God may be pleased to call backe his Angell, whom he hath sent out to smite vs.

The

The God of heauen an earth, who hath
moſt happelye bleſſed England in thus
bringing your Maieſtie to ſit vppon the
the Royall throne: graũt vnto the ſame,
the happines of *Dauid,* the wiſdome of
Salomon, the zeale of *Ioſias,* that your
Highnes and your Maieſties poſteritie,
may liue and raigne for euer, High, and
Honorable inſtruments, for the great
thinges of Gods glory, both in Church
and common wealth, to your endleſſe
renowne, and eternall happines.

Your Maieſties humble, and
loiall ſubiect,

Iohn Swan.

A TRVE AND BREIFE RE-PORT, OF THE GREIVOVS VEXATION BY SATAN, OF MARY GLOVER OF THEM-STREET IN LONDON: AND

of her deliueraunce from the same, by
the power of the Lord Iesus, blef-
singe his owne ordinance of prayer
and faftinge.

I muſt bend my ſelfe to breuitie in this
difcourſe. For if I ſhould dilate of all
actions, prayers, accidentes, circumſtances,
with the effectes, iſſues, or events of that
worke, which I intend a little to lay open:
I ſhould rather write a volume, thē be anſ-
werable to the title of this treatiſe, which
preſently I haue prefixed. For the action
being begon about 8. of the clocke in the
morninge, and not ended till after 7. at
night, And the time beinge in the meane
ſpace whollie and carefully beſtowed (the
moſt of the company not remouing all the
whole time out of the roome) in ſuch ſort
as not one quarter of an hower was free
from imployment in ſome action of the

ministers:(who were continuallye either
the mouth of God to vs, in deliueringe
sweet aud apt meditations,fitting the time
and present occasion,raised out of the blessed and comfortable worde of God)or els
the mouth of vs, to send vp our prayers &
supplications, our sighes and grones, vnto
God:it may easilie be coniectured,to what
a great bulke a booke would rise, if a man
would striue to sett downe the somme of
each sermon,the contentes of each prayer,
the actions and affections of the partie afflicted, and most of all interessed in this
worke. All which, as they are great in importance, diuers in variety, and comfortable in the issue:so it may rightly be coniectured,that the iust report of them all, cannot fall within the compas of the memory
of any one present, much lesse of him to
whom the taske was committed.Who not
withstanding being incouraged by the ex-
hortations of the reuerend brethren, and
strengthened by their promises of adding
their helpinge handes, when this my first
drawght should be offered to their veiw:
hath vnder taken to write of the matter,
as God shall enable, and his blessed spirit
shall giue direction,which I humblie craue

to

to be granted for Chriſt his ſake.

And ſeeing I am purpoſed to handle this matter in the beſt ſort I can, (to the end thou migheſt be the more fully made acquanted with all that was done therin) It is not vnfittinge (and good order requireth it) that I ſhould alſo let thee know, what the miniſters did to prepare and ſanctifie theſelues the day before to ſo great & holy a worke. My ſelfe (I confeſſe) was not at this their meetting, I knew not thẽ of their purpoſe, but hearinge ouer night of the next dayes action, I ſo fitted my ſelfe to it, as that morning I was the third perſon that arriued in the roome where the worke was performed: yet with purpoſe (as god knoweth) to be but a behoulder, and to ioyne in the affections of my hart with the prayers of the reſt, and to be partaker of their preaching. And ſo I had ſett ſtill, had I not ben drawne out of my place, as I am ſure many there preſent can teſtifie.

But touching this their preperation which I am now readie to report, although I was not (as I ſaid) preſent at it: yet I had it from one of them that could beſt tell: and hauing read it before the others, I finde it con firmed by their teſtimonies.

after

After that by consent of godly ministers,
(at the instāt request of the parents of M*a
ry Glouer*)it was resolued vppon that there
should be sett a part one day(and that pre
sently vppon good considerations)for pra
yer and fasting, that by humble supplication God might be intreated to haue mercy vppon them, and vppon his distressed
seruants of that family, especiallye vppon
the maide her selfe, who was the occasion
of the others greife: It was agreed vppon,
that on tuesday the 14. of December the
ministers (who were to be imployed in
that action)should meete togeather to ad-
uise of the order that amonge themselues
they would obserue both in prayey and
preachinge. which being accomplished, it
was thought good that one should be appoynted, who should the night before the
exercise, prepare the company that shoud
be partakers with the ministers in that ned
full and holy action.

At the time appointed of this preparation,
with much a doe they meet, some ten or
twelue, at M. *Gloners* house in Thames-
street:there they continued a space, & then
the * preacher that was appoynted : first
prayed God to direct him to speake & the
people

*M.Skelton.

people to heare, and all to prepare themfelues, that they might be fitted to come
before the God of heauen. That done, he
framed fome wordes of exhortation to repentance, and efpecially to an earneft humiliation of their foules and bodies before
the Lord, that he feeing them (efpeciallye
thofe that were moft interefled in the di-
ftrefled) truely humbled: he might in mercy and goodnes lift them vp, by givinge
deliuerance and grantinge comfort in his
good time, in what manner and meafure
it pleafed him, and that not for any other,
but his owne truth and promife fake.

The ground of his exhortation was the
10. verfe of the 4. Chapter of Saint Iames
*Caft downe your felues before the Lord, and
he will lift you vp.* which confifteth of a
commaundement *caft downe,* and of a promife, *to exalte.*

He fhewed the neceffitie of the former,
if we meane to inioye the latter, firft by
the commaundement of God, and fecond-
ly in regard of our felues, who could not o-
therwife be cured, being naturally to much
advanced in fome vaine conceites of our
owne goodnes. he defcribed the nature &
propertie of this grace & worke, he noated
the

the way how to com by it, namely, firſt by
ſerious meditation in the law of God (that
layeth open our ſinnes and Gods Iudgments) Secondly by obſeruinge the Iudgments of God vppon others, and vppon
our ſelues, Thirdly by prayer & other outward meanes ſanctified for that purpoſe,
Fourthlye, he ſheewed that if a man wilbe
truely humbled, he muſt caſt his eyes on
Gods mercies. For, feare may aſtoniſh, &
Iudgments may terrifie, but worke true hu
millity they cannot, vnleſſe God in favor
doe worke it by his ſpirit and the miniſte-
ry of grace: and therfore the ſaide preacher
ioyned this grace to true converſion, as a-
fruite to his owne tree. And this was the
ſumme of the firſt part, namely, of humb-
linge or caſtinge downe, ſavinge that ſome
what was added for the ſinceritie and continuance in this grace of God, becauſe the
Apoſtle ſaith *in the ſight of God.*
Touching the ſecond part, he obſerued the
verity and conſtant truth of this promiſe,
and ſo the exellency of it, by conſideringe
the nature & will of the promiſer, ſecond-
lye by the gratious effectes, and workes of
mercy and truth ſheewed to all his Saints,
Abraham, Dauid, Ioſeph, and our *Lord Ieſus*
Chriſt

Chrift the Prince of our faluation. Here he
thought it needfull to exhort, that hauinge
this promife of heelpe and of honor, we
fhould not abufe it, either prefcribing vnto god, the time when to performe it (fince
he hath faid it fhalbe in due time. 1 *Pct.* 5.
6.) nor the meanes, fince his wifdome is
vnfearchable and knowes how to doe it,
with meanes or with out meanes, and evē
contrary to all meanes: that the worke may
appeare to be his: or elfe by fainting in our
felues by the confideration of our vnworthines, & finne, forafmuch as god refpect-
eth his owne glory, his truth and promife
in this worke, and not our worthines, or
the meafure of our faith and repentance,
fo we haue in vs the worthines of Chrift,
and fo he concluded with prayer agreable
to this fpeach fo neere as he could.

The time when this exercife began was a-
bovt 6. of the clocke at night: wherin they
continued, in prayer, in hearing and fpeak-
ing the fpace fomwhat more then an hower: none vfinge either prayer or fpeach at
this time, but onely the minifter, who was
the mouth of God vnto the reft, & of the
reft to God, ioyning with him in prayer,
and reuerentlye attendinge the actions in
hand

hand. The maide and her mother fate nere
the preacher, religiouflye harkeninge both
in the time of the exhortation and prayer,
the father in time of prayer did fend forth
many harty fighes, which concurred fo iuft
with the wordes then vttered to that purpofe, that it might be thought by others,
that the preacher purpofly pointed at him
in his fpeach and prayer. The action being
ended, the maide and her mother came &
with fober countenaunce and gefture, gaue
thankes to the preacher. This done, they
departed with mutuall confentes to meete
the next morning at the time & place appoynted (which was not in the fame houfe
of M. Glouers, but in another place farr
diftant, for the more quyet and fecurity to
performe that good worke of prayer, fafting, and fupplication, which now I am prefently to goe in hand withall.

O n Thurfday the 16, of December.
1062. there meet together in a cer-
Miftris Ratcliefs taine *place a copany of fuch as feared god
in Shordit che. to the nomber of about 24. wherof 6. were
Preachers befide the partie afflicted: who
humbling themfelues, by fafting & prayer
all the day long, before the prefence of our
great, glorious, & moft gratious god, were
in

in the end fent away not empty, but moft
ioyfull, in that their defires were hearde,
mercy obtained, and their hopes and long-
inges fatiffied, Thus of the whole action
in generall, now of the fame in more perti-
culer fort.

About 7. of the clocke in the morninge
before it was full day light, ther were fome
few of vs come to the place, where hauing
ftaide fome halfe hower, moe were affemb-
led, and amongft others, the Parents of the
afflicted mayden: who hauing brought her
to the houfe prefented her in the chamber,
caufing her (as I remember) to come For-
moft into the roome, which mayden came
into the place not led, or fupported by any,
with very fober countenaunce, yet fuch, as
bewrayed afliction of mynd, and torment
of body, formerly fuftained, and performing very feemely and comely reuerence to
fuch as were prefent, fhee went and tooke
her place on a low fettle, at a beds fide,
nigh vnto the fire, and fo fatt downe hauinge a Bible in her hand which fhee either
brought with her, or was then and ther deliuered to her, wherof fhe made vfe fo long
as fhe could, by turning to fuch chapters as
were read, and to fuch textes as were hand-

led

led, or such quotations as were cited: wherin if she at any time failed, either by greife of body, or infirmity of mynde, or meditation, or by fayling of sight (which seemed sometimes so to be, by the rubbinge of her eyes with her hand) then a woman sittinge by, was ready alwayes in that behalfe to helpe her, especially at the instance of the Preachers, who directinge their speaches many times to her by name, would call vpon her to turne to the place alleaged, and so would stay till she had found it.

In the meane while, namely after her comminge into the chamber, vntill it was full 8 of the clock (for so long we stayed expecting the comminge of an auncient humble harted preacher, whose presence we much *M.Skelton. longed for) * one of the preachers made motiõ to spend a little time till all were cõe in reading some parts and portions of the word of God, by meditation, wherof each one priuatly might make such obseruatiõs and raise vp such thoughtes, as, wherby we might be the better fitted to the worke following. And so hauing first prayed, he did to this end, read the 4. and 5 Chapters of Iames, and after them he read the 51. Psal. throughout: which done, to helpe vs, he
poynted

poynted to some principall or especiall
poyntes therein, that seemed to him most
meet to be obserued for the present purpose, and so againe concluded with prayer
agreable. This being finished the hower of
8. was come, and the company was such, as
gaue vs comfort, and incoragement to begin,

Then the first * preacher did sett hand   M. Lewes
on the worke, and preparing himselfe to it,
framed his speech for the addressing of vs
to the more duetifull & religious carriage
of our selues in the action, humbling vs by
prayer, confessing our sinnes, our weaknes,
and vnworthines, begging pardon, crauing
gratious assistance, and an happy issue of
our enterprise, for Christ Iesus his sake,
who is blessed for euer *Amen.*

The prayer being finished, he tooke for
his text *Psalme* 50. 15. *Call vppon me in the
day of trouble, so will I deliuer thee, and thou
shalt glorifie me.* Wherin the partes obserued were 1 a precept to call, 2 the partie on
whome, 3 the time when, 4 the promise of
deliuerance 5 a duetie theruppon to be
yealded.
For the first, we are not onely allowed, or
exhorted to call if we list: but commaunded

ed to doe it, as a parte of Gods worſhip.
For the ſecōd. he noted in the party to be
called vppon, wiſdome in ſeeing all things,
willingnes to heare, and power to helpe,
and in the ſirſt poynt of his wiſdome, he
vrged his All-ſeeing eye: and preſſing the
ſame poynt vppon the parents and on the
poore maide by name, to rippe vp the ſe-
crets of their hartrs touching their liues
foreſpent: the poore ſoule the daughter, be
gan to weepe, yet moderating her ſelfe, ſhe
indured all his ſpeach, even to the end of
his forenones ſermon, wherof let it ſuffice
to haue reported thus much: ſaving that
he further added this, that God did ſee
our wants, before we aſke, he prepares our
hartes to begg, and then bendes his eare
to heare. His ſermon being done, he ended
with an effectuall & ſuitable prayer to the
purpoſe, hauing ſpentin prayers & preaching ſome hower & halfe. And truely touch
ing the man (and ſo of the reſt:) I ſpeake
not to clawe, I write in the feare of God,
to gaine glorie to his maieſtie, and not
prayſe to men, to whom belonges nothing
but ſhame) I knew him long before, but I
knew him not ſo, having neuer heard him
before. And heare I appeale to his hart, and
ſo

so to the harts of the others that succeeded in prayers and preaching: whether they did not that day finde in themselues an extraordinarie presence, and supply of God his gracious and powerfull spirit in them, in the performance of these most holy and reuerent actions.

After this action of preachinge and prayer ended, the poore creature, (being pale and wan coloured) was asked by her mother & others, how it fared with her? she acknowledged she felt payne in her body, & wept and prayed God to be mercifull vnto her, and to help her, and saide withall, that shee could and would indure further proceedinge in the begone exercise, and so satt a whyle rubbing hard, or stroaking downe with her hand, her left syde and flancke.

Then succeded the second*preacher, who should haue begone the exercise himselfe if he had come in time, but he came a little after the action was entered into by the first preacher. This man did happily second the first, and that presently without intermission, begining with a most sweete, mylde, (according to his disposition) long, earnest, and powerfull prayer: which done, he tooke for his text *Mathew* the 11. 28.

M. Evans

Come

Come vnto me all yee that are wearie and la-
den ,and I will eafe you. which being read,
he obferued in it, firft an allurement to
come,fecondly the parttie to whom,third-
ly the partties that fhould come, and laftly
a promife of eafe:of all thefe partes I could
report fomewhat,but(as I fayd)I muft apply to be breife,only this(as I reméber)he
preffed moft(at leaft it made moft impref-
fion in me)the thyrd parte. viz,of the parties that fhould come, namely fuch as in
tie of their wantoneffe could not or would
not,intend it,but being preffed with afflictions (purpofly fent) are ready to come to
the hand that gaue the wound,whofe drift
alfo was herein, to gett occafion to make
fheew of his fkill and good will to heale.
Further he noated,that ther be a great ma
ny that are laden with finne,but not weari-
ed with the burthen therof, fo endinge a-
gayne with prayer, conteyning poyntes a-
greeable to his text,and fitting the prefent
occafion: he made an end of that his tafke.
    Then himfelfe in the mildnes of his cha-
ritably difpofed minde, afked the mayde
how fhee did, and perceauing her to wax
pale coloured, weepinge, and anfweringe
faintly,he made motion that ther might be
                                a litte

little pawſe, that every one that liſt, might
walke downe a while & refreſh themſelues
diuers went, but more remained behind,
and a mongſt them, my ſelfe, who came of
purpoſe to marke (as preſciſely as poſſibly
I could) all the actions & circumſtances of
that dayes worke. In this meane time I
obſerued her, ſittinge, weepinge bitterly,
wringing her handes extreamly, complai-
ning of vnacuſtomed payne, yea caſtinge
out wordes of feare that God would not
heare vs in calling on him for her ſo wretched a creature. This circumſtance I doe
the more willingly retaine & inſiſt vppon,
to meete with a proiect of the oppoſite
Doctour of Phiſicke, who layeth it downe
for a ground, that many are cured of ſtráge
diſeaſes, (even of the mother) with a very
bare conceipt, or apprehenſion that praier
and faſtinge ſhall doe them good. For this
poore creature (as hereby yow ſee) was ſo
farr from having imbraced any ſuch ſtrong
immagination, that ſhe vttered wordes of
doubt, diſtruſt, yea, of dreadfull diſpaire,
but to returne, I will obſerue this withall,
that all this pawſe was not aboue the ſpace
of leſſe then a quarter of an hower.

Here it is fitt that this alſo ſhould not be
omited

omitted, nameliy, that she felt paynes this day, before the accustomed hower. For now they came about Nine of the Clocke, which was 4 or 5 howers before the vsuall time of her fitts, which were wont to kepe their returnes as due as the tyde. And againe, when the vehemency of the fitt began to seize vppon her this day (which was also her fitt day, being every second day) It began som-what after the ordinary time, which was wont to be before two of the clocke in the after-noone. And againe, the saide vehemency of the fitt when this day it was come, It kept not the like course as vsually before it had done. For first, in former fittes, blindnes invaded her: (and so also was it this day when the fitt came after 2 of the clocke) and this blyndnes was accompanied with a pale dead colour of face and eyes closed (yet so, as you might perceiue the whyte of them to be turned vp) *Secondly* followed dumbnes, (which also was so now) but herein they differed, that the former blindnes and dumbnes having once seazed on her, shee never cáe to haue freedome of speech till the whole fitt was ended (which was about 11. a Clocke at night) but now, they gaue place by turnes)

Thirdly

Thirdly succeeded an heaving or swellinge in the bellie, breast, and throat: *Fourthly* (on this day) followed the wagging of her chappe, which stirred much vp & downe, not with over hastie motions, but with soe leasure: *Fiftly* deadnes of the left side, with inflexible stifnes, of legg, arme, hand, and fingers: thes were also now: but they made not the like iust retournes and stayes, neither did they follow each other in their or dinarie kind of sequence: so that as one* in Rob. Midnal his notes setteth downe) ther was no coherence ot this dayes affliction, with her former fittes or passions. And thus much (as it were by the way) of the disparillitie of this dayes vexation, from the perturbations, or tormentes which beforetimes shee had sustained.

Hitherto shee had sitten vppon the Settle by the bed-side, wher at her first comming she had taken her place: But now, she was advised to remoue her seate, and to sitt about the midst of the Chamber, in a lowe wicker chaire, with her face towardes the fire, and her left side towardes the preacher. Then the foresayd aunctent preacher called for a new supplye of a third man:* M. Bridger. who in much modesty began to pray, and

C1   havinge

havinge fruitfully finifhed the fame, he
read a large text, namely *Daniell* the 9. frō
verfe.the firft to the end of Daniels prayer
verf.19. Where poynting to poyntes going before, and runninge ouer that which
he had read: He deliuered very good and
pertinent obfervations, which the very
context of the chapter doth plainly offer,
and a man exercifed in the fcriptures may
rayfe in his owne meditations, if he fhall
advifedfy & with reverence read over the
fāe, & therfore(as alfo becaufe I wilbe breif)
I paffe it over. Thus endinge againe with
a comfortable prayer agreable to his hum
bled fpirit (in which his prayer he remembred amongft other thinges; the power of
Dauids flinge in overthrowinge Goliah,
who defied the hoaft of Ifraell:) he ceaffed
for that time.

By this time (as I remember) it was paft
twelue of the Clocke: And now diuerfe of
the company called on the preachers ftill
to be doeinge, and not to giue the Lorde
any reft vntill he had heard vs, much leffe
to giue Satan any reft to harbour where
he did:and in this behalfe one of them (I
know not who) could put vs in remembrance, that *When Mofes held vp his handes*
                                    Ifraell

Israell prevailed, but *when he held the downe Amalek prevailed.*exodus 17.12. Herevp pon ther was a little ſtraininge of curteſie whoſe turne ſhould be next, either to pray or to preach. Then a fourth * preacher ſuc- ceded in prayer, who beſides the eſpeciall poyntes of the other prayers fitting the preſent occaſion. (as namely that it would pleaſe God to caſt a mouſell (that was his word)vppon the iawes of that ramping *Li- on,*that goeth about ſeekinge to devoure, wher he alſo complained, that amongſt all the miſeries that poore men are plunged into by meanes of ſinne, they ſhould be ſubieƈt to ſuch a iudgment as this was: yet he rayſed comfort in that ther was a victo rious Lion of the tribe of Iuda; ſtronger then he. ect.) I ſay beſides the ordinary poyntes of the prayers, he complained, that we might not(but in feare of men) meete together to performe ſuch dueties, and ſuch meanes as God hath ſainƈtified, and the Church heretofore praƈtiſed in ſuch caſes, for releife and recouery,of pore creatures diſtreſſed in this kinde. And ſo much of his prayer.

    Then he that preached the firſt Sermon at 8 of the Clocke in the morning, return- ed

M.Barber,

M.Lewes.

ed to his text, taken out of *Pſal.ſo.*15.(as before is ſaide)but firſt he prayed effectually for graces neceſſay, for himſelfe, for the afflicted parttie, and for the behoofe of vs all ther preſent, yea and for all the ſervantes of God, whereſoever, that done, he repeated not much of that which in the morninge he deliuered, but proceeded to hādle the reſt, & eſpecially (as me thought) he bent his force to that poynt, namelye of the time when we ſhould call vppon God, and that was, *The needfull time of trouble.* This he handled after this manner, many are the troubles of the righteons, but ſent of God, that we might call more earneſtly: and ſo by him being deliuered from thē all, he might receaue thanks of all, and for all favours. Here he noated alſo, that the wicked had their ſhare in troubles but the troubles of the one and of the other, doe greatly differ. For the one proceede from a Iudge, the other from a father: the one are light and momentanie, the other durable and the begininges of greater woe, the one to correct, to purge, and refine, the other to confound, to make more obſtinate and in excuſable: thus with prayer he alſo ended, as with prayer he began.

Now

Now was it(as I remember, and others in
their notes obſerue)paſt two of the clocke
vntill which time the maiden havinge remained in reaſonable good peace and eaſe:
I aſked one what he thought of the matter: who anſwered that his hope was, we
ſhould haue a calme ſtill,nothing but faire
weather,and that Satan would ſteale away
like a micher:wherunto I replied nothing,
as one that could haue bene glad it might
be ſo:but I doubted it,conſidering that his
mallice,who heretofore had raged in her,
wouldnot be ſo gentle, as to begon without a partting blowe:but eſpecially calling
to minde, the manner of his departing in
thoſe dayes,when the power of doinge mi
racles was given to the Sonnes of men,
(which now is ceaſed) namely that he vſed to rent, and tear, and leaue for dead:
and I imagined that his mallice was rather
growne greater towardes the end of his
kingdome,and ſo it fell out: for even a little after that time,"the poore ſoule began
to be ſencleſſe of one ſide, to be blinded,
dead coloured, and eye turned vp, to be
ſtiffe in the left legge and arme etc. (but
theſe were not in ſuch manner as in former
times, both for their ſequence & continuance,

ance, as I tould you a little before) at what
time the good ould * preacher (even with
out intreatie) fell to prayer: & hauing continued therin a good whyle, the mother
who felt the legge, and an other who held
the hand, acknowledged that naturall liber-
nes and motion began to come againe (the
preacher still continuing in his prayer) and
a none the poore creature began to gaspe,
and to striue to speake, and within a while
shee spake somewhat, but what I could not
then perceaue it was so softly vttered, and
I being further of, saw many layinge their
eares to her head to heare: but a none her
speach began to be lowder and lowder, so
that I did very well heare, a great deale
more then I can remember, yet that which
I doe remember I will faithfully reporte,
referring my selfe againe to my brethren
herein to be holpen with their additions.
The first worde that shee deliuered when
she began to labour to vtter any thing that
was like vnto speach, was, *almost, almost*: the
accent being vppon the sillable all.
But first before I begin to sett downe her
prayer, let me obserue a circumstance or
two. There did droppes of teares steale
downe the cheekes of many, often times
in

in the time of the Sermons and prayers be
fore mentioned both from weomen, and
men, yea the preachers theselues, but now
at the prayer of the damsell her selfe, they
did a bound. The preacher continued a
while praying as he began, and ceased not,
although the maides wordes were now
waxen lowde (for belike he thought shee
would presently haue ceased)but shee con-
tinewinge, this was thought to be confused, and therefore he ceased, and gaue vs
leaue to harken to her, which we were very willing and glad for to doe: he, (or another)saying further, let her a lone, you shal
see shee will doe it her selfe, she will procu-
er her owne deliuerance.

I will come to report her prayer by and by
but first one thinge more. I heard a gratious yonge * genleman(I knew him not, I   M. Osiuȳ
had no acquaintance with him, they say he
is one of the Innes of Courte) who having first heard her low voyce, and discerning what she sayd: he hasted from her with
blubbering cheeks, his tongue being scarse
able to be the messenger of his hart, sur-
charged with ioye)but at last out he brake
with the matter thus. I thanke God I con-
ceaue good hope of happy deliuerance: I
haue

haue feene her often heeretofore in her
fearfull fites, but I neuer faw or heard, that
beingonce entered into a firft fitt, fhe euer
recouered free libertie of fpeech againe,
till the laft fitte was ended, (which alfo was
vfually the moft tirrible) but remained
both blind and dumb, till then, which lafted commonly from before 2 of the clocke
in the afternoone, vntill eleuen or twelue
at night. Well, her prayer goes on, and we
giue ioyfull attendance and filence vnto
the fame, faving that many an harty *Amen*
was yelded to many poynts of her prayer,
which lafted about halfe an hower, fhe fitting all this while in her faide chaire, and
leaning backward, her face ruddie coloure-
ed, and directed vpward, her eye liddes a lit
tle opened, her handes both at once, (but
not ioyned together) continually lifted vp
and prefently falling downe at the end of
every period or perfect petition. fhe labor
ed fo in it, and that with teares, that a little
froath wrought out at the corners of her
lippes, & fo fhe continued vntill (I think)
partly wearines of her weake body caufed
her to ceafe, fo fhe refted, but as the event
fhewed, fhe was then growing to a fharper
fitte: which being perceaued, then ther was
one

one who very vnwillingly was drawne to
praye· But before I fpeake of his prayer, I
will difcharge my promife concerning the
report of hers: wherin I know I fhall faile
in remembrance of many poyntes: as alfo
for the tyme when, and in which of her
prayers each requeft was made, (for fhee
vfed 4. prayers, as you fhall heare afterwardes) but that which I will fett downe,
fhalbe fuch as I can faflye beare teftimony
vnto, both for the matter, and I thinke not
much miffinge the wordes. And herein I
will be the more plentifull, becaufe in reporting her next fucceeding prayers, I will
peradventure referr to this(as containinge
many poyntes which fhee afterwardes did
iterate)& fo eafe my felfe of labour in writ
ting, and the reader in pervfing.

O Lorde I befeech thee looke vppon me thy   Her firſt prayer
poore handmaide, with the eyes of mercy, haue
mercie vppon me for Iefus Chriſt his fake, be
mercifull vnto me and pardon all my finnes,
let them not ſtand vp as a wall to ſtoppe and
hinder thy favours from me, but wafh them
all away in the death and bloudſheed of Iefus
Chriſt, thine onely, true, and deare Sonne. I
haue ben a vile wretch, and finnfull creature,
but deale not with me as I haue deferued, re-

   member

member thine owne promise, that at what time soever a sinner doth repent him of his sinnes from the bottom of his hart, thou wilt put out all his wickednes out of thy remembrance. O lorde I reprent me of all my sinnes, I beleeue, help my vnbeleife: graunt comforte, Lord comforte, thou that art the God of all comfort and con-solation, adde strength lord to my * strength, rebuke Satan and help me: O Lord in mercy behould me and graunt me deliuerance, O Lord deliuerance, and that euen now o lord if it be thy blessed will. Neuerthelesse not my will but thy will be done, giue me patience O Lord, and strength to beare, and lay on no more then I shalbe able to beare, and confirme my hope to be deliuered when thou shalt see it good, giue me grace to say as Iob saide, Though thou kill me. yet wil I put my trust in thee. And to say, with thy seruant Dauid, If thou haue no pleasure in me, behold here I am, doe with me as pleaseth thee. Yet O Lord though thou shouldest lett Satan kill my body, let him haue no power on my soule, let the same be pretious before thee, neuerthelesse graunt (if it be thy will) that I may one day reioyce with thy seruant Dauid and say, It is happie for me that I was in trouble. And o Lord be

Her wordes were so

be mercifull vnto her by whose meanes this
trouble was brought vppon me, I forgiue her
with all my hart, even for all that hath bene
done vnto me from the begininge, and I praye
thee o Lord to forgiue her, to giue her graceto
see her sinne, and to repent, and to beleeue that
so shee may be saued. Satan was herein thy
rodde (o Lord) vppon me, and shee but the instrument, and as for the rodde when thou hast
done with it, it shall be cast into the fire. But
the instrument that hath ben (by that serpent)
abused, o Lord haue mercie vppon her, and for
giue her all her sinnes, even as I forgiue her
with all my heart. Thou knowest lord, that,
that which hath ben done against her, hath not
ben done of mallice, or desire of revenge on my
parte, but that the truth might be knowne, and
so thou to haue the glorie, and that I might be
deliuered from the slaunder of men: heare me
o lord from heaven and graunt me these requestes for Iesus Christ sake, in whose name I
further call vppon thee as he hath taught me
saying. Ovr father which art in heaven etc.
throughout to the end. After the lordes
prayer, shee added some other few shorte
petitions and so made an end, and let this
suffice for report of the cheife contentes
of her first prayer, which lasted about the
                                        space

space of halfe an hower. For striuinge to proceede, she fell into another fitt·

And then immediatlie, their was callinge both by the preachers and people, for a new man to the helme, and then was dra‐ wen forth* one(being greatlie vrged ther vnto) to praye: he yelded to that onely, for indeede he ment not to be imployed at all, but onely to ioyne in prayer with the rest of the company, and to be partaker with them of the word there taught and applyed (as appeared by his keeping him‐ selfe aloofe)but being(as is saide)vrged by the preachers and company, he began his prayer with a meditatiō out of the speech of Iacob:*Gen. 28. 16. 17. Surely god is in this place, and I was not a ware: how fearfull is this place etc.*applying the same thus,that this seare came vppon vs,becaufe the place beinge holy by the presence of God, we were vnholy in the inclinations of our hartes continually, and so he pleaded for mercy by the mediation of him,who in the dayes of his humiliation beinge taught o‐ bedience by the thinges he suffered, did send vp mighty cryes,and was heard in the thinges he feared,and therfore he beinge a faithfull High Preist,and touched with our

in·

Swan.

infirmities, could tell how to haue mercy
and help, *Heb.4.*1 5.and 5.7.&c.& in processe of his prayer he began a little to alter
the tune of the former dolfull ditties, and
began to thanke God, for mercies presently vouchsafed, vppó the preachers in their
Sermons and prayers, yea and vppon the
poore maide, whose tongue being by his
goodnes lett loose, had so spoken as before
yow heard, and therfore he began to be
bolder, and to incroatch vppon further favour, sayinge, we would take this at Gods
hands as an earnest pennie of further help,
and therfore prayed God to make perfect the good worke which he had most
gratiously begune, that with comfort we
might depart in the end, every man to
his home. But beholde this proued but
a triumph before victorie, for even then
the maid was entered againe into another
fitt, and the battle seemed to be more fear
fully renued. He therfore ryfing from the
cushion at the table, another succeded,
namely, *he that read vnto vs the 4. & 5.   *M. Skelton.
of Iames in the morninge: the summe of
whose prayer was: First a confession of
our vnworthines to appeare before the
God of heaven to obtaine mercy, Second
                                          lye

lye an acknowledgment of the Iuſtice of
God, in puniſhing the world with bodely
and ſperituall chaſtiſments, and therwith-
all confeſſed, that God for ſinnes (even
ſince our meeting) might iuſtly withdraw
his helpinge hand: Thirdly he prayed for
pardon, for favour and grace, to vs, to the
diſtreſſed, preſent or elſe wher, in hearing
our prayers, and the prayers of others, &
that not for our humiliation ſake(for that
was ſinfvll as it came from vs) but for
Chriſt his ſake, to the glórie of his owne
name, the profite & comfort of vs all ther
aſſembled, and the afflicted partie, and to
the ſtopping of all mouthes opened agaiſt
the truth of God, and laſtly for the comfort of all diſtreſſed ſoules, who hearinge
of God his goodnes to his children,
ſhould ſee that it is not in vayne to goe vn
to him in trouble, and to caſt our cares
vppon him. Then was the old * preacher agayne called vppon to fight:who
bucklinge on his harneſſe, began to crye
for help, not becauſe (he ſayd) trouble
was at hand, but becauſe he ſaw it preſent,
and preſſinge vppon vs, and ſo proceeded
with fervent vehemency as the heat of the
battle increaſed. But now (alas)his free me
ditations

M. Evans

ditations were interrupted, beinge forced
to caſt his eyes, oftentimes on the poore
maide diuerſly diſtreſſed,as alſo being tro-
bled with the confuſed outcryes of the cõ-
pany: but ſtill he continued,though now
by ſnatches(as it were)and with imperfect
periods.Yet ſee god his good mercy, who
did not lett this heavines to lye longe vppon vs, for behould even herewithall, the
maide began againe to gaſpe and ſtriue
for recouery, which cauſed the olde man
to ſay, let every one of vs help her in
our priuat prayers, ſeeing a ſett order can
not be obſerued. But in the time of his
prayer, though ſhee were deafe (as we
thought) yea dumbe and blind, yet ſhee
turned her body from him with all violence, and gaping, as if ſhe could not abide
him. So after a while ſhee ſpake, & the firſt
word ſhee vttered was (as before) with a
weake hallow, and(as it were)hoarce voice
(yet reaſonable lowd)*Once more, once more*
(making her accent vppon the word *once*)
and ſo immediatly proceeded to her ſecõd
prayer:the matter & wordes wherof were
(as I beare away)for the moſt part like the
former,but ſome things were added (both
in this ſecõd prayer, & in alſo the third, &
                                    fourth

fourth followinge) whereof I will call to minde some poyntes as well as I can. This second prayer also was continued so longe as the first, her voyce waxing stronger, & she sitting still in the same chaire, with the same position of body, countenaunce of face, and gesture of handes.

Her second prayer

O Lord thou hast begune to be gratious vnto me, thou hast done more for me then I looked for, I beseech thee o lord perfect the worke which thou hast begun, that thou maist haue the prayse, and these thy children may be comforted. Let my prayers ascend vp to thy presence, and the prayers of these thy servantes, and all the prayers that this day are made for me in any other place. Thou hast commaunded to call vppon thee in the time of trouble, and hast promised that thou then wilt heare & so haue the prayse: heare vs therfore (o lord) now calling vppon thee: in the needfull time of troble, that so heareafter I may prayse thee and magnifie thy name. Giue me an hart to submitte to thy will & to wayte vppon thee: thou knowest (o lord) my affliction, and thou canst help me, for thou art stronger then Sathan. O lord now sheew thy strength, and let vs see thy

Her words were so: and are well be-

*savinge helpe, put thy power to my * power, & thy will to my * will. fight thou for me, confound*

found his mallice, distroye his worke, and darken * the power of Satan (o lord) and lett him be troden vnder feete as dyrte (this was her very word) let not my sinnes o lord, nor the sinnes of my parents come to remembrance, which haue ben the cause of this heavie chastisement layd vppon vs, but (o lord) giue vs true repentance, and blott out all our sinnes, that they rise not vp in iudgment against vs, nor hinder thy mercyes at this time towardes vr, comfort them (o lord) and comfort me, now after the time wherein thou hast smitten vs, that I being strengthened may strengthen others, and beinge deliuered, I may comfort others, with that comforte wherwith thou hast comforted me, that so thou mayst haue from many, glory, prayse, & thanksgiuinge, forever and forever, through Iesus Christ thy deare Sonne, our onely Lord and Saviour Amen.

*inge thus interpreted: Ad more of thy power to the power thou hast already giuen me, and thy full will to accomplishe, to that right desire which thou hast formed in me.

This prayer (as I beare away) was rather longer then the other, which being interrupted (by the former infirmitie comming on) shee was presently entred into a third fitt, which also grewe more greivious then the former,. Then againe both preachers and people called for prayer, and then the vnworthiest and weakest* was put to it agayne, who began with the speech of the

*Swane

E 1   pro-

prophet, that *The fruite was come to the birth but ther was no power to be deliuered* etc. And so be moaning our weaknes. and callinge for strength from the authour of all power, he went on, stumbling and stutterring by meanes of the perplexitie that he and the company, and the poore creature were the in, powring out rather shorte requeftes then a sett prayer, even as prefent trouble enforced. Which done, he fell backe into the rearwarde of the battle, with purpose to strike no more strokes, or doe any other service then by giuinge incouragment to those that fought, applause to their well doinges, and to marke the variable inc{l}ininges of the combate, but yet even then he was thinkinge vppon a weapon or two, which he would haue vfed, if he had agayne ben sommoned to appeare before the generall. And true it is, therwas some fearfulnes noted in that partie: but I hope it was not much offenfiue to God or to them that obferved it . for (I am sure) I alfo faw, feare, and trembling, yea teares, and fobbinge, in the more auncient, expert, and experienced fouldiers & Captaines that were there. And againe let it be thought vppon what it is for earth &

ashes

aſhes,to come before the high poſſeſſor of
heaven and earth, for ſinners to come before him whoſe eyes cannot abide imperfections, yea for ſinners to be importunat,
& that at ſuch a time, when terror ſemes to
compaſſe about on every ſide, & in ſuch a
ſuite as ſeeme exceeding difficult to be ob
tayned. to this purpoſe may be remembred, that which was raiſed out of _Daniell_,
of his conſternation of minde, & feblenes
of body at ſuch a preſence. To conclude,
I thinke that feare and trembling doth bet
ter beſeeme ſuch a buſines, thē to be ſencleſſe, or without feelinge of any ſuch paſſi-
ons. Well, this whytliuered fellow being
thus recoyled, an old *experienced ſoul-   M·Barber.
dier ſteppes into the forefront, and he be-
gins his prayer, with callinge to minde a
ſayinge of one of the prophets, namely,
that, _Thoſe that are the lords remembrancers,
ſhould not giue him reſt vntill he be mo
oued
to remember his people &c._ Yet (notwithſtan-
ding his courage) in the proceſſe of his pra
yer, he bewrayed a feare and a doubt of
his owne, namely, that if the Lord were
not pleaſed to heare vs at this time, yet
that he would remember his owne cauſe,
his owne glorie, the cryes of his people, &
pittie

pittie; and releiue, and releafe tho diſtreſſed eſtate of his poore creature, when, and
where, he ſhall ſee it fitt, to make more
for the beſt, at the interceſſions and further ſuites of other brethren. And yet this
was the man, who (a little after he was ri-
ſen vp) did giue out the firſt victorious
cry, *He flies, he flies,* but vppon what occaſion he ſo did, I cannot now call to minde,
he preſſed alſo the more to be heard, becauſe *Elias,* and ſuch of gods people, by
prayers prevailed, who yet were men com
paſſed with infirmities, as we were.

After him immediatlie ſucceeded the fore-
ſaide auncient * preacher, who (I muſt remember, and I thinke he will acknowledge
to be true, that he) ſeemed to faint in his
mourninge: For beginninge his prayer, he
made moane, that the darknes of the night
now comming on, did much abate the có-
forte and courage of our mindes, and that
beinge not all this while heard, it proceeded from the weaknes of our faith, & coald
nes of our prayers, or from ſinnes not repented of. And thervppó he prayed, that if
ther were any preſent that was come with
vnſanctified affections, or kept any ſuch
corruption ſecretlie hid, as *Achan* (whoſe
smothered

M. Evans'

smothered finne impeached the Lordes
hoaft) that he might be humbled, and
brought to repentance, pardon obtained,
and fo all impedimentes remooued, we
might the better be heard and prevaile.
He vrged alfo the Lord to heare vs the ra
ther, becaufe we tooke no indirecte courfe
or vnlawfull meanes for remedie,but went
directly to him who hath all power in his
hand to help,and is readie to heare: yeelding herein obedience to his ordinance,and
relying vppon his promifes, according alfo to the practife of his Church and children from time to time in fuch cafes.
About the time of his prayer, the afflicted patient began to reviue:hauinge(in the
time of this fitt)fhewed much torment,by
her armes diftorted or writhed the outfide
inward, the left fide of her body benom-
ed,both legge & arme,her fingers ftrech-
ed a broade and ftandinge ftiffe vprighte,
inflexible as Iron, as one * (that made *M. Badger.
proofe)made prefent report,and called o-
thers to try, and fince, hath deliuered me
a noate therof vnder his hand: her chappe
openinge and fhuttinge very often without vttering any worde,(and thervppon a
preacher called it a dumb (fpirit) her eves
                                    fhut

shutt, her belly greatly swoalne, and after that, her breast bulking vp, her throat swellinge etc. And at last, (after some striuinge to vtter) she began againe to speake as she did, even with those very wordes agayne repeated *Once more, once more,* not hastelie pronounced, but with good pause & deliberation, making (as I saide) her accent vppon the word once: and then (sitting as before in her chaire) she fell to her third prayer, which continued as longe as the formers and conteyned such requestes for the most parte, and that in such wordes, as are before mentioned: and yet in this prayer she had some poynts not touched before; as namely.

Her thyrd prayer

O Lord thy mercyes haue bin exceedinge comfortable vnto me, thou hast begune to be gratious, O lorde be mercifull vnto me still, and leaue me not vntill thou hast sett me free: lett thy glory appeare in my deliuerance, and lett Satan be confounded: strengthen me (O Lord) against that Goliah, thy grace is sufficient for me, giue me power, and patience to attend thy leasure, giue me faith to beleeue thy promises, giue me victory against this mine enimy, that I and others may reioyce, and tell to others the great thinges that thou hast done for me: I beleeue

leeue, help my vnbeleife. *Thou haſt taught me
that if Satan be reſiſted he will flye, now Lord
giue me ſtrength to reſiſt, that ſo he may flye,
and I being deliuered may prayſe thee, and o-
thers that heare of it may alſo magnifie thee,
and may alwayes ſay, the lord be bleſſed that
hath done ſuch thinges for the ſonnes of men,
and ſo learne to feare thee, and call vppon thee,
and put their truſt in thy mercie. &c.*

This prayer (as I ſaide) was drawne out
much more in lenght, partly by way of repeating thinges formerly mentioned, and
partly by ſupplying other petitions, which
neither I nor the others can now call to
minde. And heere (by the way) if in all her
prayers ſhe had beatten ſtill vppon the ſáe
matters, & that even with the ſame words,
ſhe had had a good patterne of one, *who
being in anguiſh, went againe and prayed &
ſpake the ſame wordes. Marke 14. 39.* And
truely the preachers, if they had done ſo
too: it had ben agreeing with this that now
I haue ſaide: and further if it be a profita-
ble thing to preach one thing often, it cannot be vnprofitable to pray one thing often, the occaſió therof ſtill remaining, but
(to ſay the truth) the preachers had much
varietie of matter in all their prayers, neither

ther can I call to minde many *Tantalogies*, except in the time of her extremities, whē sett, or continued prayers could not be admitted.

And now it was the time of about 6 of the clocke at night, and now was come the har deſt of all the dayes labours: both in reſpeſt of the parties ſufferinges, the preachers prayers with vehemency therin, the peoples perturbation, her deliuerance, her thankſgiuing and our reioycing. And now I perceaue is come the heavieſt parte of my taſke, to marſhall each matter in his due place, and to penne it accordinglye: but hopinge for the like aſſiſtance as hath direſted me hitherto: thus I begin afreſh to ſett on the worke.

Now (as I ſaide) was ſhee entered into her ſharpeſt conflict, now had Saran appalled her ſences, eſpecially benummed the left ſide of her body, now were her eyes fearfully turned vpward, her tongue blacke and retorted inward, her countenaunce owglie & diſtorted, her mouth exceſſiuelie wyde, gaping ſometime more in length vpwards and ſometime againe more ſtretched out in bredth: her face fierce, ſometime as if it were ſcornfullye diſdayninge, ſome-

fomtimes terriblie threatning, and fo nod-
ding her head and gaping vppon the woe
men that ftood or kneled before her, as if
fhee would devoure them, then her head
toffed from one fhoulder to another, oftē
and thicke and that with fwiftnes, and was
fometime fo farr wrıthed to the one fide,
and ftayed ther fo long: as that I feared it
would haue fo remained.

Here when theˀauncient preacer prayed
God to rebuke this *foule malitious Deuill,*
fhe fuddenly (though blinde and dumb &
deafe) turned to him and did barke out
froth at him, with her head fhe fometimes
bounfed backward, on the pillow which a
preacher called for a little after the begining of this fitt, and fo laying it on the topp
of the chaire, he ftood, and fometimes kne
led behind her, with his armes vnder hers
fupporttinge her body: then fhee with her
foote and legge that was at libertie, ftam-
ped vehementlye vppon the flower, and
getting fome hold or ftay with her foote,
fhe raifed her body a loft, and forced back-
warde both the chaire and him that ftood
behind her, notwithftandinge that he and
others refifted ftifflie. In fo much as certaine of the weomen were bufily imploy-

ed inholding downe beneath to keepe *De-corum* leaſt any vnſeelines ſhould appeare.
Her voyce at this time was lowd, tearfull
and very ſtrange, proceedinge from the
throat (like an hoarce dogge that barkes)
caſtinge from thence with opened mouth
aboundance of froath or ſoame, whereof
ſome did light on the face of one that kneled by, in ſuch ſort, as his wife was mooued
to caſt him her handkerchife to wipe it of.
The noyſe and ſound of her voyce one ex
preſſeth (in his noates of obſervation) by
the word *cheh cheh*, or *keck keck*: another,
by *twiſhe twiſhe*, or the hiſſinge of a violent
Squibbe: another to an *Henne* that hath the
ſquacke: an other compareth it to the loath
ſome noyſe that a *Catt* maketh forcinge
to caſt her gorge: and indeede ſhe did very often, & vehemently ſtraine to vomitt,

* M. Bridger.   In the time of this turmoyle, another of
the preachers *kneeling downe a little on
the one ſide of the chaire: with a milde ſpirit and low voyce, began and continued a
ſweete prayer, wherevnto ther was much
attention given. In which his prayer I remember ſome paſſages of the Scripture,
wherof he aptly made good vſe, as namely, mentioninge *the ſeed of the woman* that
                                    ſhoulde

should breake the Serpents head, (who notwithstandinge would turne backe & be nibling at our heeles:) Againe he remembred the *victorious Lion* of the tribe of *Iuda*, that should daunt the roaring lion who seeketh to devoure vs: And againe he repeated the prophecie concerninge Christ, that he should overcome the great *Leuiathan* and put a hooke in his nostrills: and that he should walke *vppon the Lion and adder*, and tread the young *Dragon* vnder his feete etc. prayinge that we might see the present performance hereof, and so gather inge courage and makinge application, to raise vp in vs a comfortable hope and expectation of deliuerance: he ceased.

The afflicted partie continued still in fites, wherof some were anticke, as, tossing her head, and iettinge her shoulders, with turnninge her body from side to side: and some againe were more fearfull, as, her hucklebone standing vp in her bellie at the place of her navell, accompanied with the former disfigurings of eye, mouth, handes, armes, fingers, throat &c. And hereuppon ther were many outcryes amongst the company saying Iesus help, Lord shew mercy, Lord strengthen, Lord confound Satan, Lord

Lord send deliuerance. In this meane while
the preachers were forced to forbeare sett
prayer, because of the peoples confused
cryes: yet one of the preachers rebukinge
Sathan and calling him a foule spirit, shee
turned her face towards him (though her
eies were shutt) and did belch out spittle at
him disdainfully, as also at others that kne
led on each side of her, holding her armes,
in so much as one of them (in his large observations) saith, that he had much adoe to
forbeare spitting againe in his foule face, I
say *his* (quoth he) for that me thought, I
saw his ougly countenaunce in her then de
formed visage·

At this time the Father of the maide roa-
red right out with abundance of teares in
the disquietnes of his minde, and anguish
of his hart: and withall I came to him frō
the place where I stood (which was somewhat before the parties face noatinge how
thinges went) and taking him by the hád,
I sayde, that now I conceaued more hope
then before, for if your daughter quoth I
were not thus rent and torne, I should not
looke for deliuerance.

After this the preacher * that kneeled behind her, (thinkinge with himselfe, as he
hath

M. Lewes.

hath ſince informed me) that the pride &
rage of Sathan was but a token of his ruine
not farr of, and calling to minde the mani
feſt tokens of favour that God hath ſhew
ed vnto vs all the day till then, and alſo
the promiſe of God pſa. 50. 15. wherof he
had intreated, and grounding himſelfe vppon the truth of that promiſe:) lifted vp
his voyce vppon the ſuddaine and prayde
lowd and vehemently, vrging the parable
of the vnrightous iudge, who by meere
importunitie of a poore woman, was forced to heare her: ſo he vrged the Lorde
now to ſhew his power, and to giue check
to Satan and commaund him to be gone,
whom he often defied, and called him a
proud ſpirit and yet cowardly, leath to let
loſe his hold, and often times (with teares,
yet ſmilinglie) he cried out, *he flies, he flies,*
wherat (as alſo before) ſhe turned towards
him a direfull menacinge, (and ſometime
mockinge) countenance, and with open
mouth ſhe did caſt out foame vpward into his face, her breath enteringe into his
throat as he ſaide, and the lowder & more
earneſt that he was in his prayer, the more
ſhe raged in his armes, forcinge to riſe, and
with her ſtrength did lift him vp with her,
ſtriuinge

striuing to turne her breſt & face towards him, notwithſtandinge her eyes were ſhut as a dead bodyes, onely ſhe did lift vp her eyebrowes, which did make her to looke the more ghaſtly.

whyle he was thus contending with her to keep her from turning full round towards him, (ſhe labouring (as I ſaide)with often toſſinge the head from ſhoulder to ſhoulder,to gett her face oppoſite to his) an other preacher * began to pray:and hauing a little while continued the ſame,the maide did fall downe ſuddenlye into the chaire, where ſhee remained without motion, her head hanging downward, ſomewhat inclining towardes the ſhoulder, her face and colour deadly, her mouth and eyes ſhut, her body ſtiffe & ſencleſſe, ſo as ther were that thought, and I thinke we all might haue ſaide, *behold ſhee is dead*. Ther were that then obſerued and after conſtantly affirmed(as alſo oue of the men of good credit who ſtood nere amongſt the weomen, in his noates ſetteth it downe:) that ther was a thing creeping vnder one of her eye liddes, of the bignes of a peaſon: but becauſe it was not generally ſeene and noated of vs,it was thought good I ſhould not
much

M. Skelton

much infist vppon it.

After fhee had continued a while in this deadly eftate: fuddenly in a moment, life came into her whole body, her mouth and eyes opened, and then lifting vp her hands and ftretching them wide afunder as high as fhe could reach, the firft word fhe vtter ed was, *he is come, he is come*(looking back-warde (with a very comfortable counte-nance)on fome of the preachers, and then on fuch as ftood on each fide of her)*the co̅-forter is come, O Lord thou haft deliuered me:*

As foone as her father (who ftood not very nighe)heard her fo crye:he alfo cry-ed out and faide (as well as his weepinge would giue him leaue) *this was the crye of her grandfather goeing to be burned.* And ve relye now ther was heard amongft vs, a-plaine outcrye or fhoutinge, even like the victorious crye or fhoute of a conquering armye, and yet the fame was intermixed with a boundance of moft ioyfull teares: & even ther withall the poore partie(ftill cryinge *he is come*) did ftruggle and ftriue with all the ftrength fhe had, to be let loofe which they that held her perceiuing, yeld-ed to fee what fhee would doe, and then fhee prefentlye, and fuddainly; did flyde

downe

downe out of the chaire, and very spedi-
ly recouering her selfe on her knees, with
a countenance(truly to my seeminge) exceedingly sober, and full of a kinde of maiestie and reuerence, with handes held vp
indifferent high; her eyes verye broad o-
pen, saide to one, *he is come*, (pronouncing
it treatablie and somewhat lowd, with a little motion of her face and hands vpward,
and makinge the accent vppon the worde
come)and againe turning about to another
shee saide; *her is come*, and so to an other,
and another I thinke 6 or 7 times. Then
from that, she fell to a most sweet prayer of
thanksgiuinge, wherin shee continued long
even to fainting through feeblenes. of this
prayer I will setdowne as much as I can remember, referring my selfe herein to be further holpen with the memories of others.

Her thanksgiu-
inge:

O Lord God and gratious father, I humblie
thanke thee for thy mercies towards me a vile
creature: I am vnworthy of the least of them
all, much more of this so great a mercy vouch-
safed vnto me at this present: in giueinge me
health, strength, and comfortable deliuerance:
Lord make me trulye thankfull for it, let me
never forgett it, let me and all of vs here pre
sent, and all that shall heare of it, make true
                                              vse

vse of it:namely to prayse thee for thy mercies keept in store, and to trust to thy promises, and to depend on thy providence, who doest such thinges for thy poore servants. And now Lord, graunt that begininge as it were a new, it would please thee to take me, even like a new borne babe, vnto thy good grace that so I may become a new creature: make me to hate sinne with a perfect hatred, and detest Sathan and his workes, and treade him vnder my feete as dyrte, fill my heart with thankfulnes, fill it with the graces of thy blessed spirit, workinge in me sanctification, and newnes of life, to walke worthy so great a mercy, that so glorifyinge thee in this life, I may see and enioye thy glory in the life to come. &c. And so continuing on, iterating, and multiplying these and such like poynts, till we perceiued her to be weary: she was interrupted and bidd to favour her selfe, and to committe that duety of thankes-giuinge vnto another, who should immediatlye take it vppon him, which was done accordingly. But before that, even in the time of her prayer, one of the preachers sayde with a lowde voyce, Oh what a sweet smellinge eveninge sacrifice is this vnto the Lord? Well, another preacher*addressed himselfe to pray- M. Skelton

G 1   er,

er, fhee beinge placed againe in her chaire,
all the company fallinge downe on their
knees, & the preacher kneeling fomewhat
behinde her.

His prayer was indeede a fweet facrifice of
prayfe and thankf-giuinge, conteyninge
much varietie of excelent matter feruinge
that purpofe:In the end wherof, he added
petitions for the continuance of Gods
good hand of ftrength, and grace vppon
the partie,and namely, that he would clad
her with the complete armoure, *Ephef. 6.*
the particulars whereof, he went over and
fo drew to an end. Then alfo the firft prea-
M.Lewes. cher, * (who before ftood at her backe
holdinge her)did prefently fucceed, take-
ing the like wordes of thankes-giuinge in
his mouth, and ended with prayer, defier-
ing God, to graunt vnto vs wifdome and
difcretion in publifhing this great work of
mercy vnto the world. This laft poynt of
his prayer,concerning our care and difcretion in publifhinge this great worke of
Rob.Midnal God: the other minifters did thinke well
off and afterwards approue: even as* one
of the company alfo in his noates of remē
brance, concludeth the matter thus: For
which I pray God make me vnfainedlye
thankfull

thankfull, and bold with wiſdome to veri-
fie the truth hereof in due time.

M.Bridger

Then another preacher * offered to make
the like prayer of thankſgiuinge(and that,
as he ſaide, breiſly)but it was not admitted
fearinge time would not ſuffer.

This done, one, I thinke a kinſman, went
to the maide(ſitting ſtill in her chaire)ſay-
inge with ioyfull teares, welcome Mary,
thou art now againe one of vs: the father
alſo in like ſorte tooke her by the hand, as
not beinge able to ſpeake a worde: and the
mother went, and (putting away the hand
kercheif wherwith her daughter ſate co-
uering her blubberinge face)with like wa-
tery cheekes kiſſed her. Then ſhe was bid
to goe nere the fire: and ſo ſhee went and
ſate on the ſettle, wher ſhe tooke her place
at her firſt entring into the rhome: Thither my ſelfe went to her, and takinge her
by the hand I thanked God for her, and
bidd her grow in comforte and courage,&
ſtrength to reſiſt, if ſhee ſhould a gaine be
aſſaulted: feare not(ſaide I)the mayne bat
tle is fought, the other wilbe but a light
ſkirmiſh (if therebe any at all) ſo I left her
with the weomen ſtanding about her, whõ
I heard (a non after)to obſerue and make
knowne

knowne, that her bellye was fallen and become as lanke as it was 12 *monthes before*: then also they gaue her to drinke a kinde of posset, which she tooke & dranke with ease, to their marvile and reioycinge. For one of the men(in the noates of his remébrance) saith, that the day before,which also was her good day) he & another more stronge man,were troubled to hold her(so violentlye was she resisted)whilst she did eate a little broath, but now shee did take twise the like quantitie(with bread also in it) without any sheew of checke, or resistance at all.

In this meane while, the ministers drewe themselues to gether in a corner of the chãber, to consult on diuers poyntes meete to be considered of and agreed vppon. As

1 first, that it were good that about 6 or 7. dayes after, we should meete togeather againe, in some convenient place. there to be exercised (for the space of 3 or 4 howers) in a solemne manner of thanksgiuinge.

2 Secondlie that the names of all that were present should be taken. Thirdly that one

3 should take the paynes to penne the actions of the day now past: (and here, soarie we were that we had not taken penne and
paper

paper at the firſt, that ſome one might orderlye haue ſett downe breife noates of
thinges as the paſſed) but howſoeuer that
fell out: this taſke was committed to him
that was not the fitteſt, who yet vnder
tooke it, and (with helpe of the others)
hath done as well as he could. Fourthlye, 4
that the company ſhould be admoniſhed,
not to publiſh this that was done, as yet,
but ſtaye to ſee ſome continuance of her
eſtate, and if they reported it to any (con-
cealing the place and the perſons) to doe it
with wiſdome and with a religious hearte,
leaſt by fooliſh and vaine glorious tatling,
the cauſe might be hindred, & themſelues 5
receaue hurte. Fiftly, that if any of them
ſhould fall into the handes of any to be examined, they would then be as carefull as
might be to keepe the poore miniſters out
of danger, who looſinge (peradventure)
hereby their libertie of pteachinge. ſhould
looſe all the meanes they had of their mai-
tenance. Sixtly, that we ſhould conclude 6
with a prayer generall for the whole ſtate,
which the old fatherly ∗ preacher very well M.Evans
performed, (even plentifully & pourfully)
praying and prayſinge God for her Maieſtie, the Counſellours, Nobles, Magiſtrats,
                              Miniſters

Ministers, People, those that were present, & lastly the poore deliuered maide. Seaventhly and lastly, that to shew our thankfullnes we would seale it vp with an other sacrifice, namely, with contributinge somethinge that might be bestowed on some poore.

This done, we songe a psalme: the 34 was called for, but the 6. was chosen by that auncient preacher, which we songe with a lowe voyce, very decentlye and comfortablye. And now it was past 7 of the clocke at night, and the company began to talke of departing home. But see, the woman of the house, (whose countenance truly I did beholde before, whylst the anguish was greatest; & I did imagine that she thought what a ghest she had admitted into her house, not knowinge how quietlye shee should be ridd of her againe) I say the woman of the house had in the meane time, (namely whylst we were consulting, writing, and singing, bestirred her selfe & gote together (whether all of her owne or with helpe of her neighbours, I cannot tell) sufficient store of meate to refresh vs all, which though it were not of the daintiest, or most orderlye serued, yet me thonght it

was

7

Mistris Ratcliefe in Shorditche.

was as comfortable a supper as euer I was
at, puttinge me in minde of that, *Actes* 2.
42. *And they continued in the Apostles doc-*
trine, and fellowshipp, and breakinge of bread
and prayer.

The giuinge of thankes both before and
after meate was committed to him * who   * M. Bridger.
had before desired to succeed in the acti-
on of thankſgiuing after our comforte re-
ceaued, but beinge then as I ſaide not har-
kened vnto (becauſe it grew late, and many
thinges remained to be done) he now vnder tooke this office at the table very readily, and in his grace after meate, he beſtowed (as I thinke) ſome of his former mea-
ditations which he would haue deliuered
if he had ben then admitted. For now in
his thankſgiuing after ſupper, he very aptly recompted the ſonges of *Moſes* and *My-*
riam after the Read ſea: of *Deborah* and *Ba-*
rak after *Siſeraes* overthrowe: of the *weo-*
mens ſonge concerninge Dauid after his
conqueſte of *Goliah &c*.

By this time it was paſt 9. of the clocke
ſo riſinge from the table, we ſtood a while
talking one with another, eſpecially record
ing that of *Luke.* 5. 26. *And they were all*
amaſed, and prayſed God, and were filled with
ſeare

feare, saying, doubtles we haue seene strange thinges this day. And heere let me truly be wraye an apprehension which I had in the time of our trouble, namely, that we were the liker to speed, becaufe we were fuch meane, bafe, defpifed, and contemptible men that were imployed. For fo God com̄monly worketh, by foolifh thinges to confound the wife, and by weake inftruments to bringe downe the proud: and (as I rem̄e ber in my poore prayer I noated) Sathan is often times overtaken in his craft: for by makinge his match thus to rage in and vppon little ones (as was this poore creature in refpect of her fex & age) his foile fhould be the greater, when fuch a worme fhould be inabled to withftand his mallice, and pre vaile againft his ftrength. but to returne.

Thus though we were replenifhed with much ioye, yet we durft not departe with banners difplayed, for feare of men, but crept away by 2 and by 3. in a companye till we were all gone. But before I departed, I afked the maide a queftion or two. As firft, whether fhe did fee any thinge de parte from her when firft fhee felt releafe? Wherevnto fhe anfwered that fhe faw no-thinge, but fhe did feele fomewhat depart,

and

and withall, felt such a fredome of all the powers and faculties of soule and body as she neuer felt the like before, which caused her in that sorte to springe out for ioye.

But whether *Mary Glouer* were possessed or dispossessed, I will not maintaine. For I see, that that question growes not onely disputable, but dangerous to holde. It passeth my skill to define when a man may be saide to be possessed: for although many signes of possession (even such as the Evangelistes doe obserue) may be found in any one: yet to say how many of them, and in what degree they must concurre to make *proprium quarto modo*, appertaining to that afflictioh, I see it harde to say. And I vnderstand that a great scholler of *Camb*. disputinge that poynt not longe agoe, had even his handes full of that worke. In so much as some that hearde it, conceaued thereby, (I meane by his defence, and by the tearmes of obssession, and circumsession which he (in his sence) vsed) that not Sathan was commaunded to come out of the man, but the man was commaunded to come out of the deuill. Where also it may be remembred, that the *Heads* of the vniuersitie would not admitt his question to

be difputed of as he propounded it, namely, *nulla eft hiis diebus poffeffio ac difpoffeffio
Dæmoniorum*:but in their learned wifdome
did firft qualifie the queftion (fo makinge
an abatement of his writt) *nulla eft hiis diebus ordinaria poffeffio ac difpoffeffio Dæmoni
orum*. But if a man confider that the malice
of Sathan, the wickednes of men, and the
Iuftice of God are as great as euer they
were:he will perhapes bethinke him, whether he hath read of any abfolute revocation of any kinde of punifhment formerlye
inflicted, or threatened. Nay, our Soue-
raigne Kinge is more refolute in his *Dæmonologie pag.* 47. fayinge, *Why may not
God vfe any kinde of extraordinarie punifhment when it pleafeth him, as well as the ordinarie roddes of ficknes or other aduerfities
&c.* Againe, a man would thinke (peradventure) that thofe words of our Saviour
*this kinde goeth not out but by prayer & faft-
inge:* may be extended to a further tyme
then when miracles were wrought: efpeciallye if he doe heerewithall confider the
practife of the Church in fuccedinge ages:
whervnto alfo our Kinge in his faide book
(lib. 3. pag. 71.) giueth good allowance.

But a man may fay, why then, yea may
cure

cure Palſies, Goowt, Ague, and Lepro-
ſies,in like ſorte:I anſwer,no, we haue not
the like warrant for that *Kinde,* and Phiſitions can tell the cauſes and cures of ſuch
malladies:but if they ſuſpect *witchery;* not
finding any naturall diſtemperature of the
body:they will not meddle. VVhat then?
ſhall ſuch poore diſtreſſed creatures be left
at ſix and ſeaven, to ſinke or ſwym at Satans pleaſure? God forbid.A man(I hope)
may at leaſt, ſay Lord haue mercy vppon
them. Though ſkill of phiſicke heerin doe
fayle, yet his ſkill that taught phiſitians
theirs,can worke with,without, and aboue
meanes·and therfore is worthy to be called
vppon, both when the meanes are vſed &
when they fayle.But, as I ſayd, I will not
meddle with that queſtion:onely this that
Mary Glouer was vexed by Sathan, by the
meanes of a witch: me thinks I may ſafely
ſay it, ſith the Iurie hath found it, and the
Honorable Iudges determined ſo of it, &
therfore I cannot thinke, but that they did
a charitable and warrantable deed, that
prayed for her.
The next day alſo I aſked her whether ſhe
ever did praye ſo before, or whether ſhee
could praye ſo agayne? To which her answere

swer was, I pray God enable me to pray as
I fhall haue occafion. Agayne, I afked her
(merilie) whether fhe could nowe gape fo
wide as I might put in my fifte, (for a man
that fhall now looke vppon her, will not
thinke her mouth could poffibile ftretch
fo wyde) as it did: whervnto (with ftayed
countenance) fhe anfwered nothinge. But
(to draw to an end) Becaufe it was fuppof-
ed that the yonge recouered Souldyer
might peradventure be fett vppon agayne,
not longe after, it was thought good that
fhee fhould not be caried home to her father houfe, but fhould lodg (together with
her mother) at oneof the minifters houfes,
which was done accordingly.

The next day, ther was a lefture not farre
off, and thither came the mayde in the cō-
panye of certaine women, (religious and
matronelye Citizens) the preacher was he
M.Bridger who * that gaue thankes at the table the night
as yet lieth in before, his text was 2. Theff. 12. Grace be
prifon. with yow and mercy, and peace from God our
Father and from our Lord Iefus Chrift. whe-
cher he made a purpofed choyce of this
text or no I cannot tell, but fure I am that
from the wordes of grace (free from God)
and peace, the effect, firft betweene God
and

and man, then betweene man and man, &
thirdly found and felt within man himselfe
in his owne conscience: he rayfed and deliuered fuch doctrine and vfe, as I thinke
the poore partie prefent made good vfe
of. That night fhee with her parents were
invited to fupp with a religious Cittizen,
who (like *Cornelius*) had called to geather
fome of his kinffolke and fpeciall frendes.
(*Actes* the 10) and gaue thankes before
and after meate in very good forte, be-
yonde my expectation, to fee an ordinary
Citizen performe it fo well:but I can tefti-
fie of a truth that the Citie is not deftitute
of many fuch as are very well qualified
this way. This I doe of purpofe report,not
onely becaufe *S. H.* lybeth at his fraternitie
of holy, illuminate men, and at his *Sifter-
nitie* of mympes,mops,and idle holy weomen: but alfo becaufe this Citizen(of who
I fpeake) was bitterly taken vp by the Bi-
fhop of London, for performinge,privat-
ly in his family(as became a vertuous chriftian man)a religious duty of humiliation,
by prayer and faftinge,vppon an occafion
of an heauie croffe which at that time laye
vppon one of his children. Againe,I haue
heard iolly chaplaines in their lofttie vaine
fcorn

scornfully report the practize of prayer &
singinge of psalmes in Londoners houses,
as also deride and scoffe at their sober and
religious behauiour in open assemblies at
time of publicke prayer, and of the worde
preached.

VVell, the next day, saterday is come,
when diuers of the preachers and others
repayred to the place wher the maide had
lodged, to vnderstand how thinges went
with her, and that the rather, because a
bruyte began to be raysed abroade, that
she was relapsed into her former estat, this
beinge the daye of her ordinarie fittes,
but thankes be to God it was not so, but
being well all that day, at night shee went
with other company about halfe a myle to
supper, where appeared such a disposition
in many as was sometime in men that desired to see even Lazarus that was raysed
Iohn 12. After supper she returned to her
former lodging, and by the way homward
I noated this, that beinge weary in goinge
vp a streat, somewhat ascendinge, she was
glad to sitt downe and rest on a bench, saying, o Lord, how is my strength abated: I
could once rune nimblie vp and down our
stayres. and being sent to markett, I could
lugge

lugge home luftielye an heavie burthen
without wearines. This I obferue, that it
might appeare, it was not *reft* and *flouthful-
nes*, that caufed her greife: which yet, the
oppofite *Doctour* infinuateth in his treatife
of the fuffocation of the *Moother*.

The next day being the Sabaoth, fhe fpent
forenoone and afternoone in religious ex-
erciffes, being prefent at two publicke Sermons, and behauing her felfe there, chrifti-
anly. That day, alfo, ther was thankes pub
licklye giuen for her, by a worthy preacher
in his great affemblie, who alfo had there
many times before, prayed for her by nae.
this thankfgiuing he made, though I know
that one of the forefaide preachers of
our company was very carefull, that ad-
uertifment might in time begiuen him to
forbeare, becaufe he knew that it ftood not
with the Bifhops likinge that it fhould be
fo, even as in the time of her greuous vexations, there was (by the *Bifhope* of Lon-
dons meanes, who yet could neuer begot-
ten to *Come and fee*, although fent vnto &
earneftly mooued by certaine worfhipfull
and Honorable parfonages, to that end:)
there was I fay a feare caft on fuch as re-
forted to her, wherby they were terrified
either

either to pray themfelues, or to be prefent
at prayer for her: in fo much as at on time,
when in a terrible fite the beholders were
much a mafed, there was a gratious yonge
gentleman that called for prayer, & feeing
none ther, either able or willing to doe it,
he addreffed himfelfe to performe it, fayinge, he fawe it fitte, yea neceffary to doe
fo, though he were fure to be committed
the next day.

For my parte, I thanke God with all my
heart that I was prefent at this worke, and
had an hand, (though very little and fim-
ple)in it: For I finde (I prayfe God) therin, a labour of his loue towardes me, pro-
voakinge, nay vrginge me the more, ther-
by to performe a poynt which I begged
then in my poore prayers, namelye, that
that may be found in vs, which *Mofes*(vppon an occafion which caufed like humiliation) prayed for in his Ifralites, *O that
this people had fuch an heart in them continuallye.* And here I appeale to the hartes and
confciences of all that were there prefent,
whether they did not then finde in themfelues, a great meafure of a chriftian difpo-
fition to good: And I pray agayne (as then
and ther I did) that God would remooue
that

that iudgmeht farre frō vs, that we fhould
be like *Swine* returnning to the myre.

But (to conclude) the next wednefday fhe
was at the lecture at the black-friers: and
from thence returned home to her parents
who are religious perfons, of good creditt
and eftimation amonge their neighbours,
yea and in the Cittie of as many as knowe
them (he being accompted a man not vn-
worthy, to be the fonne of a worthy Martyr, as M. Fox maketh good and memorable reporte of) Infomuch as they are farr
vnworthy to be fo abufed as they haue bin
by the flaunderous penne of *S. H. But* as
they are not hurt in their honeft name &
good accompt by his offenfiue writing: fo
alfo their perfons together with the daugh
ter, haue hitherto well enough efcaped the
Bifhops prifons fo often and rigoronflye
threatened vnto them all, yea, and that
fince it hath pleafed God to cleare their in
nocencie, both by open triall in face of
Courte, and by ftretchinge as it were his
owne hand from heaven, in workinge the
daughters fo gratious deliuerance as nowe
I haue reported.

And thus I will heere drawe to an end of
this difcourfe touchinge this *Mary Glouer*:

com-

commendinge her to the further ſtrength
and graces of her great good God. And as
I remember I did in my prayer liken her,
to an old grandmother of hers *Mary Mag-
dalene*, who though ſhe was once a gazing
ſtocke to many, yet afterwardes, did leaue
an honorable name behinde her to many
generations: ſo now, I commend vnto this
our *Mary* (to be had alwayes in her minde
and mouth) the ſonge of a more bleſſed
Mary, the mother of our bleſſed Saviour,
*my ſoule doth magnifie the Lord, and my ſpi-
rit hath reioyced in God my ſaviour, who hath
regarded the baſe eſtate of his handmaide, &
hath done great thinges for me, by throwinge
out the mightie from his ſeate and exaltinge
the lowlye . Luke. 1 . 46.*

Now if this poore pamphlet being per-
vſed, ſhould by the allowance of my brethren chaunce to get winges and learne to
flie abroad: I ſee what diuers cenſures will
paſſe vppon it. Some will gaze at it as at an
outlandiſh Owle, and as a thinge fitter to
haue kept a forraine buſh: yet ſome againe
peradventure will ſpeake better of it. How
can it be but that I ſhould looke for oppo-
ſitions and contradictions now after the
worke done, ſeeinge before the ſame was
taken

taken in hand, mennes opinions and speaches were diuers, touchinge the parties passions: namely, in that one phisitian (vppon sight of the partie) saide, *nihil hic preter dolum*, another, *nihil doli sed forte nil preter naturam.* another more resolute, *It is either diabolicall, or at least supernaturall*: another Doctour (but not of that facultie) *That shee doth not counterfeite, I will be her compurgatoure,* another, a worthy Magistrate (who had tryed her with fire) *To tell me that it is counterfeite, I had as liese yow should tell me that my house doth walke &c.* Bnt as for this poynt concerning oppositions and contradictions of men, I am at a poynt, God knowes the sinceritie of my heart herein, the good haue perused and censered this my doinge before it came a broade, and I hane learned to be contented if I meete with that measure that my betters haue mett withall. For besides that the works & persons of worthy men of late haue ben miserablie traduced? I saw also to myne exceeding greife and feare, that even the sacred booke of God his blessed truth, could not escape the sawcie censure and audatious tongues of men, in this most mischeevous age, wherin papistes began to perke

vp

vp: Apoſtates and Atheiſts abound, and and wicked blaſphemous wordes and writinges infect the ayer and mindes of men.

It is notoriouſly knowne, how *S.H.* himſelfe hath diſputed & preached dangerous poyntes, and how in his ſaide laſt booke he brocheth a conceapt as if there were no *Witches* at all: yea, it ſeemeth by his ſo dallyinge with *Modu* his Deuill, that he his of minde ther is no Deuill at all. (Even as an Atheiſt in open Court, takinge advantage of ſome wordes of *S.H.* his Maſter, ſaide openly, *My L O R D, if any here can proue ther is a God, I will beleiue it.*) I will not ſpeake of his immodeſt ſtile, and laſcivious penn: but, (which are matters of ſequence) It is alſo too well knowne, how a man of no meane place, hath ſcurrilouſly ſcanned the ſtorie of the flood, and by pregnant demonſtration out of his geometricall proportions found out, that if that be true which is ſayd of Noahes Arke, ther ſhould be allowed to the ſtaule of a great Oxe, or of the mightieſt Eliphant, no more rhome then the bignes of a mans thombe· As alſo how like a tale it is, that *5000 men, ſhould be fedd with 5 loaues. math.* 16. Agayne, my ſelfe haue heard a man of no meane reckonning

ning, bowldly defcant vppon the ftorye of
Sampfons Foxes(*Iudges* 15) gallantly glan-
cinge at,and wantonly applyinge their being tyed by the tayles. Againe fportinge at
the fact of the fayde *Sampfon*, who (like a
madd whorfon(fo were his words,) fhould
lift off the gates of the Cittie *Azzah*, and
runne away with them(and the two poftss
and barres) to the topp of a mountayne.
Iudges. 16. (but wheiher our true *Sampfon*
of whom this was a tipe, will take this in
good parte let him looke to it.) Alfo, alle-
gorizinge on the ftorie of the fall of *Ieri-
choes walles* at the found of trumpets made
of Rammes hornes(*Iofb.*6.)and very pre-
tily and pleafantly (at leaft as he thought)
wifhed hornes on his head that would fo
literallie take it. Agayne Ijbinge at the fact
of *Iael*, as if women had more allowance
then men to committe a flagitious and per
fidious act. Item,that the doctrine of pre-
deftination,as now it is taught amongft vs
by many,is defperat, binding vp the hands
of God that he cannot haue mercy though
he would, fo that preachinge may well inough ceafe, and praying be let alone. thefe
were the times wherinto we were fallinge.
   If now the frefh witt of a luftie gallant
                                    would

would let loofe the raines of his venterous
and viperous tongue, I befeech you might
he not in like manner call into queftion
(and fo make fporte with) fuch workes as
were performed by the *Apoftles* thefelues,
& fay, the people were the deceaued (fim-
ple men) even as poore M. *Fox* was, as is
commonly obiefted? And I praye might
not the matter be out-faced, that the faft
of *Peter* & *Iohn*, (*Aftes*.3.) was much like
vnto the Creeples and blinde mans cure at
Saint Albones, the fraude wherof the good
Duke Vmphrie detefted? If this then may
befall the writtinges inditted by pen-men
fo direfted that they could not erre: what
fhall I looke for, who cannot wryte or
fpeake as I would I could.

Yet I cannot paffe over in filence, the
ftrange works of God in thefe our dayes,
who hath of late rayfed vp in diuers quarters & coafts of the land (yea, and brought
them home to our doores) a great many
of examples as prints of his prefence. And
namely, at *Northwich*, at *Woolwich*, at *Not-
thingham*, at *Burton*, at *Colchefter*, in *London*
in *Lankafhire*, and further off (as I heere)
in *Kent*, & in *Suffex*: and it may be thought
he will yet come neerer to the dwellings of

fome

some: even as if he should say, holde your peace yee poore afflicted for my names sake, I will take the cause into myne owne handes, and be revenged on the violent & wilfull oppositions of men, against the manifest workes of myne owne power.

And thus hauing reported and discoursed of this matter touchinge *Mary Glouer*, to the comfort I hope of the godly, and such as feare God vnfainedly, with a resolut purpose to liue thereafter: and hauinge giuen a caveat or warninge to others, betimes to be wise and to kisse the Sonne, before he be angry and so they perish in the midst of their ruffe: I end. Now to our mightie and eternall God, our good, gratious, and mercifull Father in Iesus Christ, to God onely wise, be yealded from all Saints in all ages, through the working of the blessed spirit, three persons and one true and euer liueinge God, all power, maiestie, glorie, wisdome, prayse and thankf-giuinge, foreuer and forever, Amen

Amen.

Pſalme. 116.

I loue the lorde becauſe my voyce,
   and prayer heard hath he:
VVhen in my dayes I cald on him,
   he bowed his eare to me.
Even when the ſnares of cruell death,
   about beſett me rounde:
when paynes of hell me caught & when,
   I woe and ſorrowe founde:

Vppon the name of god my lorde,
   then did I call and ſay:
Deliuer thou my ſoule o lorde,
   I doe thee humblie praye.
The lorde is very mercifull,
   and iuſt he is alſo:
And in our god compaſſion,
   doth plentifullie flowe.

The lorde in ſafetie doth preſerues
   all thoſe that ſimple be:
I was in wofull myſerie,
   and he relieued me.
And now my ſoule ſith thou art ſafe,
   retourne vnto thy reſt:
For largelie loe the lorde to thee,
   his bountie hath expreſte.
      K1   becauſe

Becaufe thou haft deliuered,
　my foule from deadlie thrall:
my moyfted eyes from mournful teares,
　my flydinge feete from fall:
Before the Lord I in the lande
　of life will walke therefore:
I did beleeue therfore I fpake,
　for *I* was troubled fore.

The Second part.

I faide in my diftreffe and feare,
　that all men liars bee:
what fhall I pay the Lord for all,
　his benefites to me?
The wholfome cuppe of fauinge health,
　I thankfullie will take.
And on the Lordes name I will call,
　when I my prayer make.

I to the Lorde will pay the vowes,
　that I haue him behight:
yea even at this prefent time,
　in all his peoples fight.
Right deere and pretious in his fight,
　the lorde doth aye efteeme:
the death of all his holie onefs
　what ever men doe deeme.

Mary Glouers meditation.

Thy feruant lord, thy feruant loe,
   I doe my felfe confeffe:
Sone of thy handmaid, thou haft broke,
   the bondes of my diftreffe.
And I will offer vp to thee,
   a facrifice of prayfe:
And I will call vppon the name,
   of god the lorde alwayes.

I to the lorde will paye my vowes,
   that I haue him behight:
Yea even at this prefent time,
   in all his peoples fight.
Yea in the courts of gods owne houfe,
   and in the midft of thee:
O thou Ierufalem I faye,
   wherfore the lorde prayfe yee.

Y ou that before with minds a mazd,
   in haſt did runne to ſee:
Such wofull ſightes as then were cauſ'd,
   by great perplexitie:

whoſe mournfull eyes in meaſure great,
   ſalt teares a pace downe ſent,
And tender heartes in breaſtes did beat,
   at *Glouers* chaſtiſement:

Yow that in former dayes haue bene,
   at ſuch deſerued payne:
what now for comfort may be ſeene,
   come once and view a gaine.

And come with wiſe & thankfull hartes,
   to ſee, and learne to ſay:
God doth not then reſpect deſerts,
   When troubled ſoules doe praye.

Though man be borne to miſerye,
   though ſinne be cauſe of woe,
though Sathans cruell tyrannie,
   be harde for to vndoe:

Yet ſhall you ſee the mightie God,
   hath cruſht his head in ſonder,
and quite remov'd that former rodde,
   that made yow ſo to wonder.

Mary Glouer to the godlie.

Come helpe me now to celebrate,
    the prayfes of the Lorde:
that earft bewayld my troubled ftate,
    fome comfort to afforde.

Let not this worthy worke o Lorde,
    in fcilence hidden be:
which thou in mercie didft accorde,
    in time to fheew on me.

Let all thy fainctes reioyce to heare,
    and fee thy gratious hand,
and let thy foes be fmitt with feare,
    that did thy worke withftand.

And let thy mercyes neuer fayle,
    which fheewed thou haft on me,
the force and crafte of foes to quayle,
    that wifht my fall to fee.

Forgiue them that to worke my woe,
    did try thy force and might,
A contrite heart giue me alfo,
    in prefence of thy fight.

Vnto my parents wifdome giue,
    and grace to know thy will:
Vnto thy children, fo to liue,
    as peace their dayes may fill.

Yow that did come to see my payne,
    to laugh, to mocke to iudge,
I warne yow come no more in vayne,
    let foolish fancies trudge.

But if as once yow ill began,
    so, badde yow will remayne,
as no aduised counsell can,
    reduce your myndes agayne.

If neither former hand of God,
    nor this be ought regarded,
the iustest Iudge prepares his rodde,
    his foes must be rewarded.

I neither praye nor wish your smarte,
    I wayte not your confusion:
I doe desire with all my heart,
    your sound and true conuersion.

Its easie for to carpe and snatch,
    fooles boaltes are shootinge euer:
A busie brayne much more doth hatch,
    then pen or tongue deliuer.

Did euer worke of God or Saintes,
    escape the poysoned tongues?
For proofe of this, marke many playnts
    in poore distresseds songes.

                          who

Mary Glouer to the scorners.

Who reads that sacred booke shall find,
　Chrifts actes and doctrine true:
of every wicked carnall minde,
　deemd wicked, loofe, and newe.

What then, if fome fay,alls deceyte,
　Ile pawne my foule thereon:
Ile proue it to be counteefeite,
　ere many moneths begone.

Though *Gallen* and *Hipocrates,*
　will natures workes advance,
or one as wife as *Socrates,*
　will help them lead the daunce.

Though fome faye (well) they wot not
　to iudge in fuch a cafe,　　　(what
but natures force with fome deceyt,
　may furely be in place:

Who cares for thefe or any fuch,
　truth ftandes,her foes doe fall,
God doth efteeme his name fo much,
　as thefe in vayne doe braule.

VVherfore all wife and fober mindes,
　marke well Gods hand,and fave,
thy name be prayf'd, that truth defends,
　though wicked men fay nay.
　　　FINIS.

MARY GLOVERS LATE WOEFUL CASE

Stephen Bradwell

A NOTE ON THE TRANSCRIPTION

The only known copy of Stephen Bradwell's 'Mary Glovers Late Woeful Case' is now in the British Library, where it is catalogued as MS Sloane 831. It is in a bound quarto consisting of 171 written leaves that contains no other documents. Its provenance is a mystery, and so is the identity of the person who made the fair copy we have. The W. C. who signed and dated the manuscript 21 May 1646 at the end may have been the writer, although his inscription claims merely that he read it ('lect.'). The hand appears to me to be contemporary with the author, who left no other autograph papers I have been able to locate. An insertion that is numbered as folio 128 is casually written and heavily corrected in the same hand that wrote the rest of the manuscript. This appears to be either a fragment of the first draft or a passage added after the manuscript had been written, and if this is so, then the scribe was almost certainly Bradwell himself.

The following transcription is not a critical edition. Like the printed tracts reproduced in this volume, it is essentially a facsimile of the original. I have striven to provide a text that is as close to the manuscript as possible; I have made very few changes in it and have added only a handful of explanatory notes. For instance, misspellings in English and Latin have been verified and then left as they stand, without comment, except in a small number of instances where they seemed to me to make the text too confusing. Readers will differ as to whether these intrusions are too frequent or too rare. Similarly, although I checked as many of Bradwell's references as possible and corrected his notes, I have not changed his versions of names and titles. Interested scholars will be able to find most of them easily.

For the convenience of those who might wish to consult the original, its foliation has been indicated throughout the transcription.

The one major concession to readers that I have made would not please textual purists, but it does make a difficult document much easier to understand. I have followed what has become conventional practice in editing historical documents by standardizing to modern usage some letters and orthographical conventions. Thus j has become i when appropriate and vice versa; u has been rendered as v; and initial capitals written as double lower-case letters have been modernized. Moreover, I have expanded normal scribal abbreviations and signs, rendering y^e as the and y^t as that, for instance. Punctuation and capitalization have been left largely untouched, except that I have capitalized the initial letters of sentences beginning after a full stop. Otherwise, the text appears exactly as it does in the manuscript. Bradwell's notes have been retained, but they have been moved from the margin to the end of the book. Note numbers have been placed in the text as close as possible to the position of the margination in the original. Rather than ending each of Bradwell's notes with the standard comment [marginated], I have chosen instead to flag my own rare additions with brackets or comments whenever confusion over who wrote the note might arise.

Even having set a relatively noninterventionist editorial standard, I nevertheless encountered some difficulties in rendering the text accurately. The most annoying problem was that some words and phrases proved finally illegible. This is particularly noticeable in the early folios of the manuscript, where the ink has bled through many leaves very badly. There are also places later in the text where someone has spilled liquid on the page, smudging words, or where the binding has captured parts of words. Points at which it was possible to guess the meaning of an illegible word are indicated [? illeg.] and where no guess was possible by an ellipsis and [illeg.]. The insertion at folio 128, mentioned above, is an especially challenging mixture of plain English, mangled Latin, clearly-formed words and mysterious blobs. It actually belongs at 126r, where I have placed it.

M. M.

MARY GLOVERS LATE WOEFUL CASE, TOGETHER WITH HER JOYFULL DELIVERANCE

Written

On the occasion of *Doctor Jordens* discourse of the mother, wherein hee covertly taxeth, first the Phisitions which judged her sicknes a vexation of Sathan And consequently the sentence of Lawe and proceedinge against the Witche, who was discovered to be a meanes thereof.

A defence of the truthe againste *D. J.* his scandalous Impugnations; by *Stephan Bradwell a member of the Coll: of physitions* in London.

Apoc. cap. 15: 4.

Who shall not fear the, o Lord, and glorifie thie name? for thou only art holy, and all nations shall come and worship before the, for thy judgements are made manifest.

Anno D^i. 1603

1

A brief and sincere Narration of Marie Glovers late wofull affliction effected through the permission of God by the handes of *Sathan* and the mediation of a *Witche*; from the last of Aprill to the xvith of December 1602.

Marie Glover a daughter of Tymothy Glover of litle Alhallowes in Thames streete in London, *being a mayde of fowertene yeres* of age incumbered with no corporall infirmitie, but enjoying a good and upright steete of health, was sent of her mother on Friday, the last of Aprill, 1602 upon an arrand, to Elizabeth Jackson an old Charewoman, dwellinge in the same parrish, who had (a litle before that time) conceived a quarrell, against this mayd, for discovering to one of her Mistresses a certaine fashion of her subtile and importunat begging. When [Fol. 3v] this mayd was come into her house the old woman locked the dore upon her,[1] Marie asked whie good wief Jackson the latche is sufficient for you and me, nay gossip (said the old woman) it had byn better that you had never medled with my daughters apparrell; And then rayled at her, with many threats and cursings, wishing an evill death to light upon her. And when she had geven her such kind of intertaynment the space of an hower, at last she let the mayde goe, with this farewell; my daughter shall have clothes when thou art dead and rotten. Upon her departure ymmediatelie the mayd felt her selfe evill at ease, and so testified as she went homeward, to one Elizabeth Burges, a servant of the house adjoyning; whoe perceiving her contenance and colour much altered, had asked her how she did. Assoone also as the maid was gon, the old woman went to that next neighbours house, and said, I have ratled up one of the Gossips that medled with my daughters apparrell, and I hope an evill death will come unto her. Marie Glover being thus retorned [Fol. 4r] home, languished as in a Newtrall estate untill Monday following in the afternoone; At which time, being in her Fathers shop, eating of a possit, the same Elizabeth Jackson came to the shop dore, pretending to have to speake with Mistress Glover; Marie answered that her Mother was not at home; the old woman, having fiercely beheld her, and snappishly replied, that she must speake with her, departed; Marie the same instant retorned againe to her posset, but was not now able to let downe one drop more of it, her throat seeminge unto her (as she called it) locked up. Hereupon she went to a familiar neighbours house for succour, where she was taken moreover speechles, and blynde, and so was brought home to her fathers house. The same hower her necke and throat did swell extremely, and very deformedly, and so did it thereafter every day at sundrie times, depriving her of speeche, but not much impeaching breathing. She lyked to have fingers thrust downe her throate, and could [Fol. 4v] endure how farre so ever downe any could convay their finger without any disturbance by it which all others have.

Eighteene dayes togeather she had these fittes three or fower times a day[2] in much extremitie and in all that time never receaved any maner of sustenance save by way of injection, or forcible powring downe with a spoone, and that but a litle at once, it was so much resisted in passing downe for all that, those eighteene dayes being expired, she was nothing impayred neither in flesh nor strength. The wednesday after her first falling ill, her fittes were so fearefull, that all that were about her, supposed that she would dye, thereupon her parents caused the bell to be touled for her, Which Elizabeth Jackson hearing, went againe to her next neighbours house and said, I thanck my God he hath heard my prayer, and stopped the mouth and tyed the tongue of one of myne enemies. The like words she used at Alderman Glovers house, and at another house also; adding these withall, The [Fol. 5r] vengeance of God on her, and on all the generation of them. I hope the Devill will stop her mouth. Mistress Glover hearing of these speeches went to talke with the old woman, who denyed all, and defyed them that spake against her, and yet could not forbeare but speake these wordes to her face; You have not crosses ynow, but I hope you shall have as many crosses, as ever fell upon woman and Children. All this while Doctor Shereman[3] and a Chirurgeon were used who minstered unto her sundry remedies, for the squinacy, as they then tooke it to be, but prevayled nothinge, her chiefest ease was by thrusting som finger, or instrument lowe into her throte, whereby somwhat seemed to remove downeward. Within the compasse of this time, Elizabeth Jackson sent Marie Glover an Orange, as in token of kindenes, and the maide tooke it so kindely that she kept it in her hand, smellinge ofte unto it, [Fol. 5v] the most part of that day; but afterward the same hand, arme and whole side,[4] were deprived of feeling and moving in all her long fitts, and not before.

After eightene daies her difficulties of swallowing removed and thenceforth for manie daies she tooke her sustenance freely, but now her belly was swelled and shewed in it, and in the brest, certaine movings, often in the day, with fitts of dumnes, blyndnes and deformed swelling of the throte. At the sight of which Doctor Shereman suspected som supernaturall cause to be present, yet because he was desirous, to cleere the point touching *hystericall* passions, which might be suspected, he applied himselfe thenceforth to cure the Mother of all those affects, that might raise such symptomes; but all being prooved in vaine, he pronounced and was plainely of that minde, that som cause beyond naturall was in it. Henceforth Doctor Mounford[5] was used [Fol. 6r] who ministered unto her the space almost of three monthes.

About six weekes after Marie Glovers first visitation, shee desired to eate of new wheaten lofe, which was geven her, and as she was eating of it in the shop, Elizabeth Jackson came by the dore, looked earnestly upon Mary, but speaking nothing, passed by, and yet instantly retorned, and with the like looke and silence, departed. At which doing the bread which she was chewing, fell out of Marie Glovers mouth,[6] and her selfe fell backewards off the stoole where she sate, into a grievous fitt. from this day forward, even to the day of her deliverance, she had a fitt for every sustenance that she tooke and every time that she went to bed, on her worser day; which worser day was every other day, wherein she had a long fitt, which began at a sett hower: but on the better day, had only such fitts, as came at taking [Fol. 6v] sustenance.

Not long after this upon a Sabbeth day, Mary Glover went to the next parish church to hear the sermon; Elizabeth Jackson being there first, stood up in her pew to looke upon Marie, And after that (as though she would shun the occasion of being noted) looked at her,[7] under the arm of another woman, which stood leaning upon the pew. Whereupon presently Marie Glover feeling her selfe amisse, was brought home, and fell into a grievous fitt, which was through repeticons of the witches view, increased both in strength and in strangenes dayly. In so much as *now*, she was turned rounde as a whoop, with her head backward to her hippes; and in that position rolled and tumbled, with such violence, and swiftnes, as that their paynes in keeping her from receaving hurt against the bedsted, and postes, caused two or three women to sweat; she being all over colde and stiffe as a frozen [Fol. 7r] thing. After she had ben thus tossed and tumbled in this circled roundnes backward, her body was suddenly turned round the contrary way, that is, her head forward betweene her leggs, and then also rowled and tumbled as before. After certaine dayes spent in theis fitts, she came to have exceeding wyde gapings, with her mouth, during the which, there did flie out of her mouth a great venemous and stinking blast; which one time did hit her mother upon the face, in such a feeling sorte, as she thought her eye had ben stricken out, and made her face to smart and swell very much, for many dayes. Another time it touched her mother upon the naked arme; and caused it to swell and be sore, for fowerteene dayes after. At another time, the like did smyte her sister Anne upon the face, and caused it to blister and swell. And againe at another time, the like did light upon Mistress Lumas, her face, and caused it to be very sore. The stincke whereof made her stomach sicke and held a noysome impression in [Fol. 7v] her a great while after. Upon the avoyding of these venemous blasts, she came to such ease and shortening of her fitts, as her Parents were in som hope she should have ben cleane delivered thereby, though it fell out otherwise afterward, for these seemed be procured by som extraordinary and unlawfull meanes which a Phisition in those times used,[8] as the mayd hath affirmed upon her oath. Which we would never have mentioned to the reader but for necessary regard of the truthe least any man supposing her relief to have come by naturall meanes should quit the causes of every supernaturall thing. And yet we must say somwhat more, seing we are bound to say thus much. We beleeve it had ben easier for him, if he had joyned in praier and fasting, which he so scorned and reproched, for moving it, yea though he had reaped the imputation of a Puritan for his labor; rather then to have used faithles charmes [Fol. 8r] to get the glory of a cure, which his Conscience tould him the Arte of Phisicke could not reach. But how can you beleeve saith our Saviour Christ when you seeke glory one of another, and seeke not the glory of God alone.

Hitherto the Parents kept Mary Glovers affliction secret, acquainting none therewith but som of their neighboures, like faithfull Christians also disclayming, to take any benefitt by unlawfull remedies. Whilest she remayned thus in som mittigation of her fitts, beholde, occasion was taken one day of her Mother, to have her abroad with her into the Citie. As they went, they met with that

6

wretched woman Elizabeth Jackson, After whose view Marie was
so troubled, that constrayned was the Mother to retorne speedelie
home, and so relinquish their further intended Jorney. At home
Marie fell into a double encreased fitt:[9] which dayly proceeded with
many uncouth novelties, and strange Caracters, of a newe stamp,
though out of the old forge. for about three of the clocke, [Fol.
8v] every second day, she sodenlie changed in her countenance, becoming more pale and wan, her eyes deadish, her Chin falling into her
bosome, with a stiffnes in all her parts. And being laied upon her
bed, her face upwards, there apeared in her brest, a notable heaving,
or rising, with successive fallings, very frequent, and fast going; and
lying thus, now stretched all at length, she was sodenlie and all at
once (no part moving thereto more then other) snatched from her
pillow, a foote length or thereabouts, downe towards the beds feete.
Then lying thus with her head and shoulders lowe, and at all
disadvantage, by reason of shooting downe from the pillowe, she
would gaine to arise and sit upright, without the help of any hand
thereto. Her arising being very slow, and by long degrees, with her
chin bent downe to her brest, her face and neck somwhat swolne.
When her body thus sate upright, then did her neck strech out much
longer then naturall, her face and neck apearing more lanke, at that
time, and thinner then presently before: although in her rising, as
also before, her [Fol. 9r] necke, armes and all the rest of her body,
were stiffe, yet now being risen, she could turn her head somtime
one way, sometime another; now looking sowerly or frowning,
then cherefully or smyling; her eyes all this time fast shut, and
turned upward into her head: using likewise her armes very nimbly,
somtime as though she floorished like a fencer, somtime as though
she drew a bow to shoote, and that towards sondry places. So did
she, then, play with her fingers; Now as though she had an harpe,
then as though she had a payer of virginalls before her. These being
passed, she sett her fists to her sides and lifted the shoulders,
advancing (withall) her body as though she would daunce: sitting all
this while, dumbe, blinde and senceles. Then did she performe very
nimble and strange motions of her hands, and fingers, sett togeather
somtime before her, som time behind her, and sondenly in a
moment became all over stiffe againe in which stifnes sitting, her
head and brest writhed about, slowlie, towards the beds [Fol. 9v]
head; and there the mouth made many strange anticke formes,

wrything somtyme one waye, somtime an other waie, and then
gaping strangely wyde delivered out of the throte a vyolent blast,
with this sound (*tesh*) in a long accent upon the end; the noyse
whereof amased all that first heard it. and this was thrise so repeated
whilest her head was writhed backward on that side, the aforesaid
sundry strange deformed mouthes, ever passing betweene. Then
from that side to the other side, as much backward the head was
turned, so suddenly and swiftly, as was very admirable to the
behoulders: where likewise the mouth was abused with the same
distortions, gapings and blastings, in figure and number, as before.
After this, her face and brest turned, with the same slownes forward
[Fol. 10r], as at the first they turned backward, untill her face stood
directly forward againe. And finally, her body lay downe, with that
sembable [? illeg.] slowe motion, whereby it formerly rose up. All this
is but a discription, of the severall streynes and passages, belonging to
one Course of her now double increased fitt; which course was
repeated all over, precisely, six times, before she returned to her selfe
againe, which happened at six of the Clocke in the Evening.

Two or three points, which were dilligently observed in this
kinde of fitt, are worthy here to be noted ere we passe on further.

It is here said, that her body was laide down againe, by the like
slow motion, in which it arose to sitt up. One tyme, as it was so
goinge [Fol. 10v] downe, some there present, desiring to see what
would befall, if she were thrust downe at once, did suddainely
(laying their hand on her brest) beare her body downe to the pillowe,
but as thus, her body went downe, so her foote rose up, from the bed
(the stiffenes was such throughout all her body) and their hand being
taken away, the head and brest rose up after, and the feete contrariewise went downe; like as a post or pale [sic] crooked in the midst, and
lying upon the crooked part, if a man treade down this end, the other
end mounteth up, and contrariewise. And after that the body was risen
up againe, in the same height and position it was in, when the hand
was applyed to it, it thenceforth proceeds in its owne ordinary
motion, that was begunne, untill [Fol. 11r] it fully setled downe
upon the pillow. Others againe, an other time, not thrusting her
body downe, at one push so, but yet forcing it down faster then its
ordinary pace, and so leaving her on her pillow, the body did slowly
rise againe, to that place where they began to beare it downe; and
then againe went backward, according to the first begun fashion.

8

Secondly, where her body was layd at length quietlie, betwene some of theis courses of her fitts, the company present wold somtimes fall to prayer; wherein when they pronounced the sixt petition, *Deliver us from evill,* her body would be throwen from the place where it lay, somtime to the beddes head, somtime to the beds side, likelie to have falne of the bed, save that she was rescued [Fol. 11v] and kept, by the standers about her, in which deformed throweing, her body would be strangely writhen, and crooked, backward, or sideway, and remayne so a good space. Or somtime on her belly, untill a little before her body should begin, to aryse, into a new course of abused motions and deformed gestures, as is before described. For against that instant, would the body softly turne, till it lay on the backe; and thenceforth arise by a long delayed motion, as is said.

Thirdly, one time it fell out, that the body having ben cast out of order, at the prayer, it began to rise againe in the middle, before the body was well turned upon the backe, one side so rysing before the other, which seemed would be very hard to be done; notwithstanding being both sidewayes, and her body bent round forward, her head towards her belly, it recovered up, to sitt upon one hip, but before that her head began to turne, into those deformed [Fol. 12r] motions, her body fell downe upon the right side, where it was about halfe a quarter of an hower, before it could recover up againe; her arising seeming (as it must needs be) with much inforcinge the instruments of the body. Som of the behoulders thought it was with the help of her right arme, because that in risinge they felt it beare upon the bed, but there was no reason in that, considering that in this time, all her parts were senceles and stiffe. Now returne we to our story.

After all these things thus passed,[10] Mary Glover being one day at Sheriffe Glovers house, brought thither to meet face to face with Elizabeth Jackson (on a day wherein Marie was newly before come out of one of these great fitts) before she could speak six words, in the presence of that woman, she was taken with another farr differing fitt, which shalbee [Fol. 12v] described in the last place. This kinde of fitt, and this only, she also had at sundry other times, by occasion of bringing that old woman to her: as shalbe by som instances, more specially delivered hereafter. Before we passe this place, the reader is to be advertised, that as Marie Glover was now,

9

by this incounter, before the magistrate, come to have two severall strange vexations; one called ordinary, because it kept every other day, about a certaine hower as aforesaid, the other extraordinary, in as much as it came at all howers and dayes when the old woman came to her, and not els; so was her formerly described ordinary fitt, strengthened and lengthened, yea with som new addicons, more and more augmented by her contagious coming to her. And sith that to write every degree of growing of that ordinary fitt, were to put the reader to much more paynes, and yet never the better bootie unto the truth, we shall therefore imploy the remaynder of this history, first upon the ordinary fit [Fol. 13r] as it was advanced unto his full height and strength, wherein it continued to the day of her deliverance; and then upon the extraordinary, as it was observed to fall out, both when the witch was openly, as also, when she was most secretly brought in unto her.

Every second day, about twelve of the clocke,[11] her eyes were drawen up into her head, her tongue close restrained to the bottom of her mouth, and her nether jawe, with uncouth widenes, fell open by fitts, and closed againe, her neck streching out, and she walking up and downe, betweene two persons leading her, untill her left leg becam senseles. Then was she laid upon a bed, and presently her left hand (which untill then, was at perfect libertie) was snatched into a fist, and close couched to her side: where it lay, without sense or motion, so hard held, that it could not, without som good violence, be plucked from thence. In like maner all the left side; saving that the leg lay streched outright; the toes not [Fol. 13v] contracted as the fingers of the hands, nor altogeather so stiffe. The whole side reteyned an equall naturall temper, and the pulse unchanged; except that it went a litle faster; her hearing also, on that side, perished: yet her understanding, togeather with her hearing, on the other side, remayned. But as the parts of that left side, were thus stiffe and congealed; so contrariewise, the arme and leg of the right side, were so limber and light, to move, as no resolved members use to be, nor any naturally constituted member of such magnitude, in health, can be. Yet not so at all times, alike, during the quyttnes of her fitt, but (in this respect) diversly, at divers times according to more or lesse moving admiration. After that she had thus, lyen a while, lifting up that right hand towards heaven, (which she could move, though not the arme) as craving ayd from thence, and breathing at great libertie, suddenly there would arise a swelling in her belly, as [Fol. 14r] great as a football: (the swelling not being so great there before, but a great waight very sensible to her) then, as when a man standing astride upon a quake mire, pressing downe one foote, the other boundeth up, even so, did certaine motions, betwene the belly and brest, rebounding wise, answere One an other, for five or six returnes. Which was very painefull unto her as out of her fit she would testifie. Then the mover seemed, by a visible gliding along the brest, to mount up the channell bone, where making the stay of halfe a minnute, it passed into her throate, whereupon suddenly her head was snatched backward, with her Chin upward; whereat was a stay of her breath for a litle pause, but very shortly she recovered to drawe it againe, and beate strongly on the bed, with her right leg, and upon her throate (if she were let alone) with her right hand: rebounding also with her body oftentimes, and roring with a hoarse and quavering voyce: yea, whilst she was pressed downe, [Fol. 14v] upon the throat (which usually she was at this time) with the strength and waight of a strong man; moe hands then his owne, being somtimes added unto him. After sundry, but uncertaine number of those roaring cries and tossings, whilest her throate was compressed, the swelling of her throat would geve a suddaine joult, downe into her brest, and working there as before, but a few turnes, made (againe) a speedy repasse to the throat; and so an other crying fitt, beating her body, all as before. Then eft soones fled into the brest, and eftsoones returned to the throte in one and the same maner, above one hundereth severall tymes, ere she attayned rest: every of those returns conteyning five, or six, or moe, strong cryings, and violent plungings, with her body; and allwayes when the last came, she gave a signe, at the very moment of the concluding of it, by lifting up her right hand. This storme being past, a calme ensued for more then a quarter, or (very neare) [Fol. 15r] halfe an hower. Which calme was not free libertie, but a condition of quyetlying, like that she was in, before the rising in her belly and brest began. After which time, an other rising, and moving, in her belly and brest beginneth, and proceedeth by the same passages, and returnes, in all respects, as is before described. Thus, with the intermissions of scarce halfe an hower, her Cryings and plungings hould on, from two (yea at last one) of the Clock after noone, or before, untill six, seaven or eight at night, before the whole fitt began to decline; which then was in this maner.

11

At the end of her Crying pangs,[12] in a very moment, upon the lifting up of her hand, in signe of the ceasing, the same hand which was so limber and light before, would, starting wise, pitch into the form of a dyall hand; that is, the thumbe and forefinger being extended, and the rest clasped in: at which instant, she became much alike stiffe on both sides, and was like [Fol. 15v] wise deprived of all maner sense and feeling; as by all convenient proofs, that might be made, hath ben apparant. This hand, which now, togeather with the arme, was congealed stiffe (and therefore made to natures purposes of motion unserviceable) did, even then, begin to move upwards, towards the mouth; but with such leysure, as may well be compared to the hand of a Clock, that poynteth the howers: all the rest of her body lying still, her breathing and temper quyet, and perfect, untill the hand was risen so high, as to be equall with the elbow, you could not have discerned the moving; but after that tyme, it was discernable to the eye. After halfe an hower, or three quarters, this poynting finger approached neere the mouth; somtime, in coming up, it touched first in the neck; and then (as if it knew it were wrong) it would creep up by the chin; so, when it was com to touch the nether lip, both the lipps deformedly grinning, [Fol. 16r] did open, and so soone as it touched the teeth, (which from the beginning of her start, were now so clasped, the upper range over the nether, as she could not possiblie set them so much over, when she was well, as hath been proved,) the mouth flew wyde open; in went the finger, as far as the hand could permit it, and imediatly returned, by a soft stealing pace, though not so slow as it came up: never ceasing, till it came to the very place, from whence it first began his motion: where it quyetly rested; but held his forme, position and stiffnes still; the teeth also were locked fast againe, at the very parting with the poynt of the finger. This hand being thus lodged, and the behoulders having a litle pause (as it were) to wype and ease their eyes; behould the left hand, which from two of the Clocke had remayned hard convulsed, or drawne togeather into a fist, with great leasure, thrusteth forth the thombe; and after that the forefinger; and so proceedeth [Fol. 16v] to the mouth; and againe returneth to his place, as did the right hand: with these two only poynts of difference, that this moved upwards a litle more manifestly, and constantly, without interruptions, then the other; and that this finger, spending a little longer time in the mouth, then

12

the other, was ceazed upon by the teeth, in his returne, and was ever fayne to be snatched out, by some assistant, that wayted to that purpose. Here by the way, is generally to be observed, in the going up and downe of theis handes, that if a stander by did violently (as to gaine time) thrust the hand upward, as it was ascending, or yet downward, as it was descending, it would leasurely returne to the same place it was in, before the constraint, and from thence, proceed forth to the motion it had begun. Also, if either hand were pulled out of the mouth, before the time [Fol. 17r] in it would againe, as though all complements should be accomplished. Now, when the lefte hand is lodged in his former place, then the three fingers of the right hand, which was clasped in, unclaspe, and stretch forth, one after an other, by strange order; which no sooner doe obteyne their former libertie, but she retourneth[13] againe her understanding, the same moment. The mayde being demanded, when she was out of those fitts, how she felt her selfe in all this passage, answered, that she perceaved suddenly; all her sences to be taken from her, at that start, and that they returned also againe, suddenly, but touching what time, or actions passed betwene, she utterly knew nothing. This done, the other three fingers of the left hand, opened by the same method, that the right did. Next that, her eyes; but with many workings [Fol. 17v] and motions of her forehead, twinckelings of her eylidds, and turning of the head to every side. When by such strife as is said, the sight of her eyes were neerehand brought to their proper place, then softly she conveied the right hand, which lay lower, up to the left; that they might meet about the middle of the brest. Then the eyes againe wrought a little, and the right hand was lifted up toward heaven. Next that, she strove to open her mouth, which, by little and little, she obteyned; moving her tong, up and downe, as it were to trye if it were serviceable. Then would she instantly lift up her eyes, and hand, to heaven, and with the signes of a devote minde, and fervent spirit, utter these words:[14] *O Lord I geve thee thankes, that thow hast delivered me, this tyme, and many moe; I beseech thee (good* [Fol. 18r] *Lord) deliver me for ever.* Neither hath she ben able, at any time, to change, or to ad anything to this forme, although she hath many tymes purposed, and indeaovred [sic] it, withall her power.

Assoone as the last word of the prayer aforesaid was out of her lipps, her mouth was fast clasped up againe, as before, her eyes vyolently drawen up, and the thombe and forefinger of her left hand, drawen a new into a fist. Then also appeared (afresh) those risings and reboundings in her brest, and belly, and so proceeded to torment her, and make her a like terror to all beholders; in the very same maner, as hath (already) ben described: the difference being only in this, that theis courses of pangs, after her prayer, were more strong and violent, then those before it. This done, she lyeth still, and laboureth againe, to recover her eyes, with such working in the eyes, [Fol. 18v] and forehead, as are before delivered: though not with so much a doe, but in shorter space. Yet this is added more, then in the former opening, that at the perfecte appearing of the eye, there falleth a visible motion like a bird flickering, or mouse running behind a Curten, downe from the Cannell bones, into the belly: according as in like sorte, the same maner of motion was observed, in the Loosening of every joynt of her body, towards the ending of her fitt, as shalbe said hereafter. Her eyes being now opened, she lyeth peaceably, almost halfe an hower; knowing all her frends, but not able to speake one word, nor without payne to open her mouth: presently then, in a moment, her eyes are snatched up againe, the rising and rebounding of her brest and belly returne and she is driven againe, into the former violent courses of panges; which was (at length) numbered to one [Fol. 19r] hundereth and twenty returnes, before it gave over, a most lamentable spectacle to behould.

This second course of pangs, after her prayer, being now at length come to the period, and the usuall signe of ceasing geven, by the lifting up of her hand, she againe recovereth her eyes, with that flickering motion, and suddayne jowlt downe her brest, that is before described. After this, the thomb of her left hand, which was snatched in againe after her speech, by long leysure, extendeth it selfe, and even when it is at the extent, the flickering motion, with a joult, goeth downe her brest. In ail respects so, are the next three fingers set at libertie; but then, the hande is drawen closer to the brest, then before it was, and the litle finger[15] (though now all the rest be extended) is, more strangely drawne within the palme; that joynt thereof, which maketh to [Fol. 19v] the fourming of the back of the hand, sticking out, very far, and sharp. After that the litle finger hath lyen a while, in this position, it offereth to move, but is presently checked and drawen close againe; and so offereth and is

14

Checked, three or fower times. After neere about a quarter of an hower, thus spent, somthing appearinge imediatly under the skinne, made an eminent stirring, and working, betweene the litle finger and the ring finger; not ceassing untill that finger had regayned his full strength: at which instant, the foresaid visible motion, warbleth downe the brest; but twice as great, and evident, as any before. All this strange worke, in the litle finger, hath her selfe seene, stedfastly looked at, and considered (being at that present perfect in her sight and understanding) but felt it not, neither was able to commande anie thing other [Fol. 20r] wise then she saw acted before her eyes. At this time, all her left hand was sensible, then would she winde to and fro, her wrist, her elbow, her shoulder of that side: After that, the wrist, elbow and shoulder of the right arme: for the right hand was well before: and so the joynts of both her leggs, her back, her neck; in a word all the joynts of her body she now turned, and successively loosened, every one of them: having that particular testimony, of a warbling motion, swiftly boutling downe from the Canell bones, at the gayning of their liberty: Yet was not here the end of this sorowfull spectacle: for no sooner were all her joynts thus, out of their former servitude delivered, but they were ceazed on a fresh, and put into a new livery of abusion: even as well might become that proud tyranous Lord, to whom was permitted, though for a very litle season, som such further rule in the region of her body.

[Fol. 20v] Now therefore againe, behould, her eyes drawen up into her head, but withall her armes cast up over her head, and very straight and right stretched out, not abroad, but touching neere togeather: her body and legges also, at the same moment, stretched out at length, in a suddaine stronge motion; that made all the bed to shake. At the first going up, you must imagine the palmes sett one against the other, and the fingers distanced, as wyde as may be; which thus remayning, whilst the behoulders might sufficiently consider that they saw, both the handes and arms turned, with a stately leysure, untill the back of the handes were inward, and the palmes outward; the fingers still extended stiffe, and in their former distances. [Fol. 21r] Neither must you conceipt any shrinking downe of the armes to this motion, but a full extention; nor a writhing outward of her fingers, more then of her handes, nor of her hands, more then of her armes; but that all went equally and

15

uniformly together untill the rounde was halfe performed, and somwhat more. This turne was forward, the thombes coming neere touch, in the beginning of the motion; making thus a litle pause in this uncouth position, back againe with the like statelynes, is the same halfe round turning made; And a mynnutes rest being here also afforded, whilest the palmes of the handes are againe confronted, behould, on a sudden, an other like jerking out of her [Fol. 21v] body and leggs, at length, as is aforesaid; And after that, a turning of the armes and handes, in such Luciferlike ostentation, as before. This was done, during an unruly stiffenes in all her parts, with an absolute voydenes of all sence and understanding: which now, at this period, was brought in place againe, by an arme of power incomparable; even the arme of him, who hath sett just and sure boundes, to the swelling surges of the Seas; beyond which, the proudest waves thereof shall not arise. Here her armes are layed down, decently, by both her sides; and perfect use restored unto them; her eyes open againe, with litle strife, and her handes are lifted upward, in signe of thankfulnes. When she hath lyen thus, quietly, a litle while, though yet she speake nothing, her eye taketh knowledge of her Parents, and [Fol. 22r] acquaintance, that stand behoulding her. At length, she laboreth a litle, with her mouth and throate, and then, there falleth an extraordinary great, and swyfte warbling joult, downe from the throat, to the belly. At which very time, her tongue is untyed, and her lower jawe unlocked, and she beginneth to speake, but so softly, that if ones eare had not byn laied close to her mouth, she could not have byn understood; but beinge so, she was perceaved to utter, a very good and godly prayer, almost halfe an hower continued. Which, out of doubt, was not before learned, but at the present then conceived, both because she repeated many things, and somtimes uttered her petitions, in sort and setting togeather, sutable to the ignorance of a simple mayd. For example: *Lord* [Fol. 22v] teach[16] *me a good use of this thy affliction, yet not as I will, but thy will be done.* Otherwise, and for the most part, her prayer was very fervent, to good purpose, and with great variety of spirit: As for the pardon of her sinnes, the manifestation of the truth, the glory of God, and satisfaction of his Church. Also, for the conversion of the woman, calling God to witnes, that her selfe added nothing to her owne afflictions. Againe, for patience and deliverance in Gods good time, and by his owne holy meanes. Likewise for the curbing of Sathan, if he were an instrument or otherwise, for curing the imperfections of her body. So did she geve God thanks, for all her former deliveries, and this in particular, and for that[17] he had redemed her out of the opinyon of Counterfetting; and in part, satisfied the world in that behalfe. All these, and many moe benefitts, she [Fol. 23r] craved, and thanks giving offered, only in the name and mediation of our Saviour and Redemer Jesus Christ; disclayming her owne merites, and submitting her selfe wholly to the will of God; who hath promised, that all things shall worke togeather for the best, to as many as feare him. In this prayer her voyce by degrees increased, so as at last, it might be heard over all of the bed, where she lay.

After all this, she arose, and with a litle help of leading, walked upon her leggs againe. The end of this fitt, at last, came to be about twelve of the Clocke at midnight; having beganne soone after twelve at noone: in which space, she suffered (at the least) six hundereth returnes of panges, every pange consisting of five (at least) if not six, seaven or moe, greivous, strange, yellinge Cryes, with so manie strong Compressions of her throat, and rebounding and beating with her body and right leg. Yet what time she was [Fol. 23v] fully come to her selfe againe, there remayned no memorable sorenes, or stiffnes in the rest of her body but (specially) none at all, in those principall likely parts, the throat, necke and jawes. A tender sornes only remayned then, and yet sithence her delivery doth,[18] with much tumor and hardnes in her lefte brest; which came by the occasion of one, who coming to see her, in one of her tossing and crying panges, did inconsiderately gripe that brest with his hand, whereof afterward, though she felt no payne whilest she was possessed with the strength of her fitt (for then the lefte side was senceles) yet both in the entering into her fitt, and againe ever at the coming out of the same, her payne therein was extraordinary sharp and fierce, the space of halfe a quarter of an hower.

At length we are come to an end of this [Fol. 24r] hideous and tedious fitt, but have not fully brought her to her resting place; for bee it sooner, or later, after this dayes worke, that she repaireth to her bed, even at lying downe in her naked bed she was ever taken with an other Crying fitt;[19] wherein was no deprivation of her senses, but only her eyes and tongue restrayned, togeather with such a huge extension of her throate, as was monstruous to

17

behould: with Crying yelling and stryving with her body, so as fower were scarse able convenyently to hould her. Out of this fitt, which held about one howers space, she came, by putting first the right finger into her mouth and out agayne roundly; and after that the left; having an imagination, that without so doing, she could not againe recover the use of her tongue. Yet she could not say that she removed, or placed any thinge, [Fol. 24v] with her finger. And alwaies, upon her left finger her teeth would fasten; though not so strongly in this fitt, but that she could, by bringing her other hand to help, pluck it out her selfe. Such a fitt as this, in all respects, is that, which she had at the taking of any kinde of sustenance (except it be small beare) whether it were upon her well or ill day: only the contynuance hereof was som what shorter time. Hitherto our history is furnished to geve every reasonable reader satisfaction in all needfull matters, concerning *Mary Glovers* ordinarie fitts: which came either about a sett hower, as every second day, or at an unset hower; and that both as often as she receaved nourishment, day or night, and also when soever she layed her downe in her naked bed, every sick day.

Now we will descend to the extraordinary fit,[20] which as it affordeth some moe novelties, necessary to be added to the precedent varieties [Fol. 25r] so is it accomplished, with som pregnant particularities, a litle more livelie, lymbing the truth unto us. This fitt seazed on the mayde, only at such times, as that wretched old woman came within the roome where she was. And this also requireth in a two fould sort, to be considered of: namely eyther as the mayde was well, or els evill, at her coming in unto her. For if this mayd were well, at the comming of the ould woman, presently you should have seene her dye away, by degrees, untill she became deprived, both of inward and outward senses; her eyes shut up, her mouth fast locked up; the upper teeth being so far shut over the nether, that the nether could scarsly be seene: her back, necke and limbes, inflexibly stiffe: yet her temper unchanged, and her breathing peaceable and perfect, thus would she lye perpetually, as long as the woman there continued: but if the ould woman [Fol. 25v] came unto her, as she lay upon the bed, especially if she touched her flesh, or her garments, the mayds body would (somtimes) wallow over unto her, other somtimes, rising up in the middle, rebounding wise turne over, unto her, her elbowes being

then most deformedly drawn inwards, and withall plucked upwards, to her Chin; but the handes and wrests, turned downwards,
and wrethed outward; a position well becoming the malice of that
efficient [cause]. This tumbling, or casting over towards the witch,
when she came to the bedside, or touched her, was at the first two
tryalls very palpably playne, and towards her only; Afterwards,
neither was the motion so vehement, nor perpetually towards the
woman; but somtimes towards others also: in this fitt, *the mouth
being fast shut, and her lipps close, there cam a voyce through her
nostrills,*[21] *that sounded very like (especially at som time) Hange her,
or Honge her. The repitition* [Fol. 26r] *whereof, never ceased, so
long as that Elizabeth Jackson was to be found within the compas of
that roofe; and she no sooner departed the house, but the voyce
ceased presently*: the which particular, was divers times, and dilligently observed. Againe, if the same Elizabeth Jackson were
brought unto the Chamber, during the time that Mary lay in one of
her ordenary crying fitts (which thing was upon Consultation, by
certaine discreete persons, at the least two sundry times, upon our
knowledge, attempted and done) by and by, her fitt would alter, all
motions in the belly and breast cease, all returnes of her pangs geve
over, her understanding depart, and all outward feeling be abolished. Then, by litle and litle, more and more, applying your eare
nere to her face, you might have perceaved a voyce whisperingly
com through her nostrills; which both then, and when it atteyned to
the height of it woonted audibilitie, sounded, hang her, or honge
her. This [Fol. 26v] trance and this voyce, never gave over, so longe
as Elizabeth Jackson there contynued, as hath ben said: but so
soone as she is dispatched, from the house, first that voyce
vanisheth, and after one hower, or there aboutes, those ougly
distortions of her parts, and totall stiffnes, proper to this fitt only,
by easie and visible relentings, go away; but then she returneth
(making but a pitifull exchange) into her aforesaid long and
manyfould crying fitts: which proceede, varie and finishe, in all
respects, as above we have described them.

The first experience[22] of this extraordinary fitt was found at
Sheriffe Glovers house, whither both Mary, and the witch was sent
for, on a day of the maydes ordenary fitt, and at such time, as she
was newly recovered out of the fitt: which in those dayes, was not
past fower howers long. There the ould woman, was first spoken

19

withall a parte, then the mayde was brought in, who before she had spoken six wordes, fell downe into [Fol. 27r] this fitt; when as confidently before that, she had desired to be brought, face to face, saying, she was perswaded, Goodwife Jackson had hurt her, and that they should see som token of it, at such time as they were brought togeather: and at this time it fell out, that first that voyce, hang her, or hong her, sounded, all the whyle Elizabeth Jackeson remayned in the house with her.

A second experience of this,[23] was made not long after, Sir John Harte coming to se Mary Glover, on her better day, for, by his warrant, Elizabeth Jackson being brought in, Mary Glover was imediatly taken with one of these fitts; and lying (soone after) senseles, upon her bed, at the touching of the said Elizabeth the senseles body was cast (very strangely) upon her, and that there severall times, upon so many removings of the said Elizabeth, to the other side of the bed, and againe laying her hand upon her. And this was now first observed, as a second challenge the oppressed senseles creature made, to this [Fol. 27v] wicked mediatrice of her wofull affliction.

The like came to passe in a third experiment,[24] made before the *Lady Brunckard*, and in the presence of many Divines and Phisitions. *Hetherto* the senseles body was cast, with great violence, towardes Elizabeth Jackeson, when she touched her, and towards her only: in so much, as that the said Elizabeth would be merveylously amazed thereat, as was observed by her most gastely lookes, panting breathing, choaking speech, and fearfull tremblinge: which being joyned with aboundance of outfacinge speeches, and impudent lyinge, were nothing els but notes of a ruyned conscience.

[25]The fowerth experiment was made before Mr Crooke then Recorder of London the 18th of October 1602. Who by warrant, caused both parties to appeare before him, in his Chamber, at the Inner Temple, at two of the Clocke that day in the afternoone. There the mayde and her mother, with certaine other weomen, appearing [Fol. 28r] first, were sent togeather into an upper Chamber; after that Mr Recorder had gravely protested before the mayd, that she should looke up unto God, feare him, and not make her selfe a false Accuser of any body. Soone after this, came Elizabeth Jackson, and sundry weomen with her. Mr Recorder with like gravitie, also admonished her, not to out face the truth, but

rather to acknowledge her fault. Then he choose out a woman both aged, homely, grosse bodyed, and of lowe stature, very comparable to Elizabeth Jackson. Her did he cause to put on Elizabeth Jacksons hatt, and a muffler on her face, and then brought her up into the Chamber where Mary Glover was, caused Mary to walke by her, two or three returnes, and to touch the woman once, and againe the second time; saying (then when he saw no chaunge happen) I am glad to see this Mary; I hope thou shalt touch her freely many times hereafter, and never be affrayde: with mo[re] suchlike wordes, implying, that her feare had [Fol. 28v] ben the cause of her harmes hitherto. Then he led downe that woman, and brought up Elizabeth Jackson shortly after; having on the other womans hat, with a Cloak and muffler; so as none could know who she was. And verily this woman made no sooner her first stand, in the lower end of the chamber, but the Maydes Countenance altered: but then she beying brought forward unto the mayd, and the mayde led towards her, there was no more time, nor oportunity lefte, for new maskers to enter. Thus was this senseles image throwen upon a bed, having that voyce in her nostrills, spoken of before. At this time, the bed being compassed with many witnesses, Mr Recorder sent for a candle, made a pin hot in the flame, and applyed it to her Cheeke and after that (with a new heating) neere unto her eye, to see, if she would drawe togeather her eyebrowes, or liddes, or make any semblant of feeling, but she did not. Then he tooke paper somwhat writhed, and setting fyre thereon, put [Fol. 29r] the flame to the inside of her right hand, and there held it, till the paper was consumed. In like maner he proceeded with a second, and a third paper, so as her hand (as well appeared afterwards) was effectually burned, in five severall places. When he saw this setled insensibillitie, he proved the fyre upon the Witches hand, who cryed upon him not to burne her: Mr Recorder replied, Why cannot you as well beare it as she, Who (as you say) doth but counterfett? Oh no (quoth the Witch) God knowes she doth not Counterfett. Then Mr Recorder caused Elizabeth Jackson to kneele downe, and say the Lords prayer: therein (as she ever used to doe) she skipped *Deliver us from evill* which the Recorder reproving her for, comanded her to say it againe. Which she preversly denyed but with many soft wordes, and gentle perswasions, at length, he obteyned; and when she pronounced those wordes *Deliver us from evill*, the body of the mayd rebounded in the middle, as at other times also, when any prayed by her, and used those wordes, in time of her totall [Fol. 29v] senselessenes (for at all other times her body lay quyetly to all prayers.) the rest of all this fitt, was (in all respects) like as hath ben described: and the woman being once dischardged the house, and sent to prison, the voyce in Maryes nostrills ceased, as at other tymes.

Heere, for the finding out of truth, two poyntes of advantage were well gayned, through Mr Recorders wisedome, in thus guiding this matter: the one that *feare* was not the cause of this her strange affliction, at the presence of the woman: for the first woman presented unto her, seemed as like as the second, and the second no more like than the first: and the very disguising offered matter of fear at first. Also what could she tell how many he would prove her with before he brought the suspected partie in deed? Yea so well dissembled was this carriage, as that divers weomen of [Fol. 30r] credit, neighbours that came with Mary Glover, and knew the widow Jackson well, offer to depose that they could not discerne whether the former Woman was not the second time brought up, or the Widowe Jackson, or some third. The *other* poynt gayned was this, that all might know, the mayde did not counterfett her misery.

The Fift and last experyence, of this kind of[26] fitt, was in the Session house, in the day of Elizabeth Jacksons tryall; the whole proceeding whereof, we will a litle more largely stand upon, then we have done this former instances; And so shut up this history. The first day of December 1602 Mary Glover was brought, on her good day, to the Sessions house, to geve evidence against Elizabeth Jackson, indicted there, that day, of the horrible cryme of Witch-craft: the said Mary being placed [Fol. 30v] with her face towards the bench (and not seinge the old woman who was among the Prisoners in the docke) felt a commanding power seaze upon her, and therefore, as interrupted in her purposed speech, cryed, where is shee? where is she? At which words, som of the bench cryed, shee counterfetteth: and withall, bade her proceede in her evidence: which was as she indeavored, still she was interrupted, and so againe said, where is shee, that troubleth me? Casting her hand about withall, and so, with faltering speech, sunke downe (before she had delivered xl words in evidence) into this aforesaid dead and senseles case; her body and Chinebone being so much writhed, as a with is

22

writhen, that the right huckle bone was turned forward, so far over
to the left side, as that it wanted not the bredth of a hand, of the
place, where the lefte should stand; being gone so farre, beyond
[Fol. 31r] the right line of the chinne, when she was layed on her
back. This very distortion in all respects as it is here described,
appeared likewise, in all her long fitts, both when she was in sense,
and when she was voyd of all understanding. When she was in
sense, as namely, at such times, as her body being shrunck downe,
towardes the bedds feet, in her tossing pangs, was lifted upon the
pillowes againe: and when she was voyde of understanding; namely,
when her body had lately before rebounded, at som touchings,
heretofore spoken of, or at the sixt petition of the Lords prayer,
deliver us from evill. Now also was the accustomed voyce, *hang
her*, audible in her nostrills. Thus was she carryed into a Convenyent chamber, by three strong men, who affirmed that they
never caryed a heavyer burthen. When the Justices went to dinner,
[Fol. 31v] Elizabeth Jackson was led out of the Docke, to Newgate,
it was dilligentlie observed, that for this time, the foresaid voyce in
Maries nostrills ceassed; And that after one hower, the woman
being returned, that voyce returned also. The body of Marie Glover
in the mean time, had remayned in the same plight aforesaid,
without any change. After dinner the Lo. Anderson Mr Recorder of
London, Sir William Cornwallis, Sir Jerome Bowes, and divers
other Justices went up into the Chamber, to see the mayde; before
whome went the Towneclearke, with som officers; with thundring
voyces crying; bring the fyre, and hot Irons, for this Counterfett;
Come wee will marke her, on the Cheeke, for a Counterfett: but the
senseles mayde apprehended none of these things. After the Justices
had considered the figure, and stiffenes of her body, Mr Recorder
againe [Fol. 32r] with a fyred paper burnt her hand, untill it
blistered. Then was Elizabeth Jackson sent for, At the instant of
whose coming into the Chamber, that sound in the maides nostrills,
which before that time, was not so well to be distinguished, seemed
both to them in that Chamber, and also in the next adjoyning, as
plainely to be discerned, *Hang her*, as any voyce, that is not uttered
by the tongue it selfe can be. The voyce likewise beinge lifted up
into a farr lowder accent, then accustomed. The Lord Anderson
then comanded Elizabeth Jackson to come to the bed, and lay her
hand upon the maide; which no sooner was done, but the maides

body (which untill then, had never removed from the place where it layed) was presently throwen, and casted with great vyolence. The Judge willed the woman to say the *Lordes prayer*; which by no meanes she could go through with, though often tryed; but still stood in the midle being not hable to say, *forgeve us our trespasses* [Fol. 32v] nor *Leade us not into temptation*, whereupon he caused her to say the Christian beleefe; which she began in this manner: *I beleve in God the father almighty, maker of heaven and earth, and in Jesus Christ his only sonne; which was conceived, by the Holy Ghost*, leaving out *our Lord*; which shee could not, by any meanes, be brought to bring forth of her selfe. Also when she came to these wordes *the Comunion of Saincts, the forgivenes of Sinnes*, she ever said, *The communion of sainctes, the Comission of sinnes*; and could never say the *forgevenes of Sinnes*, but only, when she was caused to speake it, after another. And it was there observed, that whensoever by anothers inducement (as taking the wordes out of their mouth) she uttered that petition, *Leade us not into temptation*, the maids body was tossed as before. The which also it did now (and so only heretofore) at the wordes *Deliver us from evill*: which words, at this time, the ould Woman could utter, leaping over the former: [Fol. 33r] Although at all times of tryall, before this day, it was contrary. In like sort, was the mayds body tossed, whilest the woman said the beliefe, at the words, *he descended into hell*.

All these Consultations being past, the said[27] woman was sent awaie, and they proceeded to their evidences. which in these principall points were urged against her. 1. The[28] maner of the maydes sickeninge, upon the Curses that this woman gave her, when she came to her howse, and the strange fitts and Cases which thereafter ensued. 2. The maner of one[29] fitt, which took her six weeks after the first, at the Coming of the woman, whilest the mayde was eating of bread: whereupon the mayd, ever had a fitt, upon any taking of sustenance afterward. 3. Her cursed and[30] prophesing threatenings, every taking effect, Which Judge Anderson observed, as a notable [Fol. 33v] propertie of a Witch. 4. Her strange fitts every[31] second day, and the wonderfull change, that ever happened to her, at the entrance of the woman into the rome, where she lay in her fitt: with the aforesaid voyce, alwaies beginning at the womans coming in, and leaving upon her departure. 5. The[32] maydes strange fitts at all other times, in the presence of that woman. 6. That a certen[33] *Preacher*,[34] willing to admonish the said Elizabeth Jackson of her lewde tongue, went one time to her house, assoone as he came in, she very intentively fixt her eyes upon him, and standing faced him; he being now prepared in minde to open his mouth, and speake unto her, had suddenly his speech taken from him, his necke became stiffe, and his Chin borne inwards into his bosome, his knees (withall) yeelding under him, as though he should fall. He thought it was time for him to rouse up his spirit, in speciall maner, and make use of his faith, and in so [Fol. 34r] doing, God gave him to prevayle: but so he departed from thence, without speaking any word, and was not quyeted in two howers after. [35]The .7. poynt urged was, that the same Preacher conferring with the old woman, afterwards in prison, could by no meanes cause her, to rehearse the beliefe, but with those grosse defects, and depravations above mentioned. Nay, she knew not the beleefe, but still offered in steed thereof to say the Lords prayer: And in saying of the Lords prayer; could never, of her owne accord, say, *Deliver us from evill.* The .8. matter was[36] the markes, which were found in divers places of her body, which were testified under the hands of the women, that searched her, not likely to grow of any disease; but such as are like the markes which are described to be in Witches bodyes. The .9. evidence was this, that one Elizabeth Burges,[37] who had once witnessed a word, on Mary Glovers behalfe, against this old woman, and had ben therefore threatned by her, to be pulled downe, coming one [Fol. 34v] day (with certaine prunes in her mouth which she was eatinge) to the said ould woman, was suddenly so taken, that she was not able to swallow one downe, but also fell on vomiting; which contynued for 3 weeks afterward, upon all sustenance of meat receaved. Among other times it happened, that once this old woman came by, and seing the same Elizabeth Burges so doing, wished that she might cast up her heart, gutts and all, adding thees wordes, Thou shortly, shalt have in thee an evill spirit too. This Elizabeth Burges, the next night following, was troubled with a Vision, in likenes of a fox; the second night, in likenes of an ougly black man, with a bounch of keyes in his hand, intysing her to go with him, and those keyes would bring her to gould enough; the third night it came in the likenes of a mouse, which troubled her more then any of the former: but by faithfull praier, assisted therein by her Master and Mistress, through the mercy and goodnes [Fol. 35r] of God, she was delivered from them all. Yea this Elizabeth Burges standing now to geve this evidence to the Jury, being faced by the witch, standing in the Docke, and bidden to speake out (with adding these words thow wilt be sicke, and cast againe anon) had at that instant, her speech taken from her, her mouth drawen to a side, and so remayned for a space unable to speake: but after that, with much contension of spirit, she had recoverd speech, and geven in this evidence, it behoved her to be led into a Chamber, where she was very evill, as the witch had threatened; and after that, was led home weake, faynte and Casting, benummed in all her body, hardly able to stand, and never yet to this day recovered her perfect libertie againe. The 10th[38] that her cursing, long before this time,[39] had ben observed to have a mischevous consequent: For having washed Clothes to one of the Lady Bonds men, and come to his lodging for money, he being then gon out of the towne, she saide, is he gone? I pray god [Fol. 35v] he may breake his necke, or his legge, before he com againe: and in that jorney, the man broke his leg accordingly. [40]The 11. that the said Elizabeth Jackson hath accustomed, to go with others, to fortune tellers; that her selfe hath confessed, she went once, with her daughter, and another time, with one Elizabeth Cooke; who as shee saith, did at that time geve xl^s to have her fortune tould her. [41]The 12 was a testimonie, geven in disproofe of their opinions, that held this maydens case but a naturall disease: which was that Mary Glover being one time, in a dead senseles fitt, in the presence of that old woman, whilest many were admiring her heavines being such, as two could scarsly lift up her head, upon a suddaine (being againe assayed) she was found more light then a naturall body, of that quantitie could be: which to prove further, a godly honest gentleman,[42] putting his armes under body, not only lifted her up from the bed, easily, [Fol. 36r] but also turning himselfe about, with her, lying upon his armes, made a shew of her, unto the rest in the Chamber, to consider; affirming to them all, of his present feelinge, that she semed to him, but as a curten throwen overthwart his armes. So he layed her downe, on the bed; and very shortly after, proving againe, found as much admirable heavines as is aforesaid. These matters, by this gentleman and the rest, beinge geven in, upon their others, *Two Phisitions, namely Doctor Hering, and Doctor Spencer*, being served by writt (according to the maner of the Court) to appeare that day, and yeeld their opinions, touching Mary Glovers case, resolutely affirmed, that they estemed it a case, which proceeded of som cause supernaturall; having stranger effects, then either the mother, or any other naturall disease hath ever ben observed to bring forth. Doctor Hering propounded[43] among many others, as fittest for the assembly to [Fol. 36v] judge of, theis instances following: The strange motion of her hand to her mouth, in her ordinarie fitt, that at the touching of her mouth with her finger, it opened and shut againe, at so strickt a measure of time; That her mouth opened at an other so curious a Circumstance, to speake so many, and such words, and no others, nor no moe: That she fell downe into a farre differing fitt, at her best times, so soone as that Elizabeth Jackson came into the house, where the maide was: That if the same Elizabeth Jackson, were brought in secretly, during the time of her ordinary fitt, she should be changed presently, into that extraordinary senseles fitt, and that uncouth voyce in her nostrills would never cease, so long as Elizabeth Jackeson remayned in the house, where the mayd lay. And lastly That in the time of the Lordes prayer, at the pronouncing of the last petition, *Deliver us from evill*; her body, if it then lay in any senseles traunce, would rebound up in the middle. Doctor Spencer[44] argued from the improbabilitie of necessary causes, in [Fol. 37r] so young a mayde, as also from the disproportioned moving in her belly, which was not so uniformely a risinge or bearing upward, but in a rounder and narrower compasse, playing up and downe, as with a kind of easie swiftenes, that certainly it did not truly resemble the mother; howsoever som accidents seemed to carie cullour that way. He stood also upon the varietie of the fitts, upon the occasion of the womans presence. Against these, stood up[45] Doctor Argent, and Doctor Jordayne, two Phisitions, with a certaine Doctor of Divinitie, men not served with writtes for the Court, as the order is. This Divine laboured to purge Elizabeth Jackson, of being any cause of Mary Glovers harme. These Phisitions sought earnestly, to make the case a meere naturall disease: and unto these, though after a certaine wavering sort, two other phisitions there present, seemed to incline; as though they would not, though they could, be contrary. But how well they acquited themselves, in the sight of God, that day, I leave it here to others, to conjecture; and to their owne [Fol. 37v] consciences to witnes. But above all others, Doctor

Jordain earnestly contended with reasons, which when they were delivered argued no somuch a naturall disease, as som minde (rather) of dissimulation, and counterfetting, in the afflicted partie: and so it was taken generally, by those that heard him. The rest which they saide, to proove it naturall; were certaine Symptomes which they picked out of her ordinary long fitt, which seemed to have some resemblance with those, that arise from certen affects of the mother: but to the great difficulties aforesaid objected, they gave no man, that we know of, any satisfaction at all. The Lord Anderson, hearing Doctor Jordaine to often insinuat, some feigning, or dissembling fashions in the maide and withall, so much to beat upon these wordes; *for these causes, I thinck it may be naturall; and these accidents and Symptoms for ought I see bee naturall:*[46] pressed him to answere directly, whether it were naturall or supernaturall. He said, that in his conscience he thought it was altogeather naturall. What do you call it quoth the Judge? *Passio Hysterica* said the Doctor. Can you cure it? I cannot tell: I will not undertake it, but I thinck fitt tryall should be made thereof. *Lord Anderson,* Doe you thinke she Counterfetteth? *D. Jordeyn* [Fol. 38r] No, in my Conscience, I thinke she doth not Counterfett: Lord Anderson, Then in my conscience, it is not naturall: for if you tell me neither a Naturall cause, of it, nor a naturall remedy, I will tell you, that it is not naturall.

After this pawsing a while, the *Lord Anderson*[47] spake to the Jewry in effecte as followeth. The Land is full of Witches; they abound in all places: I have hanged five or sixe and twenty of them; There is no man here, can speake more of them then my selfe; fewe of them would confesse it, som of them did; against whom the proofes were nothing so manifest, as against those that denyed it. They have on their bodies divers strange marks, at which (as som of them have confessed) the Devill sucks their bloud; for they have forsaken god, renounced their baptisme, and vowed their service to the Divill; and so the sacrifice which they offer him, is their bloud. This woman hath the like markes, on sundry places of her body, as you see testified [Fol. 38v] under the hands of the women, that were appointed to search her. The Devill is a spirit of darknes, he deales closely, and cuningly, you shall hardly finde any direct proofes in such a case, but by many presumptions and Circumstances, you may gather it. When they are full of cursing, use their tongue to speake mischeevously, and it falls out accordingly, what greater presumption can you have of a Witch? This woman hath that property: She is full of Cursings, she threatens and prophesies, and still it takes effect: She must of necessitie, be a Prophet, or a Witch. Their malice is great, Their practises devilish, and if we shall not convince [sic] them, without their own confession, or direct proofes, where the presumptions are so great, and the Circumstances so apparant, they will, in short tyme, overrun the whole land. The mayde now afflicted I have seene, and you have beheld. Here he repeated the tryall, himself had made, as above written; saying farther to the Phisitions; you [Fol. 39r] talke of the mother, I pray you, have you ever seen or heard of the mother, that kept it [sic] course unchangeably, every second day, and never missed; and yet that chaungeth his course upon the presence of some one person; as this doth, at the presence of this woman. Divines, Phisitions, I know they are learned and wise, but to say this is naturall, and tell me neither the cause, nor the Cure of it, I care not for your Judgement: geve me a naturall reason, and a naturall remedy, or a rush for your phisicke. The Judge having ended, Mr Recorder[48] delivered unto the Jury, the tryall that himselfe had made, at his Chamber, in the temple, as hath bene before sett downe faithfully. Whereupon he inferred, that it was neither upon fear, nor counterfetting. And as for naturall (quoth he) no man can heere prove it, nor in their greatest judgement, alleage any probable reason, but that it is supernaturall, *and in dede* through witchcraft. The presumptions and probabilities (as we all see) are [Fol. 39v] very great and pregnant.

The minds of the bench were settled, whereupon the Jewry went togeather, and shortly returned Elizabeth Jackson, guilty of witchcraft. The sentence was pronounced of a yeeres imprisonment, and fower tymes therein, to stand on the pillory, and confesse this her trespasse. Now after the witch was caried away, the voyce in the mayds nostrills ceased, and out of that deformed stiffenes, and senselessnes, wherein, for the space of eight howers she had layen tyed, her body returneth to be tossed, plunged, and varyed, with strange vicissitudes, lamentable Cryings, and most remarkeable formes of motion, as hath ben declared: untill at length, the supreme Comander of men and Angells, good and bad, did shine upon her, with his favorable countenance, as he was wont; and by this particular deliverance, and many others, gave her thirsting soule a pledge of a finall and absolute, if her faith followed him patiently, and feinted not.

[Fol. 40r] [49]As at all times, even from the beginning of Mary Glovers first affecting with witchery, her case every tyme, grewe a degree worse, that she had any meting with this wicked woman; so from this tyme, of the Arraignment, above all others, her ordenary fitt (for that extraordinary one was never seen any more, there being no occasion after this day to bringe the parties togeather any more) was augmented, both in length and strength, above measure: so as there appeared som just feare of her life, the fitt extending (at length) to about twelve howers tyme: in which, she had, at the least, six great courses of panges; every one of these consisting of one hundereth, or one hundereth and twenty short returnes; every return conteyning, five, or six, or moe grevous panges; mixed with most strang, and irresistable beating, and rebounding of her right leg, and body. We found likewise at [Fol. 40v] this season, a new and subtill stratageme of Sathan, to take away her life, although not with his owne hand, (for that, as well appeared, was beyond his comission) yet by those, who did som offices about her: for they that held downe her throat, in her panges, if they applyed not their handes timely ynough, her body would so rebound, and disorder, as that they could not be able, afterward, during that pange, in seemely sorte to rule it: Againe, if they came never so litle too soone, they strangled her. Divers, and that were accompted chiefe ones, having often well performed that office aforetime, were now, by this experience, so affrighted, that they durst no more medle with it. Which things considered, togeather with the woefull misery of the Parents,[50] and that her case being publiqly resolved to be supernaturall, for which no Corporall phisicke can serve, it might be a shame for Christians, to suffer a daughter of the Church, thus to lye in the bonds of Sathan, themselves gazing thereat, but not applying themselves to such meanes as Christ hath left in his Church, and so in their hands, to use in her behalfe: upon this (I say) and suchlike considerations, sundry godly ministers, and other devoute Christians consulted, and agreed [Fol. 41r] of a reverent assembling, and joynt humbling of them selves before the Lord, in prayer with fasting, on her behalfe. Whilest these things were ordering the adverse parties to this cause, not resting in this sentence of publique Judgement, both procured som stay of the execution, and provoked the Magistrate, to urge the Parents to deliver their daughter, to the hands of those Phisitions, which held her case naturall, and had som hope to cure her. But thus much was seene into the unfittnes of it: First, that it was unreasonable, after a publique tryall and Judgement passed, on the case, to call it into question againe, for three or fower mens sake, which contended for naturall. 2ly That seinge the Phisitions, that were to deale with her, refused to make us, that were of the Contrary Judgement, privie to their practises, it could not, but be suspicious, that rather then fayle of their glory, they would have done or permitted, some thinge more, then lawfull phisicke had taught them; especially the suspition in this behalfe, having gotten some firme grounde already, upon the practise of som other, as unsuspected, in the Comon opinion of the world, as they. Thirdly, in as much as there could be no certenty of tyme prefixed, for the proofe of their skill, it seemed not reasonable, that whilest the patience of the Judges, and those that were resolved, should be thus abused, with uncertainties, the life of the poore miserable mayd, should so longe tyme lye in jeopardie. Som [Fol. 41v] (at leaste) of these reasons were delivered to that Magistrat; and withall this offer, from som of the contrary Phisitions; that now, for further satisfaction of all men, tryall of law being made, we woulde also make tryall of arguments, with them that did resist us; referring our selves, for the ordering and determyning of the whole matter, (so that the dispute might be by writing) to the disposition of our Superiors. This course by that Magistrat, was not misliked, but whilest that stood to be signified unto, and deliberated with, others of great place, and we were preparing our minds for that purpose, the gracious time was com; wherein the eternall Phisition both of soule and body, was intreated, by poore sinners, to descend unto her succour; and by a mercy of his miraculous deliverance, to testify, in her example, how fearefull it is to offend him, how comefortable it is to fynde him, how dangerous to be out of our watch, how sure a thinge, to converse with him; what a loathsom bondage, to be in the hands of Sathan, and what an arme of unmatcheable power, is on other syde; if by faithfull prayer, in true humiliation, we wrastle to gett proofe of it, in the day of our greatest distresse: as by the history of this maydes deliverance, followeth now, in the next place to be considered (as me thinke) with great consolation.

[Fol. 42r]

A Defence of the publique Sentence of
lawe, and of the judgment, of certayne
Phisitions, that averred Marie Glovers
case to be supernaturall: againste
D. Jordens slie, but scanda:
lous impugnations
of bothe: by
Stephan Bradwell, a member of the
Colledge of phisitions in London.

Chapter 1

That D Jordens discourse was framed against
the cause of Marie Glover

Although unto verie manie of his readers this question seemeth to require no proving, yet his cautelous cariage of the matter, even from the beginning, doth necessarily impose this taske upon me, in the entrance. His professing, when he began to write, [Fol. 42v][51] unto sundry frends, that demanded his meaning, was that he would write of the disseases of the mother, as a phisition;[52] but so, as he would not touch (at all) the cause of *Marie Glover* in it. His booke cometh forth, as all men see, without once naming her: him selfe, and some of his freinds have resisted, that the readers should take knowledge, of *Marie Glovers* cause in it: Is it not (now) worthie, to be a question, whether his discourse was framed, against her cause or no? He seemeth to say it was not, and who should know better then him selfe? I confesse that none can tell, what his scope and intention was, so well as him selfe: yet because, for some reasons knowen to him selfe, he thinks it not good, to open all his heart unto us, we must be content; to seeke out his meaning, by other arguments, then som single harted man would have put us to. Let us therefore, in the first place, consider the title of his booke, which is

32

this;[53] *A Breif discourse of a disease, called the suffocation of the Mother, written upon occasion, which have bene of late, taken thereby, to suspect possession of an evill spirit, or some such like supernaturall power.* [Fol. 43r] Here he saith, that his discourse was written upon occasion; not a generall occasion of doing good, to men of his profession; and consequently, to the Comonweale, by some, if not absolute, yet well laboured discourse, of a disease that so much importeth: but a particular occasion, as namely in this particular case; that manie have misjudged a possession of an evill spirit, in stede of this disease: adding withall, that this was done of late. Now, there being som hundreths, in London, which know that Mary Glovers case was new, at that time, and that many judged it to be the worke of an uncleane spirit, against him, and a few others, that saide it was the Mother; how can we but thinke, that he framed his discourse directly against her cause? Her cause (I say) not as it was a while in question, but as it was at length resolved, by publique tryall and sentence of lawe, to be supernaturall. There hapned no other case like this of late, whereto he can so fitly accomodate his wordes, as we are verely perswaded. Also it is to be observed, that [Fol. 43v] whereas he earnestly, at that time, contended, that *Mary Glovers* disease, was but the suffocation of the mother; and whatsoever els, in it, was extraordinarie, was but feigned of her part; or voluntarily performed, to make her case seeme more strange then it was.[54] The same things hath he insinuated, in his booke: as though it had not bene ynough for him, to declare, how all the faculties, in a womans body, may come to be diminished, depraved, or abolished by that disease, except he shewed withall, how the animall functions might be abused, by our owne will;[55] and so, divers things to concurre, in such a naturall disease, through the parties owne dissembling practise, to make a wonderment. This latter poynt (all men know) was nothing pertinent to his physsicall discourse, but he gave a lash thereby, at this particular instance, which he well hoped, the reader would take knowledge of. A man would scarse looke for such subtletie, under so milde a Countenance. Againe in his epistle, shewing the reasons, which drew him to write, and publish his booke; and removing first, the false causes, he hath these wordes, *Neither did I ever finde my selfe provoked hereunto, upon any peevish humor to contradict, or to disgrace anie, who doe judge otherwise of som poynts* [Fol. 44r] *contayned heerein, then my selfe do, many of them being such, as I doe love and affect well*; and within 3. lynes after this; *I have plainely sett downe the true doctrine of phisick, concerning that dissease, which geves so great occasion, of distraction, among many good men; especially such as have not learning Sufficient, to resolve them of this point, or not that moderation and humilitie of Spirit, to acknowledge their insufficiency, and to hearken unto others, whom, in all reason, they might think able to direct them better, in such a case.* These first wordes Cited doe implye, that some familiar frends of his owne profession (for els it could be no disgrace to them, to beare his contradiction in such a question) were disjoyned from his judgement, in this cause; And this is acknowledged, throughout the citie of London. The latter words import, that his opinion was impugned, by men of other faculties and place; which he bore displeasantly, imputing it to the want, either of learninge, or humilitie in them; and amplifieng their fault afterward, by an argument of comparison, that *a Phisition ought to be rested upon, in a matter concerning the actions and* [Fol. 44v] *passions of a mans bodie, aswell as Divines and Lawiers are in their proper elements.*[56] Now I think he will not deny, that he was stiffly opposed unto, in *Marie Glovers* cause, and especially by some lawiers, to his great discontentment: whether they lacked learning, or humilitie in so doing, let that be deferred unto others; sithens (as I am perswaded) neither himselfe, nor his familiar, *D Meddowes* are competent judges. In the .4. page of his epistle, he affirmeth, that, in the case, against which he framed his writing, *some had peremptorily disclaymed the using of naturall meanes, avouching that the partie spake certayne wordes, and performed certayne voluntary motions, upon Sathans incitation, and was hindred also by him, from speakinge other wordes, which they would faine have uttered.* These things have place in *Marie Glovers* cause, and I see not, how any man shalbe able to verefie them, in any other. Last of all, he describeth the case whereat he aymeth, by .5. arguments, alleaged by some men against him, to prove, a supernaturall power inherent in that body: as namely, *insensibilitie, a dew and orderly returning of her fittes; Offence in eating and drinking; The coming of her fittes upon the presence* [Fol. 45r] *of some certayne person. And the deliverance by prayer and fasting.* All which, are so trew Circumstances, in *Marie Glovers cause*, and som of them so necessarie, and proper unto it only, that I wonder what he meant, to conceale her name, after he had once deliberated, to bring her upon the stage, by so lively a description. Thus much from his owne handwriting: whereunto if we had the consideration of his often and earnest contending, to prove *Marie Glovers cause* a mere naturall sickenes;[57] His laboring to strengthen himselfe, and make his faction strong, from all sydes; and to daunt and discountenance us, that were of the contrary judgment, by the reverent Colledge of Phisitions, and som besides, of greater power; the undertaking to write his booke, at the request of the *L B of Lond:* (as som thinke) and his most earnest and ever offitious pursuit of the matter, both at the Sessions house, and after judgment geven; as appeareth by the importunat urging of a sequestration of the mayde, from her parents, to the cure of those phisitions, that affirmed it naturall, after the sentence of law had determined, her affliction supernaturall. [Fol. 45v] If (I say) we laie the consideration of these things to the former arguments, taken out of his booke, it wilbe no credit for him, hereafter, to shrinke the shoulder from averring, that he wrote his booke against *Marie Glovers cause*, as it is judged to have ben supernaturall.[58] The strongest imployment of his witts, hath neede be in this, how he may wype away his blot of inconstancy, and somwhat els, with those, to whom he had so soberly protested, that in writing his booke, of the suffocation of the mother, he had no purpose at all, to touch the matters of *Marie Glover.* [59]*Justinus Martyr hath this notable saying: who so denyeth himselfe, to be that, he is, either condemneth, in denying, that thing he is, or maketh himselfe unworthy of that, the confession whereof he fleeth.*[60] *which thing, is never found in a trew and sincere christian.*

Chapter 2

Why D. Jorden did write in this matter. and that nether his reasons removed, nor assumed, are able to acquite him, of certayne notable defectes and blemishes, whereof he therin standeth chargeable

To know the motives, that set *D Jorden* on worke, in [Fol. 46r] these matters, and the end or scope he had therein, as we are well content to heare them, from his owne mouth (for asmuch as without controversie, everie man knoweth best what is in his own heart) so he must geve us leave, to examine his steppes, by the line of likelyhood.[61] _A wise man (in deed) will enterprise nothing without a lawfull calling, to warrant him._ For as we receave everie good and perfect gifte from God alone, so our Comission of employing the same, must alwaies be fetched from him alone: and this only, is to walke in the comfortable assurance, of a good conscience; which whosoever possesseth, as he needeth not to feare the faces of all men, so there will appeare in his proceeding, som certaine signes and markes of the same anoynting, which God, in like cases, usually bestoweth upon other men. Els, who so taketh his comission but from man, as he cannot looke for all sufficient assistance, to the accomplishment thereof; so he shall surely bewray to the sight of the wise, I say not imperfections, which all men doe, but some infallible character, of a corrupt originall. [Fol. 46v] Let us now then draw neere to behould, seeing *D Jorden* is desirous to shew, both the occasion, and intent, of all his discourse. First he saith; yea he protesteth earnestly, that[62] _he hath not undertaken this busines of his owne accord, as if he esteemed of his owne knowledge and observation, in this case, above other mens._ If not of his owne accord, who drew him to it? He doth not directly say that any did, and much lesse nameth him that did: yet he insinuateth, that it was a taske put upon him; and that in these wordes: _for if it had ben thought good, to have imposed it upon others, I do acknowledge, that there are many among us_ (he meaneth the Colledge of Phisitions)[63] _better able then my selfe, to have written in this kinde: unto whom I would willingly, have put over my task._ Well he that imposed that taske, was in all likeliehood, some person in authoritie, or dignitie; whose comand or request could not well be avoyded. If such a one did know *D Jorden*, with out a mediatour, suborned or allowed by him selfe and did perswade him to this buisines, without his first manifestation of his owne readines, to maintaine [Fol. 47r] this quarrel, then cleerely he did it not of his owne accord; but if he used the mediation of an other, to such a person, and forwardly put forth himselfe to justifie *Marie Glovers* case to be but a naturall sickenes; then, although the taske was put upon him, by such as he durst not refuse, it was nevertheles sought by himselfe, and so undertaken of his owne accord. Let the reader beleeve, that if we had not strong presumptions of these passages, we would never have insinuated them. He doth not (as he saith) esteeme of his own knowledge and observation *in this case, above other mens*, and therefore *undertooke not this busines of his owne accord*. Whie was he then so peremptory, upon so litle sight of the patient, to conclude against others of his owne faculty and Colledge,[64] who had visited her five times for his once? Whie tooke he not paynes to enforme himselfe of all accidents in the case; yea of all actions and passions, precedent and consequent, as one that feared to erre? Whie shewed he not him selfe slowe to pronounce, or at the least to contend, when he was seriously exhorted by one [Fol. 47v] of his owne profession, so to doe? Whie provoked he the Colledge, to releeve the witch imprisoned? Whie laboured he particular good men, to syde with him? Having bene (him selfe) slight, and perfunctorious, in the search of a case so abstruse, and difficult to judge of; what could be the cause, to handle the matter in this maner, if a presumption of his owne knowledge and observation, in this case, above others, had not bene as a whirle winde to carie him? Secondly he saith that *he never fownd himselfe provoked hereunto, upon anie peevish humor to contradict, or to disgrace any, who doe judge otherwise of som points, contayned heerin then himselfe doth: many of them being such, as he did love to please or flatter any person.* Fourthly, *nor as taking upon him to reforme the mindes of men which are not under his charge.* The last of these I am well content to let goe; but the .2. former he cannot so easely cast away. Of his spirit of Contradiction what manifest or overture, will any man require, then his proceedings, from the first, to the last, do sett out unto us? Before the Sessions, as [Fol. 48r] he was verie readie to accept everie occasion, apertly, and directlie, to affirme *Marie Glovers* case to be nothing els but the mother, whereas others, that were of contrary judgment, would make choise to whom they shewed their mind, and also pronounce more doubtingly of the matter; One day, there hapned betwixt him and one of his opposites, some large reasoning of the case; wherein he calling for a Character of supernaturall, to be shewed him, had one geven him, whereof he could render no reason, but betooke himselfe (as his best shifte) to denye the instance; which we have manie sound witnesses to avouche. The other Phisition looking into his minde, by this loopehole, came in the end to this earnest motion with him, that seeing the case conteyned apparant difficulties, and that time

37

would be able to discover more, they should both be content
to enjoye their owne judgements, without labouring others, to
draw sydes and factions, that peace might be mainteyned amongst
us, and occasion of dissension taken awaie. To this he seemed
to assent, for that time, but within few daies forgot himselfe,
[Fol. 48v] taking part or joyning, in earnest courses, to deliver
the witch out of prison;[65] being occasion to som of his opposites,
of some hard and disgracefull speaches, for the matter, and drawing
manie of the Colledge, to speake and stirre in it against us.
Afterward, when publique justice had taken his course, himselfe
had bene heard what hee could saie, to the cause, manie wise and
experienced men had looked into it, with all the eyes they had, and
the sentence of law passed formally, with our judgment, yet this
man is never the more satisfied. Nay, even the day of the maids
deliverance, which was by the imediate finger of God, without any
meanes of phisicke at all, to geve it the least colour of a naturall
dissease, his brest could not be mollified, one jot to receave the least
impression, of quiet perswasion but, though all sorts of arguments,
like starres from heaven, had, in their courses, fought against him,
he obstinately persisteth to sing his ould song still. And because his
audience fayled him dayly, mens minds growing generally setled,
after publique sentence, he sendeth abroad his booke, that it might
infect the minds of men, in corners, and so raise [Fol. 49r] up a
broode of new partakers, filled with misconceipts of that, which can
no more be seene to controle them.[66] So hath the spirit of
contradiction seemed to double, and treble upon him; whatsoever
himselfe protesteth to the contrary. And so must, by his occasion,
now, the Judges, Justices, divines, phisitions and other abundant
witnesses, their learning, gravitie, experience, zeale and dilligence,
be weakned, traduced, annihillated, by a sorte of carping paradoxists,
malignant papists, and brother afflictinge newtralls, in all practise of
religion: rather then D. Jorden could thinke himselfe, possible to be
overseene, in a poynt, wherein the most learned phisitions, in this
latter age of the world, have ofte overshott themselves, and bene
deceaved. As much to be beleeved is he, when he saith, *he wrote not,
in a humor to disgrace any, who judge otherwise.* For in that earnest
insertation, that he useth in the second page of his epistle, against all
such, as did not rest in his Judgment,[67] and his associats, his words
are those, (let the reader see, I abuse him not) *But disclayming both*

hony and gall, I have plainely set downe the trewe [Fol. 49v]
*doctrine of phisick, concerning that disease, which geves occasion of
distraction among many, good men. especially such, as have not
learning sufficient, to resolve them of this point, or not that
moderation and humilitie of spirit, to acknowledge their Insufficiency,
and to hearken unto others, whom, in all reason, they might thinke
able to direct them better, in such a case. for if it be true, that one
man can not be perfect, in every art and profession, and therefore in
cases out of our owne callings, we do depend upon those, which have
ben trayned up, in other particular subjects, beleeving men in their
owne professions, why should we not preferre the Judgments of
phisitions, in a question concerning the actions and passions of mans
body (the proper subject of that profession) before our owne con-
ceiptes, as we doe the opinion of Divines, Lawyers, Artificers etc. in
their proper elementes?* What place (I beseech you) in all this
passage, doth he afford the Phisitions that were of contrary
judgment unto him? Were the Judges, Justices, Jurie, and all sorts of
men so hastie, and headlong, in the cause of *Marie* [Fol. 50r] *Mary*
[sic] *Glover*, as to refuse and sett at naught, according to this
insertation intimateth, all such direction and light, as from phisitions might be geven them? Then it seemeth that those phisitions
which contested with him, in the session house, and others abroad
(whose opinions he well knew stood against his) were not worthie
anie accompt, in his estimation: for if they were worthie any
accompt in his eyes, he could never, with any face, thus have
expostulated, as though the judgment of phisitions had ben so,[68]
against all reason, refused in the proper subject of their profession.
Is it not as much, in effect, to reason thus? The judgment of *D
Jorden* and his concurrents were not preferred, in the triall of *Marie
Glovers* cause; therefore the Judgment of no phisitions was accepted
therein. This insufficient induction could not grow out of his
ignorance, that other phisitions were embraced; for he knew that,
by as evident meanes, as his senses of hearing and seeing could
procure him. It must [Fol. 50v] needs (therefore) come out of the
superlative thoughts, of his owne selfe love; which in that passion of
jealousie, he was then in, (fearing his estimation would stand too
low) blinded his eyes, that he saw not, how he bore downe, and
trampled us under his feete, whilest himselfe, thus, strove for a
place, somwhat more eminent among the people. And least any man

of favorable affection to his cause, should deme that we presse him too sore, by this one place, contrary both to his meaning and words, in others let us see unto him further, and if all other places, touching us, be not sutable to this; that is, disposed to cast some disgrace upon us, we will be content to let fall our suit in this point hereafter. In this first chapter, setting his course to declare, that the disseases of the mother have manie times, so strange symptomes, as deceave not only *the comon people*, but also phisitions:[69] *such as are not verie well exercised in the practise of their profession* [Fol. 51r] maintaineth the same by .3. texts: one out of *Cornelius Gemma*, the second out of *Avicen*, and the third out of *Hippochrates*: but pursueth that of *Hippochrates*, as most excellent for his purpose, to make the reader thinke, that even the auntient father of our phisicke, long agoe, condemned all phisitions, that were of our opinion in this case, to be guiltie, either of ignorance,[70] *and want of experience, or els of a worser humor: as being loth to bewray our owne defectes, through pride and arrogancie, and not knowing what to praescribe, for cure of such cases, have therefore wholly relyed upon praier and fasting; like as those heathen phisitions did upon expiations, incantations, sacrifices etc. cloaking our ignorance under these shadowes etc.* as followeth in that place verie lightsomly to be applyed (as he presumeth) in everie point unto our dealings: although the cases be nothing like, as will (at full) appeare, when it shall heereafter be discussed to his double losse. What? Doth he by a counterfett foyle of an unlike comparison, labour to impose upon his reader, so stronge a delusion as to [Fol. 51v] think us, men, of no better rank, then are heere decyphered? It is too plaine: for there followeth no healing for this hurt; no exception, nor direction, to make the stroake fall short, or go beside our heades. Nay he followeth on, soone after, with an other as good, lest (perhaps) that former blow, should yet have left some life in our credit: and saith;[71] *Thus much in explanation of these .2. arguments of Hippo: against the errors of his time; which notwithstanding hath ben continued in the mindes of men untill this day, and no marvaile, unlesse the same corruption which bred it at the first, had been removed out of the world. If he had not intended, to guide both his readers hand and eye,* to applie that comparison of *Hippocrat*: corrupt phisitions, to us his opposites, in *Marie Glovers* cause, he would either have made his reddition more particular, noting out properly some other Persons whom he ment; either else have designed as some speciall protection, or house of harbour, amongst honest and good men; that we, whom he ment no disgrace unto, might have [Fol. 52r] stood secure, whilest such buzzing bolts were flyeing at random in the aire. Heere I look for no better replie at his hand, then this: *if your conscience hould you guiltie of these thinges, then I mean them unto you, otherwayes I have said nothing to you at all* but he may not so wype his mouth and go away: for when all men, that were acquainted with *Marie Glovers* case, doe likewise take knowledge, not only of the difference amongst the phisitions, but of the principall parties also in that difference; can they read these things of *D Jordens*, whom they acknowledge and principall partie heerein, denyeng causes supernaturall, but they must needs understand us, the principall parties on the other side, affirming supernaturall? Seeing (I saie) he hath lefte no cautionarie clause, at all for us; or to direct his reader otherwise. Here therefore, he hath not walked by the rule of charitie, neither towards us, nor towards his reader: not towards us, because he doth no where sett us forth in the cloathing of sincere men; that by such a signe we might be passed by, when ignorants and depraved [Fol. 52v] minds were taxed: nor toward his reader, because he hath craftely conveyed, and set in his waie a subtile insinuation, as a stone of offense, to make him fall into misconceipt; when as it lay in his power, plainely to have prevented it. How litle cause there is, that our Consciences should be touched with his great oversight in abusing the authoritie of *Hippochrates* against us, shall in a fitter place, hereafter be made manifest. Yet he hath one place moe, which argueth either his disgracefull heart, or hand towards us, and that in the end of his first chapter. Where coming to his conclusion both of his authorities and examples, produced to prove, that manie times, both the Comon people and phisitions thinke fitts of the mother to be a possession of the divill: he draweth to his drift with these woords: *These examples maie suffice, to shew how easelie men unexperienced in those extraordinary kindes of disseases, may mistake the causes of them. When through the admiration of the unwonted and grevous accidents they behould, they are caried unto magicall and meta-phisicall speculations.* [Fol. 53r] *But the learned phisition, who hath first bene trayned up in the studie of Philosophie, and afterward confirmed by the practise and experience of all maner of naturall*

41

disseases, is best able to discerne what is naturall, what not naturall, what præternaturall, and what supernaturall: the three first being properly subject to his profession. And therefore they doe wrong unto the facultie of phisick, and unto themselves, and oftentymes unto others, who neglecting that light which we[72] *might yeelde them, do run headlong and blindfold into manie errors and absurdities.* If his conclusion do comprehend his premisses (and it were immodestie for us to suspect him, in such a point of learning) then he saith in effect thus; [73]*These examples of ignorant and arrogant phisitions, recorded by Hippochrates, but remayning in succession to this day; as also those of the comon people, by sundrie other Authors testified: may suffice to shew how easely etc.* to the end of the whole period; which only teacheth [Fol. 53v] the reader, who they be that cannot judge in these matters, and what it is that transporteth them. Then he turneth himselfe on the contrary to shew who should be hearkened unto, in these things. *Who but the learned phisition?* Which, because the reader might have a *quære* in his head, to aske how may we know him? He proceedeth in the next words sufficientlie to describe him, and so appropriateth unto him, the matters in this Controversie, as the very element wherein he liveth. From these things he draweth this consectarie, *therefore they doe wronge unto the facultie of phisick etc who neglecting the light which we might yeeld them etc.* Now we must desire to know of him, *who neglected this light* he speaketh of: if he be able, let him tell us. We looke for a pregnant instance: as eather the Justices of the bench, or Jurie, or els (at least) the generall number of ministers, lawiers, other schollers and professed christians, which before and after the [Fol. 54r] sessions, came to see the maide in her afflictions. But all men know, that the Justices were not without the direction of Phisitions, in their proceeding. And the rest of the people, at other times, did often finde some of those phisitions, that were most observant of everie thinge, that hapned in her case, and clerely in judgment contrary to him; and to their judgments they clave. Therefore it is false that *phisitions were neglected.* O but now I better remember my selfe; his words are these, *Who neglecting the Light which we might yeeld them etc.* Here the word (*we*) must needs implie himselfe and his Concurrents in *Marie Glovers* cause; which nether the bench nor Jurers, nor the generall number of schollers and understanding of people, that came to behould the maide, did beleeve. What then? Doth he restraine the description aforesaid of *a learned phisition* to himself, and those only that concurred with him in this cause? Art all other phisitions excluded? I am far from that thought. Surely he excludeth none, that are within the compasse of the description. Why [Fol. 54v] we take our selves to be such also for we have so instituted our studies from the beginning, and our yeeres and practise are equall to his. Alas, but we are not fallen out of his opinion, and therefore must needs be excluded in this place: And being here excluded whether doth he thrust us but among the route of *Hippocrates* ignorants and ill minded meanie. Now we appeale to the indifferent readers conscience, whether *D Jorden* have caried these matters for our disgrace or no: he protesteth that[74] *he did not ever finde himselfe provoked to write his booke, upon anie peevish humor to contradict, or to disgrace anie etc.* Some adversarie here might reply to him, that although he did not ever finde himselfe so provoked, yet sometimes (as it seemes) he did, and so in such a humor wrote his booke. But we are perswaded that although his writing be cautelous in other points, yet that in this place, he intended not to overreach his reader, but meant simply, that *he never found himselfe provoked etc.* To which we answere, if he had (in deed) never beene, by so impure a minde provoked, then could not *de facto*, such and so manie hard passages [Fol. 55r] of speach, reserving no comfort for us that were his cheife opposits, and necessarily inferring disgrace to som that were his opposits, have issued out of his pen. This rule stands for ever *Out of the aboundance of the heart the mouth* (and so the pen) *uttereth*. In that he saith *he never found it himselfe*, it doth but increase his blame, as arguing either none at all, or verie slight examination of his owne conscience, those dayes that he applyed him selfe to this busines. For we do not allow of his presumed consequence; he never *found himselfe provoked of any peevish humor, therefore he was not*: Manie things escape us when we stand upon our watch most dilligently, and much more if we grow secure, so as We delight in the companie of the ungodly, especially if the dere love of truth decaie in us; for then many false loves will crowde into the place thereof and principally that selfe love, which corrupteth all the judgment. His other motive which he doth so scornefully hurle from him in these words[75] *Neither upon any fawning humor to please or flatter anie person whatsoever which*

I do esteeme more base than begging. Will not [Fol. 55v] be removed from him, upon plea of his integritie only: but it behoved him either to have used moe and more artificiall arguments, or els, to have left us none, or fewer occasyons, to suspect him, in the whole cariage of his cause. First therefore we desire the reader to consider, that to write a booke, after a publique sentence of law, in way of defence, to the end the subjects of the kingdom generally may be seazed of the equitie of the sentence, and deterred from doing evill in like case, is the formall and usuall proceeding of the magistrate in some causes of great consequence. But for anie privat man to write a booke, against a just determination of law, proceeded in by the lawfull magistrates, (none of them parties to the cause,) and by an usuall course of tryall, can have no good report in it; nor spring out of anie roote of equitie or good Conscience. And we are assuredly perswaded, that of his owne disposition he is far from doing anie act, that may likely procure him anie displeasure, from the magistrate. It must needs be therefore, that he had to his writing some procuror and Abettour of an other streine. And that must be one of such [Fol. 56r] place and power, as either would command him, or els by faire entreatie provoke him to do it.[76] But comaund him no subject could; therefore he did it by entreatie. If he were but entreated he might have refused; especially seing he testified to divers, his own unwillingnes therein. What could then be the cause that he wrote his book but to please, not himselfe, but the humor of an other. Perhaps he will defend him selfe thus, albeit in yeelding to write, I was willing to please (as you say) not my selfe, but an other; yet in my writing I sought not to sooth up any man, but the truthe only. If this be silver, let us see, how it will abide the teste. If he sought not to please him that sett him on worke,[77] even in the maner of his writing also, then can we not ceasse to wonder, to what end *counterfeiting* comes in so often: especially sith that upon his oath, and protestation of his conscience, he cleered *M Gl* of all imputation of Counterfeiting, in the Sessions house. In his 4th Chapter which teacheth [Fol. 56v] how the animall facultie maie be offended, in disseases of the mother, (which truely is his phisicall taske) he bestoweth very neere a whole leafe, to proove that the *animal functions may be abused by our owne will*, and so consequently manie actions, or passions, straunge and incredible, be performed, both to the counterfeiting of disseases, and possession of *Divills.*

Why, what should these things do there? To the doctrine of the suffocation of the mother they perteyned nothing. O but one will saie, he delivered not his discourse of that dissease indefinitely, but with a peculiar relation to a late case, that gave occasion of his writing, not of that dissease in women indifferently, but of that dissease in this woman particularly. Well we wote he reached at *M Gl* in the rest of his book particularly, namely to make his reader beleeve, it was a naturall dissease, and nothing els: if in this pointe we should admitt his eye willingly glaunced at *M Gl* What shall we thinke of his contrary protestation before the judge? Certaynely therefore [Fol. 57r] unto us, in this ambiguitie, it seemeth most reasonable to esteeme, that he wrote this according as he was inspired by his taske master, and not out of his owne sense and judgment. If here againe he flee from us crying out of wrong, and desiring that these things may be understood in *Thesi* and not in *hypothesi*, perhaps all righteous Judges will refuse him, as aman [sic] not craving the lawfull favor of the Court, but partiall indulgence. And thus they will shew it him, sayeing; this place last cited out of your booke, being but of an impertinent to the dissease you handle, and altogeather concealed in your title, is either utterly idle, or els brought in, to help to furnish your naturall symptomes, so as they may be able to comprehend all things, that may be objected out of *M Glo:* case. But we will not thinke that you have abused us with idle stuffe. Moreover if you meane that some others have counterfeited possession of evill spirits, by adding straunge voluntarie actions beyond the power of their dissease, but yet do in your conscience exempt *M. Gl.* according [Fol. 57v] to your former protestation to the Judges, then it stood upon your honest reputation, to have set down, in the same place, a peremptorie exception in her behalfe. Which, because you have not done, you can with no cullour of reason, looke for anie such favour in this matter as you require. To be rid of all the bondes at once, when he seeth no cunning can help him, we are affraide he will betake him to this kniffe, and saie:[78] I was in deede of that perswasion, what time I so protested before the Bench, but since that, upon further consideration, my minde in that point is altered: so as now I thinke, that *Marie Glover* was one of those; who willingly and of purpose [was] observed to do certaine actions in their fittes, to stirre up admiration, and to breed, and nourish in their behoulders, the opinion of possession of Divells.

45

Som what to this sense in deede he spake of late, to *M Gl.* and her mother. And this is valiantly with *Alexander* to cut the knott, when he cannot unknit it: but withall declining *Silla*, to fall into *Charybdis*: for so shall he [Fol. 58r] joyne hands, with men of fearfull condition; with whom it is not possible in mans ey, to hould conformitie, and keepe therewithall [on] the path of truth. I saie, I am affraide he will do thus, because I hate him not (as the Lord knoweth) but covet his return if he be in declining: and would be grieved in my heart, to see him, not only to *walke in the counsaile of the ungodlie, but also to stand in the waie of sinners.* This I have saide, to bring him unto an earnest consideration with him selfe; who is, in his epistle, so earnest with his reader, to *discerne truthe from counterfeiting,* in this our present course. For if he yet will have his reader thinke, that *M. Glovers* case was partly counterfeiting; we must rowle him up (though against our wills) in the scrole and Catalouge [sic] of such, as Care not, how impudently they open their mouthes, when they have a purpose to oppresse the truthe. Now when we see, that this was not *D Jordens* judgment originally, but that he came to it, by the contagion of evell companie, we cannot see reason to thinke, but that a fawning humor did sett in foote, among other motives to the writing [Fol. 58v] of his booke. Perhaps he will not strive in his owne defence thus, that I am not altogeather of their judgment, it may appeare by myne owne words following in that epistle, if you would but affoord me indifference of interpretation. For there I saie, *I doe not denye, but that God doth in these dayes work extraordinarily, for the deliverance of his children, and for the endes best knowne to himselfe; and that among other, there may be both possessions by the Divill and obsessions and witchcraft etc. and dispossessions also through the praiers and supplications of his servantes, which is the only meanes lefte unto us for our releife in that case.* We are glad where we finde him speake in Orthodox language, and have no doubt, but that he knoweth and is perswaded of the truth in these things, touching the generall: which maketh us to marveile so much the more, why then he runneth after them, so fast in the particular instances; which if they might gaine as easelie at other mens handes, as (it seemeth) they do at his, [Fol. 59r] they would shortly make their induction so well replenished, as they would constrayne him to eat his word, touching possession of Divells and witchcrafte. That he over easilie

46

assenteth to them, in denyinge instauces of Demoniacks, it is very evident in his next sentence, where he speaketh so like their language, that he marreth the grace of all that he said afore. These are his wordes:[79] *But such examples being rare now a dayes, I would in the feare of God advise men to be very circumspect, in pronouncing of possession, both because the impostures be manie, and the effectes of naturall disseases bee straunge to such as have not looked thoroughly into them.* This is to plant with one breath, by positive affirmations in the generall; and supplant with another breath, by privative negations in the particulars. In the former he speaketh like D. Jorden; in the latter like his taskemaster. But you will say, his negations are not so absolute; we grante it; he sheweth himselfe a fearfull scholler, yet a scholler: who hath more cause to boast of his timiditie, then of his facilitie. But in earnest, [Fol. 59v] doth he thinke, that *such examples are rare now a daies?* and that *Impostures are manie?* If he had sayde *In those kingdomes where Antichrist beareth swaye, such examples are rare in comparison of the Impostures,* we could have lent some eare unto him, and further have attributed som authoritie to his travailinge times, to have recounted to us, what pageants he saw either in the *Santo in Padua,* or els where, amonge all the romish rowtes that he passed. But to saie, that now *a dayes, such examples are rare, and impostures manie,* maketh such an universall untruthe, touching this kingdome, and layeth such a lumpe of scandalous corruption, in the way of truth, which he had uttered before, as it is much, that a man of his wate and meanes, could be so charmed, or enchaunted rather. To prove the truthe on his side, I trust, when we come to instaunces, all men will yeeld, that it lyeth him in hand, for everie one of our trew examples, to produce three, or two at the least, of such as were counterfeit. If he make the number but equall, he is found to beare false witnes, if inferiour he must be taxed [Fol. 60r] with grosse over reaching. But if we bring five trew for his one false, what epithite wilbe added to his name? Let him now beginne when he left, we will never withdrawe one foote from the chalenge. Provided alwaies, that the soveraigne power, give us equall hability, to discover and discredit, wheresoever we shall finde any *farded* face of craftie disguised image, maliously erected to outface the truth. In tracing him hitherto, we finde him not cleere in his enterprise, of manie corrupt causes, thereunto inciting him howsoever he entred into the lists, with his solemne protestation, disclayming everie one of them. What then? Shall we thinke, that only by the instigation of som great man in this world, he did presume to turne the streame of universall credence, sent forth now, with so strong a current, from most lawfull trialls and proceeding? Nay, but he adjoineth moreover, that *being a Phisition and judging in his conscience that these matters have bene mistaken,* he thought it good thus to write, both to rectifie mens understanding, that they might not hereafter, erre in judgement, touching these matters, and to [Fol. 60v] preserve them from *abusing the name of God and holy prayer.* And certainely, this is as fayre, as copper [or] silver to the eye: but let us come to more artificiall examinations, and then we shall see, what aloy it conteyneth. If a good conscience sett him on worke to reduce a multitude erring, it must be because, either the errour was grosse, or els his diligence had surmounted in discovering of it. For if either the misjudgment were not manifest generally and yet neglected or his diligence had not exceeded all others, so as he was able to open the eies of the blinde, in this cause; there was no other reason in the world could urge his conscience to this service, for either the neede must be great that calleth forth a man meanly qualified, or the knowledge must excell, that taketh upon it to alter such a multitude. But so farre of was it that the errour or misjudging on our syde (if there were anie) was apparantly grosse (howsoever one man at the sessions, with greater audacitie then judgment, avouched the symptomes to be the same with the mother, *and not straunge to phisitions*) that *D Thauris* and *D Selme* before the judgment seat (seeming fearfull to displease som men) bare witnes yet, that the case had manie [Fol. 61r] straunge and wonderfull things in it, so as they could easelie have inclyned to thinke it extraordinarie, but that they were rather resolved, for that time to suspend their judgments. Now then, if the matter were difficult, so as it made wise men to suspend their judgment, although they were unwilling to crosse his opinion; and that difficult things, require much attendance, studie and observation, if a man meane to make a good ground for his conscience, when he shalbe called to testifie thereof, his dutie both to God and men, did bynde him,[80] (if he thought himselfe called to interpose himselfe in this cause) to have visited and considered the patient often, with long musing and meditation as schollers doe in difficile matters, and poynts of surmounting reache, to have

48

numbred all the symptomes, seene all the varieties, and weighed them in the balaunce of well advised comparison. Also to have enquired diligentlie, into all causes precedent and consequent, absent and present, privately and positively. But that D Jorden did not bestow all necessarie diligence this waie, both his seldom visitations, and litle time affoorded with the sicke, (whereof there are manie witnesses) as also his roving, loose and undigested discourse (as shall particularly be shewed hereafter) doe [Fol. 61v] publish and notifie unto all the world. And therefore it could not be a good conscience, that did comfort him to undertake his taske: as neither was it, to testify before the bench, having not the ordinarie calling of the Court, but by his owne meanes, came thereunto. We graunt that he held *Marie Glovers* cause to be naturall; and in that respect, spake and did what was in his thoughts, but not according to a right conscience: which never suffereth the mouth to beare witnes in a matter of facte, but whereof it is privy, that some of the outward senses, have taken knowledge before: nor in a matter of opinion or Judgment, but according, and as far forth only, as it is assured, no requisit meanes of right conclusions, have bene neglected in it.[81] We grant a man may (with a good conscience) yeeld his opinion being asked of a matter, not so exactly considered before; but to undertake opposition in it, and so forwardlie compere, to induce judges and jurers in it: Yea and when the cause had receaved sentence against him, and had been cleared finally, with a testimonie from heaven, to write (then) a booke, to seduce the subjectes from giving credit to it, seemeth so unsutable [Fol. 62r] to the proceeding of a good conscience, as that this his professing of it, to his booke, can but occasion his reader to think, that he well understandeth not what a good conscience meaneth. Moreover as his conscience here is reproved, for want of such a ground of knowledge to settle upon, as his faithfull diligence might easelie have attayned; so is it no lesse blame worthie, for unsincere, yea plainely unfaithfull handling of the matter. In the 4th page of his epistle dedicatorie, pretending to answere the argumentes which we used, to prove the case super-naturall, he produceth five, but unsincerely:[82] the 3 first being such, as we never alleaged to such purpose, then growing to his conclusion, thus he windeth up his clue: *Manie other such like instaunces they may produce, according to everie ones severall conceipt; which were in vayne for me to repeat particularly, unlesse I knew wherein*

49

they would principally insist. Did not *D Jorden* know? Was he not
privy in his conscience, to moe arguments then these; and wherein
we did principally insist? He must pardon us; we cannot believe
[Fol. 62v] him. He knew them from us, by conscience, and from
sundrie others, that opposed against his judgment during the time of
the maides affliction. And if these were not meanes sufficient to
make him know them, yet I hope the Sessions, were abundantly:[83]
Wherein first *D Herring* beyond the poynts aforesaid, objected
unto him, those remarkable motions of her handes to her mouth
and the opening of her mouth in such a methode, to speake such and
so many wordes, and none other, nor no moe. And that in the time
of the Lords praier, at the pronouncing of the last petition, *Deliver
us from evill,* the maids bodie, (if it then laie in a senseles trance)
would rebound up in the middle: And if in such a time; the widow
Jackson were secretly brought in, the bodie would be changed into a
farre different passion. After him *Dr Spencer*[84] reasoned against his
opinion of the mother, from the absence of the causes in so younge
mayde; from the deformed moving of the belly and brest, not like
that uniforme rising, which is in the suffocation of the mother. And
from the varieties both of the fittes themselves, and of the symptomes in every singular fitte. These were (I trowe) infallible causes,
to make him privy to manie moe of [Fol. 63r] our instaunces, then
he would take upon him to answere in his booke. From effects
(likewise) we will prove that he knew moe: namely in that he hath
geven answeres to some men and rendered reasons (such as they
were) for the altring of the bodie at the coming of the Witch, and for
rebounding of the bodie, at the using of the Lords praier: Which
reasons though he was afrayde to sett downe in his booke, yet we
will not be afrayde to shew the unsavourines of them in place
convenyent. Againe, his verie booke, in the same epistle, doth
witnes against him in this point. Where he sayeth that *som*[85] *avouch
the mayde* (in her fitts) *spake certayne wordes, and performed
certaine voluntarie motions upon Sathans incitation, and was hindered by him, from speaking other thinges, which she would fayne
have uttered.* These wordes (although he deliver them unsincerely)
do prove a verie materiall instaunce of ours, whereto he was privie,
although he was much wiser, then to trouble himselfe with the
answere of it. To conclude therefore, seeing *D Jorden,* touching the
causes of writing his booke, cannot come to quit him selfe of

certaine unworthie Corruptions, nor to justifie his calling thereto, nor conscience therein, to be good, in respect of sundrie great [Fol. 63v] and greivous exceptions, which everie where, lie in his waie, to hinder his passage, as above is declared. We would in the feare of God, advise him, to be more circumspect hereafter, then in this busines, hitherto, he hath bene. And first if he accompt it a reputation, such as his soule desireth to be zealous of Godds truth, that he busie himselfe, with all his witts, to discerne with whom the truth standeth, lest he be found to fight under wrong colours. Casting up his reckoning thus withall, that there can be no zeale of truth, that conteyneth not hatred of errour, and of all malicious abettors thereof, according to that sentence of *David*:[86] *Doe not I hate them O Lord that hate the, and do I not earnestly contend with those, that rise up against the? I hate them with an unfeigned hatred, as they were my utter enemies.* Secondly, that in a Christian Commiseration of his afflicted bretheren, he be affrayde to strengthen the hand of iniquitie against them wittingly, and ashamed to be inveigled to doe the same unadvisedly. Last of all seeing the fairest motive that made him [Fol. 64r] write, was the instigation of a sinfull man, and that he was not, otherwise, qualified with anie better callinge from God, unto it; let him now at length (better late then never) seriously consider, what a sinne he hath entred into, thus to contradict and cancell (to his power) the grave sentence, in a just proceeding, of the reverent judges, togeather with the settled perswasion, of manie godlie and wise Christians, in a cause of such truth, as is witnessed unto by him selfe in the generall; and from heaven, in the particular. Which particular, (as halfe an eie maie see) is not persecuted and oppressed, for it selfe (the parties being not such as can be touched of like evill) but only for the cause of the generall, to deny possession and dispossession of divells; that so they might spoyle all sincere Christians, of some parte of their Crowne and glorie in this life, even the sweete fruit of their faith-full praiers, a testimonie of their acceptance with God in Jesus Christ. Not (as I think) of purpose, to hinder mens salvation; but, as by all meanes, to put out the light of that *antithesis*, which both in præcept and practice, doth dayly argue their dissolute profesion.[87] *Blessed is the man which putteth his trust in the Lord; and respecteth not the proud* [Fol. 64v][88] *nor such as to turne aside to lies.*

Chapter 3

How D Jorden hath written in this cause and first in generall

Now that we have seene, how nether justly nor necessarilie (whatso-ever his words are)[89] *D Jorden* hath written against *Marie Glovers* case, as out of a most lawfull and orderly tryall, it was sentenced: Let us come more neere hand to consider, how well he behaveth himselfe in the cause, and upon what good grounds it is, that he thus presumeth, to draw men awaie, from that truth, which by so faire, lightsom and well conditioned meanes they have received. First we will take a generall view of his platforme; and after that, examine the speciall points and parts of workemanship in it. *S. H.* (the letters for his names and the man for his manners, both apt to intimate shame, to his readers) having the stomach of an archennemie to disgrace this cause, but wanting a fitt patient, and place sutable, to sett up his forge [Fol. 65r] in; made his recourse yet, to an other of his Machivilian tricks, to succour him in this desperate distresse, namely to write a booke against the Cousinages, that are used in the synagogue of Antichrist, and therein by opening, amplifying and resolving all things for his purpose, yea sometimes with an impu-dent comentarie; he instilleth here and there, unthought of, into his readers cogitation, those contagious suggestions, of everie where counterfeiting and cousening, in all cases of this nature: presuming certainely thereby, to infect some moe, or, at least, to retayne those manie, that are alreadie of that leprouse judgement, with him; and to hinder the weake and Comon multitude, from admitting anie impression of truth, as it is in this our case: Not respecting the learned writings of all ages despising the observation of judges,[90] and trampling under his feete, the assertions of our most learned and experienced King in this behalfe. *D Jorden*,[91] although I accompt him a far better man, hath yet handled his matters too like him, in this affaire. So it is [Fol. 65v] to converse with the ungodlie, and to touch pitche: so good Joseph, by living in Ægipt, learned to sweare by the life of *Pharao*: And so hath he, doubting the yssue of an encounter, with *Marie Glovers* cause in playne, fetched about, with manie circuits and traverses, to tell with strange dissease the mother is, how all the faculties may be hurt by it, so as somtime physitions have thought the Divell to have bene a cause in it; and therefore much more easelie maie it deceave the Comon people. Especially perturbations of the minde concurring, and som litle tricks of counterfeiting being mixed withall, to augment the wonder. All this stuffe, he contriveth and setteth out, with chapters and divisions, of the sundrie wayes offended faculties, and incredible varieties of symptomes, in the suffocation of the mother, illustrating many things with examples, and adorning the whole with verie copious quotations of good writers; though they but prove that, which will do him no good when it is granted him. So by this meanes, he comforteth himselfe, with great hope, that albeit he, in no place expressely writeth that [Fol. 66r] *M. Glovers* case was in all poyntes, thus, or so; yet that manie of his unwarie readers, would apply it so, and take it for granted. And namely seeing that howsoever, in the front of his booke, he modestly professeth therein, but a declaration *of divers straunge actions and passions of the bodie of man,*[92] *which in the comon opinion are imputed to the Divell, to have there* [sic] *true naturall causes and to accompanie this dissease*; which I would not greatly sticke to grant him; Yet in his first chapter, and second page, loosing all the reignes of goverment unto his pen, thus inconsiderately he delivereth; that, *whatsoever straunge accident maie appeare in anie of the principall functions of mans bodie, either animall, vitall or naturall, the same is to be seene in this dissease.* For seeing that, all most all extraordinarie actions and passions of the Demoniacks, arise from the suffring of these principall functions, discomposed by the Cunning and power of *Sathan,* how is it here [Fol. 66v] imposed upon the reader to thinke (although *D Jorden* speake it not, in so manie wordes) that all and everie accident, in *Marie Glovers* case, had no other mover in the world, but the mother? Yea and by these wordes he provideth verie cuningly; that albeit, in his enumeration of the severall symptomes of that dissease, (to be accommodate [sic] for satisfaction, to everie instaunce of our case urged against him) he shall not satisfie the expectation of his reader in everie particular (as it wilbee shewed, that he doth not (almost) in anie one) yet this generall rule shall serve, in sted of all; that so far as anie function of the three principall faculties, animall, vitall or naturall, may be made accomptable to diminution, depravation or abolition, so far this rule shall reache to gather all such accidents, within the compasse of suffocation of the

53

mother. He presuming (that which is alwaies probable) that the readers apprehension will excell his judgment; and that which taketh hold first of the fantasie, will soone after settle in the understanding: the number of those that [Fol. 67r] are seasoned with prudent discourse, being not great; and few of them affoording time of dew consideration, in reading such things. By this rule likewise, his unwarie reader, must interpret another sentence of his, which els would labour of manie insufficiencies; namely in the conclusion of his epistle; where he excuseth his owne slipping awaie from the combat, upon pretence of ignorance what weapons we woulde use, he telleth his reader this tale, and so departeth: *But in the discourse following, I have as neere as I could, described all the Symptomes, of this dissease; whereby every man may readily find answere to his severall objections.* Which is as much to saie; beinge not willing to beare the adventure of the field himselfe (although he was Chalenger)[93] to entreat the bystanders, to supplie his place, promising that he would send them all sorts of weapons. Thus wise he is in deede, to sleepe (himself) in a whole skin, and of such a conscience, as to leave a thousand others by the eares. And if the victorie fall not out for him, in our singular contentions, yet by this meanes, [Fol. 67v] hath thus much to answere for himselfe; his weapons were unskilfully handled. Without doubt his conscience tould him; if he should himselfe have made application of all those symptomes of the mother, which he thinketh accomodable to *M Glovers* case; which had been plaine and righteous dealing, he should both have bene put, to verie much expence of his witt, (whereto I blame him not to be unwilling) as also to verie imminent hassard of som fall of his reputation; which everie man abhorreth naturally. Therefore chose he rather, by the waie of implicative generalities, and insinuated analogies, as things considerable, either in naturall passions, or els in counterfeit actions, to make all his readers disputers in this question: yea, in a sort, to enforce them. As when they shall read, that the disseases of the mother are able to alter, or disparage all the senses, and to disorder anie waie, and in everie degree, all the instruments of voluntarie motion, togeather with all the regnant powers of womans bodie, which his [Fol. 68r] 2. 3. 4. and 5 Chapters are wholly employed to prove, and that an incredible increase of wonder may accrewe, to all the offences of the animall functions, if in their fittes, they can also counterfeit, and add

Mary Glovers Late Woeful Case

somthing by dissembling: which by manie examples he setteth out in his 4 chapter. Shall not he that readeth be compelled (without further examination of differences) under the excessive spread of these generalities, to argue the comprehension of all our particulars? At least, if he shall make anie use of the *D* writing: and so (as mans wit is by nature like the fier, ever moving) make applications, and draw in Conclusions by himselfe, without the daunger of Controlment, which, if the Aucthor (as it was his part) should have done, by expresse writing, it must needs have drawne upon him further trouble to defend it. It was his wisedome therefore to leave these imperfections in his writing, for manifould more advantage to him selfe. First to transferre the imputation of unskillfull applieng anie of the particulars, from himselfe to [Fol. 68v] all such readers as should be inveigled by his writing. Secondly they would be boulder, and lesse circumspect then he durst be, and so passe by all pracise [sic], examination and weighing of differences, which himselfe might have been drawen unto. Thirdly if he had applied *Marie Glovers* particulars to his generalls, the reader would then have tyed himselfe to his applications, and so should easely have seene the uttermost poynt of his game, and goodnes of his cause to judge betwixt us. Whereas now, there being no bounds sett, only great occasion of intermedling geven to his reader, it must fall out, that according to the happynes of everie ones wit, the matter wilbe judged, and, so manie as applie matters to his purpose, become contenders for their owne judgments, and consequently, as men engaged, defenders of him. And as, by this hooke of generallities, he pluccketh to himselfe this imoderate gaine, so hath he a crooke of analogies, also, to suspend his reader, least he fall from him. For where his symptomes of the offended functions, and tricke of counterfeiting, rehearsed by divers [Fol. 69r] instaunces, fall short in his enumeration, to match with such a case as *M. Glovers* was, there is yet insinuated, that by way of analogicall proportion, whatsoever is defective to the eie, may be supplied in the minde, by discourse of the readers owne wit. Thus hath *D. Jorden* fared, like the rich men of this world, whose hearts being wholly sett upon gaine, care not, what indirect meanes they use, so they may have it. But evell gotten goods must be restored, if he meane to be a penitent *Zacheus*, as I hope he will.

55

Mary Glovers Late Woeful Case

Chapter 4

Wherein his generall platfourme is more specially reproved

The project and image of his minde being seene; and the reasons whereupon as piles he hath pight [sic] his foundacion, being discovered, and already reproved by their parralels; it is time to come unto the more speciall examination of his whole platfourme, and so descend by degrees, to the ripping up of every part. Thus he would have his reader [Fol. 69v][94] conceive him:[95]

Whatsoever affliction had all the actions and passions thereof proceeding from the Mother, feare, and counterfeiting, that is not supernaturall.
But Marie Glovers affliction had all the actions and passions thereof either from the Mother feare or counterfeiting;
Therefore Marie Glovers affliction was not supernaturall.

His proposition hath light in itselfe. But his assumption is darkenes it selfe. How will he prove it? I trow thus:

If the mother feare or counterfeiting, severally or mixt, are able to bring forth the like kindes of actions and passions that Ma: Glo: had, then were all hers but of such originall,
But the Mother feare or counterfeiting severally or mixt, are able to bring forth the like,
Therefore all Ma: Glo: were but of such originall.

Heere you have the full and naked view of all his magnificent building. Fcure [i.e., secure] it is in shew; but yet peradvanture paper walles; not fit for [Fol. 70r] habitation. Let us therefore goe into it, and behould the substance, coping and provision for weather. His Connexive proposition, the maine pillour of his building is manie waies unsound, and unable to support the roofe, if a man do but walke upon it. It reasoneth from the abilitie of naturall efficients supposed pressent, to conclude the absolute privation of supernaturall efficients. Againe when he speaketh of bringing forth like actions and passions, there first he presumeth, that from a similitude of effectes to naturall efficients manie necessarilie be concluded a dissimilitude of effects to supernaturall efficients. And

56

secondly under the latitude of likenesses he abuseth his simple reader with unlike comparisons. I will therefore first declare the inconsequence of his proposition in generall and after that defend *M Glover* from all his presumptions and disproportions in particular. Whereas he supposeth by placing naturall effects to call in naturall causes, and by admitting naturall causes to exclude supernaturall out of dores, he is much deceaved. For supernaturall efficients can doe all the naturall maie and much more. Which thing forasmuch as it is best able to be discerned [Fol. 70v] by instaunces, I will not flee the paines for the better cleering of my answere to set him downe some competent store, and that of such instaunces as shall not digresse one haires bredth, from the verie cause we have in hand. Namely such, wherein supernaturall causes were necessarilie admitted, although the effects were none other, then such as meere naturall causes can and doe at other times produce. Amongst the unspeakeable miracles which our Saviour did on earth, the Evangelists do record his soveraigne casting out of Divells, and amongst others of them, some of those persons were such, as had none other shewe or character in them, then such as meere physicall causes can, and daiely do bring forth. As namely, one that was dumbe;[96] another is set forth to have bene blinde and dumbe,[97] another is described in all respects, as one, that had the falling sickenes;[98] and a fourth I observe, which had least shewe of all the rest,[99] a woman that had long time ben crooked and could not erect her bodie. If these afflictions were caused by the Divell,[100] and yet were none other, in all shew, then naturall sicknesses [Fol. 71r] it is manifest that *D Jordens* proposition is destroyed. But albeit these instaunces from the scripture, were abundantly sufficient, to take awaie the necessitie of his consequence, yet because, I know he will strive to maintayne this hould, as long as he can (it being the strongest fortresse he hath) let us suppose he is not satisfyed, with these examples from the scriptures, as not set downe at large, and therefore the signes might be wanting which did discover them for Demoniacks: He might have knowne this truth, by manie writers of his owne profession, if his eye in reding, had ben as indifferent, as it was diligent. *A certaine man* (saith *Fernelius*)[101] *through heat of weather, vehemently thirsting in the night season, arising out of his sleepe, and missing to fynd drink, met with an apple; the which as he was eating he felt his jawes to choke, and to be clasped togeather as*

with ones hand, and therewithall the Divell entring was possessed.
He semed to see himselfe devoured in the dark by a great black
dogge. All which thinges, after the time of his deliverance, he
rehearsed in order unto us. Manie out [Fol. 71v] *of his pulse, heat*
and roughnes of tongue pronounced a fever, and from his not
sleeping and perturbations of mynde, judged simplie a raving or
frensie. Joannes Langius telleth,[102] *that whilest he exercised physick*
at Bononia, there was a certaine woman vexed with an ulcer, and of
the nature of meliceris, about her secret part, and ever when the
hope of healing up was neerest, with the Chirurgion, suddainely, a
new filthie matter would plentifully break forth, in substance like to
honie; untill at length the Devill wherewith she was possessed, being
by divine deprecations expelled, that same night, no signe of a scarre
being lefte, the ulcer closed up of it owne accord. Cardanus[103]
maketh relation of a case altogeather as admirable, *of a woman of*
note, the storie whereof being by him verie largely sett downe, for
the readers ease I will contract. *She laboured of a mighty burning of*
urin and perpetuall desire of making water [Fol. 72r] *wherefore .7.*
of the principallest physitions of the citie being called togeather, they
conjectured all causes, and devised all remedies, and applied the
same inwardly and outwardly, not sparing to open the part with
instruments, and that often, for the finding of that which offended,
and satisfying everie one in all their suspitions, but all in vayne.
Seaven moneths togeather she was thus tormented, and desperately
lefte of all. All the secrete parte being now ulcerate, and partly
through the heat and sharpnes of medicines applied, and partly
through their importunate using of instruments; and all her bodie
consumed as by her anatomies face, it well appeared, to everie man
that saw her. No hope remayning by physitions, there came unto her
one Josephius Niger Grek lecturer, but a noted magitian; he instructed
a sonne of this woman, who was his scholler, that looking in a
threesquare chrystall, he should saie, that he saw three ugly Divells,
standing on feete, before his mother, and another divell on horse-
back, much taller then they; with a threefork in his hand, who did
pinnion the other three, and binde them to [Fol. 72v] *his stirrops,*
and so lead them away. Hereupon the woman slept, her payne went
away, with all her buring and incessant desire of making water. Her
lively colour and flesh returned, so was she perfectly restored to
health and conceived with child. D Jorden abuseth his reader with

this example, bringing it in among such as were cured (being put into some good conceipt) by their imagination only. *Cardan* in deed, in the same place, where he writeth the storie, maketh question, whether she was cured by the divell, or by her imagination or faith, as he calleth it. And therefore reasoneth the matter thus. *If the boy spake true what he saw, and Joseph did but dissemble, this prompting of him, to cover the truth of his other doinges, for feare the law should take hould of him, for a conjurer, then was she cured by the Divell. But if the boy were warned before in a word, that he should affirme he saw whatsoever Joseph would ask him, then craft was used to procure the health of the mother, and so it is* [Fol. 73r] *manifest, that by imagination and faith she was healed. Only it is marvaile if craft were used, why he refused reward: for the kindely end of the fraud appeareth not, where no reward is sought for. And whether the matter should succeed, or not succeed, he was sure to hazard some estimation it it. Therefore it is more likely she was made wholl by the Divell.*

Behould how *Cardan* did cast in his minde, what causes were most probable to effecte this cure, and refusing that, wherein he saw no light to lead him, concludeth with the other which had all the likelyhood lefte unto it, when all things should be dewly examined. What reason (I pray you now) had *Dr Jorden* to deliver this narration in such words as he hath done? Namely thus. *Cardan tells of a gentlewoman, who finding her selfe vexed with many greivous symptomes, imagined that the Divell was the aucthor thereof, and by Josephus Niger was cured, by procuring her sonne to make her beleive, that he saw three Divells in her looking glasse, and one great one to drive them out.* Certainely he ought to be put in minde, [Fol. 73v] of divers corruptions and oversights, in this short passage. 1. that he maketh not relation of it sincerely, when he saith, that the *gentlewoman imagined that the Divell was the aucthor of her infirmities,* when there is no word in all the narration tending that waie. 2. he was weake in judgment, when he brought this instaunce in, among his malancholike conceited patients, cured by fallacies. For hers began not with imagination, but reall paines, and other symptomes, which consumed her wholl body. 3. that he would so smoothly turne *Cardans* tongue to tell the tale for him, contrarie to his setled purpose. If he would out of the storie, by reason have enforced it, (as seeing further then *Cardan* did) he should have lefte

59

us his reasons. 4. he was ignorant, that *Cardan* upon further information in that matter afterward, hath put us out of question, that it was by the worke of the divell: certiefying us in these wordes.[104] *It is manifest, that the* [Fol. 74r] *woman of whom we spake in our bookes of subtilitie, so manie waies vexed, and at length healed by Josephus Niger, was healed by the Divell, according as afterwards we understood, althoughe the man at that tyme did denye it.* I think I have, made a sufficient band of instaunces, to evict, that the Divell maie be found, to have his hand in sundry bodely afflictions, which have no supernaturall symptomes to discover them. Learned Physitions have afore me, bene of this minde:[105] and namely *Johannes Echtius* and *Hubertus Faber*; who els would never have adjudged that Nunne to have bene afflicted of the Divell; who complayned of nothing but a swelled belly like as in the dropsey. And avoyding stones by urin, as fragments of bricke; some as great as haslenutts, some lesser. Yet *Wier*, saith these .2 (whereof one his praiseth to be ἰατρὸς πολλῶν αθταξιος ἄλλωμ) did conclude so, after they had exactly scanned, and weighed every thing, by the just beame and ballaunces of art. And as thus, by the aucthoritie of instaunces, the stateliest pillour of all this platfourme, is pulled [Fol. 74v] downe, so by good reasons it cannot be builded againe, For naturall and supernaturall causes maie Concur, to the production or generation of sicknes, as they may likewise to the curation of them; and are not contraries that expell one another, as his argumentation supposeth. Also *Sathan* the Ocean sea of subtleties,[106] can, where leave is given him, hide his own ougly shape, under the leaves of ordinary symptomes; and make good advantage thereof, for exercising his mallice there the longer, and more securely. They whom God enlighteneth, shall (notwithstanding) fynd him out. Let no man make haste in these things, under pretence of doing good: Nor think, they can be discerned assoone as a tertian fever. *As one saide wisely of the word of God:*[107] *It hath shallowes in it, for silly lambes to wade in, and it hath depthes, able to drowne the huge Elephant.* So say I, of these workes of God, in like maner: there be manie of them apert and familiar, for meane capacities to discusse; and others againe, so abstruse and farr set of, as that the greatest witts in the world, maie [Fol. 75r] dayly finde reasons to admire them, but never to understand them. I hope *D Jorden* will not skorne, to make use of these thinges, with me. As touching his like actions and passions, which he speaketh of, and scattereth here and there, throughout his booke; The reader is to understand, that he taketh very dissolute libertie in his likenings, so as he might, with as good reason oftentimes, compare a Jacke an apes to a man, as manie of those symptomes of *Marie Glovers* affliction, to such actions and passions, as he layeth by them. Neither can I conceive what other use, he maketh of them, then, as by much trampling, of purpose, to raise a dust, to hinder his readers eies from seeing the perspicuitie of truthe.

Chapter 5

*That feare was no force, and
counterfeiting had no colour, in
Marie Glovers case*

D Jorden having engaged him selfe before the judgment seat to make this good; namely, [Fol. 75v][108] that *M Glover* was only sicke of the dissease called the mother, and that all the admired accidents observed in her case sprang of that only, and from no other originall; yet when he came to write in the cause (which I wish for his owne sake he had never ben drawne unto) he well found, that neither all his bookes, observations, nor freinds, were able to drawe out, the just limitts of that dissease, so farre, as to comprise and satisfie all the objections, which his readers would be readie out of her case to presse him with. He hath therefore added feare and Counterfeiting to amend his matter, intending, that when his reader shall remember how, at the presence of the witch, the maiden was afflicted, he should satisfie himselfe, with thinking, that it might spring out of feare. And if there come into his minde, anie other uncouth thing that all those reasons reach not; some voluntarie action by her dissembled, must make up his mouth. And thus he thinketh, he hath fullfilled his promise made in the conclusion of his epistle [Fol. 76r] in these wordes: *But in the discourse following,*[109] *I have as nere as I could, described all the symptomes of this dissease; whereby every man may readily finde answeres to his severall objections.* The symptomes of this disease, would never have served his turne, if he had not eiked them with these two peeces: as neither

61

now shall they doe, by the grace of God; if the reader will but lend
his willing eare indifferently: Let all prævaricators, when I have
done, speake and spite, what they can, to the contrarie. What
straunge mutations in the bodie of man, perturbations of the minde
are able to bring forth; if we had not the assent of the learned
philosophers of the world, yet the records of time, experience of all
ages, and daiely observations of our eies would evict [sic], confirme
and seale up the irresistable truth thereof.[110] And in deed the soule
being the soveraigne Comander of the body; as she is able, by
her continuall quyet motions, sciantally instituted, and dewly
accomplished, without impeachment [Fol. 76v] of adversarie, from
the highe throne of the phantasie, to defend the scale of the
conspiring faculties without rupture or disorder, even till she come
to the lowest and basest functions in the bodie, according as her
daiely dispensations doe demonstrate; so she being transported by
passion in her institutions, or interverted by adversarie occurrents
in her proceedings, breaketh the order of her scale, and putteth out
of tune the harmonie of the members: for even so, doe the ofte
events, of her maniefould erroures, like as manie trumpets
proclaime in our eares. And seing this is no singular, which maie not
make a rule in art, but comon to all men, in this our depraved estate
from Adam, that no discipline is able so to temper, and moderate
the maners of a man, or to settle and keepe downe, the tumultuous
motions of his minde, but that he is allwaies driven and tossed in
their waves and tempests, therefore have wise men, and that
worthely [Fol. 77r] placed these unrulie perturbations of the
minde,[111] amongst the evident and necessarie causes of disseases.
Notwithstanding as the soule, by her destinated powers, working
most regularly, is not able to exceede her latitude of atchievements;
which are bounded within the compasse of well knowne effects: So
neither maie it be thought, that her oversightes, and transgressions
in working, can have larger territories,[112] then particular oppositions to those effects, graunted them. Now then it seemeth naturally
deduced, that we must in all these matters, sayle by our certayne
compasse; and not suffer our ship, to be caried of everie windie
conjecture, to wrack our judgements, upon the sands of loose
conclusions. The moderation of our affections, conduce to health
and long life; their imoderation to sicknes and speedy death.
Neither of them priviledged with habilities to all maner purposes:

both of them marked with signes of their immediate presence, in the operation. How then should we feare, to meet with this Doctors allegation of feare? Certainely [Fol. 77v] although he joyne anger unto it,[113] we are resolved to abide the encounter. Now let us heare him, in his owne wordes, and at full, *Perturbations of the mind are oftentimes to blame both for this and manie other disseases.*[114] *For seeing we are not Masters of our owne affections, we are like battered cities without Walles, or Shippes tossed on the Sea, exposed to all maner of assaultes and daungers, even to the utter overthrow of our owne bodies. We have infinite examples among our historio-graphers and phisitions of such as have dyed upon joye, greife, love, feare, shame, and such like perturbations of the minde: and of others, that upon the same causes, have fallen into grievous disseases; as women delivered of their children before their time upon feare, anger, griefe etc.*[115] *Others taken with the falling sicknes, apoplexies, madnes, sownding, palseis, and divers such like infirmities upon the like causes.* These his and c. [etc.] and his divers *such like infirmities* are but overslight handlings of so serious a matter: or els to walke in craftines towards his reader, as laying traynes, to drawe into [Fol. 78r] his imagination, manie other things besides, which himselfe dare not mention. As [to] put case [to which] the reader could not applie his minde, to referre the fashion of *Marie Glovers* Case to the fitts of the mother, then he might yeeld it to the falling sicknes, or apoplexie, which manie men, women, and Children have ben surprized with, either through feare or some other passion, and if not one of those affects, yet some other of some such stamp, or kinde of resemblance. And how farre soever the thoughts of a man can runne in analogies, so far will he geve his reader leave to reave, so that himselfe be not held guiltie of his particular guiding. If this were his fetch, it discovereth great malignitie of minde; if not, it is to be marveiled at, whie in trading the doctrine of the suffocation of the mother, he could so fowly transgresse the law of καθ'αὐτὸ, as to offer us to looke upon examples, of unproper and impertinent natures.[116] As in his third chapter [Fol. 78v] where he undertaking to shew, how manie waies the mother may offend the vitall facultie, bringeth us to see, certaine examples of men, troubled with beating of the heart; which notwithstanding, had never the suffocation of the mother in all their lives. Againe in his 4 Chapter, being to declare how sundrily the animall facultie maie become offended by this dissease, he bringeth in a Catalogue of slovenly rouges and coosening copesmates, which by long practised impostures, and other worth-lesse peeces of skill, could raise admiration among the people. If these digressions have not the same reach in them, that I lately spake of, then the *D* sometimes slept as he wrote; but he slept not as he wrote: witnes the laborious quotations, even in those verie places; therefore the remaynder (for ought I can see) must lye upon him. Thus in trasing the digresser (which I cannot be excused to omit) I am somtimes constrayned to digresse, my self. Let us heare his more [Fol. 79r] pertinent exemplifications. *And concerning this dissease whereof we doe entreat Johannes Montanus tells us of a patient of his, who fell into fittes of the mother upon jealousie. Forestus of another, who had her fittes whensoever she was angred. And of another that upon love fell into this dissease. My selfe doe know a gentlewoman, who upon sight of a particular man, would alwaies feele an uterine affect. And another upon feare of being chidden, or seeing another in the fitt of the mother, would also fall into it her selfe.* Thus he setts before his reader divers covered dishes, and goes his waie. Well let us looke into them. It is a pitifull default, in the case of so miserable a famine of reasons, which this cause in controversie hath raised, to be fed with such pescod shelles as these, at the handes of so great and resolute an undertaker. His example of jealousie must here be rejected like as that of love. *Marie Glover* had neither of those *capriecies* in her braynes. Feare and anger [Fol. 79v] we admit, that they might have made suffocation of the mother in her, like as they doe in others, but we denye that they did so. Upon these reasons.[117] First touching feare (which both he and others do principally make choyce of to object) it was not there, in anie such degree (at least) as is requisite to the raising of such an affecte. For not everie measure of feare, but an excessive, (if not such as bringeth to consternation of minde) must worke this feate. But this mayd denyed, that she feared; both when she was encouraged by anie of us, at the coming in of the Witche, and when she was demanded of the same, at other times. Secondly if she had greatly bene afrayde of the Witche, she would have sought occasions, as much as lay in her, to have shunned and avoyded her. But this she never did, there being sundrie times, their meetings procured, well knowne to the maid. And saie, that it lay not in her power to shun them, yet it laie in her power to seeke shiftes [Fol. 80r] and doe her best to shun them; and it was not in the power of one, so fearfull as they pretend, to be without this propertie. To prove that she sought not to shun her, at any time, both there are manie witnesses, that will stand forth for it, and also one of their meetings which was at Alderman Glovers house, doth verie specially confirm it. For thither both the maid and the woman, being sent for, on a daie, and hower, wherein the maide was newly recovered out of her ordinarie fitt, *Marie* might have made manie excuses for that time, for going out of dores to her, if she had ben affraid to see her. But to shew the plaine contrarie, she not only went readely thither, but when she was there, desired confidently; to be brought face to face with her.[118] .3. Feare (like as the rest of the passions) cannot raise the mother or make anie such notable mutation either in ould or young, save in bodies disposed.[119] But *M. Glovers* bodie, was neither plethorick nor cacochymous, nor yet attayned to seminall or menstruall ripenes;[120] therefore not a subject [Fol. 80v] disposed for passion to worke upon.[121] .4. This feare, defined to be a suddaine, and unrulie revocation of the bloud, and spiritts, from the outward partes, unto the heart, bringeth in a chilling could, trembling and palenes in the outward parts, and causeth a small, slow, rare, and weake pulse to be felt; easie and familiar signes to prove his presence by. This maid had no more palenes at these times, then at other fitts without the presence of that woman, but besides that no cold, no trembling in her members, yea an equall temper of heate, even when deprivation of all sense and moving ceazed on her. Her pulse large, lively, strong, equall, and without fault; except that somtimes, in the fitt, it might be observed over fast going.[122] Therefore feare must not be admitted in this operation. 5. Feare was sufficiently disproved at Sergeant Crookes Chamber, at that time the Recorder of London. If the maides feare had done the deed, then had she fallen downe, when he brought in unto her, the same woman (for [Fol. 81r] ought she could tell) muffled and disguised; which were some occasions, to strike feare into anie one. But albeit the Recorder, caused her to touch the woman diverse times, using words, such as implyed, it was that woman; saying he hoped she should thereafter, never more have cause to be affrayde of her, and dwelling somwhat long upon the matter, the maid for all this, remayned as she was before, and was not altered. Most certaine it is, none of them in the chamber were privie to the Recorders counsaile, there was no dissimilitude in the outward forme of the person. It was verie easie for the maide to thinke it was that verie woman, when as all her neighbours that were with her, protested that they tooke it so. And who could tell how manie others he would disguise, before he brought the right one. 6. Let us consider, how at the judgement seat, when this maid stood forth to geve in her evidence, not seeing the woman (who stood in the dock a pretye distaunce of, and manie persons betweene) yet before [Fol. 81v] she could utter .xl. words, as interrupted, she cryed, where is shee? *'Where is she that troubleth me'*. and so fell downe.[123] Was this likely to be feare? Or rather a comanding power, which she felt, at that instaunt ceazing upon her, even whilest she resisted to the uttermost that was in her. Lastly to the quitting of feare, and anger and everie passion els, I reason thus: If these thinges threw her into that ougly fitt, at the presence of the widow Jackson, then could she not fall into that fit, although that woman were present, whensoever the occasions of those passions were truly prevented. But the maid, *Ma Glover*, fell into that same kinde of fitt, at the presence of that woman, at such time as the occasions of all such passions was truely prevented. Therefore neither feare, nor anger, nor any such was cause thereof. Manie sought meanes in deed, at sundrie times, to cleere this [Fol. 82r] pointe. And at length it was. 2. severall times,[124] by sundrie godlie and discreet men so ordered, that upon the suddaine, in the time whilest the maide laie cast into her ordenary fit, no notice being geven to the Parents, or anie of that familie, that infamous ould woman, was secretly brought into the Roome, which usually in those daies, was well filled with men, women, and Children, behoulders of a terrible spectacle. But verie shortly after her coming into the roome, although she neither spake to the maide nor came neere her, but only was quyetly kept within the Chamber, behould the body, that even now, being miserably plunged and tossed, yeelded forth lamentable crying and yelling, turned by verie sensible degrees, into an universall stiffnes and insensibilitie, the outward temper of her flesh nothing altering therewith. Also her inward senses were abolished: and by litle and litle increasing degrees, a voyce groweth [Fol. 82v] in her nostrills, first, whisperingly, and at length audibly, as though she should say, *hang her, or hong her*: according as in all these fitts, at the presence of that woman, she alwaies accustomed to have it.

Here could be no occasion of feare. Here could be no opportunitie for perturbations of the minde to take hould. Once I know *D Jorden* was urged with this argument, and had nothing to answere, but suspected the truth of the Narration. But there are manie witnesses, and such, as against which, no exception can take place, among so manie godlie men as know them. Therefore since that time (as I understand) he hath thought it fitter to shape this answere; that peradventure the maide at such times did heare a noise of a coming in of manie at once, by an extraordinarie shuffling and trampling of feete, with roome making, and such like thinges.[125] And thereupon feare might surprise her, lest the said widow Jackson were entred in: I will not [Fol. 83r] conceale that I have heard of this answere and thus I replie; put case it should have bene, as he saith, yet could have ben no absolute feare, but a suspition at the most or doubtfullnes. But where doubtfullnes is, there is som contradiction in the minde, and striving on both handes: and consequently no tirannous perculsion of the minde could grow from thence. For (as it hath bene shewed) it is not anie meane or remisse degree of feare; but the highest of terrour, that striketh as the lightening, is able to bring such a thing to passe. Therefore this answere, even when he hath too much favour given him, can gayne him nothing. Yet againe I say withall, if it could have bene able to have gott him gaine, he must have lost it. For the christian wise reader, will not by and by, be lead, by his bare surmise, who speaketh to maintaine his owne argument, that those men who tooke care, and set in order manie things, to attayne to the cleering of this pointe, would (when they had so secretly caried [Fol. 83v] the rest, that neither the Parents nor anie of that houshould, were privie to that purpose) so grossely erre, in this last act of it, as to come into the chamber, with an *o yes* before them. My selfe at this same tryall, stoode at the bed side by the maide, and, I protest before the righteous judge of heaven and earth, (there standing much people betwixt the bed and the doore, so as I was not able to see her) I did not, at all perceive her coming in. As for the noyse of feete and such other signes, let the reader know moreover, that there, it was an usual thing, daily, in times of her ordinarie fitts, to have manie behoulders, coming in and going out, sometimes by troupes of .8. or .10. at once; and persons of worship and honor, which had waye made for them. And therefore such noyses were ordenarie and no noveltie, if so be they had bene at that time, as in deede, and truth they were not. So that this answere of the Doctor, to so weightie an argument, is but as the [Fol. 84r][126] cavilling shifte of some malignant minde, who not being able to satisfie with reason, casteth yet a stone in the waie, for the truth to stumble on. And would to God, I were able, but in this one thing, to resemble him unto a man of malignant minde, I should not then have ben put unto it, to defend this cause from the imputation of counterfeiting, as now (even greived for his sake) yet wholl minded for the truthes sake, which I love more) [sic] I must, and cannot choose. For in the .4th. chapter of his booke,[127] where he undertaketh to declare, how the animall facultie, maie manie waies be offended, in that disease of the mother, after a litle entraunce made, he findeth a pretty occasion, to deliver us a speciall difference, of the animall facultie, from the vitall and naturall, thus: *This animall facultie hath this peculiar difference from the vitall and naturall faculties, that the functions of it are subject to our will, and maie be intended, remitted or perverted, at our pleasure, otherwise then in the other faculties for no man can make* [Fol. 84v] *his pulse to beate as he list, or alter the naturall functions at his will and pleasure. But these animall functions maie be abused, both by our owne will, and by the violence of some dissease, and by both, as Galen testifieth li. 2. de sympt. caus. cap. 12. That it may be abused by our owne will, he proveth also in another place, where he bringeth an instaunce of a servant (servi barbari) who killed himselfe, to anger his master by houlding his breath,* and so, having found so much wast place, to set up his stall, [he] openeth a large fardell of such like instaunces; at least, to make his reader stand at the gaze, although he list not to buy. And amongst the rest of such good ware, maketh shew of this faire jewell; *that some have counterfeited possessions, either upon meere deceipt, or inticed thereto, through the conceit of som dissease, wherewith they have ben troubled.* And what then? Though *Rachell Pinder* and too manie such have done this; what is that to us?[128] Forsooth he geveth this ynkling in another place; *Wherefore* [Fol. 85r] *it behooveth us,*[129] *as to be zealous in the truthe, so to be wise in discerning truth from counterfeiting, and naturall causes from supernaturall power.* What? But is it possible, that *D Jorden* is willing, his reader should imagine, *Marie Glover* did counterfeit? What els? I am out of doubt of it. See what he saith, where he telleth

his reader, what arguments we use, to prove *M. Glovers* case
supernaturall. *Another maine argument of theirs is the deliverance*
upon fasting and praier: which we will imagine to be so in deed,
without anie counterfeiting in the pointe. To be thus quit of
counterfeiting in one point, what is it but to enwrap her in the guilt
thereof in other poynts? If he had meant generally to absolve her, he
would absolutely have said, *We will imagine it to be so in deede*
without any counterfeiting, leaving out the other wordes: which
restrayning his liberalitie, to one part of her cause, implieth a
denyall of so much favour to the wholl. Also since his booke
writing, he hath charged this maide to her face, that she did
dissemble som things, what [Fol. 85v] then shall we conclude of *D*
Jorden, in this poynt? He hath sworne before the publique seat of
judgment,[130] that *M Gl* (in his conscience) did not counterfeit. He
hath written it unto all posteritie, that she did counterfeit. I will not
(for my part) stand long wondring at this thing. I will beleive his
oath; and help to my power that posteritie maie interpret this
difficultie, according as I think, in my conscience, the case doth
stand. A gentleman of good understanding, that wrote the arraing-
ment of the old woman, that bewitched *M Glover* setting downe *D*
Jordens evidence, hath these wordes. *But when the bench saw him*
at first, undertake to prove it a naturall dissease, and marked that all
his speach tended to make it a counterfeit (as though he had eie
rather to some private instructions and resolution, then to his owne
proposition, and the tenor of his oath) the Judge interrupted him etc.
In these wordes (I am perswaded) is the nayle smitten upon the
head: namely, that he spake not in that sort then, nor hath not
written thus [Fol. 86r] since, fully out of his owne heart; but
enchaunted by the charmes of privat instructions, the bane of manie
a just cause; and so, the concluding not of an evell man, but of a
weake man, will grow upon him. But be his weaknes what it wilbe,
yet seeing that in his weaknes, he hath ben wonne, to scandalize this
cause, by the waie of counterfeiting, so, as manie from him, have
taken it into their mouthes, I fynde my selfe called to stand a while
longer, in this place; to heare, and to answere whatsoever he is able
out of his contagious instructions, to object. It must be heere
remembred, that in one place of the narration, is described, the
manner of the maides affliction, at the presence of the suspected
woman. And namely, that when the maide laie, all stiffe and

senseles, if then the woman touched her with her hand, the maides
bodie would wallow over, or tosse and rebound up in the midle.
What it is also added (according to the truth of most diligent
observation) that this *tumbling or casting over towardes* [Fol. 86v]
the witch[131] *(when she came to the bedside or touched her[)], was at
the first .2. tryalls, verie palpably plaine, and towards her only.
Afterwardes, neither was the motion so vehement, nor perpetually
towardes the woman; but somtimes towardes others also.* Hence
must arise his worthie demonstrations of Counterfeiting:[132] I had
like to have called them ridiculous. Now let the reader be judge;
whether I had sufficient cause. In one fit, wherein we had the old
woman present, *D Jorden*, after he had sene manie of these
touchings, called alowde, to have that woman againe, to touch her,
but withall, silently poynted unto another to doe it. At the touching
of this other, the bodie rebounded up in the middle, in the like sorte
and so in like maner did it .4. or .5. times togeather, sundry persons
touching her: somtimes the old woman being called upon, somtimes
not called upon before. Hereupon was great insulting for (I know
not what) discoverie: but in deed a rash insulting, upon poore
prejudiced truth. Yet forwardes they goe, well weening to gaine the
consequent: which was, that calling likewise alowd, to have the old
woman [Fol. 87r] now, caried out of the house, and yet secretly
retayning her, the maide might have geven over, the uttering of that
voyce by the nose, which sounded *hang her*: but alas that did not
succeed, (dissemble as they could) untill such times, as filled with
those pastimes, they let the woman go from the house in deede. My
selfe stood by, all this while, and saw this wittie comedy. What I
thought, I did not forbeare to tell the Doctor himselfe afterward.
But now, am constrained, to tell him againe in the eares of manie;
and that with som advauntage, or increase of answere to it. And, to
doe it in order, (which we love in all things) let us first laie downe,
the supposed gaines, that he hath gotten by this passage, and then
deliver our satisfactions distinctly. Two maine pointes hereby, he
would have his reader thinke, he hath evicted [sic]. One, that *Marie
Glover* had her sense of hearing in all times of her fittes. An other
that this chalenging motion of her bodie, at the presence of the
woman, was voluntarily performed, and held by observation, to
accuse the woman, and raise up admiration. That *Ma: Gl* had her
hearing all times, he coveteth here, as also in sundrie [Fol. 87v]

places of his booke, to draw upon his reader: because it serveth him
to threed his needle, to peece up other breaches hereafter. As it is
delivered in the historie, or narration, of her affliction, there were
divers times, wherein she could heare, and divers times, wherein she
could not heare, in her ordinarie fitt, but in this extraordinarie fitte,
(which never hapned but when this woman came unto her) she was
utterly deprived of all her senses. Which we are induced by these
necessarie consequents to beleive. All the while she could heare,
only halfe of her bodie laie spoyled of feeling and moving:[133] the
other halfe had serviceable feeling, though the moving was not so
good. When soever she gave no signe of hearing then only, all her
bodie was universally voyd of feeling. Againe when one side was
deprived of feeling, then one eare (namely of the same side) was
deprived of hearing. Proved thus: We laide a finger under her arme
pitt, or upon her shoulder, or upon her eare or temple, on the
afflicted side, and called upon her, to answere [Fol. 88r] by signe,
whether she felt our hand or noe. To hould up her hand of the
better side, was the signe affirmitive; not to move it at all, was her
negative. She denyed to feele it. Then we would remove, or draw
our finger forward, toward her brest, throate, nose or forehead,
according to the first placing of it, keeping a right line; she never
(being oftentimes demanded) gave signe of feeling untill the finger
came at the line, which devideth the bodie into .2. equall partes
according to the longitude. Then we stopped the right eare, that was
the whole side, and called upon her to geve answere to our
questions: but all the while we stopped that eare there was no more
signe geven to anie question. Which declared plainely that as she
moved not, nor felt not, so she heard not on her afflicted side at all.
And then by verie just consequence it followeth, that at what time,
that same deprivation of feeling and moving, invadeth both sides, at
such time also, [Fol. 88v] there was a totall privation of hearing
withall. For the proportion must needs hould true in both alike;
except he can geve us som good reason of a difference. As to the
moving of her bodie, at the touching of the woman aforetime, and
now of others, which should proove, she was taken with crafte, and
so laide open in her malice and imposture. It is but as a dreame,
wherein men (somtimes) build castles in the aire, but find them not
habitable, when they are well awake. By manie experiments of
pintchings, and prickings with pinnes, some before, some at that

time; and after that, of burnings with fire; it was made as cleere as
the sunne at noone day, that the maid was voyd of feeling, in all that
kinde of fitt. What then avayled it, for anie to touch her, to the
purpose that they intended? And as she had no feeling, so neither
power of anie voluntarie moving, her whole bodie and partes [Fol.
89r] lying (as is sett forth in the story) in an incredible stiffenes and
deformitie. In somuch as when it did rise up in the middes, as if it
would rebound, it fell not downe againe, as in voluntarie motions,
but stoode halfe waie crooked still, as ruled by a straunge power.
And this it did, at that verie time they speake of; the bodie
remaining betwene their touchings, halfe bended upwardes, with a
side way crooking, so as one might easelie, put their arme bet[w]ixt
the bed and her. I aske therefore where was their *acumen?* Nay
where was comon reason? Had not an eager desire of carping and
traducing infatuated them? Els they would have called their wittes
togeather, and reasoned thus: If she do of purpose move, at the
touching of this woman, as chalenging her to be consenting to her
harme, then it behoveth, that she have the sense of feeling, to
take knowledge when she is touched: but (presently would have
come in there mindes) she hath no sense of feeling, and so this
conclusion, therefore that must needs be a vaine tryall. The rest of
his concurrents [Fol. 89v] there that were not Phisitions, might
readelie thus have foreseene their absurditie. But the Doctor him
selfe, should have ben able, to have seene it, in this that followeth
likewise. Where voluntarie moving must be,[134] there must be first a
libertie of the joynts; but here is an universall and strong rigiditie in
all the joyntes; therefore here is no voluntarie motion to be
expected. Paradventure then it wilbe here demanded, if this were
not a voluntarie motion, what was it? I answere, that, seeing for the
reasons aforesaid, it could not be voluntarie; nor from any dissease,
because it answered to their purpose: it must needes follow, that
some supernaturall power had so much commaund at that time,
over her members. If supernaturall, then either a good or an evill
Angell: but not a good; because it perverted the ordenance of the
Creator, in the position and motion of all the members of the bodie;
therefore an evill Angell, even that uncleane spirit, who hateth the
works and glorie of god, was there. And he it was, that by such
tossing of the maides bodie, [Fol. 90r] and moving that voyce in her
nostrills, chalenged that wicked woman, as a compartener, or

abettor in that worke. But readely will Mr Doctor here returne upon me, to knowe, how then this came to passe, that the maides bodie tossed at the touching of others besides her? Nay I will help him with this much more, that it tossed, at that time, at the touching of others, and stirred not when she touched. My selfe made that e[x]periment, a litle before *D Jordens*: taking the womans hand in mine, and laying it first upon the maides hand, and then upon her face. But she stirred at neither. Yet instantly, sundrie others touching her, she moved at them all. To this demand therefore I make this answere. *Sathan* being a thousand fould deceiver,[135] can well skill, (when leave he is geven him) by one act, to serve himselfe of divers turnes. And so it is hard for man, to sett downe in anie certaintie, whie or to what end *Sathan* should so carie it; both at this time and thenceforth, to make the bodie tosse at the touching of others, and before that time, but [Fol. 90v] at Widow Jacksons only. Yet I will not sweare, to shewe my conjecture freely, togeather with the reasons thereof, let the reader consider, and so geve sentence, whether I kepe within the compasse of probabilitie, or not. Betwene Witches and their Divells a compact or covenant ever intercedeth. The Witches promise to do their service and sacrifice to him.[136] He geveth his sure word, to gratefie them againe, with their desires. By which word of his, although their obligation be no better, then if it were sealed with butter; yet he will not stick, to make a goodly shew for it, in divers particulars, which maie not hinder his essentiall attempt of their ruine. When therefore, he hath receaved Comission from God, to seaze upon the person of a man or woman, and hath drawne into the conspiracie, some of these destitutes, of Goddes favour and protection, if, in his tormentings, he discover the witch, by som signes taken notice of, (which he seldom faileth to do and as in this case he did notoriously) he will not stick [? illeg.] (that he may retayne her faster) to gratifie [Fol. 91r] with the chaunge of a signe, wherewith shee is too too [sic] much troubled. And this may seeme to be one mayne motive unto *Sathan* in our present instance. The old Woman, in .2. severall encounters before this, had ben mervaylously agasted, at this maner of chalenge, made to her, and to no man or woman els, so as all the people cryed out upon her; therefore now, she had desired her good servant (or Master rather) to use that trick no more. And so he condescended to this new composition; namely, that thence forth the maides bodie

73

should either not move at her touching, or not at hers only. A verie like case to this fell out, in that notable witcherie, of Mr. Throgmortons children at Warboyse in Huntington shire.[137] For there, after sundrie lighter chalenges, one daye, the Divell caused the Children to accuse mother *Samuell*. More specially, by this; namely, that they were ever in their fittes, and would not be well in any place, but in the presence and companie of mother *Samuell*. Whereupon, that [Fol. 91v] witch, being greatly encombred, as constrayned to tarie, at Mr Throgmortons house, among the Children; One daye, she got leave to go home for a litle time; meane space, some of the Child[r]en fell into their fitts, and the *spirit then talking with them* (as it used to doe) saied; *that now Mother Samuel was feeding of her spirites, and making a new League and composition with them; which was that although now she came againe to the house, they shalbe no whit the better, but rather the worse for her being there, because she would not remaine any longer there: which thing seemed to be true that the child spake; for so soone as she came againe the children which were in their fitts at her coming, so continued, and they that were not, after her coming fell into their fittes, all of them crying out, that now Mother Samuel had made a new composition with her Spirits.* And surely, in this our case of *M. Glover*, *Sathan* purchased a large field of comodeties, by so doing. For he seeing som present there, that were setled in incredulitie, and knowing, there were greater ones abroad, that laie in the winde for som slaunderous calumniations, to blemish this cause with, stood [Fol. 92r] the handes of both, in this oportunitie. And by that means, satisfied his good dame, brought to passe, division among the behoulders and witnesses, slaunder to the innocent maid, scandale to the truthe, securitie to his longer inhabitation, and prevention (as he hoped) to that casting out, which might much advauntage the cause of the Church, and give glory, unto the God of most unserchable mercies, everlasting power, and infinite wisdome. Neather did *Sathan* in seeking so great a purchace, departe from one pinne of his game in the seelie woman.[138] As nether did he, in that other example of the witches of Warboyse. But as there, he discovered mother *Samuell*, in her new composition, so did he here; both by making all touchings waste, but when the witch was present, (which had ynough in it still, to accuse her by) and by pursuing her with that goodly voyce in the maydens nose, so longe as ever she made her abode within that roofe. The which voyce at that time when this wise discovery was somuch presumed upon, seeing it hold [Fol. 92v] on without interruption, untill the witch departed the house, and at that time ceassed; notwithstanding all the policies they could invent, to make it alter, it must remaine a good demonstration for it selfe, and also conclude another argument, For the former point, that nether action was voluntarie, and so by consequent nether counterfeit. Which things well considered, it will (as I beleeve) proove a bile in his conscience one day, thus far to have broken the nynth precept of the royall law of God, sinning against his neighboures good name, Which *Sollomon* prized at so great a rate. Whether it grewe from his owne Corruption, or from other mens malicious instructions, let him looke unto it, if he love the peace of his conscience. For as these reasons will not support him, whereupon he adventured to ground himselfe, so all other inducing considerations crie shame on him.[139] First the forepassed life of the parents was not such, as ether to bring up the Children and servants, in wayes [Fol. 93r] to abuse the world with counterfeiting. 2. the maides education was like other mens of his qualitie; in her booke, sampler writing and other houshold laboures, according to the necessities of her parents. 3. her affliction came suddainely, not without an overture of supernaturall causes, but altogeather without cullour of teaching or trayning to it. And namely for this reason that her fittes greatly varied, after so many behoulders came dayly to observe her, so as she could not cleanly learne any new trickes, without being espied in her first raw acting of them. 4. For that Phisitions and Chirurgeons were used seriously from the beginning of her affliction, and for ten weekes space continued, untill they pronounced that there was something in it, beyond the compasse of naturall causes; and some of them sought to use supernaturall meanes to succour her. 5. If there had bene imposture, there must needs also have ben lucre. But that stood only in charges upon Phisitions, and [Fol. 93v] sought remedies, and in sundrie losses and spoyles, which could not be but often comitted, by such multitudes of daylie commers unto them, for divers monethes togeather. If anie shall suspect there was mony geven them. Let them take but the wholl truthe with them, and I graunt it; Which was this; some personages of honour and sundrie worship, when they had seene the sad spectacle, and considered their wofull miserie, could not but in comisseration leave somthing in their handes when they departed: Not that the Parents made anie signe of seeking it (for my selfe was present at the chiefest time, and was consulted with by the givers, whether it might be convenyent, in respect of the scandale, to give any money or no: As also I had ben manie dayes before that; by the father; whether he should take anie thing, at the handes of certaine Ladies and gentlewomen, that enforced him) but that noble mindes think it a disparagement to their reputation not to doe it. I am assured therefore that the Parents tooke litle [Fol. 94r] mony, and no gaine: not for that I presume they followed my counsell, but for that the summe beinge afterwardes exacted by an oath of them, came not to Six Poundes from the begining to the day of her deliveraunce. Which I hope can be no argument of seeking lucre by counterfeiting; without which yet, counterfeiting can be but verie could. 6. We are manie witnesses of the pitifull groanes and sighes of the parentes daylie, and of the vehement prayers, with cryes and teares, of the wofull father, unto him, that was not to be jested withall, at anie hande. 7. There are sufficient witnesses, that the maidens prayer at the end of her great fittes, as it was mixt with thankes givings, so was it also, with direct protestations in this behalfe. As namely, she besought God,[140] *to manifest the truthe, to his glorie, and to the satisfying of the Church, and called him to witnesse, that herselfe added nothing to her owne afflictions.* 8. When anie waies of tryalls, or to sifte out any poynt, have bene [Fol. 94v] devised upon, or undertaken, the Parents have nether resisted, nor sought shiftes to put them of. 9. Nether have they in her fitts, used any whisperings with the maide, nor anie such like suspicious cariage; nor bent them selves to be much with her, but comonlie rather gave libertie, for all straungers to stand next about her. 10. In the dayes of her sequestration, from her Parents, by the hand of aucthoritie, she was with all thirstie diligence, examined upon everie point, and winnowed, as far, as anie lawfull proceeding could stretch; and at length dismissed, with no fault found in her. Lastly, that most fearfull, and withall most joyfull day of the maides deliverance, whether you consider therein, the maner and measure of her passions, the spirit and power of her prayers, and the proportionable sequences of the Divills casting out; with everie particular severally, and all sett togeather joyntly, it doth proclayme it, both

Mary Glovers Late Woeful Case

with a lowde voyce, and with much evident authorities from the Author of truthe himselfe, that she was innocent in this behalfe, [Fol. 95r] and unwoorthie, that the least insinuation of counterfeiting should be offred unto her. If *D Jorden* did not ponder all these thinges in his minde, before he set his hand to write his booke, he is shallow and rash headed, unworthie to be employed in grave and weightie affaires: especially seeing all those thinges, that I have noted, were passed, before he wrote, and as recoverable for him, to have set before his eies, to consider of (if benevolence or equabilitie had possessed him) as now they were at hand with me, to make him see them, to his just reproofe. Againe, if he did recount all, or moste of these things in his minde, and yet applied his hand in writing, to dispose his readers minde, to thinke of counterfeiting; Alas, what pitie is it, that an honest man, should be somuch corrupted with evill companie? O that he had remembred, what it is, to be *a brother in evill, or to be a partaker with other mens sinnes*, that he might have [Fol. 95v] taken the counsell of the Apostle and so have kept *himselfe free.* Also,[141] *he that condemneth the innocent, and justifieth the wicked, even both are alike abhomination before God,* saith the wise man. He is guiltie of the former here by good proofe; and he standeth chargeable therefore, with the latter, by an inevitable consequence. Let him pardon this my vehemencie, in the behalfe of truth and innocencie. If he had spoyled them of their goodes, there might have ben easie restitution; but the publique blemish of their good name, he is never able to satisfie. For howsoever the wound is healed, yet the skarre remaineth: and there is an advauntage lefte, by him that inflicteth such a wound, for everie lascivious tongue, to make it raw againe. For this therefore, even for this mischeife, God provided a preservative warnon [sic] in his word,[142] saying *Thou shalte not walke about with tales among thy people* for such is humaine corruption, that a testimonie of goodnes in our neighbour, is either not at all receaved, or els (at the moste) not [Fol. 96r] much regarded: selfelove and envie sitting as partners in our heartes. But if an evill note be once raised up, be it never so false and Calumnious, mens affections are, not only ready handed, to receave it, but tickled with delight, to spread and multiplie it. A heathen man spake divinely in this point,[143] when he saide *A calumniation (or a crime unjustly imposed) is a thing most greivous; as in which, there are 2. doing wrong, and one receaving it.*

77

For the Calumniator doth injurie, in accusing the absent, and even so doth he who giveth credit to the accuser, before he truely knoweth the matter: but the absent partie is injured both by the Calumniator himselfe, and also by others who, lending so light an [sic] *care unto him, esteeme evill thenceforth, of the partie that was traduced.* But certainely, it never becometh a good man, either to deliver a calumniation himselfe, or to receave it from another. One saith well:[144] *Whosoever giveth credit to calumniations, is himselfe either defiled with evill conditions, or els hath plainely but a childish* [Fol. 96v] *wit. Manie (saith Rheginus) have receaved more hurt by calumniations then by enemies;*[145] *and more hurt is done to manie, thorough* [sic] *the infirmitie of their owne eares, then by all the strategemes of their adversaries.* Seeing then this sinne is great before *Jehovah*, and is withall, an easie trap of *Sathan*, for sinnefull man to fall into (as men out of meere naturalls have acknowledged) it standeth all in hand, unto whome this cause shall come, not to receave into their mindes anie impression of Imposture which the *D* insinuateth; if they love to keep their Conscience uncorrupt, free from the taynt and guilt of slander and oppression.[146] My selfe am neither kinsman, nor of any ancyenter acquaintance then their late affliction; wherein my paines taken, as manie will witnesse, was without reward: therefore were they nothing interested in me. Againe they were of low ranke, among the people, and of meane mainteynance, therefore there is no worldly thing that I could hope for at their handes. On the other side, they that hated them in this cause are mightie, and will hate me for their sakes, therfore there is danger towardes me, [Fol. 97r] by this testimonie: furthermore in publique I have (untill now) said nothing; and therefore not engaged my selfe, further, then that I might have, (if time had shewed the truth to stand on the other side) with sufficient safetie of my reputation, withdrawne my foote: wherefore it can be no wisdome of flesh and bloud, that hath drawne me into their defence. Only the truth, whose free servant I am, hath called upon my conscience, my conscience hath awaked my spirit, my spirit thenceforth hath incessauntly supplicated to the Author of truth, and father of spirits, and upon these grounds, and causes, and upon these only, and none other, (as he that knoweth the heart, can witnesse) have I delivered my present testimonie in this point. They that speake, or write otherwise thereof, if the wise shall well winnow them, shalbe found (if they have not leapt for a benefice in it) to have done it, either out of ignorance, of *M Gl:* case, in particular; or els out of malice, against the cause of possession and dispossession of divells, in generall.

[Fol. 97v][147]

Chapter 6

That Marie Glovers affliction was not the Suffocation from the Mother

Seeing then, that these two peecings (feare and counterfeiting) which made his cause an imoderate extente, are cut away from him, and that there remaineth no more help, but the suffocation of the mother, to compas all his purpose by, he must have patience now, to have his writings in that also, weighed by other mens balaunces, aswell as by his owne. For having found him, in the former, worthie to be taxed, we have cause in the latter, to looke more diligentlie into his behaviour. Which if the attentive reader, shalbe pleased, with patience, for a while to condescend unto, I beleeve, we shall finde his defects, touching this point, prove as evident, as we did his depravation in the other. In manie thinges, he hath well delivered the doctrine of Physick, touching the passions from the mother, according to the cheiftayn [Fol. 98r] writers in our profession; and in deed much varietie of symptomes maie appeare, and manie waies affected maie the principall functions be (able to raise som admiration to the unlearned) in those affectes, which are saide to have their originall from the mother; which thinges, in som measure, also, we ought to know; and it is not verie probable, to those that are acquainted with us, that we should be so grossely ignorant in them, as he would fashion his reader to esteeme. Notwithstanding, it is not sufficient for him to saie, sundrie, great, and deformed symptomes, may spring from Hystericall passions, and upon such or such causes; but he must withall, conclude the same in our particular subject; and demonstrate the same, by the causes and signes, not comon, but proper to that part, so affected only. And especially, seeing he so premptorily calleth for a Character of supernaturall at our handes, It ought to have come into his minde,

79

by the law of equall right, to geve us such pathognomonicall signes out of *M Glo.* [Fol. 98v] case; as might be able to induce such as have their senses exercised in those thinges, to beleeve, that the mother ill affected, was the cause of all her evell. Yea, considering these times, wherein so hot contentions are growne amongst us, touching the power of *Sathan*, in vexing the bodies, as well as the soules of men, he might well think, that his oblique insinuations could satisfie no man, but such, as had alreadie, captivate themselves, unto the negative partie. If he wrote not to satisfie, but to put scruples, whie intermedled he? With what conscience could he do it? He hath said, *that he valeweth our judgmentes (that are contrarie) at a verie low rate*: We mervaile not now, thereat; seeing that the truthe and peace (oh, what can be so precious on earth [? illeg.] to a good man?) are both misprized by his writing. For sith there is nothing in the world of his booke,[148] able to cleere one pointe in our controversie, and yet verie manie thinges, geving [Fol. 99r] men occasion to stumble at the truthe, and go awrie in judgement; he must needes be guiltie of misprision against the truth. And the disturbance of the peace of the Church, is such a consequent thereto, as all the powers of men cannot avoyde; much lesse I, by this my defence, can, though fayne I would promise to atchieve anie matter of moment to that purpose. Only this I will endevour, that in contending for the truthe, I maie geve no just occasion of encreasing the strife. Which if apert and plaine handling, of that which he hath intricately enwrapped; and a diligent producing and discussing [of] all things, that fall within our compasse, to the best satisfaction that I can procure, maie be able to bring to passe, I doubt not to doe it: or, at least, so as honest men shall acknowledge, I have made no sleight attempt for it. Let our cause then, come before the readers eies, in this sort: *D Jorden*, and I, visited, and considered [Fol. 99v] *M. Gl.* in her late affliction; he out of his best judgment, pronounceth; that it was nothing els, but the suffocation of the mother, wherewith she was troubled, I (not a litle sorie that we so dissent) say, it was not that dissease. Thus he disputeth for the affirmative.

Whatsoever affects are but a diminishing or abolishing of the animall, vitall, or naturall faculties, or the functions depending upon them, those same are meere naturall affects.

But all *M. Glovers* affectes were such:
Therefore all *M. Glovers* affectes were meere naturall.

And then, forasmuch as it wilbe graunted, that in some passions of
the mother, all the principall functions maie be diminished, depraved or abolished, his meaning is, that his reader should deduce it
hypothetically, that all *M Glovers* affects, sprang but from that
principall, which is called the suffocation from the mother. Namely,
as if he had thus delivered it:

> If the suffocation of the mother be able to diminish, deprave,
> or abolishthe animall [Fol. 100r] vitall and naturall faculties,
> and the functions depending upon them, then all *Marie
> Glovers* symptomes, sprang from the suffocation of the
> mother.

But the first is true:
Therefore the later is true also.

Of my sinceritie, in this drawing to head, his loose scattered
disputes, and subtillie insinuated driftes, I willingly make the reader
of his booke, my judge, as whether, I have, or not, made it speake,
in the perfectest language wherewith he endewed it. First I will
answere to his simple sillogisme, and after that to his compound, as
it falleth in order. His proposition and assumption are both false;
therefore his conclusion must have no place. To his proposition I
answere more precisely, by distinguishing, first, of the *naturall
affectes*: which comprehend the causes and effectes, the dissease and
symptome, the outward appearance or figure, and essentiall being
or fourme of such thinges. For as *affectes* [Fol. 100v] implyeth both
the dissease as cause, and symptome as effecte; so naturall intendeth, both the outward appearaunce of such, by their fashioned
symptomes, and the essentiall being of them, by the causes formally
producing them. And so, that maie have the semblaunce of naturall,
touching the outward figure, which is supernaturall, as touching the
cause. The offended functions therefore, whether it be in diminution, depravation or abolition, maie be of sorte, to be raunged with
such, as flow from ordenarie sicknes, and yet for all that have an
efficient *trans naturam*, or (as we use to speake) supernaturall.
Examples hereof abound; and I have affoorded him a competent
number in the .4. *chap*. Before we depart here, his proposition must

81

be branded with this evill note; that it strengtheneth miscreants, to denie some of his glorious workes, and darken a part of the loving kindenes of our God, to his people; which from time, to time, he hath testified, by this casting [Fol. 101r] out of *Sathan*: so as if the gainesaying Jewes had heard him in those dayes, they could have given a more slie censure, and more likely to have hindred Christs estimation among the people (which they earnestly sought) then to saie, *he cast out divells by the power of Beezebub, prince of the Divells*, they would have saide,[149] he cureth bodily disseases, through the credulitie of the people, (whose imaginations cure them) but doth not cast out divells; for these were not Demoniacks; as appeareth by their symptomes and signes of meere naturall infirmities. His assumption taketh upon it, that all *Marie Glovers* straunge actions and passions were a diminution, depravation or abolition of the animall, vitall or naturall functions and nothing beyond them. Namely the rebounding of her bodie at the .6th. petition of the Lords praier. The voyce *hang her*, delivered by the nostrills, her mouth being fast shut and that only during the time that *Elizabeth Jackson* was in the house. Also the altering of the fittes, [Fol. 101v] at the present coming in of that woman. For howsoever he maie labour to raunge those motions, amongst the depravations of the facultie of moving, yet to be done, at such times, only, and infallible then; maketh them transcendent poyntes, above his reach. Now, to his connexive sillogisme I answere, denying the consequence of his proposition, upon these reasons following. Let us suppose (for the present) that the signes of a supernaturall cause had not bene so pregnant in this mayden, and that there had ben nothing before the Doctors face to consider of; but such symptomes, as argue the diminishing, depraving or abolishing of the naturall vitall, or animall functions; which the ordenarie disseases, incident to this our mortalitie, do daily laie before our eies: Must it therefore follow, of necessitie, that her dissease was the mother? What is the bond of this connexion? In all his booke, I see none other, but because she was a [Fol. 102r] woman *pauca considerantes facile pronunciant* was there no more to be saide, for finding out of the part affected, then so? *Jachinus* saith,[150] that *The symptomes of the mother are maniefould and greivous, yet physitions should not be such maner of men, as whatsoever affect hapneth unto women, to referre the cause thereof unto the mother: as whether their head do* ake, *their stomuch be windy, their belly payned, or their breathing be short and difficult; when as all these may spring out of other causes.* D *Moundford,* who,[151] (both for the worth of his judgment, and for that he was one that ministred physicke unto the maide, in her affliction) is as meet to be heard, in this case, as *D Jorden;* affirmed plainely, that her dissease was not the mother; but rather conjectured of some other parts affected; And forbeareth playnely to pronounce of anie. Men should do *D Mounford* wrong, to think he did not enquire, about the parte primarily affected. And surely his meanes to know it, were incomparably greater, both in respect of the sucesse of his ministrations, which he would daily observe, to get still further light; and of the time (which was [Fol. 102v] above .2. moneths) pretie large, to visite and consider every point and parcell, that might lead him to his seeking or lend him addresse, to finde the fountaine of her evills. The like thinges I urge from *D. Shermans* testimonie, as is alreadie sett downe in the narration. Seeing then, that the principall functions maie ether faile,[152] or come to be evell perfourmed, by some disease in the fountaines from whence they flow; as well as by a second devise, and consent to Other partes, that first seduce them, and againe, although their hurt should happen, but at second hand, yet that there are more regions and partes of the bodie, besides the mother to be examined upon the felonie, as he knoweth well ynough, that in the cases of the falling sicknes and melancholie, all good aucthors, in our profession doe testifie: it stood him upon importantly, if he meant to help and not to hurt his reader, first to have set downe the signes that doe distinguish betwene those offences which are unto the principall partes from the mother, and those which grow from other inferiour partes besides; or els chalenge their originall, in place, where the facultie it selfe, makes [Fol. 103r] his residence: and then the second place, to have accomodated his generalls, unto their appliable particulars, in our individuous subject, or case in question. The same likewise I chalenge to have bene his duetie to doe, concerning the causes of the suffocation from the mother. For it nothing avayleth us, for the finding out of this truth, to be remembred by him, that of monstruous bloud, or seed, or other refuse humours, transmitted to that part in women, the princelie faculties maie receave those damages that he recompteth; except he shew us withall, the signes of a true cohærence, of such causes and effects, to

83

have ben in *M. Glover*, of whome we speake. Thus therefore he must mend his course hereafter, if he meane to chalenge us with a second booke. In the meane time, although it were ynough for me, in answering (if I should follow his example of slight handling) to content my selfe, with the pursuit of his proofes, and, where I finde them faile, to call for sentence against him; yet I, having learned to seeke better things, then myne owne glorie, [Fol. 103v] even victorie unto truth, edification to the Church of Christ, and a pulling downe of every stone, of the synagogue of *Sathan*, wheresoever it standeth, [I] am resolved, er I passe this place, sitting downe (as it were) under the shadow of the readers patience, to enter into some more curious disquisition of this cause: as namely, First whether there were anie probable reasons to induce a Physition to suspect the passions of the mother in *M. Glovers* case, or no. And secondly, what I have to shewe to conclude all her affliction to be raysed and wrought by the hand and work of the Devell. But thus much by the waie, albeit I could here get advantage of his handes, by the notation of the name, which hath not compasse ynough, to include all the affectes he hath layde under it. Yet I am content, to take the *suffocation of the mother*, in this present controversie, as a name comprehending all hystericall affectes, or passions of the mother. Yea this much will I gratifie him moreover; that, if he can raise more advauntage to his cause, out of the whole catalogue of [Fol. 104r] naturall diseases, let him hereafter amend his plea, I will not binde him, as his booke hath done, unto the mother. I willingly confesse, that the passions of the mother, do offer themselves oftentimes, to be considered, under such numbers and varieties of straunge symptomes, especially of the actions offended, of some of the principall members; that it is verie hard for a wiseman, to set downe one enuntiation of them, that shall stand for a scientiall theoreme, as having a perpetuall truth in it. And therefore *Fernelius* saith[153] *They must be discerned by an observation of all the affected parts, and by the consent of all the signes.* And *Mercatus* thinks,[154] concerning manie of them, that there is none other reason, more certaine, to know that they proceed from the mother, then that they kept no law, nor have no unifourme nature to be known by. Neverthelesse there are some certaine moodes and fashioning in them, if they be often seene and considered, by a man that hath his senses well experienced in [Fol. 104v] such things (who is not lead by the literall name of the

84

symptome which ever carieth too great a compasse of generalitie in it, but houldeth the expresse Image of it, in the same dimensions as he receaved it from sound precedent observations;) that will chalenge a certaine proprietie, in the cause, and part, from whence they came:[155] and therfore an excellent phisition can (as touching finding out of diseases) perfourme more himselfe then he can demonstrate to another: his eye being better able to infourme his understanding, then his tongue or pen to utter forth his cunning. The difference that is amongst us in this guift of imaginative, maketh the disaccording, that is so much noted against us, in determining of diseases or parts affected. Which if it be daylie seene in cases, meerely preternaturall and comon, much more may we looke for it in this of *M. Gl.* Like unto which, and having no cause in it supernaturall, I would fayne see anie man, out of all the recordes,[156] that have ben kept from *Hippochrates* dayes, produce us but one [Fol. 105r] instaunce. Some thinges I know there were in it, which at the first blush, gave suspition of some passions of the mother; to wit, a certaine rising in her belly, resolutions, convulsions, Croakings in the throate, and fittes upon meats receaved. But when a man looked more neerly upon everie one of them, (viewing (as I maie speake) both their owne attire and eke their equipage;[)]] and then matching them in just comparison, with those, that he as an exercised physition first thought of in his minde; the longer that he considered (if strong prejudice stood not in his waie) the further he should finde him selfe of, from concluding his first inhabited apprehensions. As to goe further in these named particulars (with which I would have joyned moe, if I could have found likely anie moe) if that rising, which was seene to be in her belly, be layd to the measure and shape of that rising, which appeareth in fittes of the mother, they wilbe found more disproportioned, then a Camell and a mule are one unto another. The rising of the mother in naturall sicknes, is uniforme, beginning from the lower part of the [Fol. 105v] belly: and so with a certaine equally augmented fulnes, bearing up towards the stomach, and *diaphragma*. In this manie times, ones hand held upon it, maie feele a kinde of resistaunce, as a bolting or bownding against it, from the place of the mother. And in this verie time, the sounding and suffocation happeneth to the patient. Againe, during the continuance of this motion, it is proper, and pathognomonicall, that the pulse be litle, slow, rare, unequall, or inordinate; sometimes tensive, and defective and fayling.[157] Which diversities *Josephus Struthius* doth in this sort explicate:[158] If the humor in the mother be thick, cold, much in quantitie, and sharpe qualited out of putrefication, there is added unto other thinges, some Convulsion; and then the pulse is tensive. If the matter be more melancholicke, it bringeth forth sadnes and sounding; And then the pulse is litle, slow, rare. Also forasmuch as the disease is cold, it is agreable that the pulse should be such: and moreover unequall and [Fol. 106r] inordinate, through the faculties oppression. But if the sicknes too far prevaile, the pulse becometh frequent and deficient, and at last, if his crueltie persevere, the pulse faileth utterlie and is abolished. Hitherto *Struthius* explication. I saie, some of these kindes of pulse is proper and perpetuall to this rising of the belly; and this kinde of rising in the bellie is also (with the differences of more or lesse) proper and perpetuall, to that kinde of passion of the mother, called *The suffocation*: as *Johannes Gorhæus*[159] hath judicially written, and daiely experience doth confirme. Now the moving that was in *M. Gl:* bellie was after this sorte: It began in the middest of her bellie: it moved as if it had beene some living creature, or ones hand within a bed, first obscurelie lifting up the cloathes, and then more manifestly; so did it make the middest of her bellie to lifte*[160] upwardes, from her back; not arise upwardes, towards her stomach. Againe everie returne of this motion in her bellie, had an answerable rebownd in her brest; As when a man standing astride upon a quakemire, pressing downe one foote, another bowndeth up, and so by turnes; even in like sort, [Fol. 106v] appeared this mutuall motion, betwene the bellie and the brest, rebownding wise to answere one another, for a five or six returnes. Then the mover seemed (by a visible kinde of gliding up the brest) to amount to the Channell bone; after which ensued Convulsions etc. It seemeth unto me, that, the comparison betwene these two motions, being soberly and seriously made, by anie man of experience, and unforestalled minde, there should no great suspition of the mother arise, or, at least, continue; but rather an apprehension of a note, of *Sathans* vexation; according as it is, with a trewe discerning eie, set downe by his excellent majestie,[161] our gracious Soveraigne, in his *Dæmonologie*: whatsoever S. H.[162] out of his great penurie, both of divinitie and honestie, hath written to the contrarie. As touching the pulse, which so properlie appertaineth to the rising of the mother, it was never to be found in this maide; but alwaies a good pulse, moderately large, equall, and ordinate: [Fol. 107r] sometime a litle too frequent; but never slowe, nor rare; and much less tensive, or deficient. The second of these questionable symptomes, is an unmoveablenes in her right arme, which seemed unto some men, to chalenge the palsey or resolution, as the stock, from whence it descended. But it was a verie bastard, as might well be conjectured by his straunge conditions. For whereas in a preter naturally resolved member, the moveablenes is lesse, and the waight rather more; as *Fernelius*[163] and daily experience sheweth; having attendant thereupon a litle pulse, slow, rare, languishing and softe, in some, fast going, unequall, and somewhat inordinatelie intermitting: in this maide, the arme was (at sundrie times) so light, to be removed or tossed with ones hand, the pulse remaining sound and perfect, as it seemed, by good right to require some hand of help, of a higher nature, then anie such as *Asa* trusted unto in his sickenes, was able to yeeld her.[164] The third [Fol. 107v] generall symptomes, that seemed to laie some clayme to naturall sicknes, was convulsions, which certaynely she had; both universall and particular; but such as (I am perswayded) the world hath hetherto never seene, in natural sicknes. She was turned round as an hoope,[165] with her head backward to her hippes. And after that, her bodie was suddainely turned round the contrarie waie, to wit, her head forward betwene her legges; and in both these positions, her wholl bodie rowled and tumbled, with such violence and swiftenes, as that their paines, in keeping her from receaving hurt against the bedds head and postes, caused .2. or .3. women to sweat. *D Jorden* (perhaps) will make no bones, to acknowledge these for .2. species of convulsions, called *opisthotonus*, and *Emprosthotonus*. This is soone saide; but let no man be perswaded by such rash answeres, untill he can resolve them withall by what meanes, such violent rowling and tumbling proceeded, whilest the whole bodie was brought in such straunge positions. Also her bodie was at the same time cold, stiffe as a frosen thing and sencles [Fol. 108r] which insensibilitie hapneth not in these Convulsions.[166] But come we neerer: what kinde of Convulsion will he make, of that monstrous distortion, of her chine bone, wherein the right huckle bone was so far turned over to the lefte side, as went beyond the right line of her brest bone, (her bodie lyeing plaine upright) and came within the bredth of iiii [sic] fingers, to the place, where the left huckle bone should have ben found, according to the lying of her bodie? He can nether call this *Emprosthotonus*, nor *Opisthotonus*, nor *Tetanus*, much lesse can he give anie propper convulsions name unto it. What will he do? Will he saie it maie have a name geven unto it? And that it is no reason to denie a thing for lack of a name, so long as the nature is present or to be found?[167] I am not one that will contend for names, so that we finde the substance. But even in this point (o indifferent reader) staie a litle, (I beseech thee) and consider, seing this [Fol. 108v] must be confessed, hitherto, to have no proper name, being (as you see by the description) so notorious, and that Aucthors in our profession have accustomed, so much curiositie in names, as to notifie thereby propper Convulsions, such as were lesse of note then this (as *strabismus* in the eie, *Trisinus* in the Chapp; *Cynicus spasmus* in the mouth, and *satyriasis* in the masculine member)[168] Was not this a verie competent occasion to make modest men doubt, whether it were of a preter naturall or supernaturall cause? when as in our bookes we could not finde it. They that were so peremptorie before the judgment seat, for naturall disease, did not even this point, put upon them a necessitie, either out of booke or observation to have produced some pregnant instaunce; or els in a reverence to the truth, (which a christian will feare to scandalize) to have laied their handes upon their mouthes? But I have more to abate their confidence withall, then this. [Fol. 109r] For they must geve us reason, wherefore she felt no paine, for this monstrous distortion of the back bone, whereas everie man in anie comon cramp feeleth paine. I confesse that in epilepticall convulsions, because there is withall consternation of the minde, the patient doth not afterwards complayne of paine; but where feeling and understanding are in force, there, great Convulsions, or distortions of the members (and what could be greater then this we speake of) must needes afflict with vehement paines.[169] Let them not tell me that *M Glover* was voyde of sense and understanding, at all times, when she suffered this straunge distortion: for there are abundant witnesses, that even in her ordinarie fitts, in such times as she laie with halfe her bodie in sense, and her understanding good; so as she was able to answere us by signes, and take knowledge of all her acquaintances, by their voyces; even then you might have seene her [Fol. 109v] lying in this uglie distortion of her Chine bone. And if muscles, which are involuntarily moved towards their beginninges, and draw the members in consequent with them, according to the law of their naturall inflexures, do suffer paine; much more in this case, where nether the muscles nor their joyntes, moved towards their originalls, nor kept anie correspondence with the lawes and ordinaunces of their creation. Furthermore, the seeker of truth must here be instructed thus much, as touching Convulsions. That all voluntarie motions of our members, are atchieved by the muscles. So as, when the muscles, (according to the will) withdraw them selves toward their heades (which we call there [sic] beginninges) thitherto also, are those parts or joyntes withdrawne, whereto they are infixed. If some affect arise in the bodie, that setteth them in this motion, the fashion of that motion wilbe like unto the naturall;[170] and yet must be called a Convulsion, because it is involuntarie; that is against the will. And [Fol. 110r] therefore is utterly no difference betwene the naturall motions of the muscles and their Convulsions,[171] but this, that the one is involuntarie, the other is ruled by the comandement of the will. By this doctrine, universally receaved in physick, it will presently be made cleere, that this winding about, of the chine bone, whereof we speake, was no Convulsion. For there, the joyntes were not turned according to their desinate motions, as neither were their muscles contracted towardes their originalls. And if this be evicted (as I beleve none will resist) then *D Jorden* wilbe terribly puzled, to finde out some classicall symptome, under which he maie raunge it. If he can reduce it to no head in physick; let him yeeld, and not merit the imputation of pertinacie. Touching the other Convulsions; as of her lefte hand, and the shew of an *opisthotonus*, in her ordinarie fitt; I saie, the pulse consented [Fol. 110v] not, to conclude them within phisicall speculation. For *M Glovers* pulse, both in the entring into it; and in the verie passion of the Convulsion it selfe, was utterly deprived of all notes of a Convulsarie, pulse as hath ben saide. For that, as *Galen* describeth it,[172] necessarilie taketh his name of the affect, and is like unto it in deed: that is to saie, consulsive, as if a hollow bodie, such as is a gut, were by two handes twitched towardes either of the endes, by alternate extension.[173] Neither is here either *Diastole* or *Systole* explicate, but a certaine confusion rather, of both togeather. Also *Galen* sheweth the reason,[174] whie the pulse must needes be such in Convulsions.

For the heart (saith he) *transmitteth arteries to the braine, for a bond of their societie: the brayne likewise sendeth sinewes to the heart, for a pledge of like good turne; which although they be not great, yet sufficient for that service, to carie the message of reason thither. Moreover unto every arterie, fibres are deduced from the synewes, to make a fellow like coherence and* [Fol. 111r] *mutuall accord, not only of their actions, but also of their affectes. And therefore no mervaile, when as the whole yssue of the sinewes, have in all partes, conjunction with the arteries, that their affectes appeare also in them.* Yea so farre *Gal.*[175] urgeth this pulse, in all proper Convulsions, as that even in the lighter sort of *Epileptick where nature is but meanly molested, and therefore no exceeding great mutation made in the pulse, only there the arterie* (saith he) *of right, is stretched towardes both endes as in those that suffer convulsions*: quitting it there, of inequality and strong tension, with litlenes, raritie, faggednes, and other worser differences, which a greater power of that affect prevailing, bringeth forth in the pulse. Which last alledged texts of *Galen.* I must here a litle longer insist in coming (as now) to examine a third difference of Convulsions in *M Glovers* case; namely the universall one, in her extraordinarie fitt which, both because it was universall, and also joyned [Fol. 111v] with a totall privation of the understanding and sense,[176] it must be referred, (if to anie thing of the mother) to the passions *epileptick* thereof, and not to the suffocation: wherewith it held no proportion in the world. Now then, I praie you, must not the pulse in this fitt, have ben found, such as is in a strong *epilepsie*? I will yeeld him the cause, if he can prove it was such, as *Galen* saith (*of right*) must be in a weake: that all men maie see, what good notice the *D* tooke of this matter. But he was not only overseene in the pulse (if this be referred to an *Epilepsie*) but in the verie fourme of the Convulsion, in that disease: which is not only a contraction of all the members, as this maids was, with a permanent and abiding stiffenes; but a concussorie motion in them, arising from[177] *the fountaine of the nerve, and endevouring to expell, that whatsoever offensive thing, transmitted unto it, from the part affected.* And therefore is that striving motion and beating togeather of the partes [Fol. 112r] convulsed, which appeareth daylie in all forcible fittes of the falling sicknes. If *D Jorden* seeing these inconveniences, shall here start from us, and renounce my references; thinking to help himselfe from some *Lethargie, Apoplexie, Catalepsie*, or other such; Let him know, that the longer he seeketh, the lesse he will finde; and the more he taketh up, the more he wilbe forced to laie downe againe, with double disadvauntage. Also the same arguement that I used, concerning the distortion of her Chinebone, the same must *D Jorden* here, in like maner, be pressed withall, touching the distortion of her Elbowes, up to her Channell bones, in her extraordinary fittes. That was no legitimate Convulsion, for the reasons afore alleadged, and much lesse a *Catalepsie*, or anie other præternaturall affect that he can name. Thus much of those symptomes, that might seeme to have some [Fol. 112v] reference to the Convulsion. The next notable thinges are, her Choaking, and fittes upon meats receaved. To the former I replie; there was utterly no shew hereof in her extraordinarie fitt; as neither was there, of those motions in her bellie. In her ordinarie fitt, and in those that she suffered after sustenance receaved, there appeared some such thing; but with speciall notes of difference from that suffocation which importeth the mother. In that choaking which is from the mother, first we are to conceave a twofould difference. 2. shew their natures, and .3. bring our comparisons. The difference of the Choakings is in the more or lesse, as *Mercatus* noteth[178] and dayly practise observeth. For in some cases all sensible respiration is deprived, as in the vehement fittes; in some againe, but hindered, as by a certaine catching, or Convulsorie motion in the throat, touched by *Galen*,[179] and [Fol. 113r] likened to a kinde of *angina*, but unjustly pretermitted by a multitude of other Writers.[180] For as there is a strangulatorie respiration, in the passion of the mother, which is declared by the manner of their breathing, to be a convulsion in the muscles of *larynx*; so doth that measure and degree proove unto us, what is the formall cause; of that totall deprivation which hapneth with a number of others; not as the *Neotoricks* comonly write, the expression of the aire in the longes, and restraint of attraction of new, through the compression of the midreife by the mother, and inferiour bowells. (*Galen*[181] hath worthely confuted that locall rising.) But a Convulsive twitching togeather of the top of the Wesand, which is the vocall organ,[182] at the same time, as the vapors of the mother make such turbulent motions in the bellie. And this, is the fourme of Choaking, comon to these two differences or degrees, of more [Fol. 113v] or lesse; ever testified, by the parties,

Afterwards, reporting of a sensible drawing togeather of that part, as if some string did bynd it. Now the reader is to understand, that *M Glover*, although she felt at the end of those reboundings in her bellie, a suddain strangling in her throat, in her ordinarie fitt, yett was it principally by the occasion of the plucking backward of her head, which at that time hapned, neither therefore with an *angina* like noyse, in drawing her breath; as in the remisse fittes of the mother, nor deprived of breathing, as in the stronger ones is seene; but, as if the omission of one breathing space had bene allowed, to that divellish *opisthotonus*, (that is a convulsion of the neck backwards,) she fetched her breath afterwards (and cryed) freely; whether her throat were helped by compression of mens handes (which was comonly used) or she were left at libertie to tosse which waie soever; as more then once was proved. Also here againe was wanting a correspondent pulse for such a suffocation. And as for that vexation in her throat which came in her meat fittes, that [Fol. 114r] was with such a monstrous tumor in her throat, suddainly rising, and bloud flowing into her face, even to blackenes, and going away with certaine noyses, like uncouth barkings, no motions in the belly going before; as that I beleeve, no booke, nor physicall observation can exemplifie it: *D Moundford, multis parasangis*, a great waie beyond *D Jorden*, in time and practize; confessed he never saw the like. And this fitte of the throat, was that they called her meat fitt: which came not on her, some halfe hower, or hower, after sustenance receaved as in fittes of the mother it useth to doe, (having first geven them leave to eate what they lust) but tooke her even in her meat eating: so as she was constrayned (her stomach serving well) to post downe her meat, when once she beganne, almost without chewinge. Neither came this fitte upon meat only, but ever when she laide her downe in her bed also; on the sicke dayes night. And that in everie Circumstance, nothing being altered. Whereby *D Jordens* reason fetched from the mother is utterly defeated, and made of no power, to geve satisfaction to anie wise man. [Fol. 114v] Thus you see, what credit these vagabound accidents ought to have, in that they clayme kin[d]red of the passions of the mother, which is a free denizon of the Comon wealth of phisicke. Is it reason, that Apes should chalenge the priviledges of men, because in some features, limbes, and maners, they carrie some pretie resemblances of men? Albeit *Sathan* is more

92

apt to beguile us, then all the apes in the world, yet if we rightlie stir up the guift of God,[183] which is in us, we shall in some measure, be able to encounter him in all his deceipts. There is a founten of wisedome paramount: none maie presume to drinke his fill of that, but he that hath renounced the service of himselfe.[184] If our heartes stand right with him, the scales of obscuritie shall fall from our eyes, and we shalbee made to see, that, wherein manie others are blinde. Me thinke *D Jorden*, in this place steppeth forward to except against me in this wise: *Seeing these symptomes by your owne confession, have some* [Fol. 115r] *similitude with those which are observed in passions of the mother, was it not fittest for Phisitions to referre them so? Rather then to seeke newe causes, as though we would multiplie species, against the philosophers rule? And I mervaile what moved you not to be so minded with me.* Thus I will endevor to satisfie him; opening the thoughts of my heart (for this point) freely unto him. I had read manie things, and meditated much on such like cases, before: And I found, that as the Comon people are over Credulous, for want of judgment, to direct them; so the phisitions were too incredulous for want of humilitie to adorne them. Insomuch, that (whatsoever *D Jorden* hath written, of phisitions mistaking supernaturall for naturall sometime) I will joyne issue with him in this, if he please; to prove, from all written records; that three phisitions have erred in his cause for one in myne. Whereof not only *Psellus* sheweth the reason to be[185] *because they know nothing, but that which is subject to their sense.* But also the learned *Valesius* confirmeth it saying:[186] *But certainely as those which are ignoraunt of Philosophie, are wont through their* [Fol. 115v] *ignorance of manie naturall thinges, to be verie credulous, and superstitious; so they who are overmuch addicted to naturall philosophie* (*as who but Phisitions*) *are ever readie to discredit all thinges, which either are not bodies, or the motions of bodies.* And *Cornelius Gema*,[187] from whome the *D.* taketh some hart, (because he saith, sometimes Phisitions are beguiled in matters of the mother) even he acknowledgeth, that they make themselves manie times infamous, by devising ridiculous reasons in supernaturall causes: which the events that follow, force them afterwards againe to relinquish. When I therefore had seene these testimonies, and found withall, such principall men of our profession,[188] as *Antonius Benivenius, Jo. Fernelius, Hieronimus Cardan, Johannes Langius, Jacobus*

Hollerius, and *Rennerus Solenander* (beside a number of others, whose merit these do testifie) to have confessed themselves gulled and beguyled in this kinde, by that maniefould deceaver of mankind, from the beginning: I remembred me of the brasen serpent,[189] who hath broken the head of this serpent, and of that power and wisedome, which [Fol. 116r] is *allsufficient, to him that seeketh him in uprightnes of heart;*[190] *and geveth to every such bountifully, casting no man in the teeth.* Then I looked about, to consider, other observed cases of like nature;[191] and I sawe, such circuler convulsions of the whole bodie, with rowling and tumbling; spoken of before, such movings or reboundings in the bellie, *and breast,* such huge swelling of the throat, and shutting up against the receipt of susteinance; with other like, to be harsh symptomes in the mother, but curraunt in dæmoniacks. Wherefore me thought, it laie me upon, (being called to this case of *M Glover*) to seeke (by the help of him, by whome *St Paule* saide,[192] he was able to do all thinges) to finde a difference, both for my selfe and others, in the verie symptomes of the mother, from these, by which the wilie serpent beguiled unwarie mindes, with some shewe of Conformitie. And thereupon I made that diligent disquisition aforesaid: with what successe, let all those, that have obteyned that wisdom,[193] which is pure and peaceable, judge. Moreover when [Fol. 116v] I had found it no phisicall case, by the symptomes, I entered also into the consideration of causes; to see if such were present in *M Glovers* case, as all the learned agree of, to be either in passions of the mother; or anie other naturall sicknes whatsoever. And here I found matter of Confirmation, not only for my selfe, but for everie one likewise, that seeketh the truth in these kinds of questions. *Hippochrates*[194] carefully constituteth this Cannon, which he repeateth more then once, for the guiding of phisitions, enquiring into the diseases of weomen: *he that will rightly handle these matters of women, it behoveth him, that first he beginne from God (who is the principall cause in the diseases of man kinde) and next, to discerne the natures and ages of women, togeather with the oportunities of tymes, the season of the yeere, the places, and the windes.* Here we see divers pointes put downe for a phisitions direction, in the cases of women. Some governe him to find the disease, some the parte affected, and other some of the causes. *The* [Fol. 117r] *natures* implying the temperament and constitution[195] insinuate what natured sicknes is there to be looked for; *ages* shew the particular inclinations; *the oportunities of times* the prædestinate motions of nature or sickenes: the rest further and procure, or els hinder and hold backe the causes and their fruits. The maide of whome we treat was by temperament hot, as by the colour growth and temper of her haire and skinne, largenes of vaynes and strength of pulse can be proved:[196] Therefore neither Convulsions, mother, fallinge sicknes, *Catalepsis, caros*, nor anie such cold diseases likely to fall into her. And if they should there cast their seed, yet not to bring forth fruit in the highest degree, as in this was seene: for if it were *the suffocation from the Mother*, yet *D Jorden* himselfe never saw, nor read of the like degree, if his booke maie be taken for a testimonie. The season of the yeare made resistance likewise. For where as it is noted even by the *D* himselfe,[197] that winter and cold seasons with moisture, are the [Fol. 117v] times wherein weomen are most attainted with this disease, it contrariewise, set upon this maiden in *Maie*; and encreased his strength at *Midsomer*. Certainely this must have ben much more dangerous to her life, to have ben so highely afflicted with a disease,[198] so contrarie to her temperament, and to externall resistant causes. The same I argue also from her Constitution. Which was so good, that she lived before this affliction befell her, not only in health simply, but in a strong perfourmance of the functions of every part, which phisitions call a good habit,[199] as a degre beyond simple health: the accidents and measure whereof, are serenitie, and constancie in accomplishing the functions of the bodie. Which, who so possesseth, cannot be denyed to have a good Constitution: and this good Constitution cannot be in phisick denyed the honnour of the highest place, of those things that resist, all causes of diseases, both inward and outward; be they sadnes, or anger, or care, or watchinges, wet or drie, or whatsoever els, as [Fol. 118r] *Galen* speaketh more at large. We grant you (will *D Jorden* saie) that for these reasons rendred, to behooved the causes of *M Glovers* sicknes to have ben most potent, mightie and stronge, and therefore those that we delivered (if they be rightlie considered) are no lesse. I am content to approch as nere, to the consideration of his causes, as he would have me; for I feare not narrow sifting, in this Cause, yea rather I seeke it. But when we shall have more exactlie weighed his causes, not in *Thesi* only, as he doth, but in our *hypothesi*, as reason willeth; I beleve they will not

95

only be found to light, for those affects that should be fathered of them, but also bewraie his overmuch slightnes, and rawnes, in a matter that merited so much maturitie of deliberation. The principall causes (I know) whereupon he setteth up his rest, are these two; bloud and seed; encreased and retained above natures dew. I willingly graunt that these two are, by their evill dispositions, able to bring forth great [Fol. 118v] garboyles in humaine bodies; to the proofe whereof he might have spared much of his paines, and employed him selfe rather to prove, that either bloud or seed, were in quantitie or qualitie, at that time offensive, in *Ma. Glo:* bodie. Which if it had ben in his power to do, as his booke sheweth it was not, it would have come (I confesse) somewhat nearer to the scope, yet neither had it beaten the nayle upon the head: for I must have brought him to this *Quære* moreover; whether the quantitie or malignitie of bloud or seed are able to produce such affects, as in *M Glover* were seene. Against which point, not so much (perhaps) to prevent him, as to breed him an appetite, I will dispute more copiouslie in the Chapter next ensuing. The rest of the Chapter I am resolved to spend, in disproving that former Conclusion, which is so necessarie here to be understood, namely, that either bloud or seed, offending in quantitie or qualitie, could probablie be accused in *Marie Glovers* miserie. In the discussing of which causes, we shall have need to repaire againe to that canon of *Hippochrates*: and as we [Fol. 119r] have at his Counsaile alreadie, cons[i]dered the nature of the partie, and the season of the yeare, so nowe moreover, to weigh the age, and oportunities of times, for the framing of our judgments. Her age you have heard in the storie, to have bene xiiii [sic] yeeres, when she was thus made a spectacle to men and angells. This being the second septenarie (as *Hippochrates* calleth it)[200] is the first period or terme, wherein nature ordinarilye, sendeth forth her first chalenges and procurations, in weomens bodies, for menstruall bloud and generative seed: it hath no similitude to truth, that nature in her first addresses to womanhood, should be so much surprized with a sudden over ruling adversarie, made of one of those, which er while, were so familiar and derely beloved unto her: so as no strength of temperament, no armor of good Constitution, and healthie habit, with well conspiring passages and destinated enunctories, were able to cast out, suborne or countervaile them; but that they must, so ignominiously, insult on her, and [Fol. 119v] leade her in triumphe, as it were, with one daies victorie.[201] I gladly subscribe to the learned, that women are subjecte to manie straunge passions, through the deprivation of these two humors; but I can never think, that these two, can come to erect so highe a trophee of depravation, in a living bodie;[202] otherwaies, then, by manie vitious proceedings, and importunate interruptions of the naturall functions, to breed there Corruptions, first so farre, as that the faculties, with the insited heat and spirit, cannot anie longer chase or overrule them; and secondarilie, that they thenceforth, abuse naturall heat, to their owne advauntage, and by further fermentations, circulations and graduations, attaine puissaunce to passe each court of guard, and to encounter the principall faculties in their verie fountaines. Which worke to atchieve, presupposeth both a concurrence of enabled causes, to act; a correspondent disposition of the subject to admit, and a competent intermediall time, [Fol. 120r] to the obteyning of the enterprise as it doth, manie sensible offences of the functions, sundrie and often Complaints of the partes, with various and remarkeable Chaunges of colours, for witnesses of so wofull a Conquest. And namely as touching the generative seed,[203] what though the second septenarie, which is the xiiiith [sic] yeare, do bring in the first presentative thereof? Hath it so daungerous a Consequent, if it be not, by and by, accepted to the finall use? The fathers of our phisick never saide so, and his booke conteyneth no example for it. Nay, albeit in that age, there be in womens bodies, that inward præperation, for bud and blossom, of a shortly ensuing spring to be expected; outwardly also warranted, by certaine proportions, growthes, and customes of nature; yet are these myres, but as those whayish crudities, by which after the blade is shott, the eare of Corne getteth outward fourme, but yet lacketh time and sunne, to concoct and seperate the graine. Now everie thing that wanteth maturitie, hath [Fol. 120v] yet somewhat, whereon natures operations should further proceed; and therefore is no burthen, nor offence, but sweet and kindelie to the partes conteyning it. According to this is it, that *Aristotle* saith in the place above cited, that in the third septenarie, is afforded the seed, that hath power and meetenes for generation. And *Cordæus* plainely confirmeth me, in these wordes:[204] *Seed therefore in the second septenarie,*[*205] *the corne being eared, (as I may speake) albeit not fitt for generation, yet cometh to the place by natures instinct, even as do the monthely*

Mary Glovers Late Woeful Case

customes also shew themselves, not without some plenteous gathering togeather of bloud and humors: I yeeld also, that all are not ripe in one certaine yeere, but some earlier, some later, according to the temperament, region, diet, and education. A latitude is allowed in all such determinations. But I saie, that in England, among the ranke of meane people, where everie one must worke for a living, and are not pampered with full and daintie fare, nor courted and enchaunted with companions of luxurious spirites, [Fol. 121r] there to finde a mayden, at xviii [sic] yeeres of age, sicke of such a surplus of this humor, as that it is turned through long keeping, to the nature of poyson (as all good Aucthors yeeld it must)[206] I hould it impossible, and whosoever looketh upon those instaunces, which *D Jorden* hath laide downe,[207] for his purpose in this point (the youngest of them being xviii yeeres old) will thinke I have no cause, to alter my Judgment, for his impertinencies. With me likewise, and not with him, concordeth *Mercatus*, whom he so much hopes in:[208] *In maydens* (saith he) *which are not immodest, nor have exceeded the xxvth yeere of their age, verie seldom do these diseases grow, out of corruption of the seed; notwithstanding that through conversing with men, and evill institution both of life and diet, it may sometime come to passe, and so must greivous accidents happen thereupon.* *Solenander*[209] had sometime a case of the like nature in his handes, whereof writing unto *Johannes Echtius*, a learned phisition, and his familiar freind, he saith, he could not suspect it to be of seed, *for what seed* (saith he) *beyond nature hurtfull, can there be retayned,* [Fol. 121v] *in a maid that gaddeth not abroad, about xviii yeeres of age, and not acquainted with such use of it?* Whereto he addeth, *Galen and others look for this in widdowes, though I likewise saw it in a maide at Lovaine of xxviii. or xxx. yeares old, impatient of delaie* (which measure of growth in this matter, *Jacchinus*[210] likewise assigneth:) *as also at Lyons in a handsome nunne, but both of these having differing symptoms from this.* And so saie I; that which *Solenander* telleth of, was farre short in admirabilitie of symptomes, of *M Glover.* Yea so straunge was hers, to be compared to the Mother, that a gentleman and scholler, of some understanding and sort, receaving but by the eare, some description of *M Glovers* straunge vexation, which then at London was in everie mans mouth, first answered, that he beleeved it was but the mother, and that himselfe had a sister, as straungely vexed as she. But being perswaded, and drawne to see *M. Glover*, with his owne eyes, he resolutely afterward pronounced [Fol. 122r] that there was no comparison to be made betwene them. This I have added upon occasion of *Solenanders* last wordes: the rest of his text declareth, how unlikely a thing, a man of much experience thought it, that a maid of xviii years old, of privat or modest education, should have those passions of the mother, *D Jorden* speaketh of, through default of this humor. And if not in the middest of the third septenarie, then maie I well hould myne owne, for the beginning of it.[211] And as her age, with mete appurtenances, denyeth the generative seed this mischeevous operation, so was there no signe, by sounding or privation of breathing, which *Galen*,[212] or, by the effluxe of humor; or externall coldnes (I meane in her cheifest fitts) which others speak of, not to notifie the same. You see then, that there are manie difficulties, and of much moment, that resist the admittance of this cause in *M Glovers* case. The other of [Fol. 122v] menstruall bloud wilbe asmuch encombred. All experience in deed subscribeth to *Hippochrates*[213] wise observations, and descriptions, of womens maniefould afflictions, through the imoderate delaies, and unkindly empeachments of these courses. But none of them all, have anie kindly congruitie, with *M Glovers* miserie. Besides if it be trew, that the worst kinds of *Hystericall* passions grow, from the former cause, and not from this; then sprang not *M Glovers* from hence; so evill a case as which, *D Jorden* (if his booke maie judge) did never see. Also it is not ordenarie for maides to have these thinges, even at the finishing of their second septenarie; and if they have, yet not in great quantitie. Then doth beginne (in deed) a redundancie of bloud, in their bodies, and a resort thereof to those partes, as though their destinated uses should now enter Chalenge. But this is done by slow and stealing steppes, and according to an old principle of [Fol. 123r] nature, who abhorreth all violent and suddaine mutations.[214] And because (as we have considered in the seed) this maturitie hapneth not to all maides, in the same age, but we must graunt, here also, a latitude of time, for the reasons aforesaid; we will busie our selves, here a little, to examine, whether this mayden (who before her affliction had never this course) was therein defrauded of her right or no. When one seeth a garment on another mans backe, he maie have some gesse, whether it make offence or not, but the partie that weares the same, can only put the matter out of Controversie. So

D Jorden and my selfe might suppose that *M Glover* needed the custome of weomen at that age, but because nature it selfe could tell us best; it is fitt, that we both put our selves upon natures decision. For as that created power in humaine bodies, which we call nature,[215] dispenseth all thinges, both in the functions and humors, in dew time, and order, if it be not impeached, as by an æconomicall wisdome, [Fol. 123v] that erreth not: and if it be empeached, it hath meanes of parties and oportunitie of regions, to expell or subdue all mutinies or insurrections of rebellious humors, that make head against her: so likewise, where inward adversaries,[216] by correspondence of outward causes, escaping first her ordinarie watch,[217] gather a hand, and do, at length, defeat her decretories; ther, nature suffereth no sooner such contempts, but she hath her proper language and cryers to proclaime it, as to call for outward succoures, likewise, (the Phisition) to remedie it. [218]*Menstruall courses not proceeding, the bodies of weomen become diseased*, saith Hippochrates. He doth not saie, there is bred a formall sickenes at an instant, but with time. Nothing passeth from one extreame unto another, but by the meane or middle degrees, that lye betweene them. Betwixt upright health and downeright sickenes, there is a newtralitie, as well of decidencie, intercedent in the falling, as there is of Convalescencie, or amendement, in the arising, to be well [Fol. 124r] againe. In this newtralitie of decidencie must needs be *morbosus apparatus* presupposed,[219] as cause thereof. And as everie existent in nature hath his cause, whereof he was raised, so that he his properties and notes to be acknowledged. *Morbus fiens* (as they borow leave to speake) is to be discerned as well as factus. And if in anie other disease in the bodie, then is this trew in those, that grow out of menstruall suppression especially. Therefore *Galen* sheweth,[220] besides that signe of milke in the brests, (which is a token of this defecte in some maides) that it is to be discerned, by a heavines of the whole bodie, loathing of meate, and a certain shivering in their bones: A Corrupt appetite of evell thinges, paynes in their loynes, necke and forepart of their head. *Hippochrates*[221] by his curious observations of these matters, traceth (as I maie speake) and discovereth all the tracts and footsteppes, of these defectes, from moneth to [Fol. 124v] moneth, both in maides and women, even from the first *morbosus apparatus*, thereof growing, as from the egge, untill it be come to his full consummation of the setleld mischeifes, as to the flying byrd. In like sorte *Mercatus*,[222] following his steppes, doth thus deduce it; out of *Hippochrates*, speaking of the narrow veynes in maides: *Besides that the bloud, which is prepared thus to be vented, is somewhat thick, and by litle and litle gathered in the veynes of the mother,*[223] *those veynes also being streight, no mervaile though they be altogeather stopped up. By which occasion it cometh to passe, that maides are so discoulored, and often caught with slow and obscure fevers. But if those said courses doe altogether transgress their due time and keepe awaie, when age requireth them, then come more evident fevers and greater obstructions, which doe not only beset the mother it selfe, but the nutritive partes, yea* [Fol. 125r] *almost all the bowells likewise. By whose consent moreover either the principall members are then affected, or els the young woman, by litle and litle is brought unto greater evells. Besides, if that menstruous bloud, which aboundeth now, being retayned beyond natures time, do get some qualitie of putrefaction withall, then they are miserablie afflicted, with yet more vehement and forcible fevers. Like as also, if that bloud become in some otherwise affected, without putrefaction, then, for to have them often payned in their heades, with gnawings in their stomaches, tormentes in their bellies, wearines in their bones, and verie manie other diseases, I take it by observation, for a thinge most certayne.* If then it stand both with reason and our best Authors, that menstruall suppression worketh not such height of evells, on a suddaine, but litle and litle, in the bodies of weomen, and also that those evill degrees,[224] according as they grow, doe from time to time, notifie themselves [Fol. 125v] by some agreable affects flowing from them (*Nam dum intus manet aliquid causæ, et symptomata aliqua illorum restant.*) Then seeing M Glover stood in perfect health (as I have shewed before) within three dayes before she fell into this miserie, and was but then at such tender age, as that nature could not reasonably be suspected of empeachments, but rather of unripenes; I am much deceaved, if I have not better reason, to conclude, that *M. Glo:* was not defrauded of natures dew, in this point; and so consequently, had not the mother, through menstruall suppression; then *D Jorden* hath, to affirme it, upon this only ground, that manie young women, have it, through this cause. Furthermore, if *Ma. Glovers* affliction had growne from this cause, then must her fittes have ben more strong and vehement, at those monthly periods, and againe more meeke and remisse, in the intermediall times; because a disease more urgeth in *hora motus materiæ quam quietis*.[225] So speaketh reason, so confirmeth aucthoritie, so ratifieth experience [Fol. 126r] daiely. But there was utterlie no such to be observed in *Ma Glovers* case. Therefore she was not sicke of this defecte. [An arrow pointing upwards in the manuscript indicates the position of the following insertion, which is written on fol. 128: [Fol. 128r] (arrow pointing up) moreover, he is here to understand, that which (perhaps) he never enquired, that *M. Gl.* bodie enjoyed this dew of womanhoode about the end of Julie next after the day of her heavie visitation: and from thenceforth continued by orderly periodes, well encreasing measures, for a yeare after, that I was privie unto and so to the daie of her death, for anie thing I know. Here then *D. J.* must needes be much encumbered: seeing so manie hundreds will witnes that iii monthes after that time, *M. Gl.* case began to grow to such extremities the fittes having holden her for the former six monthes in farre more tolerable tearmes:[226] For *Hippochrates* hath these rules against him:[227] *Convulsioni solutio est, si mulieriæ principio apparent, neque febres acceserit. 1. It is a solution to the convulsion if the course of women appear in the beginning; and here be no fever. Agayne, Plurium vero morbi pueris judicantur alii quidem quadraginta diebus, alii septem mensibus, alii septem annis alii autem ad pubertatem accedentibus. Qui autem pueris perduravient et non fuerint finiti circa pubescentiam, aut fæminæ cum menstrua ermirpunt, diuturui fieri erumpent consueverunt. Verie manie diseases ar judged in children; some in 40. dayes, others in seven monethes, othersome in 7. years. And there be that reache unto stripling age. But those which continue in boies, and finish not about such time as youth doth bud, or, in maides, when ther monethes breake forth, such use to stick by it and become of long continuance.*[228] Now to applie oure instaunce to that first sentence; *M. Gl.* had no fever; her courses came, about iii monethes after her first visitation, not long after the antick convulsions beganne; yet no solution nor ease of that dissease ensueth them. [sic] The other, *Aphorisme*, hath a double overthrow by it. For nether had she cure by the coming of her monethes, as the first part thereof intendeth; nor yet did her dissease, by escaping that opportunitie of natures crisis, become inveterate, and of aged continuance, as the latter part though doth playnly affirme. These aphorismes were not only true in *Hippochrates* times, but in *Galens* also,[229] as he beareth witnes in sundrie places. And that oure times avouche no lesse, heare ii or iii of the best, in the name of all the rest. *Brassavolus*[230] uppon this cited aphorisme writeth thus: *Nos multos comitiales morbos in hac ætate finici vidimus, et multæ pustulæ sparsiæ per corpus, et in mulieribus multas præfocationes, quæ errumpentibus menstruis sanatæ sunt.* That is, *we have seene manie falling sicknesses finsih in this age; and manie pustules dispersed over the bodie, and in women, manie suffocations from the mother, ar healed by the coming of the tearmes.* Hollerius *hath these wordes:*[231] *virgines et convulsione cum comitiali, tum proprie' dicta, aliis quoque mortis pueritiæ vindicari, quo tempore primum menstrua errumpunt, Hippochrates scripsit, et experientia confirmata res est.* That is, *That gyrles ar quit of convulsions, both epilepticall and propper; as also of other disseases of childehood; at such time as there monethes doe first breake forth; both* Hippocrates *hath written it, and also by experience it is a thing confirmed.* Whereto this maie be added out [Fol. 128v] of Vaselius:[232] *Nihil magis medicus receptum, et experimento congitum, quam pueriles morbos, fluentibus menstruis, mulieribus, pueris vero, in adolsecentia, finiti. 1. Nothing is more received among phisitions, and knowne by experience; then that the disseases of childehood are finished by the menstruall fluxe in young women, and by the entering of youthfull age in boyes.* I think now, that it standeth *D.J.* greatly in hand if he will not here fall out with his old masters rules, to set us downe some sound and commodius reasons first which in *M. Gl.* was nether cured of her precedent suffoc. from the mother ther at the coming of her monethes; but hold it still, yea grew farre worse, within iii monethes after and secondly, whie she was afterward, so cleare quit of it, whereas by the rule it should here have continued upon her incurably.] Againe if menstruall defect had made the obligation at first, then menstruall fluxe must have come to the solution at last. But so it did not, therefore her sickenes had no dependance there upon. But will he saie, this is no necessarie consequent. For the solution of the disease cometh not, alwaies, with evacuation of the humorall cause conjunct, no not in our *hypothesi.* I saie it doth, in ours especially; admitting no exception but this; where the matter is translated to some other region. Which then cometh to one of these two issues; either there to be evacuated (as *per vomitum vel secessum etc.*)[233] or els to breed another disease, which cannot then be called a Curation, but rather transmutation of the sickenes. This *metastasis* was not to be found in *M Glover* by nether issue: therefore my argument standeth [Fol. 126v] good. The like maner of argument I fetch, from the evill chaunge of windes, namely into the South; which *Hippochrates* proveth, by argument *a majore* to make hurtfull alteration in such diseases.[234] To conclude, as effluxe of humor in the declination of the fitt, is an argument of the generative seede degenerated into a cause of the evell, so a croaking noyse, spreading over the bellie, is a signe of declining of the menstruall suffocation: like as, often risinge, or breaking winde by the mouth is comonly seene in ether fitt; and geveth ease to both the kindes. All which things, being utterly absent from *M Glover*, do with the rest, both of signes and causes, averre, as much as I have taken in hand to proove, and more then ever *D Jorden* dreamed thus to heare; namely that *Marie Glovers* case was not the suffocation from the mother.

[Fol. 127r][235]

Chapter 7

That Marie Glover was vexed with an uncleane spirit

By these things maie the judicious reader perceave; that, seeing this one Canon of *Hippochrates*,[236] hath brought forth the consideration of so manie matters, of no small emolument or value, to the purchasing of light for the finding of truth; it is too probable, that if his minde had not bene taken up, aforesaid, with[237] præjudice, and so his taste marred with other mens opinions, *D Jorden* would, (out of his learning, which in no wise I extenuate) have deduced, from this, and manie other rules, both these and manie other such arguments, to have led him peremptorily and conducted him cleerly out of the maze of those *maie bees*, wherein plainely he hath lost him selfe. Notwithstanding all that is hitherto said, I see where he is not setled, and perceave with *Hippochrates*, [Fol. 127v][238] that it is *necessarie to bring manie arguments, for the removing of opinions,*

*which stick fast in mens mindes if a man intend to bring his auditor
from his first receaved opinion, to beeleive him.* Now therefore I will
turne me from the negative proofes, to that taske of the affirmative;
which *Dr Jorden*[239] (with no litle confidence) imposeth upon me, in
these wordes: *where as all other diseases are knowne by their notes
and signes which resemble their cause, as choler, flegme, melancholie
etc. have their proper markes, corruption and putrefaction their
proper notes, and malignitie his character, so there must be some
note or character of a supernaturall power in these cases (as
extraordinarie strength or knowledge or suffring) or els we have no
cause, but to think them naturall.* I have alreadie[240] uncoupled this
consequence both by reason and aucthorities heretofore. Howbeit,
for his characters of supernaturall, in anie particular instaunce, I am
also provided, if he be reasonable, with sufficient store to satisfie
him: For as in the former Chapter I have proved, that neither
generative seed, nor menstruall bloud, were offensive [Fol. 129r] in
M Glovers bodie, so I purpose here, to publish such effectes, as
those causes, howsoever they had ofended, could never have
produced. To pratermit that huge swelling in her throat, with the
monstrous motions in brest and bellie, that uncouth rowlinge round
of her bodie, and uglie distortion of her hucke [sic] bones and chine
(though they be characters of transnaturall causes) as thinges
sufficiently spoken of, upon a just occasion, in the former Chapter;[241]
I will here beginne with the beginning of her evells; the first
shutting up of her throat against swallowing, and held for the space
of 18 daies; with sundrie fittes in everie daie of Dumbenes and
blindnes, gaping often wide, and receaving downe her throate, as
farre as anie bodie could thrust their fingers, without anie offence or
provocation, either of Choaking or vomitting: and this upon sight
and speech with *Elizabeth Jackson*; one not suspected then, but
convicted since of witchcraft. Here went but a thin paire of sheares
between soundenes and sickenes. The maid was eating of a posset,
she hath but a short parliaunce with this woman, she is instauntly
unable to swallow one drop more; and presently [Fol. 129v] after
that, taken dumb and blinde. Doth not this meeting togeather, of
such symptomes and Circumstances, discover some character of
supernaturall? And that not so much to the Comon people, as to the
phisitions:[242] for, that there is no naturall disease, that carieth that
stamp upon it, either in the beginninge, or processe of so manie

105

daies. And all the booke cases and private observations, which *D Jorden* bringeth, when they are compared with thus, are but idle and addle instaunces. But like this hath ben seene in other demoniackes, whereof *Wier* bringes us more then one, which here I will not sticke to set before the readers eies. One, is of certain Nunnes devoted to *St Bridget*,[243] not farre from *Xantes, which being manie other waies vexed by Sathan, had, by fittes also, their jawes so taken, as that they could swallow no meate. Another among the monkish maydes that were possessed, Wierus saw*,[244] *by the name of Judith, who besides the cruell convulsions she suffred, had her jawes so shut up, as that she could admit no meat; and her tongue sometimes holden that she could not speake. Prosper Aquitanicus* writeth,[245] that [Fol. 130r] *at Carthage, there was a certaine christian maide, who being in the bathes, and unmodestly behoulding a picture of venus, with feigning her selfe like it, was presently possessed of the Divill, and namely in her throate, that for 70 daies and nightes togeather, she was not able to swallow either meat or drinck.* These cases in deede come neer to *M Glovers* prehension, and do confirme our first character, gathered out of some signes and circumstaunces set togeather. Another like to this,[246] maie thus be collected: when this maid was amended the aforesaid *Eliz. Jackson,* some six weekes after her first ungracious salutation,[247] came to *Glovers* shop dore, and bestowed a double view upon his daughter, who was then eating a peece of bread, the fruit whereof was, that the bread then in chewing fell out of the maides mouth, and the maid from her stoole into a new greivous fitte; which fitt she kept afterwardes, to the hower of her deliverance, for everie sustinaunce that she tooke. Adde hereto, that her fittes had, after that, divers such other encreases, by divers such interviews, as appeareth in the Narration. And when as [Fol. 130v] that old woman did heare the publique brute, that *M Glovers* matters stood in these evill termes, she gloriously tooke upon her the matter, *geving her God thankes, that heard her praier, and stopped the mouth and tyed the tongue of one of her enemies.*[248] *I hope an evill death will come to her.* And at another time and place; *The vengeance of God on her, and on all the generation of them. I hope the Divell will stop her mouth.* Now that this woman, had a good servant, attendant upon her curses, maie appeare both by those wordes, and by this consequence, which we have from a testimonie geven in evidence, before the bench of her tryall: thus

namely; that to a certaine man, who ought her a litle mony, being
out of towne when she came for it, she prayed God, he might
breake his leg, or his arme, before he came home againe; and it came
to passe for his arme breaking, accordingly. Out of this, I thus
collect my Character: here was a straunge sicknes; no naturall
causes precedent (as I have [Fol. 131r] shewed in the former
chapter) it encreased at everie meeting with that old woman: who
was a cruell Curser, and therefore a fitt mistresse for the Divill, and
who did assume to her selfe the maydens affliction; as the effecte of
her imprecations. A third I have of the same suit.[249] One daie,
Elizabeth Jackson sent to this *Marie Glover* an orange, as in a
qualme of kindness. The wench tooke it no lesse, and kept it in her
hand,[250] smelling often to it, the most part of that day; but after
that day (it was observed) the same hand, arme and wholl side were
deprived of feeling and moving, in all her long fitts; and not before.
Now here was not the womans presence, but her token, no feare,
nor anger, but contentment and good liking; yet even so, the
mischeife was well increased. Fourthlie[251] her neck would sometime
be stretched forth much longer then natures stint, her face becoming, meane while, much lanker and thinner then before.[252] Fiftly,
lying in a fitt [Fol. 131v] her face upright,[253] and her bodie stretched
out at length you might have seene her whole bodie, all at once,
suddainely snatched downe towards the bedds feete, a foote length,
from the place, wherein she laie before. Here we have a question
about the second generall kind of *motus*,[254] which is *Latio* or
Localis: for here is a bodie removed, from a place where it was laide,
to a place where it was not laide. It is to be enquired how it
commeth thither. The meanes must needs be one of these two,[255]
and in ward proper power, in it selfe, that so did move it,[256] or some
outward force that caried it. By anie proper power in it selfe that
motion came not, for asmuchas it was altogeather, and at once, the
motion of the whole beginning at no one part. Which thing is
contrarie to naturall, in all sense, and common experience. For none
of us can go or leap, or turne our bodies being laide, otherwise then
by thrusting forward, to our purpose, the whole, by some one part
at the least, and that one part removeth last, and not with the first.
This motion therefore could be no action of the maids [Fol. 132r]
but rather a passion and suffring of some externall straunge
vyolence. That could not be the suffocation from the mother, nor

anie other naturall symptome, therefore heere we have a supernaturall character. Sixtly[257] The variable weight of her right arme in
all her long fittes, so as sometimes you might tosse it, as if it had
bene made of cloutes, but slightly lapt togeather; sometimes againe
it held waight proportionable to his magnitude: also of the whole
bodie, at some times proved; as appeareth by Mr Sharpes deposi-
tion, before the bench. Seaventhly[258] In the time that she gaped so
wide, as farre exceeded naturall use, and which she could not come
neere, by anie willing endevour when she was well; even then, a
violent blast brake out from her throat, sounding *tesh*, with such
accent as amazed as manie as first heard it. As likewise was froath
spit out of her throate, in the time of like gaping, at her deliverance.
Let the reader consider the places in the narration, and then judge,
[Fol. 132v] first, whether anie man can so doe; and especiallie the
maide, in that insensible condition, wherein she then laie. Secondly
if it were not voluntarie, what symptome it can be named, and unto
what disease it apertayneth. If it can be referred to none (as I beleeve
verelie it cannot) we must take it for the character of some straunge
guest, whose workes are wordes of blasphemie, and abusion of the
creatures of God. Eightlie,[259] I observe that coupling of con-
trarieties, more then ever is seene in kindelie sickenesses: as in an
extreme rigiditie of the whole bodie and abolition of the Comon
sense, to have certaine partes move scientiallie and in methode. Such
as were the rising of her bodie about the midle, and doing those
anticke gestures, spoken of in the [blank] page of the narration; the
carying of her handes to her mouth, and back againe with the
opening and shutting of it, at such direct and strict moments of
time; with the uttering of so manie and such wordes, and no others,
nor moe, nor fewer, as is to be seene in the [blank] page of [Fol.
133r] the Narration. And the lifting up of her armes over her head,
in such curious fourmes of exact and inimitable gestures, described
in the [blank] page of the Narration. Here againe we come to
examyne locall motions, that we may finde at length, whereunto
these pretie ones must be referred. If here was no supernaturall
cause, then were these actions either *secundum naturam* or *præter
naturam*: that is, either according to nature working freelie and at
libertie, or els, as she is by some diseasefull cause diverted, or
impeached. If by nature, then volantarie; but such were not hers, of
whome we speake, for she laie (now) voyde of all sense. If by

diseasefull causes, perverting the faculties or instruments of moving, that symptome, must have bene shewed in one of these two fashions: *diminution* or *depravation*:[260] but all weakened or lessened motions stand raunged under voluntarie actions, and must here be cassiered with their Captaine: depraved motions are of fower sortes,[261] *trembling*, [Fol. 133v] *convulsive, panting* and *yerking out of or foyning.*[262] As for trembling, panting and foyning, everie man will quit them in this case. Now if we finde it not in Convulsion, then it is no where within the Physitions compasse. Convulsion in deede, hath this in Comon, both with his fellow symptomes, and this our case, that it is *præter voluntatem*, and beyond his fellowes, hath thus much more comunitie, with our motion in question,[263] that is a drawing of the muscles towards their originall, and consequentlie moveth the member after the waie of naturall motion. But here then, I shew an essentiall difference betwixt them; that *Convulsion* is a rash inconsulted motion, from the beginning to the end, destitute of all direction, and scientiall guiding to anie shew of use. Ours on the contrarie, was an ordinate ruled motion, scientially limitted and guided, from the first to the last, to an apparent shew of use. Therefore this methodicall motion, that I speake of, in this place, was no Convulsion, and consequently nether to be found within the Jurisdiction of phisicke; nor yet in the whole [Fol. 134r] Comon wealth of nature; taking nature as we do in this discourse. Wherefore we have here no remedie, all thinges being diligentlie considered, but to resume againe, that member of our connexive distribution, which was layed aside; whilest other appellant causes might speake for them selves, and were shined upon, with as much favour of the Court, as they could deserve. Which although I heere abandon, geving sentence on the side of supernaturall, yet to the end they shall complaine of no injustice in me, I leave them with this hope; that if they bring anie advocate, that shall better prove their right, this sentence shall not debar them hereafter. In the meane time, let their fautors geve me leave, here to pronounce a Character of supernaturall; chalenging that spirite of pride, maliciousnes and blasphemie, as the cause of these. Ninthly[264] that noted motion of a warbling or flickering joyned with a certaine joult from the throat downe into the brest and bellie,[265] which hapned in the declination of her fitte, at the loosing and setting free everie joynt and member of her bodie, which before had ben holden [Fol. 134v] voyd of feeling and moving, as is to be acknowledged by sundrie places of the storie. As also it appeared at the asswaging of everie pange. This was neither of bloud nor alliaunce, to any symptome of the moving facultie, and that being so, is worthie to be excluded all the coastes of our profession. It is likely rather, that here *Sathan* was willing to insinuate with some ostentation, the place of his abode, during the time of quyet betweene her fittes: whereof also some shew appeared, in that the bulke of her bellie kept bigger then naturall, all the time of her affliction, and fell as manifestly at the moment of her deliverance. Tenthly[266] that straunge fitt, which the maide was ever cast into, at the open presence of that same *Elizabeth Jackson*.[267] For both, that was no fitte of the mother, in anie kinde of resemblaunce, and it came at the presence of no visible creature, but of hers only. This is no new note of witchcrafte,[268] but hath bene observed of others before this time. Eleventhly,[269] that at the touching of the said *Elizabeth Jackson*, the maides bodie had tumbled and wallowed over unto her, in Chalenging wise, [Fol. 135r] so oftentimes, and to none others touching, for manie trialls; yea and perpetually to none others, except she were in presence. The maid could have no advantage hereto, by the sense of feeling; for of sense and understanding she was utterly deprived, at this present, as I have declared otherwhere.[270] And therefore this was as good an evidence of supernaturall, as to have a dead bodie, bleed at the presence of the murderer, or looke at him with the eyes. 12ly[271] that at the secret presence of the said *Elizabeth* brought in, when the maid was, in one of her ordinarie fittes, the bodie instauntly altered, from a dimie into a totall deprivation, of sense and moving; as in those other fittes, which began at the open presence of the witch. 13.[272] the voyce *hang her*, or *honge her*, in the maides nostrills began, soone after the Coming in, of *Elizabeth Jackson*, and continued (without intermission) for everie breath, one repetition, until she was clerely departed the house againe. A man can not [Fol. 135v] say precisely, those were the words, but that the voyce sounded neerest them of all other wordes. And that it did, sometimes more, sometimes lesse, as the storie delivereth. At that time, when the *Lady Brunkerd* was present, there was with her, a certaine gentlewoman, altogeather setled, to ascribe whatsoever she saw, to the passions of the mother; I never saw anie more manifestly possessed with præjudice; when

110

she had listened long at a tyme, and often, to the sound of this voyce, I pressed her with some importunitie, to declare openly to us, what that voyce was like, in her best judgement; and finding her still loath to speake to it, I urged her thus, it is not likest that she saith, *hang her*? No, quoth she, but *hunger*. By this the reader may perceave, what manner of voyce it was; and seeing it so pursued that woman, and none els, whether it were a character of supernaturall or no, I recomend it to the reader. 14.²⁷³ Is the tossing of the maides body, at the saying of the sixth petition of our Lordes prayer; only at those times, as she laie voyd of [Fol. 136r] all sense; and at none other. For at all other times, when prayers were made, she would shewe by the gesture of that hand which she could move, that she devoutly joyned in them in her minde. At the time of Elizabeth Jacksons arraignment, the body was tossed also, at these wordes, *Lead us not into temptation*;²⁷⁴ namely when *Eliz. Jackson* was caused to saie the Lords praier; as also at these wordes *He descended into hell*, when she said the christian beleefe. These be things that *Galen*, (no, nor *Hippocrates*,) never saw in phisick, and therefore I am sure, he must no more then they, that can assigne them place within the compasse of our profession. But well doth this signe, challenge his fire, by other like cases reported of *Demoniacks*, by *Wierus*,²⁷⁵ and the booke of the witches of *Warboys*: where, at the invocating the name of Jesus, the parties afflicted were suddainly moved, or tossed and one especially, I finde to have bene troubled, at those verie wordes, in like sort, *deliver us from evill*.²⁷⁶ This manie badges have I found of supernaturall causes [Fol. 136v] in *M. Glovers* case, before that joyfull day of her deliverance. And as no daie cometh to us, without some profit, if it be well imployed, so how should this day, be unserviceable to our purpose; wherein Sathans proud armies were so gloriously vanquished, by our Lords humble hoste? Not marching in the strength of flesh and bloud, nor using the weapons of worldly warfare, but by the soveraigne power of Jesus our King, and by his sanctified weapons, of faith and fervent supplication. Let us approach neerer (then) to the view of this daie, and see what it affordeth further, to the augmentation of the former number. 15.²⁷⁷ The fitte that daie was notoriously altered, in these .3. circumstances: in the time, in the whole fashion, and in vehemencie. First for the time, it began about .9. of Clocke in the forenoone, which was an anticipation, holding no proportion with the præcedencies. For her former ordenarie fittes, began first at 3. of Clocke, in the afternoone, and held them constantly to that hower, until divers trialls were made, of the presence of that old woman, so often named; by every one of which, her fitt both [Fol. 137r] anticipated; and was ecked out in length. But all by litle and litle; so as in a .3. moneths space, it had gotten almost .3. howers time in sooner coming, and extended it selfe further, by .6. howers space in continuance. Which the prudent reader must be intreated to note,[278] to understand the reason, whie the writer of the report of *M Glovers* deliverance, saith her fittes were wont to begin at .3. or .2. they did so in deed, but he knew not, that they came at length betwene xii. and one. This by the way. But to my purpose, seeing now this dayes fitt, is testified to have begon about .9. of the Clocke, here must be graunted a marvelous disproportion, betwene this fitte, and the præcedents, touching the quantities of anticipation. The like I conclude (though in a contrarie sorte) for the length of the fitt. Which by how manie howers it began earlier, by double so manie it was cut of sooner. God declaring by the first part of the daie, that he approoved their enterprise, by his gracious presence: making it an intollerable terror, yea a furious agonie unto [Fol. 137v] the adversarie; and by the later part, geving them a pledge of his victorious arme, and sweet acceptaunce of their sacrifice; by casting out *Sathan*, the implacable enemie of mankinde, in the verie middest of the battaile, and in the height of his most raging encounters.[279] Thus much for the time Now to the fashion. 16.[280] This was neither like the fitte called ordenarie (which should have come that daie) nor extraordinarie, which she was throwen into, at the presence of the Witch. The dissimilitude, more particularly set fourth by the author of the *Report*, I will here comprehend in these two principalls: the symptomes chaunged, and the tenor interrupted. The chaunge of symptomes, some being absent, namely those motions of her handes to her mouth, of her armes over her head, and of those warbling joultes downe her brest. Others present, and that other such, as in former times she had, though not of .3. moneths space,[281] or els new, that never appeared before that daie: such were the wagging of her Chap, with huge gaping [Fol. 138r] and foaming. The moving of her bodie from the preachers, and uglie Counteinaunces made towards them, as menacing or storming them etc.

The tenor of her fitt here was interrupted .3. times, everie one affoording a long praier of the maides betweene; a playne noveltie on her case; and an excellent demonstration of *Sathans* forcible repulse. 17.[282] The vehemencie of this fitte (likewise) above others, was notable, as whosoever readeth and compareth shall easily finde and see, especially in the last conflict, wherein the Divill (as it seemed) set all the handes he had, to worke, and bestirred him to the uttermost; to quell her life, or keepe his hould. When *D Jorden*, or anie other for him, shall, from his *suffocation of the Mother*, or anie other sickenes, render some competent reason of these alterations, which this day brought unto her fitte; then will I wype these .3. last out of this catalogue of supernaturall characters. Untill then, they must be reckoned worthie place, (at least) [Fol. 138v] in this our subject, what intertainment soever they shall finde, in all other cases of like nature hereafter. 18.[283] In asmuch as this cure was atchieved by spirituall meanes only, the corporall laid aside, and that herein doing, a principall man of the action in his prayer,[284] *urged the Lord to heare them, the rather for that they took no indirect meanes or course for remedie, but went directly to him etc.* In a case of naturall sicknes, it had ben unlawfull to have said so, but the answere of God proved that this contestation was true and allowed; therefore this also was a signe of supernaturall cause. 19.[285] Both the praiers of the maid, when she reverted, and of divers of the preachers, were directed unto God, expresly for the casting out of *Sathan*. This course, yf the case had stood otherwise, had ben so far of obteyning a blessing, as that it must needs have provoked, the displeasure of our Lord against them, for so perverting his holie ordenaunces, and offring up the sacrifice of fooles unto him. But contrarie to this, our most gracious heavenlie [Fol. 139r] father, was so well pleased with their importunate praiers and vehement cryes in this behalf, through his deere sonne, our Lord Jesus, in whom they were accepted, that never men departed with more rejoycing spirits, nor with greater assurance that God had heard their prayers, and was well pleased towards them in that daie. For further confirmation whereof, maie be added, that some of them, after their trembling praiers, others in the middest of their wrastling with God, were so inflamed in their spirits with strong and joyous assuraunce, that they cryed out, *he fleeth, he fleeth.*[286] A thing well knowne, to all that are exercised in the heavenly psalmes of *David*, to be sutable to the worke of Gods spirit; namely to geve a kinde of warrantize to the conscience of him, that rightly powreth out his deprecations unto God, that he becommeth manie times, as certainely assured, of the thing he hath asked, as if it were, even then, alreadie accomplished before his eyes; so as even then also, he geveth thanks, before [Fol. 139v] he ariseth up from prayer. And so did these christian soldiers at this time, upon the like ground, with these encoraging acclamations to their bretheren, insult upon,[287] *that foule malicious Divill* as another in his praier, rightly tearmed him. 20.[288] Her bodie shunned the preachers that prayed, as if she could not abide them: and with most monstrous gapings, and sundrie other detestable Counteinances, turned her face toward them, as to out face and disturb them, that most confidently called for help against Sathan.[289] In so much, as when one of the preachers, in the middest of those blasphemous abusions of Godds goodly image, prayed God to rebuke that foule malicious divell, she suddenly (saith the storie) though *blinde, dumbe and deafe, turned to him, and did bark out froath at him.* So did she to others that stood over her, *cast out foam, up to their faces; her mouth being wide open.* There is no cause, that I can understand, whie the suffocation of the mother should have been in such a chafe. 21.[290] *There is a condition which we dayly meete withall in the practise of phisick, called ultimus naturæ conatus. When* [Fol. 140r] *the sicke partie is verie neere unto death, and a litle before his departure, hath a suddaine alleviation or lightning (as they call it) as though he should presently recover.*[291] *This is when the soule, having gathered togeather the remnant of spirites, not yet wholly spent and dissipate by the sicknes, fortifying with them the most indigent faculties, to her power, chargeth the disease full causes, everie where, upon a suddaine: as to take awaie once for all, her feare, of that unwilling seperation from her bodie. And by that meanes, albeit she prevaile not utterly, yet such a repulse she geveth the sickenes, at that time, as procureth an apparent cessation. How be it having now paid the price, of the losse, of all her men of armes, for this litle poore victorie, she of necessitie, geveth place at the next assault, that the sicknes maketh.* Even so (according as there is a resemblance in Contraries) *Sathan* in this poore patient, being at this period, invaded by the Angell of God, in every corner of his habitation, and finding no abilitie to keepe his hould anie longer, enlargeth yet his malice, to the [Fol. 140v] supplie of his might,[292] and desperately attempteth, as his uttermost act, being cast out himselfe, to carie out life with him. For so it followeth here in the storie *that she fell downe suddainely into the chaire*, with all signes of death accomplished. In which case she remained not long, er life was put into her againe; and therewithall, the heartes of everie one filled with gladnes and thankesgeving.²⁹³ Like as²⁹⁴ *when the Lord brought the captive multitude of Sion We were like them in that dreame* (said the Church) *then was our mouth filled with laughter and our tongue with joy etc.* Some demoniacks in the gospell,²⁹⁵ cured by the word, of that eternall word, had this signe at the ejection of *Sathan*. But in no curation, by praiers, of any naturall diseases, hath it so hapned at anie time, that ever I could see, read, or heare of. If *D Jorden* can furnish us with some instaunce he maie doe well. And it is not safe for his cause, to detract to do it except in the sted thereof, he deliver us good reason, how in thus curing of the *suffocation of the mother*, this might happen [Fol. 141r] To conclude, the maid felt something depart out of her;²⁹⁶ *and therewithall felt such a freedom in all the faculties and instruments of her soule and bodie, as caused her to spring out for joy*, and break out into this new and heavenly note, *The comeforter is come. O Lord thow hast delivered me.*²⁹⁷ Having then in her owne happie person, the practicke feeling, of everie waie universall truth;²⁹⁸ *Where the spirit of the Lord is there is Libertie.* And againe²⁹⁹ *if that sonne make you free, then you are free in deed.* Yea herein had she an experimentall proofe of that promise,³⁰⁰ of *the sending of the comforter*, which the everlasting truth hath made, to all that aske in his name. And herein her lott was made like to her grandfathers,³⁰¹ in necessitie of Comfort, and receaving it in due time; but her testimonie the verie same; *The comforter is come. He is come. He is come.* Hereunto I adjoyne, that then, so observable countenaunce of majesticall comlines; which by the waie of *antithesis*, in contrarie causes, the Lord our mightie redemer, was pleased to affect their eies withall, to asmuch comfort and rejoycing, as they had, not long [Fol. 141v] before, conceived sorrow and heavines by the contrarie. That hereby all naie be taught, not to feare the malice of *Sathan himself* (therefore not of lesser enemies) so long as we have faith in the Lord of life, but be assured, that all his rage and stormes against us, shall finally be frustrate; and how defourmed and shunned soever, he maketh us, in the daies of our humiliation, yet we shall finde a full recompence of glorie in that daie of exaltation. And although to the children of this world, the exercises, schoolings, and afflictions of the righteous, seem to lye in equall balaunce with the wicked, or els to be more horrible; yet the end shall tell of great difference; and preach the plenteous mercie of the lord, to all that in faith and patience, importune and waite for his seasonable Coming. And where the Lord, by such successe, and shining of his Countenance, both inwardly and outwardly, is pleased thus to notifie the happines of his benevolent favor, and propitious presence to his peoples enterprise, there doe I beleeve, hath bene no errour, neither in the substaunce nor end of their [Fol. 142r] supplication. Now the substance here was, that this maid might be delivered out of *Sathans* vexation: therefore I conclude, that by the hands of *Sathan* her bodie was then tormented.

Chapter 8

Answeres to certayne objections, made against some thinges, in the later ii chapters

My Catalogue of supernaturall Characters,[302] in this case, thus accomplished, *D Jorden* will require, no further answere (as I think) to the aucthoritie of *Avicen*,[303] *of the Divells perverting the complexion into the nature of black choler, himselfe departing.* If he doe, I turne him over to the learned *Valesius*, who hath answered it alreadie, and is able to save me this labour. In the first chapter of his booke, *D Jorden* urgeth out of *Hippochrates*, these two argumentes. [Fol. 142v][304] The first, that Characters of a supernaturall cause cannot in this case be rendred. This is now answered. His second which he professeth as eagerlie is, that *these symptomes do yeeld unto naturall causes, and are procured, and also eased by such ordenary meanes, as other diseases are; and therefore they must needes be naturall etc.* Although *D Jorden* in these words and all that page following, speaketh directly of the *suffocation of the Mother*, and the symptoms thereof, shooting verie wide from his marke, as I will shew in the Chapter ensueing, yet forasmuch as in this place, he hath an eye also to our present instaunce, I must take knowledge, that by these wordes; *these symptoms do yeeld unto naturall causes, and are procured and also eased by such ordenary meanes as other diseases are,* he meaneth some symptomes (at least) in *Ma. Glovers* case, although not all, nor many. Which thing he declareth more plainely in these wordes afterward: demanding, *what equalitie of contrarietie, either in* [Fol. 143r] *degree or in power, can there be, betweene a supernaturall suffocating power, and the compression of the bellie and throate.* This seemeth to touch our case; for asmuch as in the rising of that mover to the throat, that so rebounded first in the brest and bellie, the maids throat was usually compressed, with great strength of mens handes. Now he reasoneth thus; forasmuch as diseases are ever cured by their Contraries, what contrarietie can here be assigned? Then he addeth further: *These are disparates in Lodgick, but not contraries. For contrarietie is betwene such as are comprehended under one generall. And where one is opposed unto one alone, and not indifferentlye unto manie. Neither do I thinck that any man well advised, will say, that by compression of those partes, he is able to suppresse, the power of the Divell.* These things to shew, (although there were none other) that his booke was published *non præmorsis unguibus;* with too little premeditation. For [Fol. 143v] first, it doth not follow, that whatsoever affect yeeldeth to naturall helpes, doth it selfe spring out of naturall Causes. *Saule*[305] his melancholik madnes, was raised of an evill spirit, sent of God. Yet was his vexation often eased by *Davids* harp, which was a naturall meanes. Manie learned men affirme,[306] some of them out of experience, that dæmoniacks may receave ease by phisicall helpes.[307] And that for this reason: the divell inflicteth hurt in way of diseases, when he hath lycence thereto; Distempering, depraving and Corrupting the outward aire, and the inward humours in manifold maner, especially disposing them unto melancholike habit; which humour *Jerome* calleth the Divells bath. Against these molitions, maie phisicall darts at sometime, be so happely hurled, as mai, if not defeate, yet enfeeble or hinder their fallfilling [sic]; and so bring some releefe to the Patient. But *D Jorden* will say, here is the rule of Contraries, [Fol. 144r] rightly houlden in the curation; whilest so distemperatures are altered, redundancies evacuat, obstructions opened etc. But what have you contrarie to the divell in that Compression of the throat? I aunswere Compression (in deed) of the throat, and such a supernaturall worker, and disparates in Lodgick, but so were Davids harp, and Saules evill spirit. And so is Corruption of menstruall bloud or generative seed, matched with compression of the bellie, in the right suffocation of the mother. Yea so you shall finde it oftentimes, if you compare remote causes with immediate helpes; and consider not the Logicall affection of Contraries in their next immediat *genus*. For example *Davids* musick and *Saules* evill spirit are in the balaunce of discretion, dissentaneous arguments, in deed, such as both in reason, and nature dissent, and therefore opposits; but yet intertayning no greater discord one with another, then both of them doe with heat [Fol. 144v] or cold, blindnes or eloquence, distention or obliquitie; and therefore maie well be disparates, whereof one may be opposed to manie; but cannot be contraries, which fight in single combat togeather.[308] But if it be weighed, that *Sathan* prepared first a seat of black choler, and thereof, as out of foggie combustion, raised black terrifieing vapoures, which affrighting the phantasie, might raise expressive feare and furie, then are we led, as by a threed, to finde, 2. subordinate causes; the object of delight and consolation and the object of terrour, and vexation, defeating and conquering one another. In matters more phisicall, and not transcendent, the same opposition may be observed. As, what contrarietie in degree or power, can be found between the *Tarantula*,[309] whose byting ensueth such monstrous exorbitant symptomes, and the pleasaunt sound of musicke, which presently appeaseth all? The *Tarantula* itself is not avoyded by musick, [Fol. 145r] therefore then are not contraries, that expell one another, but the operation of musicke, and the worke of her poyson, are set in extreme opposition without anie intercessour at all: the poyson chasing the spirits into their fountaines, and so insinuating itself, there to surprize life; and the musick calling the spirits from their center, and with them, exhausting the venome, from the fountaine and tower of life, and cunningly intertayning it, in the outward baser partes, till there insited heat, assisted continewally with influent [? illeg.] spirits, have scattered, and cast it out againe, by the pores. From materiall medicines likewise we are furnished with examples, to illustrate this doctrine. As, hath rubarb anie formall contrarietie, or variaunce in nature, with the *Tertian* fever? Nay, it is rather like it. And doth not therefore availe, to the cure of the fever properly, but only by a Consequent, in asmuch as it evacuateth the matters of obstruction in the [Fol. 145v] first veynes, whereof the fever was inkindled.

118

And, to exemplifie from outward helpes also there is no right contrarietie, betweene vapoures ascending, from diseasefull causes in the mother, and that compression that is made above the navell; for if these had a proper or immediat repugnancie, then should that compression prevaile at all times, when vapoures thence ascended: but that is refuted by all hystoricall epilepsies, and melancholies:[310] therefore is the contrarietie in deed, and directly, betwene that compression, and the distention or swelling of the lower bellie upwardes, whereby the vapoures are not kept below; but the daungerous oppression of the vitall parts, by the violent bearing up of the *Diaphragma*, is, to the great ease of the patient, thereby much prevented. In much like sort, standeth the case, that *D Jorden* here toucheth; for that compression of the throat in *M Glovers* fittes, was a right and immediat contrarie to the distention thereof, whereby she was eased; and withall, a meanes, of a more comly [Fol. 146r] keeping the position of her bodie, to the better satisfaction of the beholders. But me thinkes I heare *D Jorden*, or some other, rather, of lesse judgement, thus muttering: whether that distention of her throat was done, by *Sathan* ymmediatly, or els by materiall causes, raysed in her bodie, by him, yet could the compression of mens hands make anie resistaunce to the power of the *Divell*, and so procure her ease? Is anie man able to represse the power of the divell? I answere by distinction of this power; as it is considered at large, or els limited. In the former respect, all flesh is unable to match with him: but according to the later, men maie be able to prevaile against him in particular resistaunce, so as sorteth with that divine providence and dispensation. For albeit his power, be as the power of a mightie Angell, according to his creation,[311] yet his rebellion and fall considered, he remaineth in a perpetuall bondage; having now all the moments of his might [Fol. 146v] exquisitely limited towards all creatures: both as touching the effecting of the worke,[312] such only, as it is designed him; as also, touching the extension of his might, in everie singular thing, so far only, as is permitted him. I doe not beleeve there is anie man, well instructed in the schoole of Christ, that wilbe found so unadvised, as to denie this. Then do I, therhence, thus gather, and conclude: Wheresoever Sathan hath leave to torment the bodie, he hath for everie action therein, but such a proportion only of his power, permitted him to use, as our soveraigne God then leaveth at

119

libertie unto him; and more then that, he is not able at that time to employ. And we may see it to be so, in all Dæmoniacks; in whome his malice would, and his might could, rather unjoynte their members, then writhe them; and burst out the skinne, then stretch it forth. Yea those that he tossed upon a bed or floore, he could as easely throw up into the aire. And [Fol. 147r] such as trouble six to hould in Comlines, he could make impossible for a hundreth men to retaine amongst them. It is then no unadvisednes to affirme, that the Divell cannot effect so much in everie point, in the partie, that is houlden by strength of men, as he can in such, as ly at libertie and receave no succour from the strength of men at all. For his power was proportioned before; to extend but so far, when as no externall might should be added, to assist that creature; therefore it must needs fall short, of that uttermost degree of acting, so oft as it is encountered with a greater then the ordenarie degree of resistaunce. And so was it with *M Glover*. When she was not houlden at all, then did her throat swell more, and her paine was greater; then also was her bodie throwen, and tossed sundry waies, yet the uttermost of all was, but somewhat more a grevous spectacle of this extremetie by the [Fol. 147v] outward compression, thus far shorter his action was advanced, as that she was kept upon her back, and had not the extension of her throat so great. *D Jorden* doth not thinke, Demoniacks are not holden; for that were against Comon sense. He will not saie, houlding can in no wise availe; for that were as much against all experience. He must graunte therefore that the Divells limitted power maie be a little restrayned in the uttermost point of the outward acting or moving of the members, so ofte, as it findeth there a further proportion of resistaunce then was that; against which, the dispensation was at first extended. Thus have I also dispatched his second argument out of *Hippochrates*. For that which he addeth there further, of *Cupping glasses, and sweet plasters, applied beneath, and evill smells above*, his meaning is not to accomodate, to the case of this patient, (whom no man can avouch to have ben eased by them) but to denie by them, such an [Fol. 148r] opinion as (I thinke[)] no man ever held. Of which matter, you shall heare more (by the grace of God) in the next Chapter. Against my .9. Character is excepted thus: the Convulsions and Cataleptick prehensions of the partes, in her fittes, came of hystericall vapours, spreading by Courses, through out the bodie, and insinuating them selves into the joynts; and so againe on the Contrarie, by the falling downe, of those vapours, into the place of their originall (*ad fontem mali*, as they speak) every member and joynt, obteyned his free libertie againe. Save that I am sure of the honestie of the reporter, I could not have beleved that a Doctor of Phisick, who had ben first trayned up in the studie of philosophie and afterwards confirmed by the practise of it [? illeg.] would have said thus. All concrete humors would have their motions downewards to the place of the waterie element, which is next the earth: but being dissolved into vapors, they chalenge straight, the [Fol. 148v] region of the aire for their habitation. And as water ascendeth not upward but by violence, so vapours have no naturall motion downewarde, neither can they descend, but by some externall agent forcing them. And as is perpetually trew in the great world, so hath the same necessarie bond of resemblance, in the litle world of mans bodie. Out of the fermentation of malicious humors in the matrice, arise vapors (I graunt) much afflicting sundrie waies, both heart and brayne; but to yeeld, that they returne thither anie more, after they have wrought their mischeife above; is to imagine them, like the devouring beasts of the nighte, which returne againe to their dennes, in the morning: and yet more absurdly;[313] because the beasts have their naturall motion to returne by; vapours are barred, by the strong law of nature, to goe downe anie more. *Valesius*[314] therefore that learned Commenter upon *Hippochrates*, geving reason for the vanishing of certaine convulsions which are spoken of in that text, writeth thus; [Fol. 149r] *Defecerunt convulsiones, quia abritror, incoeperunt iam excuti [sic] a nervis in carnes, et deturbari a capite, ad uterum excrementa unde acciderunt sudores et menstrui fluxus.* Here he acknowledgeth the waie of the vapours, to be, out of the sinewes, (not to revert to their fountaine but to passe forth) into the flesh, and so be discussed [sic] by the pores in the skinne. The remnaunt, that yet reteyned there humorall fourme, by other decretorie passages, according to their kindly motion, were sent downeward. And thus were both braine and synewes,[315] delivered of their Cloying excrements. I need not here draw in manie testimonies, where reason is so lightsome: especially where *M Doctors* owne testimonie, maie stand in the sted of twentie. In the .7. leafe and second page of his booke, declaring how the partes of the bodie, aswell as by proper affects growing in themselves, maie also be drawne to consent of suffring with others, and that either by an absolute, or consequent communitie: coming to shew how substaunces maie be transmitted insensibly from part to parte geveth instaunce from the fittes of fevers, in these words. [Fol. 149v] *Where a vapour arising from the part affected, disperseth it selfe thorough the whole bodie, and affecteth the sensitive partes with cold or heat, the motive parts with trembling, the vitall partes with fainting sounding inequalitie of pulse etc. The naturall partes with dejection of appetite subversion of the stomach etc. untill* (what? the vapor be returned unto his originall?) no: but *nature have overcome and discussed it.* Againe in his 21. leafe, 1 page. speaking yet more properly for my purpose, where he searcheth out, with good judgement, the cause of those soddayne fittes, women have of the mother, he saith, that the *humor; being at first crude expecteth his concoction in our bodies, and geves no signe of his presence, untill such a proportion of it be digested, and resolved into vapors, as, for the offence thereof, the part affected is not able to brooke; and for the weaknes of the expulsive facultie, not able to avoide out of the bodie, but filling the veynes, arteries and the habit of the bodie, is comunicated to the principall partes, diminishing or depraving their functions so long, untill that portion of vapours* (what? returne againe [Fol. 150r] to their fountaine?) no: but *be discussed through naturall heat.* Manie will wonder, (yet they will not think it to be a miracle,) that men of such ranke, should be so overtaken in contradiction. But they will cease soone after, they have considered; that in this investigation of causes, the spirit of his minde discoursed freely, as being not tasked to the mainteynaunce of some formerly enamored Conclusion: but in the other answering, his passion seemeth too strong for his judgment, so as, it made him mistake likewise, selfe love for conscience: which in another place,[316] so earnestly he pretendeth, to be the cause of his writing. For what els could transport him, or force him to forget him selfe, when he was demanded a reason of the flickering motions, downe from the throat into the bellie; Let godly wise men judge. Against my 10. character, some make attempts to this evasion. That it is an argument of a strong *antipathie* (in deed) but not [Fol. 150v] of witchcraft. *D Jorden* in the later end of his sixt Chapter, would laie that whole burthen, upon perturbations of the minde, which in my fifte chapter I have disproved. This exception seemeth to be of a higher nature and to soare above the eagle, so as the wing that must surmount it, hath need to be imped with some feathers of divine intelligence. In deed manie curious subtleties are comprised in the Comon place of secrete properties, whereof *antipathie* is a principall member. I am not he that will enterprise to sound all those depthes, being well inough privie to my owne imbecillitie for such attempts. He that professeth full abillitie thereunto, cannot want the note of arrogance and impudencie, saith grave *Gorrheus*. Yea *they that reduce all things to the manifest qualities of elementes, are nothing els themselves but Elementes*, saith one of the sharpest philosophers.[317] But here we shall not need to enquire, of other *antipathies*, then that [Fol. 151r] only, which is betwixt two individuous species of one kinde an old woman and a young maide. What secrete discord in nature could be betwen these? I denie not, that there are in certaine men, certaine peculiar qualities, which are consequently necessarie[318] to the proper mixtion of their first materialls; and that either in this whole bodie, or but in some part; namely the stomach, braine or other. Whereupon some men are evill affected by cheese, some by a rosted ducke, others by hot milke, honie, and sundrie such like: as also at the sight or propinquitie of a Cat; but these are species of other kindes. Againe in mankind, and for the same reason, some two men have a principall correspondence in their natures, to consent and love togeather. And some other two fynde the contrarie. But yet these thinges come not neere the case in question. [Fol. 151v] For here this maide, at the presence of that old woman, is made, not onely voyd of all sense and understanding, but also an uglie spectacle of monstrous symptomes, unsutable to all kindely sicknesses. He that affirmeth this to be from phisicall *antipathie* is also of opinion that God made some men to be towards others, as the woolfe is to the sheepe, the kite to the Chickens, or rather (as Pline saith)[319] the *Catoblepes*, and the *basilisk* are towards man, which kill him by sight, without anie further delay. Or as the *Triballians Ilirians* and *Thibians* who having in one of their eyes two pupills and in the other the figure of a horse can bewitch, yea and kill, those whom they wistly [sic] looke upon.[320] Whereupon he thus concludeth *See how nature, having engrafted naturally in some men this unkinde appetite, to feede* [Fol. 152r] *commonly (like wild beastes) upon the bowells and flesh of men, hath taken delight also, and pleasure to give them inbred poysons in their whole bodie, yea and venome in the verie eyes of some, that there should be no naughtines in the whole world, but the same might be found againe in man.* Thus in deed writeth *Plinie*; but he collecteth like a prophane pagan, ignorant of the true God, and of the creation of the world by him. If any amongst us, have taken hould by his writing, I advise them to let go that hould againe, and to learne from the soveraigne scripture, that man consisting of bodie and soule, was created in the image of God:[321] which image shined perfectly and yet doth shine in part, both in his soule and body, by sundry resplendant sparkles, and beames, as symboles of divine and heavenly perfections: yea verie remarkeable in this grace of his innocence,[322] and harmelesnes towardes [Fol. 152v] others by his naked and unarmed birth; having no part fourmed us to hurt withall; as other creatures have. A native badge of vacuitie of all inbred *poysons*, and naturally engraffed harmfullnes, so as *Plinie* writeth. And if either our creation or birth were otherwise, certainely then, it must have followed, that God had geven unto men a lawe, which manie of them must have broken against their wills: which leadeth us unto a verie blasphemous absurditie; howsoever *Wierus* saw it not.[323] In consideration whereof I both accept and joyne with that religious exclamation of *Erastus*;[324] *Quae ergo dementia sit credere aliquos a Deo factos esse qui ex oculis præsentissimum venenum, lingua etiam et voce, interitum adferant aliis? Magna (crede mihi) et detestanda est hæc superstitio, in multorum animis etiam nunc radices agens.* In English thus: *Therefore what madnes is that to beleve that God made some men, such as should poure* [Fol. 153r] *forth most present poyson by their eies, or with their tongue and voyce, bring suddaine destruction unto other men? This (beleeve me) is a great and detestable superstition.* (He might have said heathenish prophanenes) *Which yet to this day ceaseth not to maintayne his rootes in the mindes of manie men.* But (to set foote to foote with them, and prove their armes) If this could be a phisicall antipathie between *M Glover* and that evicted witch, we must finde the discord in one of these twayne: in their fourmes or in their qualities. *Fracastorius*[325] is of judgment, that fourmes can extend and propagate themselves, beyond the Circumscript line of their matter; whereby the fourmes of two discordant bodies, at competent distaunces, meeting in the mid way, doe expell and labour to destroy one another; even as, on the contrarie; in agreeing fourmes so constituted, there is a mutuall reaching forth of handes for conjunction: which is that sympathie which so manie singe of. But *Scaliger* findeth these difficulties in that waie. *In the eyes of* [Fol. 153v] [326]*the Cock (say they) is a contrary power to the eyes of the Lyon, therefore if that fourme maie goe forth, so maie the fourme of man doe likewise. And so it shalbe generable and corruptible in part, wherefore also in the whole for it were foolish to saie, it dilateth and contracteth it selfe like a sponge.* This (he saith) is the greatest argument. *Another not much lesse is this. For so shal the fourme of a man be in the aire. Therefore then the aire is man. And that the matter of the aire is indewed with two fourmes, to wit the fourme of the ayre, and the fourme of man. By this meanes shall the aire be full of fourmes going forth and one fourme piercing another, and passing beyond, through all sorts of passengers everie waie and from everie place, going hither and thither this waie and that waie. Ether therefore the aire must be infourmed with all fourmes togeather, and neither with this fourme nor that, this nor that part, but the same part with manie, or else the same fourmes with mani both in the subject and without the subject, abstracted and not abstracted both togeather.* Thus far *Scaliger* well disproving the meeting abroad of their [Fol. 154r] fourmes we speake of. But as he againe saith, that albeit fourmes be denied, yet the egression of accidents are liable to this imputation, without anie heynous trespasse against philosophie [smudge]. So here at least our excepters will hope to help themselves and shall not want the assistance of *Pomponatius* and *Paracelsus*[327] to presse the matter to the furthest in their behalfe. Which because they doe it in many particulars, transgressing my theme, or (at least) exceeding the compasse of my waste time, I will leave them to *Erastus* and *Codronchius*,[328] who have both traced and overtrodden them, in everie circumstaunce, alreadie. Only for the readers sake, I will hereto speake a litle, enclosing all my matter within this small circle. If that afflicting presence of *Eliz. Jackson* towards *M Glover*, came through a Certaine Corrupting and destroying qualitie, that was in her, oppungnant to the nature of that maide, I would aske (then) whether this qualitie was originally inbred, or in her life time acquired. I am sure they can not vouch it [Fol. 154v] inbred, for that would have ben found in her, before she came to this age, towards some others; or in this age, and towards *M Glover*, at the least: who was familiarly acquainted with her, and that without this daunger, untill that falling out of theirs; whereupon was threatended and executed so heavie a vengeance. If they graunt this qualitie acquired; then doth it rest to be enquired, how she came by it. This active abilitie, in this kinde to offend another; that is, by her verie presence, to cast into a greivous affliction of the bodie, must be either without the consent of her will, or with it. The former waie can be by no other, then contagion. Now a disease cometh through Contagion, when as anie one that carieth about himselfe, some rotten or infectious disease,[329] doth by the meanes of hurtfull breathes, or aires flowing from their bodie, or Cloathes, smite some other with the like, whose bodies are prædisposed to receave such an impression. But by this meanes did not *Eliz. Jackson* offend *M Glover*: First because [Fol. 155r] she her selfe had no contagious disease upon her. 2. because the disease which they say the maid had, to wit, the suffocation of the Mother, cometh not by Contagion. 3. if it could come by contagion, yet could she not have it of her, for asmuch as the said *Elizabeth*, had not the suffocation of the mother her selfe; and she could not geve that she had not. 4. if by rotten aires issuing from her bodie, she could have infected others, she must needs have infected some others besides that maid in like manner; she conversing and standing in the throng, of so manie hundreths, at sundrie times, as manie can witnes she did, in those her daies of tryalls. 5. if the maid had ben hurt properly by contagion, her disease would have proceeded the same with her, although the externall efficient were removed; like as of all contagious diseases in deed, the whole profession of phisick beareth witnes. But this maid was never in this manner of affliction, but thorough the [Fol. 155v] presence of that *Eliz. Jackson*. For at all other times her fitts bare other fourmes, which had no re-semblaunce with this. Therefore without her will, as by phisicall contagion things come to passe, this could not happen. If then, that mischeife were inflicted, with her willing consent, it was either absolutely out of her owne wrath or malice effected, or els by some adventitious power contracted and combined. To do such a thing by an absolute malicious aspect, is impossible, and manie waies absurd to affirme, 1. because malice or wrath are not, in their nature, transient, and operative in another subject, but tarrie alwaies at home, so long as they have any being, to bring mischeife to the brest that bred them. And albeit the eies sparkle (as we saie) with furie, and desire of revenge, yet the partie against whome they are so enflamed, sleepeth never the worse, if he list him selfe. For although I should graunt, that our seeing is made by the going forth of the spirits (which were most advantage for their cause) yet are not those spirits, become animate wights, now enabled, in [Fol. 156r] a forreigne subject, to worke the designes, of that mischeevous appetite that sent them. For if they were, then all men that are angrie towards others should easily worke their owne revenge incontinently. And if you will saie, that is not a naturall propertie of wrath, but only proceedeth from a peculiar and excelling degree thereof. What degree can be imagined to have been in that sillie Woman, that hath not ben seene manie milions of times in men of hotter bloudes, of haughtier and more copious spirits, more highly and incomparably provoked and enflamed then she was? 2. Againe if one passion by the simple propertie of his nature or graduated to some great height, by manie doubles of reflexions, can forinsecally affect thus; why should not other passions by the same reason, effect the will of their sender in the like sort? And so the wicked lover, compasse his lewde love, upon the chastest matrone that he can behould? 3. Let us consider, what can passe forth, with those seeing spirits by the eyes, unto the object [Fol. 156v] whereunto they are sent. Could it be anie other, then some abstract species of a foule disease, first conceaved in the imagination, and then furiously impressed in the visible spirits, to be by them convayed unto the evill wished object? I denie not that fearfull fantasies and imaginations of monsters, maie easelie hurt the partie that conceaveth them, and I am content also here liberally to graunt them, that as the eies do then become witnesses of the inward perturbations, by their froward [sic], furious or gastly aspects, so they be portes likewise to let out the flashing sparkes, that break out from the inward flaming spirites. But what then? How shall these to the like in a forraigne subject? By what dore shall they enter; yea by what commission and power shall they proceed? Guided they can not be by the will of the partie, out of whose eyes they issued; for the soule is bounded within organicall regiments and will, or intelligence of their owne, they had [Fol. 157r] none: being at first but idle abstracts, things that had no consistence in the world. And such shadowes as they were first made, such kind of being did they loose, so soone as the act of imagination left them, which must needs be assoone as Ever they went out of the eye, at the uttermost. 4. If that godlesse old

127

woman, had by these meanes inflicted that fitte, then did it lie in her power, when she should see it, to be her best advantage, not to have inflicted it. But she could not avoyde it possibly; iii or iiii [sic] experimentes in iii moneths space being made: in anie one of which, it had ben greatly for the Witches advantage, if the maid had stood up well. Therefore not by anie efficacie that flowed out of her selfe absolutely, could she cause this crewell spectacle. 5. There be manie witnesses of one of those experiments, which my selfe, being at that time present, did observe; when that witch was secretly brought into [Fol. 157v] the roome where the maide laie, afflicted with her other kinde of fitt. She was not brought to the maide; but caryed to a Corner of the Chamber, and manie persons standing then betwene them, she could not possiblie fix her ey upon the maide, to smite her by that meanes; and yet was she by and by, as surely smitten as at other times. Here their witts are quite dried up, and all their magicall constellations, will not make one shower to moisten them. Let *Pomponatius* and *Paracelsus*, or whosoever in favour of them or of their doctrine, in this poynt, have leant their helping hand sometimes in disputations, consider Whether an adventitious power be not here enforced by a necessarie consequent: Seeing those things that are here disputed, can neither be referred to the knowne qualities,[330] nor secret properties of nature; for then it behoveth that more potent causes be searched out, by which such effects can be atchieved. Those powers [Fol. 158r] which surmount the powers of nature, must either be God, or Angells good or bad. Now then we are to trie, of what spirit she could be that did these things. She could not be assisted in this busines neither by God, nor good Angell;[331] for that, it was the seeking of her private revenge, and the accomplishing of her curse; it was the hurt of her neighbour; and she a woman of no faith Which I proove by iii infallible reasons. 1. she could not pray, but as other Witches doe; that is leaving out that petition, *deliver us from evill*. Which thing was discovered to be a symbole of the Covenaunt between the Devell and her, by that rebounding of the senselesse maides bodie, at the use of those words in prayer, Pronounced at such times, by anie there present. 2. As she could not praie that petition, which made against her God, soe could she not make profession of that faith which should vouch her, to stand for the true God: which among sundry other, I principally [Fol. 158v] argue by these two poynts: when she should have saide, *and in Jesus Christ, his onely Sonne our Lord*; of her selfe, she would ever leave out, *our Lord*. And when she came to saie *The holie Catholick Church, the forgivenes of sinnes*: she would saie thus *The holie catholick church, the comission of sinnes*. Wherein we maie trace the verie foot steppes of *Sathan*. For betwene these wordes, *forgevenes* and *comission*, there is no similitude of sound whereby she might easely mistake the one for the other; and the Word Comission, was the aptest word, that could be put, in that place to blaspheme the Christian faith withall. This can with no colour of reason grow out of ignorant simplicitie, but must rather be referred to the institution and schooling, of the Divell her confederate. 3. As she could not praie to, nor confess the trew God, so by her Works, she proved the Divell to be her God. For she had before times, sought his help, by Witches and Soothsayers; as was proved at her enditement. [Fol. 159r] It is manifest therefore, that not God, nor good Angells, were that supernaturall hand that assisted her, in the smiting downe of that poore maid, by her presence,[332] but *Sathan* the enemie of Mankinde and high blasphemer of God, in all his workes. Loe what at length, their *antipathie* is found to be: even a combination with the divell; wherein she had vowed him her faith, renouncing Christ her Lord, and he againe promised to serve her in such turnes, when she would call for him. That the Divell will not doe this for everie wicked person, but for such only, as are becomme his Covenaunt servants, all men of sound understanding will easily acknowledge. What could then the reverend Judges, and honest jurers otherwise doe then finde her guiltie of, and geve their sentence for Witchcraft; When as they had seene, with their owne eyes,[333] so lamentable a spectacle of *Sathans* worke, whereof that divellishly addicted old woman [Fol. 159v] had sufficiently proved her selfe a mediatrice? The same kind of antipathie likewise, and none other is to be yeelded unto those *Triballians*, and others, which *Plinie* affirmeth could bewitch by their lookes. This needeth never to be yeelded unto them, as if God had geven them above other nations, that peculiar guift of wonderfull working, as *Fernelius* and *Wierus*[334] seeme to let it goe; but God having revealed him selfe unto them; by his workes of the Creation; sufficent to make all flesh unexcusable,[335] and being not sought unto by them, nor worshipped accordingly, gave them up, as he doth all such others, unto a reprobate minde, even the God of this world to blinde their eyes

that as they receaved not the love of the truth, that they might be
saved, he might geve them, by an efficacious working, strong delusions, to beleeve lyes; that all might be damned which beleeve not the
truth, but have pleasure in unrighteousnes. Neither let anie [Fol. 160r]
think it straunge, that young and old of some whole nations, and
that in manie descents, should thus be cast out of Godds protection,
and marked in a Covenaunt, for the bondslaves of *Sathan*; this
present age of ours, is not destitute of examples to confirme it.
The *Brasilians* of whom *Lereus* writeth among his travells,[336] have
not only their bodies, both men, women and Children, possessed
with Divells, in the daies of their solempne Ceremonies, but, at all
other times also, are under such an yron bondage, of intollerable
servitude to them, that (as if God had cast of all care of them) they
are almost continually permitted to his corporall whippings and
beatings, without anie power or hope to get out of his handes. But
we need not sayle into *America* for such merchandize. The *Nevrians*
[sic],[337] part of the *Livonians* which in times past were called [Fol.
160v] *Nervians*, so much abound with this filthie frie at this daie,
that yearely, in the daies, next following that, which the Church
observeth for the nativitie of Christ, (we call them the twelve daies)
there is a generall calling of them togeather, by a warning crie, of a
lame footed boye. After the boy, followeth, not longe, a certayne
tall man, with a whip of yron lashes in his hand; which he so
premptorily bestoweth upon them, that foresloe to appeare at that
first summons, as that for a long time after, with grevous paines the
smarting sting and scorches thereof remaine upon their beastlie
hides. Assoone as they are in readines to follow him, they seeme
transfourmed all, in to the shape of woolfes. They are some
thousands of them, that thus assemble togeather. The Whipping
Captaine goeth before, and all that goodly rout followeth, supposing themselves are become Wolfes. As they march forward in their
waie, they fall upon and worry, all Cattell that they meete, and
spoyle as much els as [Fol. 161r] they can, Only men they can not
medle with. When they come at a River, their Captaine parteth the
waters with the stroake of his whippe, so as they seeme to divide a
sunder, and leave a drie patch, for his heard to follow him. And after
the twelve dayes thus well spent, havinge kept the Divells Christ-
mas, their Woulvish semblance departing, the Wretched slaves
returne to their homes, and to their (a litle) better witts againe. The

Pilapians also, a people inhabiting the frozen sea, have hitherto above the memorie of man, and record of stories, worshipped wood and stones for their Godds. When they go on hunting, or fishing, or begin anie other worke, they first meaning to consult with their Godds, endevour by certaine adjurations, to move them from the places where they stand. If their Godds move easelie towards them, it is taken that they favour their enterprise, and promise successe, if they go back from them, they denie successe, but if they will not move at all, they are [Fol. 161v] offended. Then must they please them with some sacrifice, which straight waie they doe, by the meanes of a brasen drum and frog, which they use in that conjuration, the Divell shewing unto them, what kinde of beast, foule, or fish they must sacrifice unto him. The head of that beast, they hang upon a tree, which they count holie, the Remnaunt they boyle and spend amongst their freinds. And all of them wash themselves in the broath, wherein the sacrifice was boyled. Thus they thinke to have all thinges prosper and goe well with them. Moreover if anie straunger with them, desire to know the state of his houshould, or freinds, they will make him certefied thereof, within .24. howers space, though the place be .3. hundred miles of distaunce. And that in this manner. The enchaunter that undertaketh it, after that with his usuall ceremonies, he hath called upon his conjured Godds, suddainely falleth downe as dead, and so remaineth with out all sense, moving or shew of life. This caution [Fol. 162r] goeth with all, that some doe continually attend to his bodie, feare least the Divells do carrie it awaie. After 24 howers expired, the spirit being returned, the breathlesse bodie wakeneth with a groane, as out of a deepe sleepe, as though it returned from death to life againe. And thus being restored answereth unto all the parties demaunds, and to geve him the better assuraunce, reckoneth up something in speciall, whereby the partie may assuredly acknowledge that he hath bene in his house, or in the houses of his freinds, after whom he enquireth. Verie great is the number and power of spirits that appeare, walke amonge them, banket and talke with them, so as they can not be rid of them. Sometimes they are much terrified and troubled, as with the ghostes of their kinsfolks dead, which to be quit of, they burie their bodies under their hearth. Which is their only remedie; and that being neglected, they are miserably infested and disquieted, with their shadowes in all places meeting them. At this day are there

131

fewer incantations, then have ben in times past; the king of *Sueden*, having [Fol. 162v] severely prohibited the use of such things amongst them, and cared, as much as is possible, to instruct them in our religion. The ministers of Finland and other Countries adjoyning, goe to them in the winter season, when it is yce, (for at other times they can not) and such as they can meet with, they instruct and teach to praie; baptising likewise such as they can fasten anie competent instruction upon: the aged sort, of which, do comonly dy within vii. or viii. daies after baptisme. These things writeth *Pencerus*, a man verie godly, learned and grave of yeares, being of himselfe, slow to beleeve such things; and therefore professeth that *he hath found these thinges to be true, (although of long time, he had not beleved them) by most sure and explorate indications of witnesses worthie credite.* And that the Children of such Parents,[338] are oftentimes wofully geven over, to this corporall servitude of *Sathan*, if plentifully proved, by him, that is well able to speake to these matters; havinge in xv yeers space, ben at the conviction of nyne hundereth [Fol. 163r] witches in the Countrey of *Loraigne*. Agreably hereunto saith *Peucer*,[339] in another place, *That these witches doe not onely vow themselves to Sathan, but even their children also, in their wombes, or new borne, do they dedicate unto him; yea give in mariage their daughters to the Divell, like as in old time they burnt their children to the Idoll Moloch.* Thus farre hath the misticall exception of *Antipathie* geven me occasion to enlarge my selfe (as I hope) for the better strengthening of the truth against her enemies. The next objection is *D Jordens* owne. *That, for that voyce in the maydens nostrills, it is nothing to be accompted of; himselfe could fashion the like.* Cato (they saie)[340] would not admire anie mortall man: No more doth *D Jorden* any symptome. But when he shall have made therof proofe; before some of those that heard it, in *M Glover*, and shall obteyne their lawfull testimonie, [Fol. 163v] then shall he gaine thus much at my hand by it, that I will yeeld, he can counterfett a very straunge thing.[341] *D Jorden* (belike) is in his younge bloud still, nothing is straunge, nothing is difficult in his eies in all this case; which so manie els, that have seene some things also in their dayes, had in no small admiration. I must entreat pardon for [not] beleeving him, for these 2. reasons. 1. because himselfe was not sufficiently enformed in this matter. 2. because he avoucheth therein an impossible thing. It had ben good

D Jorden, had called to minde before he wrote, how one *Crescens* (who would have ben accompted a great Philosopher in his time) was condempned, by *Justine* the *Martyr*, for no philosopher,[342] but for speaking of the Christians, things that he knew not. I will sett no such censure upon *D Jorden*, but by his patience, I will enfourme the reader, of more then *D Jorden* seemeth [Fol. 164r] to know. If the maid had uttered this voyce willingly, as in passion, (for so he would have us think) then would she have set forth the voyce suddainely, with moving or spreading of the Nostrills, and some contention of the brest. But contrariewise, her brest and breath went peaceably, the nostrills never moved at it, the noyse, to those that diligently applied their eare verie neere to her face, beganne a far of, with a sauft whispering, as if it had ascended out of her bellie: and in deed at the first offer of it, there would beginne a litle motion in her bellie, as the beginning of one of her pangs: which motion went stealinglie up into her throt and so,[343] from saufte whisperings, it proceeded, it proceeded by stronger and lowder degrees, till it grew to a voyce, audible to manie. I cannot think that *D Jorden*, if he [Fol. 164v] had diligently observed all these circumstances, would either have made so light of the matter, or yet have affirmed that he can do the like himselfe. 2. But especially if with these he had likewise weighed, all other concurrents of her case: namely, that the maide was in all that time, voyde of all manner sense and voluntarie moving, as hath ben proved. And that the Witch was sometimes, brought into the chamber secretly, of purpose to finde out, if there were anie fallacie. Whereof the case was so cleered, as that (beyond all I have heretofore saide) at the Sessions house, whilest the Witch, for dinner time, was caried to Newgate, the voyce in the maides nostrills ceased; but in the afternoone, that same kinde of voyce was returned againe, before anie in the Chamber with her, knew that the Witch was returned into the Sessions hall: so as the Coming of the voyce againe, was the first motive to make them enquire whether that woman was [Fol. 165r] come into the judgement place:[344] and so they found it. Let the reader now be judge, whether *D. Jorden* hath in this point taken upon him an impossible thing. It seemeth that he oftentimes practised to fourme such a voyce, when he was by himselfe; and when, in his owne judgement, he had attayned somwhat neere it, he had by and by, asmuch as he looked for: nether considering how it would sound, to those that had heard *M. Glover.* and much lesse how he might prove, that the maid had anie apprension actually, and in use, or abilitie of will, to dispose of anie action: and least of all what might be the reason, that the voyce could both come and cease at the presence and departure of that woman only; and could not be shifted nor altered by anie device. He soonest geveth his verdict, that deviseth but upon a few things. The same defecte wilbe found in him, in his next observation to my .14. Character. For thus he saith to it: *At the pronouncing of that* [Fol. 165v] *petition, Deliver us from evill; the maid was put in mind of that woman, by whom (as she thought) she had receaved hurt; which remembraunce, moved her passion, her passion then, caused that suddaine tossing of her bodie, either as in waie of detestation and shunning her; or as to challenge and accuse her.* Some Reader maie think, that by thus reasoning, he chargeth the maid with a voluntarie acting of this, to make the case seeme more straunge and wonderfull; which tendeth to imposture. He, being in deed thus pressed by some sought to salve it thus: *those wordes of the petition give her (as in the twinckling of an eye) a fearfull apprehension of that woman, that apprehension moveth the bodie, before anie discourse of reason can enter to staye it.* So that he will make it but as a start, which hapneth to a man upon incogitancie; when some warme thing, that would not burne him toucheth his skinne, at unawares. But [Fol. 166r] here his ignoraunce of the case, which he judgeth, cometh againe to be taxed. For he knew not, having not attended so diligently, that the tossing of her bodie was proved iiii [sic] times at one prayer, *Deliver us from evell*, being so manie times repeated, and her bodie rebounding at the same. If the first motion had taken her suddainly, the second did not: and if the second had, yet the third and fourth could not do so. The case is like in the former similitude. For if a peece of brasse or yron, being some what hoter then his flesh be layed upon a mans hand at unawares, it maie cause him to start at the first, but if it be done so iii or iiii [sic] times, he will contempne it, as being secure, that no further hurt can grow thereof. 2. I saie, that if the remembrance of that woman could be such a startling to the maide, whie was it not the same, in all other parts of her fitts, when as there was evidence, that she understood what we saide, the same praier being used? Because I know, he will shifte as farre as he can, I suppose he will answere: *She did not the same at those other* [Fol. 166v] *tymes, because then, the discourse of her understanding stood more free; but now it was verie feeble and slender.* But I replie againe, if her discourse were at this time, feeble and slender, whie did she startle at those wordes *Deliver us from evill?* For to pick out *Elizabeth Jackson* out [sic] of those wordes, in the twinckling of an eye, hath need of a verie quick discoursing braine. Here behoved the logicall part of reason, to be free on foote, to descend the scale of *genus* and *species* so swiftly and to ascend againe from the affecte to the Causes, and among them to finde out the instrumentall, with such dexteritie. Call you this a feeble and slender discourse? Nay, surely, this matter was brought nearer unto her hand before, in those words of our Lords praier, *forgive us our trespasses, as we forgeve them that trespasse against us,* for here the consequent fell very direct from that generall, *forgive them that trespasse against us* to this particular namely, *Elizabeth Jackson.* Also it was manie times nearer in the ministers praiers, wherein evermore God was besought to defeat the worke of *Sathan.* For, from the Divell to his instrument, was a [Fol. 167r] far shorter discourse. Yea beyond all this, it is more probable she would have moved rather at the plaine naming of *Elizabeth Jackson,* in tyme of this her weaknes, then at those wordes, which offred so far fetched occasion to think upon her: and yet that, oftentimes having ben done by those that stood about her, at such verie times, did never provoke anie motion of her bodie. Furthermore these reasons pretend that this motion was but a meere start, suddaynly stayed againe; but it was somtimes a straunge rebounding with wallowing; and that namely at the session house, where *Eliz. Jackson*, being brought into the Chamber where the maid laie, and comaunded to saie the Lo[rd's] praier, at the pronouncing of these wordes *deliver us from evill*; (with which much adoe she was constrayned at length to speake) the poore senselesse maide, lying at that time, in verie ougly distortion of her armes, and extreme rigiditie or stifnes of all her bodie, was bowed upward in the midle, as a halfe Circle, and then throwne over unto the woman, so far, as if *Judge Anderson* himselfe had not staid her, she had fallen over the bed, on [Fol. 167v] the same side, where that woman stood. This amounted to more then an inconsiderat starting. On the other side if it were voluntarie, as in detestation, then would she not have moved, towards the Witch, but from her ward: if to chalenge or accuse the

Witch, whie not much rather, before she fell into her fitt, at such times as that woman was brought in unto her. If he saie she did it thus, rather, to make the matter more wonderfull, he accuseth her againe of imposture. Which if he will (at length) rely upon, to succour him selfe (for he hath done as much as that, alreadie in this cause) then he falleth into the ruynes, which I have brought upon his cause, in my fifte Chapter: And there let him ly for me, untill he have repented of his pertinacie. Lastly against her extraordinary deliverance, he affirmeth, that she receaved no succour, in that day, beyond that which was naturall: And that was twofould; *abstinence*, and *a confident persuasion*: both which, are oftentimes observed, effectuall for such cures. First touching abstenence, let him not be angrie with me, that I [Fol. 168r] compare him to that notable witchwarder *Reinold Scott*,[345] (sith him selfe blusheth not to use his authoritie sometime) who stretching his treble to sing a note above *Pharaos* inchaunters, would have his reader imagine, that if they had knowne asmuch as he, to wit, that mans greace will in short time ingender lice, they might peradventure, have gone further in one point, with *Moses* then they did. He never considering that this must have required some daies (besides manie other difficulties unanswerable) both for the anoynting of all the *Ægiptians* bodies, throughout the land, as also to have ben alowed for the production of that vermin afterward; and so could not be matcheable with *Aarons* stroak of the rod, which turned the dust into lice, at once in everie house and quarter. For in like sort doth *D Jorden* reason here, with asmuch advyzednes, and as litle defensible, when he saith that fasting helped *M Glover*. For albeit fasting be convenyent, in such a Disease as he supposed hers to be, yet I am assured his meaning is not, that fasting from one meale can do the feate. Againe he is overtaken with ignorance of the case; for if fasting could have turned her, there was a time wherein, for the space of [Fol. 168v] 18. daies togeather, she lived in much more exquisite abstinence, then *Cælius Aurelianus*,[346] or any of the *Methodicians diatrites* would have exacted at her handes. But this is too grosse to spend time upon. The other hath some kinde of subtilitie in it: *that a good conceipt cured her*: like where unto, another man of great edge said, *Imagination hurt her, and imagination helped her*. To both I answere, if there were not in other occasions, and times, greater weight of wisdome, and solid judgment to be expected, and hoped at both their hands, certainly, neither the one were fitt for the bodie, nether the other for the soule, to take anie charge or cure thereof. It is true in deed that Patients are much comforted at the presence of their phisition, of whom they are well perswaded, both touching his knowledge and good will towards them, because by such a one, they hould themselves assured, (having first made up their reckoning with the Almightie) that they shall receave asmuch succor as the ordinarie meanes can afford them. If such a one therefore geve them a comfortable report of their disease, they conceave straight waie a good [Fol. 169r] imagination. This good imagination taking place, more and more, in their minde, thrusteth out feare, which before was seated, either as the originall of their sicknes, as it is in some; or else as companion adding strength thereunto, as it is seene almost in everie one. For even in those, in whom their sicknes hath not the whole dependance upon feare, yet partly through love to live still (which alwaies hath a jealous eie at everie paire of sheeres that are caried by their threed) and partly through ignoraunce of their remedie (which causeth them comonly to suspect their daunger to be greater then it is) although feare was not in the beginning to make them sick, yet it joyneth soone after the entraunce, and geves the sicknes greater settling. For which cause it is, that Phisitions first put their patients in good comfort generally, that so they may have fewer causes to fight against. But especially if they see feare have taken full possession, then they make their tongues as the combes of honie to drop and infuse into their patients minde the sweet imaginations of recoverable health. Which good conceipt once fastened, doth then proffit, more or lesse, according to the greater or lesser dependancie on that passion, not by [Fol. 169v] an imediate encountring the mayne disease, but only by putting out that passion, that either bred or nourish it. Hereupon the cure succeedeth, without anie other then refectorie phisick, and that (ofte times) with great expidition, if feare were the solitarie cause and new; if it were but accessorie or old, the releefe yet further dependeth upon the rest of the phisitions skill well performed. For other morbificall causes, will not be, by a good imagination, removed. And to accomodat at these things unto the present instaunce, of *M Glovers* cause, I will admit she was touched with such dread as is comon to all sicke folkes, and suppose withall (for the present) but not graunt it, that this dread was removed by a good opinion taken in, at the beginning of their prayers; but what (I pray you) removed the residew of diseasefull causes, to wit, generative seed or menstruall bloud, enforced upon us by *M. Doctor* in this case? Did a good conceipt worke this feat also? Verely I hould him a more reasonable man then so to saie. [Fol. 170r] For that can but displace feare as I have said whereof [? smudged] ensueth a quiet dispensation of the faculties, which before time were disturbed, and therefore weakened; the fruit whereof is, a good disposition of the bodie, to admit all phisicall cure. If any man urge, That so, the conjunct causes might be quit also, I answere, dayly experience is against it, in other like patients, as he supposeth this was. And besids that, here followed no evacuation of anie such materiall causes in her curation, as I have proved, in my .6. Chapter, of necessitie, must then have ben. So that even by this he gaineth nothing, though I should geve him, that she had a vehement apprehension of help by that daies meeting. Whereas yet it playnely seemeth otherwise, by the report of that day of her deliveraunce, when as a pauze being made, after .2. Preachers had prayed, and interpreted the scriptures, she fell into weeping, and wringing of her hands, *complayning of unaccustomed paine, yea casting out wordes of feare, that God would not heare them, calling on him for her so wretched* [Fol. 170v] *a creature.* By this passage maie be seene well ynough that the maid was unfurnished at that time, of that good imagination of her helpe, which we speake of in this place, and then much more, of *that confident perswasion D. Jorden* speaketh of,[347] which is of the substaunce of faith. Which if he resume here, to urge me withall, putting it in place *of good imagination or apprehension,* which tearmes to his purpose, he rather should have used; I know that faith, when it is pitched on a true object, and other waies well conditioned, overcometh all things.[348] And hereby *M. Gl.* (at the length) triumphed in victorie; but then he falleth upon his owne sword. For faith is a supernaturall thing. If he yeeld she came to her former health by that meanes, then he falleth into the lapse of my former conclusions in the .7. Chapter, If here he strive, to finde a difference, betwene faith and confident perswasion, I know none but this, that faith hath but one roote, or foundation, whereon it standeth fixed, as a columne that cannot be removed. But confident perswasion is a thing that walketh on 2. leggs, a right and a lefte, and therefore maie be pitched wrong, as well as right. When it setteth forward the right leg, fixing it upon the word and promise of God, then [Fol. 171r] it is faith; but whensoever it proceedeth with the lefte leg, fastened at randome upon other objects, it is presumption. What object here he assigneth to *M. Glovers* I wish to know his minde. If subordinat meanes, then she sinned *Asaes* sinne,[349] whose Confidence was in his Phisitions. And such would her reward have ben. I hope he hath no thought, that she trusted to inordinat meanes, as they that put confidence in Charmes and enchauntments, for that had ben *Saules* high rebellion and blasphemie against the Eternall.[350] Whether [sic] then will he turne himselfe? If he wil have his tearmes of *confident persuasion*, extend no further then a good imagination, then he speaketh unproperly, and is answered, before. Finally, and for altogeather, if good conceipt could cure her, then would the entrance thereof, have brought in, with it, present ease and mitigation, but not a violent encrease and exacerbation of the symptomes. Witnes his owne examples of the Countess of *Mantua* and some others. *The Countesse* (saith *Marcellus* his Author)[351] *being afflicted with hypochondriack melancholie, but imagining her selfe bewitched, was through the prudent counsell of her phisition,* [Fol. 171v] *cured by casting into the egestions of her purging (unknowne to the Lady) nayles, feathers, and needles, and causing her woman afterward, to shew it all unto her, with a glad counteinaunce. Her Ladie in joy cryed out, I perceave I was not deceaved, when I thought I was betwitched: and after that, daily, she became better and better.* Such are all the cases that *Trallian* bringeth,[352] being moe then the *D.* rehearseth. Yea such are all that *Marcellus* was able to gather, both out of experiments and aucthorities: he being a great learned man; and writing a Volume of merveylous histories in phisick; wherein he sheweth (amongst the rest) verie great reading and observation. If then *M. Glover* was cured by a contrarie passion; the first as cause, being feare, and the second as remedie, being a cherefull apprehension, whie had she new paynes, and sooner approaching? Whie was that fitt more tumultuous and violent then anie? How happened thereupon, those ougly, outfacing and menacing countenances; with falling dead and suddaine integritie out of that? And for this suddain, *Trallian* yeeldeth,[353] that where passion, as primitive cause, bringeth the sicknes, and the sicknes it selfe be of no long continewance, there the cure maie be so suddaine, as in those examples he setteth downe: But if it continue long, and the imagination go into a habit, such artificiall devises will effect but a litle; at the least (I would ad) not effect such suddaine integritie. But all men know that *M Glo.* affliction continued the space of seaven moneths and a halfe. All which things considered, these objections are gone,[354] turne them which way soever, and all their imaginations vanish into vapour.

Finis.

Lect. 21°. Maii
1646. W.C.

Notes to Bradwell, 'Marie Glovers'

1. The meanes of her first being taken.
2. The maner of her first fittes for the space of 18 dayes.
3. Doctor Sherman used for her cure.
4. How her lefte arme became more specially affected.
5. Doctor Mounford used for her cure.
6. The second increase of her fitt.
7. The third increase of her fitt.
8. A reliefe by Charmes.
9. The fourth encrease of her fitt.
10. The fifte encrease of her fitt.
11. Her ordinary fitte in the last degree of his growth.
12. The maner of her cominge out of her fitts.
13. All her senses all this while deprived.
14. Her short praier which never could be altered.
15. The post brashial bone where the little finger is set.
16. Her larger prayer at the end of her fitte.
17. These were her wordes.
18. The cause of her sore brest.
19. Her bedfittes and meatfittes.

20. Instaunces of her extraordinarie fitte.
21. [Clover-like symbol].
22. Experience at Sheriff Glovers.
23. 2. Experience before Sr John Harte.
24. 3. Experience before the Lady Bronkard.
25. 4. Experience before Sir John Crooke.
26. 5. Experience in the tryall at the sessions.
27. The Indictment.
28. The 1: point of evidence.
29. The 2.
30. The 3.
31. The 4.
32. The 5.
33. The 6.
34. Mr Lewes.
35. The 7.
36. The 8.
37. The 9.
38. The 10.
39. namely in July 1603. the time that last S. Br. spake with her.
40. The 11.
41. The 12.
42. Mr Sharpe.
43. Doctor Herings Evidence.
44. Dr Spencers Evid.
45. Dr Argent Dr Jordayne Dr Medowes.
46. [Clover-like symbol].
47. The Lorde Andersons Speech.
48. The Recordo Speech.
49. The case of M. Glover after the day of the Arraignment.
50. The occasion of the prayer and fasting which were used for her.
51. Folios 42v–45v are headed with the running title, written over the verso and facing recto, 'D. Jorden wrote against, M Glovers cause'.
52. D.J. said he would not touch M. Gl. case.
53. D.J. booke was framed against M. Gl. case.
54. D.J. speaches writings and protestations in this point ever contradictorie.
55. In his .12. page.
56. D.J. displeased that his judgment was not receaved of the Magistrate.
57. None so busy to perswade others as D.J. was in M. Gl. case.
58. D.J. liked to work underhand.
59. [Clover-like symbol].
60. Just: Mart: in his apol: for Christians.

61. [Clover-like symbol.] A wise man ever walketh in his calling.
62. D.J. motives to write his booke.
63. D.J. was put to write.
64. DJ gave judgment before he was thoroughly acquainted with the case.
65. We probably conceive it thus, out of the effectes.
66. D.J. strangely hardened against this truthe.
67. His writing tendeth to disgrace his opposits.
68. Selfe love doth blinde the eyes.
69. fol. 2.
70. Hipp: had no thinking of the Mother in that place.
71. fol. 4.
72. [Clover-like symbol] he meaneth which D.J. might yeeld them.
73. fol. 4 p. 1.
74. first page of his Epistle.
75. Whether D.J. were free from fawning.
76. An insolence in D.J. writing.
77. If he sought not to please another he could not so contradict himselfe.
78. Perhaps D.J. when he wrote his book beleived M Gl did also counterfeite.
79. D.J. against possession and disposs. of Div.
80. D.J. not diligent to enforme him selfe in the case.
81. D.J. ill advised when he wrote.
82. D.J. delt not sincerely.
83. D. Herringes arguments.
84. D Spencers argumentes.
85. .4. page.
86. psal. 139 .21. 22.
87. psal. 40.5.
88. Folios 64v–69r are headed with the running title, written over the verso and facing folio, 'The generall shape of D.J. writing'.
89. Epist. dedic. p. 1.
90. K.J. in his Dæmonologie.
91. D.J. handling of his matter too like S.H.
92. D.J. kept not within his promised compasse.
93. D.J. maketh his readers disputers.
94. Folios 69v–75r are headed with the running title, written over the verso and facing recto, 'The lively image of D.J. Booke'.
95. The summe of his booke.
96. Mat. 9.33.
97. Mat. 12.22.
98. Mark 19.17.
99. Luc. 13.11.

100. Naturall symptomes may have a supernaturall cause efficient.
101. Fern. de abd. rerum caus. lib. 2. cap. 16.
102. Lang Epist. med. li. 1. Epist. 38.
103. Cardan li. 19 de subtil within the first leafe.
104. Cardan, de varietate li. 16. cap. 93.
105. Joh. wierus de præst. dæmonu. lib. 5. cap. 14.
106. The Divell can maske under the shew of a naturall sicknes.
107. [Clover-shaped symbol].
108. Folios 75v–80r are headed with the running title, written across the verso and the facing recto, 'That feare had no force in M. Gl. affliction', which is occasionally miswritten.
109. All the symptomes of the mother will not serve to make good his promise.
110. Passions of the minde what and how they worke.
111. Fern: de morb. caus. li. 1. cap. 18.
112. Everie passion worketh not everie fashion.
113. chapt. 6. 7. he alleaged it likewise unto me in our private conference.
114. Fol. 15. pag. 2.
115. Fol. 16. pag. 1.
116. D.J. out of method.
117. That feare wrought not this evill in Marie Glover.
118. See the narration pag. [blank].
119. Erastus disput. part .1. pag. 95. 96. 97.
120. not when she fell sick.
121. Fernel. de morb. caus. li. 1 cap. 18[;] Cardan. de subt. li 14. tit. de anima et intell.[;] Gal. de symp. caus. li: 2.
122. As in the narration pag [blank].
123. see the Narration pag. [blank].
124. see the narration pag [blank].
125. D.J. shifting answere taken awaie.
126. Folios 84r–97r are headed with the running title, written across the verso and facing recto, 'No colour of counterfeiting in M Glovers case'.
127. That M. Glo: counterfeited nothing.
128. For Pinder, see *The Disclosing of a Late Conterfeyted Possession by the Devyl in Two Maydens within the Citie of London* (1574); Matthew Parker (1853) *Correspondence of Matthew Parker*, ed. J. Bruce and T.T. Perowne, Parker Society, Cambridge, pp. 465–6; Thomas, *Religion and Magic*, 483; Barbara Rosen (1969) *Witchcraft*, London, pp. 231–9; Reginald Scot (1964) *The Discoverie of Witchcraft*, ed. Hugh Ross Williamson, Carbondale, Ill., pp. 124–5 (VII, iii).

129. Epist. dedicat. pag. 3.
130. D.J. inconstancy through weaknes.
131. pag [blank].
132. How D.J. argueth M Gl a Counterfeit.
133. That M Glover could not heare in this fitt.
134. There was no possibilitie of voluntarie moving.
135. The reason searched out whie her bodie now moved at the touching of others besides the witch.
136. Dæmonologie [;] Erastus de lamiis [;] Bodinus dæmonomania [;] Remigius dæmonolatria.
137. For accounts of this episode, which lasted from 1589 until 1593, see *The Most Strange and Admirable Discoverie of the Three Witches of Warboys* (1593) London; Rosen, *Witchcraft*, 239–97; Walker, *Unclean Spirits*, 49–52.
138. Marke how the witch was chalenged still.
139. The imputation of counterfeiting a notorious slaunder.
140. Narrat pag. [blank].
141. Prov. 17. 15.
142. Levit. 19. 16.
143. Heredotus li. 7.
144. Menander.
145. Rheginus de amicitia.
146. The Aucthor his testimonie in this case subject to no just ecception.
147. Folios 97v–126v are headed with the running title, written across the verso and facing recto, 'M. Gl. disease was not suffocation from the mother'.
148. D.J. encombreth and perverteth but cleareth nothing.
149. These namely in Math. 9. 33 and 12. 22. Mark 19. 17. Luk. 13. 11.
150. in 9 Rhas. Cap. 69.
151. D Moundford.
152. D.J. unsufficient handling of this matter.
153. Fern. de part. morb and sympt. cap. 16.
154. Merc. de morb. mul. li. 2. cap. 2.
155. Juan. Huart exam. de ingenios. cap. 12.
156. No book case like M. Glo.
157. Gal. introd. in puls. and de causis puls. li. 4.
158. Josephus Struthius sphyg. art. li. 4. cap. 32[;] Gorrhæus def. medic.
159. Gorhæus def. Medicinal.
160. *you must ever understand that in this case she laye along uppon her backe.
161. K. Dæmonologie li. 3. cap. 4.

162. Declar. of pop. impost. pag. 137.
163. Fern. li. 5. cap. 3.[;] Gal. introduct. in puls. et de caus. puls. li. 4.[;] Joseph Struthius li. 4. cap. 29.
164. 1 Cronic. 16. 12. [i.e., 2 Chron. 16: 12; cf. Jer. 17: 5].
165. Narrat. pag [blank].
166. Jason Prat. de cerebri morb page. 53.
167. Gal. meth. med. li. 1.
168. Joh. Gorrhæus def. medic.
169. Fern. li. 5 cap. 3.
170. Gal. li. de trem. palp. et convuls. and againe de loc. affect. li. 3. cap. 3.[;] Fern. loc. citato.
171. Gorrhæus def. med.
172. Gal. introduct. in pulsus. also de caus. puls. li. 4.
173. Joseph. Struthius li. 4. de art. sphyg. cap. 28.
174. Gal. li. 2. de caus. puls.
175. Galenus Introduct. in pulse Also li. 4 de caus. puls.
176. Gal. loc. aff. li. 3. cap. 3.
177. Gal. loc. affect. li. 3. cap. 5.
178. Mercatus de mul. aff. li. 2. cap. 3.
179. Gal. prorrhet. 3. com. 27.
180. Fernel. Path li. 6. cap. 16.
181. Gal. loc. affect. li. 4. cap. 5.
182. Paul Pereda schol. in Pascall cap. 58.
183. 2. Tim. 1.
184. Luk. 9. 23.[;] 1. cor. 3. 18.[;] Ja. 3. 13. 14. 15. 16. 17.
185. Psel. de oper. dæm. cap. 14.
186. Vales. de sacr. phil. cap. 28[;] Item Math. Durastantes probl. 1. li. 5.
187. Corn. Gema cosmocr. li. 1. cap. 7 [i.e., *De natura divinis*].
188. Anto. Ben. de abd. 8. Hist de spectr. pag. 112. 113.[;] Wierus and Solen cons. med. pag. 312.
189. Gen. cap. 3.
190. Jam. 1. 5.
191. Ant. Ben. loc. citato.[;] Wierus li. 4. ca. 11. id. cap. 6. li. 5. cap. 31.[;] K. Dæmon. cap. 4.
192. Phillip. 4. 13.
193. Jam. 3. 17.
194. Hipp. de nat. mul. sect. 1. 1 and de morb. mul. li. 2. sect. 4.
195. Hipp. de nat. hum.[;] Gal. aphor. 2. li. 3.
196. Gal. de temper. li. 2. item de art medic. Gal. de temp. li. 3. and de loc. affe. li. 6. cap. 5. Gal. de sanit. tuenda. li. 5.
197. Cap. 6.
198. Gal. meth. med. li. 7.

199. Gal. lib. de opt. corp. constitutione opt. corp. habitu.
200. Hipp. li. de carnil...[;] Arist. hist. anim. li. 5. cap. 4.[;] Clem. Alexandstrom. li. 6. ex Hermippo Berytio et Solone.
201. Hipp. de virg. morb and morb. mul. li. 1.[;] Gal. de ven sact. ad Erasise li. 4. de loc aff. li. 6. ca. 5. et com. in Aphor. li. 5. 57.
202. How diseases take ther breeding in the bodies.
203. Generative seed no cause.
204. Mauric. Cordatus in Hipp. de virgina libris 3.
205. *adventante pubertate I translate by this metaphor.
206. Gal. loc. aff. li. 6 cap. 8[;] Merc. aff. mul. li. 2. pag. 205.
207. In his .1. and .4. chapters.
208. Merc. de mul. aff li. 2. ca. 3. pag. 188.
209. Solen. consil. medic. sect. 3. cons. 2.
210. Jacchinus in 9. Ras. cap. 69.
211. Menstruous bloud no cause.
212. Gal. loc. aff. li. 6. cap. 5.[;] Fern. path. li. 6. cap. 16[;] Solen loc. citato[;] Mercatus loc. cit.[;] Ghorrhæus def. et alii.
213. Hipp. de morb. virg. et de mul. morb. li. 1. Item de morb. epid. li. 3. sect. 3. 11. 12.[;] Valesius coment. in eundum[;] Mau. Cord. com. de morb. virg. pag. 63[;] Gal. loc. aff. li. 6. cap. 5.
214. Hipp. li. de vict. nat. in morb. ac. nu. 17.[;] Item li. 2. Aphor. 52.
215. Gal. de natur. fac. et de atra bile[;] Item de dieb decretorius li. 1. et 2.
216. Hipp. li. 4. de morb.
217. Hipp. de Septim. partu.
218. Hipp. li. de genitura. Item Gal. de ven. sect. adv.[;] Erasistr. loc. et alibi. Item Hipp. Aphor. 1. lib. 3. 57.
219. Gal. li. de totius morb. temp.
220. Gal. de loc. aff. li. 6. cap. 5.
221. Hipp. de morb virg. Item de morb. mul. li. 1. et de natura mulibre.
222. Merc. de mul. aff. li. 1 ca. 3.
223. Mauric. Cord. de morb. virg. Item Vales. com in Epid li. 3. sect. 3. ægru. 12.
224. Vales. also in li. 3. epid. sect. 3. ægr. 7.[;] Gal. meth. med. li. 2.
225. Vales. in epid[;] Hip. li. 2. sect. 3. sub init[;] Hip epid. li. 3. sect. 3. ægr. 11. 12.[;] Vales. com. in eundem.
226. [Much of this line is crossed out and overwritten, and hence it is barely legible.]
227. Coac. præn.[;] Hip. li. 2. sec. 23.
228. Aphor sec. 3. 23. item li. 5. 7.
229. Gal in li. 3. Aphor. 28. et de morb. vulg. li. t. com. 5. tex. 26.
230. Brassavolus in eund. aph.
231. Holl. in coac. præn. Hipp li. 3 sect. 3. 23.

232. Vales in li. 6. epid. sect. 5. text. 25 a.
233. Hipp. de morb. mul. li. 1.
234. Hippo. de morb. sacra. sect. 15.[;] Nicol. Roch. de morb. mul. cap. 5.[;] Paul Ægin. de re med. li. 3. cap. 71. comp cum propr. observ.
235. Folios 127r–142r are headed with the running title, written across the verso and facing recto, 'M. Gl. was vexed with an uncleane spirit'.
236. See above pag. [blank].
237. Folio 128, an insert, is folded into the text here [editor's note].
238. Hip. li. 4. de morb. sect. 32.
239. Ch. 1.
240. pag. [blank].
241. The 1. Character of supernaturall.
242. Bapt. Codronch de morb. ven. li. 3. cap. 13.[;] Alsaravius cap. 34. de Epilep.
243. Wier de præst dæm. li. 4 cap. x.
244. li. 4. cap. 12.
245. Prosp. Aquit. li. 6. de prædicet et premiss. ref. Wiere li. 5. ca 31.
246. The 2. Character of supernaturall.
247. Nar. pag. [blank].
248. Nar. pa. [blank].
249. A 3. Character of supernaturall.
250. Nar. p. [blank].
251. The 4. Character of supernaturall.
252. Nar. p. [blank].
253. The 5. Character of supernaturall.
254. Gal. de nat. fac li 1. et alibi.
255. Gal. de us. part li. 11.
256. Gal. de sani. tuenda li. 2.
257. Nar. p. [blank][;] The 6. Character of supernaturall.
258. Nar. p. [blank][;] The 7. Character of supernaturall.
259. The 8. Character of supernaturall.
260. Gal. li. de symp. differ.
261. Tremulus convulsivus.
262. palpitans vibrans.
263. Gal. loc. aff. li. 3. et li. de Trem. palp. et conv.
264. The 9. Character of supernaturall.
265. Nar. pag [blank].
266. The 10. Character of supernaturall.
267. Nar. pag. [blank].
268. Bapt. Codronch. morb. ven. li. 3. cap. 13.
269. The 11. Character of supernaturall.
270. cap. 6.

271. The 12. Character of supernaturall.
272. The 13. Character of supernaturall.
273. The 14. Character of supernaturall.
274. Nar pag [blank].
275. Wierus. li. 4. cap. 11.
276. Fincelius de miraculis li. 3.
277. The 15. Character of supernaturall.
278. A seeming contradiction taken awaie.
279. which was about .6. of the Clock in the Evening otherwise the fitt had continued untill midnight.
280. The 16. Character of supernaturall.
281. Antick gestures described in the Nar. pag. [blank].
282. Report pag. [blank][;] The 17. Character of supernaturall.
283. The 18. Character of supernaturall.[;] Arculanus in 9.[;] Rhasis cap. 15.
284. Report. pag. 37. [Cf. Swann, *True and Briefe Report*, p. 37, for the actural wording.]
285. The 19. Character of supernaturall.
286. Rep. pag. 6 and 45.
287. Rep. pag. 41.
288. The 20. Character of supernaturall.
289. [Clover-shaped symbol].
290. The 21. Character of supernaturall.[;] A lightening before death.
291. [Clover-shaped symbol].
292. Mark 9. 20. 26.[;] Isidor. Sentent. li. 3. cap. 5.
293. Rep. pag. 47.
294. Psal. 126. 1. 2.
295. Mark 9. 26.
296. Rep. pag. 56.[;] The 22. Character of supernaturall.
297. [Clover-shaped symbol].
298. 2. cor. 3. 17.
299. Joh. 8. 36.
300. Joh. 14. 16. 26.[;] Joh. 16. 17.
301. [Clover-shaped symbol] *Rob. Glover matyr, see Acts and Mon. pag. 1712.*
302. pag. 3.[;] cap. de melancholia.
303. Phil. sacr. c. 28
304. Folios 142v–171v are headed with the running title, written across the verso and facing recto, 'Satisfactions to there [sic] objections'.
305. 1. Sam. 16. 14. 23.
306. Corn. Gemma Cosmocr cas. mirab. etc.
307. Wier de præst. dæm. li. 5. cap 28. li. 4. cap 25[;] Bapt. Codron. li. 4. cap. 2.[;] Franc. Vales. sacr. phil. cap. 28.[;] Saxonia li. de Plica cap. 45.

308. Gal. de symp causis 7.[;] Dom. Peon. li. 3. sect 1. cap. 8.[;] Vales. sacr. phil. cap. 28.
309. Alexand. ab Alex. gen. di. li. 2. ca 17.[;] Wierus de præst li. 4. cap. 29.
310. Marcat. de morb mul. li. 2. cap. 2. 4. 5.
311. Ephes. 2. 2. cap. 6. 12.[;] Psal. 34. 7.[;] Psal. 91.[;] Math. 18. 10.[;] Heb. 1. 14.[;] 2 Pet. 2. 4.[;] Jude. 6.
312. Job. 1. 2.
313. Gal. de natur. fac. li. 1. cap. 13.
314. Val. in Epid.[;] Hip. li. 3. sect. 3. ægr. 11.
315. As Math. de Gradi cons. 81.[;] Albert Bollonus de morb. mul. cap. 41 and manie others.
316. Epist. dedic.
317. Gorrheus def. med.[;] Jul. Scaliger. exerc. 345. 9.
318. Erast. disp. par. 1. pag 50.
319. Plin. nat. hist. li. 8. c. 21. li. 29. c. 4.
320. Pl. nat. hist. li. 7. cap. 2.
321. Gen. 1. 27.[;] zanch. de op Dei. p. 3. li. 3. ca. i.
322. Idem de hum. creat.
323. Wier. de præst. dæm. li. 3. ca. 36.
324. Erast. disp. par. 1. pag. 96.
325. Frac. de symp et Antip.
326. Scal. de subt. exerc. 344. 3.
327. Pomp. li de incantationibus[;] Parac. de caus. morb. invisib.[;] Paragrano li. 2. ad Athen. et aliis locis plurimis
328. Erast. disp. cont. Par. part. 1[;] Codronchius li de morb. venef[;] Casmannus Angelographia par. 2. cap. 24
329. Gal. diff. feb. li. 1. cap. 4.
330. Erast. li. de Lamiis. pag. 13.
331. Jam. 3. 14. 15.[;] Jam. 4. 3.[;] Heb. 11. 6.
332. Remigius dæmonol. sag. li. 1. ca. 1. li. 2. ca. 2 et alibi[;] Erast. de lamiis item cont. Parac part. 1. et Goddel. de lamiis passim.
333. See the Narrat. pag. [blank].
334. Fern. abd. rer. caus. li. 2. ca. 16[;] Wier de præst. dæm. li. 36.
335. Ro. ca: 1:[;] 1 Cor. 4. 4.[;] 1. Thes. 2. 9. 10. 11. 12.
336. Joh. Lereus hist. nav. in Brasil. cap. 15.
337. Casp. Peucerus de Theomonteia[;] Godelmanus de lamiis li. 1. cap. 6. p. 51.
338. Remigius dæmonol. li. 2. cap. 2.
339. Peucer. li. de. divin. gen. tit. de divin. ex som. sub finem.
340. Dion, in Pompeie.
341. Arist. Rhet. li. 2. cap. 28.
342. Just. Mart. apol. 1. ad sen. Rom.

343. As M Scot of the temple also witnesseth, that he observed at the sessions house.
344. Test. M. Scott in his report.
345. [i.e., Reginald Scot] li. 13. cap. 18.
346. Cæl. Aurel. li. tard. pass.
347. Epist. dedic. and pag. 25.
348. Heb. 11.
349. 2. Cron. 16.
350. 1. Sam. 28.
351. Marcel. Don. de med histo. mirab. li. 2. cap. 1.
352. Alex. Tral. li. 1. cap. 16
353. loc. cit. si morb. inveteravit.
354. Both Divine and Phisition.